Building A Lasting Dream

1909 to 2009
A History of the
Rockford Park District

by
Webbs Norman

with
Geri Nikolai & Tim Dimke

AMPHITRYON PUBLISHING

DEDICATION

*This book is dedicated to the Nicholas brothers —
Bill, Dan and Ab —
for their support of the Rockford Park District
during its first 100 years and their generous lead gift
to the Nicholas Conservatory and Gardens,
the symbol of the district's next 100 years.
The Nicholas brothers have led the way in improving
the quality of life of past and future generations.
The citizens, commissioners and employees of
the Rockford Park District are deeply grateful.*

ABOVE: Bill, Ab and Dan Nicholas (the three men in center left) line up with their families to break ground for the Nicholas Conservatory and Gardens on August 4, 2009.

OPPOSITE: The Nicholas Conservatory at night, reflected in the Eclipse Lagoon. (Photo courtesy of ThompsonDigitalimage.com)

Building A Lasting Dream, Copyright 2011 by Rockford Park District Foundation.
All rights reserved.

Printed in the United States of America.

No part of this book may be used or reproduced in any manner whatsoever
without written permission except in the case of brief quotations embodied in
critical articles and reviews.

For information, go to Amphitryon Publishing via thomasfranklinwarren.com.

ISBN: 978-0-9669045-1-2

Book design by Michael Bugler, Bugler Design Inc.
Printing by Willowbrook Printing

All book sale proceeds will go to the Rockford Park District Foundation.

The mission of the Rockford Park District Foundation is to assist the Rockford Park District
by securing philanthropic support on its behalf and enhancing awareness of
the District's benefits to the community.

ACKNOWLEDGEMENTS

Winston Churchill once said that writing a book goes through five phases. In phase one, it is a novelty. But by phase five, it becomes a tyrant ruling your life.

I found that to be true, given my experience of trying to write my first book. Without all the wonderful people who helped to make this book a reality, tyranny would have won — hands down!

I started thinking about having the history of the district written in the late 1990s, realizing the district's 100th birthday was getting close. I explored the market and found it would cost between $300,000 and $400,000 for a professional writer. We didn't have the funds. So I considered writing the history. Having never written before, I talked with two close friends who were published authors, Jon Lundin and Tom Warren. Both encouraged me to write on the belief that I knew much of the history. I thought so, too, until I started writing.

My next move was to engage two longtime friends of the district, Bob Kirkpatrick and Jan Herbert. At the same time, I persuaded Barb Bailor to come out of retirement and take care of scheduling and other tasks for me so I could devote myself to this book and fundraising for the Nicholas Conservatory.

Bob and Jan, with support from Barb, did a super job of researching and laying out a plan for the book. The only problem, as we learned more about the district, was that the first design did not fit. We wanted to tell more stories of the people who guided the Park District, not solely what decisions they made.

That is when I called on Geri Nikolai and Judy Emerson to join the team. Their years of journalistic writing were just what we needed to enhance the material we had accumulated. The commitment of Bob, Jan, Barb, Geri and Judy cannot be overstated.

I also am grateful to Paul Elmer, Lowell Hamilton and Robert E. Cryer, whose earlier works on Park District history were enormously helpful; Jean Lythgoe and staff at the Local History section of the Rockford Public Library; Shonnie DiGiovanni, Dave Schultz, Chuck Sweeney and Eleanora Smith of the Rockford Register Star; Frank Schier of the Rock River Times; local author Pat Cunningham; Tinker Swiss Cottage staff and volunteers; Laura Furman of Midway Village Museum; Don Swanson, educator and author; Ruth Little; and several people who talked with book researchers about their knowledge of and experiences with the Park District. They include Rolf Thienemann, Jo Baker, Ed and Vi Carlson, the Dahlquist sisters, Loren Johnson, Miggie Perrone, and Kristin Lyons Gonzalez.

As the book progressed, so did the need for additional, specialized help. Special thanks to Jodi Carroll, Karen Weis, Vance Barrie, Steve Reichensperger, Cindy Rathke, Denise Delanty, Sara Saunders, Nathan McDonald, Ben Wiegel and Sue Englund. The final work was done by Michael Bugler of Bugler Design and Sadique Isahaku of Willowbrook Printing. Their individual and collective strengths were superb, and their special skills and talents rounded out the team.

I could not have found a better adviser, ally and friend than Tom Warren. Tom saw the value of this book long before I did. He encouraged me and, at times, came close to nagging. Thanks, Tom. Without your advice and persuasion, this book would never have turned out this well. I am eternally grateful and I know that Jon Lundin is proud of our efforts.

I am indebted to all the members of the Park Board for appointing me the district's volunteer historian. All of you, as well as Executive Director Tim Dimke and his staff, have supported our efforts at every turn.

Finally, I want to thank my family for their tolerance, support and patience throughout this long process. To my wife Mary and all of our kids and grandchildren, thank you for making our past full of rich memories, our present full of joy, and our future full of great dreams. I love all of you, especially how each of you has enriched my history.

The Park District's Washington Park Community Center provides activities for youth and families.

TABLE OF CONTENTS

Introduction 4

Chapter 1: *The Dream Takes Shape* 1909 – 1928 7
　　　　　　First commissioners laid a strong foundation by
　　　　　　stressing promises, professionalism and partnerships.

Chapter 2: *The Dream Grows* 1929 – 1944 65
　　　　　　People need park services whether times are good or bad.

Chapter 3: *The Dream Seeks a New Level* 1945 – 1971 87
　　　　　　Returning WWII veterans were catalyst for great changes
　　　　　　in society, park districts.

Chapter 4: *The Dream Reaches Out* 1972 – 2006 145
　　　　　　Park District staff gives best service to public by working
　　　　　　effectively with one another.

Chapter 5: *100-Year-Old Dream Still Has Vital Role* 2006 – 2009 273
　　　　　　Executive Director Tim Dimke shares how district past
　　　　　　guides current decisions, future plans.

Prologue to Appendixes 297
　　　A: Maps of the Rockford Park District 298
　　　B: Rockford Park District Growth for 100 Years 302
　　　C: Park District Directors 304
　　　D: People Who Made a Difference 306
　　　E: Distinguished Service Award Recipients 312
　　　F: Allen Sapora Plaque 315
　　　G: IPRA/IAPD Community Service Award Recipients, Individuals 316
　　　H: IPRA/IAPD Community Service Award Recipients, Organizations .. 322
　　　I: Staff Development Instructors 324
　　　J: Rockford Area Golf Hall of Fame 325
　　　K: Major Awards to the Rockford Park District 326
　　　L: Letters from Patrons 328

Bibliography 334

Index 335

INTRODUCTION

This book centers around one person's dream and shows just how important one person's dream can be. In this case, the dream was to build a park system in Rockford, Ill.

You will learn how that dream became reality and how the core values established by the first Park Board continue to influence decision-making in the district.

You will see why citizens came to trust the board and why that relationship is so important and continues today.

You will meet all 49 commissioners who served on the board since its inception. I worked for 22 of them.

You will get to know each professional director and their challenges and achievements. I was the fifth of them.

You will understand how and why the board remained non-political while it established a level of professional leadership and service.

You will discover the unique role the Rockford Boys Club played in bringing tax-supported recreation to the district in the middle 1950s. Our own University of Illinois led the way in the struggle to establish recreation as an equal partner with parks to provide the balanced and broad-based core of services taken for granted today.

You will read about tragedies, personal failings and mistakes. The human factor was, of course, a part of Park District operations.

You also will see how the human factor led to great progress: a mother's refusal to accept the standard outdated program for her disabled son; a board member who was one of the first to see the fitness movement coming; skaters, soccer players, swimmers and other local athletes who needed fields, ice rinks and pools; the deep commitment of volunteers who refused to see a park close; and the generosity of people who gave back to their hometown through the Park District. All of them, and the board's wisdom in responding to their needs, combined to make our Park District something special.

You will learn how the board and executive director handled a five-week strike by district police and maintenance staff and how that strike became an opportunity to broaden the district's

leadership role locally, statewide and nationally. The book has been prepared in a way that illustrates why ends and means are equally important, that how we do something is as important as what we're doing. It provides considerable evidence that we cannot do externally what we cannot do internally, and how the strike helped all of us learn how to talk with each other. That was essential to clarifying our internal concerns and establishing common and shared goals.

ABOVE: *The $80,000 public library, built in 1904, with Memorial Hall behind it, and a dozen or so rowboaters enjoying the river in 1909.*
OPPOSITE: *Crowds gathered for an ice skating festival on the frozen river in downtown Rockford in 1910.*

You will read many little-known parts of history that will broaden your understanding of the community, such as why golf became an important element in Park District programs.

This book has been written in five different eras of history. In each, you will see how the board responded to shifting cultural and economic trends while handling its ever-changing local challenges.

Our 100 years of experience illustrates that our community is composed of three sectors, the private, public and non-profit/social. To achieve and sustain the most effective service at the least cost, all three must work toward a common goal. Certainly that has been true in the past three decades when global economic and political changes required successful communities to operate in an interdependent manner. The new and emerging global community will be enhanced by the health and wealth of the many parts of communities that constitute the whole.

It is our hope that the readers of this book will gain greater insight into how quality of life issues such as park and recreation services have provided great opportunities over the past 100 years for thousands of people. Park services have enabled them to establish meaningful and lasting relationships with their families, their work colleagues and their fellow users of park services.

This book is intended to broaden your understanding of the district, stimulate discussion about the value of park and recreation services, and, we hope, increase your participation in healthy recreation and support of your Park District.

We had space limitations and could not cover everything. If you think we omitted something important, please let me know. I'm not sure what we will do with responses but I promise we will, at the least, file them for future reference. Just mail them to me at Webbs Norman Center, Rockford Park District, 401 S. Main St., Rockford, IL 61101.

Webbs Norman

CHAPTER 1
The Dream Takes Shape
LATE 1800s – 1928

First commissioners laid a strong foundation by stressing promises, professionalism and partnerships.

Levin Faust Shares His Vision

If you have ever watched the sun set over Levings Lake, walked the path along the Rock River or taken children to a neighborhood playground, you have done exactly what a young man named Levin Faust envisioned when he made his way to Rockford in 1887.

Faust, a Swedish immigrant, dreamed of cashing in on America's promise with his inventive mind and work ethic. He dreamed of becoming "somebody" in a nation where successful risk-takers are rewarded with wealth and prestige. And he dreamed of living in a community where residents enjoyed places of beauty, rest and play.

"After a long week of toiling in the shop, a working family should be able to spend their free time in the green grass under the shadow of trees without fear of their children playing in the streets," he said.

It was that dream, which Faust shared with anyone who would listen, that led to creation of the Rockford Park District. It is the dream that inspired hundreds of park facilities and programs that today serve a population of 210,000 with services second to none.

This is that story, but it is not just a recital of programs or series of events. It is about the men and women who, like Faust, had a vision of what a well-run Park District could bring to this community. Some were non-paid elected commissioners, some were paid staff members, and many were people who simply gave of their time and expertise because they shared a passion. They were innovative, persistent and dedicated, committed to a high standard and making the rules as the need arose. They chased cattle out of Sinnissippi Park, nearly went broke feeding a ravenous elephant, "educated" many a

OPPOSITE: The refectory, an out-of-fashion word which translates to concession stand, was built in 1910 in Sinnissippi Park. It was refurbished in the mid 1990s, thanks to the Rock Valley Kiwanis Club (now Rock Valley Heritage Kiwanis). Service clubs have provided significant support again and again in the Park District's history.

RIGHT: Levin Faust

naysayer, and weathered political battles, the Great Depression, wars, and social and cultural upheaval.

Although I didn't come on board until decades later, I can tell you the cast of characters was diverse from the get-go. Now and then we weeded out a crook. We had many individuals of honor, courage and great energy. We suffered tragedies. We made mistakes.

Through 100 years, we tried to do what was right for the right reasons. The park district that developed is one of the major positive forces in this community. Ask anyone about Rockford parks, and you'll see what I mean.

It was difficult to cross a downtown street with the mix of horses, streetcars and automobiles in the early 1900s.

Rockford Club Adopts Park as Mission

Rockford was positioned to make Faust's dream come true in the early 20th Century.

In 1895, the Illinois Legislature provided the framework by passing the "Submerged Lands Act," which enabled towns and townships to establish park districts if voters so chose.

Faust and a few others, former Mayor E.W. Brown among them, were eyeing 80 acres of woodland and river shore just north of the city as the ideal public park. Brown sought approval to buy the land during his six years as mayor in the 1890s. Aldermen refused. They declined again, five years later, when Faust urged the city to make the purchase for $16,000.

Aldermen may not have seen the need for public parks but others did. Many were influenced by the work of Joseph Lee, a wealthy, Harvard-educated Bostonian who spent his life studying and promoting the concept of play and recreation.

Lee was intrigued with a Boston charity that built "sand-pile" playgrounds in the city's slums. He built playgrounds of his own to study children and the impact of play.

"Play is not a luxury but a necessity," Lee concluded. "Play for adults is recreation, the renewal of life. For children, it is growth, the gaining of life. It is not simply something that a child likes to have; it is something that he must have if he is ever to grow up."[1]

Lee's philosophy resonated in communities around the nation. If a city wanted to grow, many believed, it needed to show that it valued recreation and beauty, as well as manufacturing and a work force.

The Dream Takes Shape • Late 1800s – 1928

Faust judged the time for Rockford to act was right in 1908. Just back from a trip to Sweden, he joined the newly formed Rockford Club, a group of influential men. Some enjoyed the club strictly as a social outlet. Not Faust.

"I really did not understand the purpose of the meetings, because nothing of importance was discussed and subsequently nothing was done," he wrote in his diary.

Faust talked to club members about the 80 acres north of Rockford he and former Mayor Brown wanted the city to buy. The plot was called Rood Woods. Faust described his vision of parks, green with grass and trees and filled on Sunday afternoons with adults relaxing and children playing.

FROM LEFT:, *Levin Faust, Pedter Frechuer and Bert "Fish" Hassel in a 1920s photo.*

Faust appealed to the egos of his fellow club members, telling them such a park would be a fine legacy.

"I indicated that if the Rockford Club could bring this goal to realization, the members could look back at this with pride, even if that was the only thing the club ever could accomplish," he wrote.

Former Mayor Brown, president of the Rockford Club, quickly endorsed Faust's idea. Industrialist P. A. Peterson moved that the club adopt as its goal the building of a park, and the measure passed unanimously. The club appointed a committee of three attorneys to determine the best approach for acquiring the land. They recommended that the community form a park district governed by its own board.

Faust and other Rockford Club members circulated a petition for a special election to create such a body. They needed 100 signatures and quickly obtained 250.

Judge Louis M. Reckow set the election for Saturday, March 27, 1909. Voters also would elect five park commissioners to serve on the first park board if the measure passed. Reckow established the boundary of the Park District as that of Rockford Township.

It was time to see if Rockford voters were willing to pay taxes for parks.

A Need for 'People's Country Clubs'

There was reason to be optimistic. The average daily wage in machine shops and furniture factories was $2 to $2.50, enough to feed, clothe and house a family. It wasn't easy, of course. Workers put in 10-hour days, six days a week. But they looked around and saw a city with promise.

Approaching a population of 45,000, Rockford boasted a Carnegie library, a six-story "skyscraper" at State and Main, a new City Hall on Walnut Street built for the exorbitant sum of $100,000, a growing

Levin Faust as a young man.

Robert H. Tinker built this Swiss Cottage in 1865, 44 years before he was elected to the Park Board. The cottage today is a Park District museum.

number of manufacturers, and the new Memorial Hall, personally dedicated by President Theodore Roosevelt.

In part, the vote hinged on how electors felt about children and childhood. It is somewhat startling to think that, just 100 years ago, many people didn't see play as a vital part of child development. The old Puritanical belief that children should be kept busy being useful still prevailed.

While researchers were learning about the need for play as part of healthy childhood development, child labor was still a fact of life. It was increasingly frowned upon but would be tolerated in the United States until the 1930s.

Children not born to wealthy families seldom went to school beyond the sixth or eighth grades.

Rockford was paying more attention to the needs of children, however. The Children's Home orphanage opened in 1905; the Boys Club started in 1908. Newspaper stories reflect concern about wayward youth. A coalition of women's clubs wanted the county to turn over a farm for use as an "industrial training school for delinquent boys." State reform schools took miscreants from the ages of 10 to 21. A speaker in Rockford in 1907 noted that 39 Rockford boys had been sent there since 1893.

The Rockford Club and local newspapers made the value of parks and playgrounds a part of local conversation.

"Rockford needs public playgrounds for children," declared a Morning Star editorial in 1909. "In a city so given up to manufacturing as is Rockford, playgrounds are absolutely necessary … young people must have a chance to play and a place to play. It is health protecting, it reduces crime. It makes better boys and girls and, in the end, makes good citizens."

Local papers carried stories about other cities that had created parks. Juvenile judges said their caseloads went down when parks and organized games were provided for young boys. "There was a time when play was looked on as mere pastime. Now the physical, educational and moral value of play and games is coming to be appreciated…" said a Morning Star article.

The Star added that the idea of city parks, while still a new concept in the United States, was fast becoming a trend with 300 cities building playgrounds in the past two years. Some called municipal parks the "people's country clubs." The belief was that public park systems could bring to the common people the type of recreation — golf, tennis, picnicking and swimming, or bathing, as it was commonly

> *"A park will not directly pay dividends in gold. But you cannot build a city on the dollar alone."*
> – ATTORNEY ROBERT REW, FROM MORNING STAR, MARCH 21, 1909

The Dream Takes Shape • Late 1800s – 1928

called — that wealthier people paid for at private clubs.

Rockford at the time had made few provisions for the play of children. There were some "parks," the largest being Fair Grounds. Others were mostly squares and triangles of land donated to the city over time.

The city lacked the money and the inclination to develop parcels into play areas. Some were maintained as flower gardens by neighbors and children were warned away with "Keep off the Grass" signs.

About the only maintenance seen at Fair Grounds, the largest city "park," was the occasional mowing of hay.

One year, the council had to cut $20,000 from its budget; the first cut was $1,000 for parks. At least one alderman complained at a council meeting that parks were sorely neglected.

City officials focused on providing the streets, sewer, water, police and fire services that a growing community needed. Parks were extraneous.

Some families paid a tragic toll for the absence of public play areas. Newspapers carried stories about children and teens who were injured or killed by trains and streetcars. Homes of workingmen were small; many families had small yards or none at all. Streets or railroad tracks were the only places many children had to run and play.

Vote "Yes" for your Children

Besides support from the all-male Rockford Club, park campaigners received an endorsement from the Rockford Woman's Club. Although women in the city could not vote until 1915, they understood the need for parks.

"The problem of providing playgrounds for the children demands immediate attention," the club said in a public statement. "… the streets are unsafe to play in and vacant lots are closed to children…"

Passage of the referendum, however, was not a sure thing.

Then, as now, Rockfordians questioned the need for another governmental body

> *"Parks should not be disfigured with the sign 'Keep off the grass'…"*
> – FRED CARPENTER SPEECH, MARCH 2, 1909

Fair Grounds Park was the site of the Winnebago County Fair until the early 1900s.

These boaters were fishing for clams while the factories along the river belched smoke. The photo is from 1915.

and another tax levy. Detractors contended that Rood Woods, at the north end of the city, was so far away from residential neighborhoods that no one would go there. Others thought the whole notion of green space for relaxation was wasteful. They believed children needed to be kept busy at work or in school, not turned loose to play. Still others were suspicious of the businessmen leading the campaign.

Faust reported in his diary that the parks referendum "met with strong resistance from the Socialist paper, which claimed that the "capitalists now tried to trick the poor workers in purchasing of a park so the rich people could make use of it." The Socialists argued "the poor people needed their few free hours for sleep after working in the 'cave mills'," their term for the factories and shops.

After reading that, Faust and his fellow club members took their message directly to the workingmen. As the Rev. C. A. Wendell said at one gathering, "We ourselves could get along without the parks … but coming generations could not." In other words, be a good father and give your children and grandchildren a happier and safer childhood than you had.

Faust noted that wooded and open spaces were rapidly being closed to the public as the city grew. Public parks and playgrounds were as much a necessity for a city the size of Rockford as light and water, he maintained.

At a forum held at Svea Hall on March 19, 1909, just eight days before the vote, the Rev. Wendell said parks were needed to combat the physical and mental health ailments that afflicted people forced to live in congested cities. Parks could transform dirty and dangerous cities into ideal places to live, he said. An executive for Greenlee Brothers Manufacturing and Rockford Club member took the floor to predict that all cities, Rockford included, would soon look upon parks as vital parts of neighborhoods. The only question, he said, was whether to start now when land was available and affordable, or wait until later when it would cost more.

The last speaker was Robert Rew, an attorney and club member who explained that park commissioners would receive no pay and have no special privileges in the Park District.

The Rockford Morning Star reported that Rew got the most questions of any speaker. A show of hands indicated that everyone at the meeting was in favor of a park, but many questioned the authority and taxing power of a park board. Rew said the tax levy could not exceed four mills, which worked out to 10 cents for every $250 of property. For a home valued at $2,500, which was around the average in that time, the tax would be $1.

The mainstream press solidly championed the referendum. In an unsigned newspaper opinion piece one suspects was written by Faust, the writer says, "Vote for your children and their children ... Should we let a few dollars stand in the way of the happiness and enjoyment of thousands of people for hundreds of years to come?"

'Rockford is All Right'

March 27 arrived and 25 percent of voters went to the polls. By a margin of 1,232 to 705, they said yes to creation of a park district. The Register Gazette reported that 14 of 17 precincts rolled up majorities in favor of the district. Rockford that day became the 12th region in the state to establish a park district.[2]

The five candidates on the ballot were selected as the first board commissioners.

Families lived upstairs in many of these buildings along Seventh Street. Photo circa 1900.

Levin Faust

George Roper

H.W. Williams

Fred E. Carpenter

According to the Gazette, "A few scattering complimentary votes were cast for various (other) citizens but no organized effort was made in favor of any other aspirant for membership and the quintet suggested by the club was endorsed…"

All five of the men were solid citizens and businessmen. As board members, they guarded the public's dollars as closely as they guarded their own. They knew the community and its needs, and they passionately wanted the city to grow. It was, after all, their home and the place where they wanted their business investments to flourish.

Rockford Club member Rew knew all five. They had been put on the ballot by the club. In endorsing them, Rew described them this way:

"Uncle" Robert H. Tinker, he said, was one of the city's best mayors, "knows the ins and outs of public business and is one of the most skillful landscape gardeners in Illinois."

Tinker, born in Hawaii to a missionary couple, came to Rockford in 1856 to work for the Manny Reaper Co. After traveling in Europe, he built the Tinker Swiss Cottage (now a Rockford Park District museum) in 1865. Known as "Uncle Robert," he was mayor in 1885, became a father at age 71 when he and his second wife adopted a son, and was elected to the Park Board at age 72. A skilled landscaper, he was deeply involved in designing early parks of the district. He did much of the landscape work and planting himself, referring to his efforts as "Tinkerizing." He served until his death, which occurred on his 88th birthday.

"Colonel" George Roper, said Attorney Rew, "is one of our leading business men; he is energetic and intensely patriotic … he is thoroughly interested in parks and in beautifying our city."

Roper, born in Springfield, might have understood the need for safe play areas more than most; as a child, he was playing on railroad tracks when a train ran over him, severing his left arm above the elbow. While Roper did not let that stop him from anything he wanted to do, it must have been a factor in his thinking regarding parks.

Roper came to Rockford as a young man and founded the Roper Corp., which

> *"no precedents to follow … they must create precedents."*
> – ROBERT REW ON THE FIRST PARK BOARD

The Dream Takes Shape • Late 1800s – 1928

Robert Tinker

became the world's leading manufacturer of gas stoves.³ Roper served two years on the Park Board but remained interested in it all his life.

His nickname was "Colonel Roper," a tag he acquired because of his patriotism and civic contributions. Perhaps inspired by the "Black Hawk" statue on a river bluff south of Rockford, Roper donated a large statue of Chief Black Hawk to Camp Grant during World War I. The 86th Infantry Division, which was formed at the camp, was called the Black Hawk Division. Roper purchased thousands of emblems of the United States flag and its history and sent one to each school in Illinois, as well as every Elks lodge and Rotary club in the nation.

Rew ranked Fred E. Carpenter, the "cosmopolite," among the leading attorneys in town. The new Park Board, Rew realized, would need an able lawyer.

Carpenter grew up on a farm near Rockford. As a young man, he taught school in the winter and farmed in the summer until he got a job with his uncle, a lawyer, and decided to follow in his footsteps. Admitted to the bar in 1899, he entered the public arena when he was elected to the Park Board. He became its first president and then served as lawyer for the board. Carpenter later became a county judge and probate judge.

Newspapers referred to him as a "true cosmopolite" because of his travels and open mind. Carpenter loved horseback riding, boxing, hunting and mountain climbing. Although he was not a golfer, he pushed the board to make a golf course one of its first projects because he believed that pastime should be available to everyone, not just those who belonged to country clubs.

The inspiring Levin Faust, described as a self-made businessman, "likes flowers, shrubs and trees, and believes in playgrounds and parks," Rew said.

Faust was born in Sweden, coming to Rockford at age 24 and quickly making a name for himself as a machinist, inventor and business man involved in at least a dozen local manufacturing companies. He was Park Board president nine years and was on the board until his death in 1936.

One of Robert Tinker's many hobbies was making furniture out of twisted tree roots.

15

The Faust Landmark building, once the city's grandest hotel, was named after him.

When Faust died, tributes came from around the world. Carl Milles, perhaps Sweden's greatest sculptor, recalled coming from Chicago to Rockford in 1930 for dinner with local dignitaries and Faust. Milles became engrossed in conversation with Faust and went home with him to continue the talk. He intended to stay a few hours but spent most of the night. "I look back on that evening as one of the most inspiring I spent in America," said Milles. That was high praise of Faust's intellect, considering that Milles had been an assistant to the sculptor Rodin and had lived in Paris, Munich, Rome, Stockholm and Austria.

The high-spirited H.W. Williams "is a bundle of restless energy, and his home shows he admires the wild woods and flowers," according to Rew.

A Rockford native, Williams learned the insurance trade as a messenger for Rockford Fire Insurance. In 1896, he was instrumental in starting a firm that operates today under the name Williams Manny Insurance.

Known for his outgoing personality and love of nature, Williams also enjoyed a practical joke. The Rockford Historical Society reports that Williams caused great excitement in the National Avenue neighborhood where he lived because of what he kept in a storage box in his entryway. If you lifted the lid to the overshoe compartment, you would find a snake peering out at you. Williams was on the Park Board from 1909 until 1917.

> *Vote is "GREATEST FORWARD STEP CITY HAS EVER TAKEN."*
> – ROCKFORD MORNING STAR

The shelter at Sinnissippi Park stood from 1910 until it was demolished to provide space for Park District headquarters in 1971.

The Dream Takes Shape • Late 1800s – 1928

Commissioner Robert Tinker helped design this rustic stone bridge in Sinnissippi Park in 1910.

I never met any of these men but I admire them. They were ingenious about getting things done. If cows needed chasing, Faust chased them. If plants needed tending, Tinker tended them. They were highly-skilled professional men who didn't hesitate to get their hands dirty if a job needed doing.

The Rockford Star couldn't have been more pleased with voters after approval of a park district.

In an editorial headlined, "Rockford is All Right," the paper said the vote "is the GREATEST FORWARD STEP THE CITY HAS EVER TAKEN. It means a better and more beautiful town. Resultant there from will be a bigger and grander Rockford. The people have done well. They have lifted a too conservative Rockford on the plateau of progress … an era of enterprise has been launched."

'Keep Our Promise to the People'

The new Park Board met at the law firm office of (Fred) Carpenter & St. John on April 20 to get organized. Commissioners drew lots to establish length of terms: Tinker, five years; Faust, four years; Williams, three years; Roper, two years; and Carpenter, one year. The board elected Carpenter president and designated him as the board's legal adviser. Frank J. O'Brien was appointed secretary and Martin Kjellgren was named treasurer.

The board was ready for business and, once again, Levin Faust led the way.

When Roper suggested the Park District concentrate on building a boulevard along the east river bank, and promoted his idea with store window displays, Faust countered by noting that the campaign for the district had centered

The sunken gardens at Sinnissippi Park were popular attractions. Fair Gounds Park had a similar garden.

on creating a large park on the Rood Woods land. To Faust's disappointment, the newly elected board was not as enthusiastic as he was.

When Faust suggested the board approach the owner of Rood Woods with an offer to buy, "the other members laughed at me…" he wrote in his diary.

"I was the only Swede on the board and the other members did not seem to have very much respect for the 'foreigners,' as they called us immigrants," he said.

Faust stood firm. Prodded by board members about cost, he insisted that even $100,000 would not be too much to pay, if necessary.

"…I was convinced that we should pay the price and, as park commissioners, keep our promise to the people," he wrote. "Somebody asked if I was willing to back the debt if the park was purchased. My answer was that I would take it as an insult if I was excluded from the responsibility for the purchase."

Any disagreement about making Rood Woods a priority soon ended. Park District minutes show Roper making a motion on May 1 for Carpenter to investigate buying the land. Carpenter got an answer and things moved quickly.

Edward Waller of Chicago, who had spearheaded that city's establishment of parks, owned the property. He asked $600 an acre, or $47,500, for Rood Woods. Park commissioners considered that a bargain price and agreed to it. But having just been established, the board had collected no taxes and had no money.

A Rockford Morning Star article on May 13, 1909, reported that commissioners used their business contacts and "just-do-it" attitudes to get the job done.

The Dream Takes Shape • Late 1800s – 1928

The option to buy Rood Woods for $47,500 was to expire on May 12. Waller, park proponent that he was, was a businessman also and not inclined to renew the option at the same price. Both Waller and the commissioners knew that private developers, eager to get their hands on the land, would pay substantially more if given the chance.

In early May, Park Board members visited three local banks — Winnebago National, Third National, and People's — to secure a loan for the amount needed. Commissioners Faust, Roper, Carpenter and Williams signed for the loan; Tinker was out of town. The four promised to repay the loan with their personal money, should that become necessary.

Board minutes reflect some questioning of whether that was the proper way to handle public business but commissioners were determined to move ahead.

"This board considers it would be a distinct loss to the people represented by it, if said premises should be purchased by private individuals and used for private purposes," the minutes state.

This was at a time when more than 170 factories, some large and some small, lined the river in Rockford. Private interests had already taken most of the riverbank, but Rood Woods remained available.

According to the Star, the quartet of Faust, Roper, Carpenter and Williams journeyed to Chicago on May 12 and met with Waller. They signed the papers and came home thrilled to report that the Park District now had 80 acres of beautiful land, with woods, a hill and a river bank, just north of the city limits. It would be dedicated to public use. By grabbing up that land, the board ensured that generations of residents would be able to walk, run, picnic and fish along the river close to downtown.

Had private parties gotten the land, such activities would have been restricted to those lucky enough to build homes there or those who paid fees to commercial enterprises that sprang up.

Instead, citizens became owners of this splendid river resource. For 100 years, they have enjoyed it from dawn to dusk. Bordering busy North Second Street, it is a landmark of the city and a central meeting place. See you at Sinnissippi Park.

Cattle Evicted from Sinnissippi

In 1909, Rood Woods was a stand of trees, a bog and a pasture. The board hired a retired fire chief to clear debris. It seemed Faust's dream of a park was becoming reality when an unexpected set of obstacles — the four-legged, bovine type — presented themselves.

When Faust went to Rood Woods one Sunday, expecting to see families enjoying nature, he instead found a herd of cattle.

He reported this to the board, which immediately ordered the owner of the cattle to take them elsewhere. But when Faust checked again, the animals were still enjoying the green grass that belonged to the Park District.

Faust found the retired fire chief and let him know he was not pleased. "I asked him," Faust wrote in his diary, "if he worked for the Park Commission or the cattle owner."

The chief said he had not been told to oust the cattle. So Faust issued the

Levin Faust wrote his diary in Swedish.

order himself and then helped the chief remove a gate so the cattle could be driven out.

"With this done, I thought everything was ready for people to come out and use the property," he wrote. "Next Sunday when I came out, the gate was put in place again and the cattle were still there, and so was the fire chief. I asked him to help me take down the fence and we took down about 200 feet.

"It had its effect and the cattle were moved," Faust wrote with satisfaction. "People began to use the property more and more."

Faust's diary does not mention a "fierce bull" which was pastured in the woods, according to posted signs intended to keep people out.

Professional Leader Signs On

Acquiring Rood Woods fulfilled a major promise the commissioners had made to voters. But it was just the beginning of an ambitious period as the commissioners worked on park development as aggressively as they pursued business.

Even more importantly, the commissioners established values and standards that proved vital to the district's long-term success and that prevail today.

They insisted on a professionally run agency that had service as its highest priority. Service to citizens, the first board made clear, meant working cooperatively with other agencies, public or private, as long as taxpayers benefitted.

Board minutes show that philosophy was firmly established when the district was just a year old. In the summer of 1910, the district helped buy and plant shrubs around the then-new John Nelson School at 623 15th Street. A local nursery firm complained that the Park District took over what could have been a job for private companies.

The nursery owner received no sympathy. At a board meeting, Roper moved, Faust seconded and the board unanimously asserted that Park District staff could help a school or charitable organization as long as the board president consented.

Through its history, the Park District made cooperation an art form, expanding the concept into partnerships that led to major programs and facilities the district could not have handled on its own. The end result, as the first board understood, was that the community reaped benefits both in the form of expanded services and in efficient use of tax dollars.

In keeping with their values and standards of professionalism, the first commissioners looked for a high degree of competence in their first superintendent. In February 1910, they hired a Swiss-born man who had worked in Yellowstone and other parks in the then-fledgling National Park System. Paul B. Riis was a gifted forester who advocated the use of natural materials and species in landscaping and park structures. At a starting pay of $100 a month, he helped establish an efficient and service-oriented park system in Rockford. Riis stayed on the job for 17 years.

'Nature's Best Handiwork'

The commissioners didn't wait for Riis before they went to work on Rood Woods. Soon after buying the land, they named the property Sinnissippi, the Native American name for the Rock River. Translated, it meant clear flowing.

Paul B. Riis, first executive director, then called superintendent

THE DREAM TAKES SHAPE • LATE 1800s – 1928

Tree canopies covered many streets in the city until Dutch elm disease hit in the 1950s.

The board passed a tax levy of $35,000 and issued bonds of $100,000 at 4 percent interest. The action provided the means to buy 40 acres of adjoining land from the Cassidy Estate for $402 an acre, and six lots south of the park from W. W. Sawyer for $960.

With those purchases, Sinnissippi was a park of 126 acres with wooded lands, known as "the hills," on the east and riverfront land on the west. Beloit Road and two railroad lines separated the two parcels.

The board recognized that Sinnissippi already had much of what it needed to be a superior park. As local attorney Rew said, "Having traveled extensively, I have never seen Sinnissippi's equal for natural advantage. Nearly all city parks are artificial, while Sinnissippi is nature's best handiwork."

The board kept that in mind in choosing O.C. Simmonds, a Chicago landscape gardener of some renown, to draw up a design for Sinnissippi. Simmonds believed that good landscape design was achieved through the use of native plants and landforms that naturally existed.

To accommodate a growing form of transportation, the automobile, the board ordered construction of a one-mile road, of bricks laid on edge on a concrete foundation. The road, with asphalt between the bricks, was believed to be the first brick road in a park in the United States. It cost $22,000.

Motorized vehicles had been around for about a decade but a horse and buggy was still the common mode of travel. Acknowledging this, commissioners had 40 hitching posts installed.

In the first two years, the board erected a playground for boys, picnic tables, rustic stone bridge, stone shelter house and refectory (concession stand). To encourage picnicking, the district built cooking grates and furnished firewood.

Under Riis' supervision, the Park District became a growing organization in both programming and land. A tradition that continues today began when the Rockford Military Band performed the first Sinnissippi Band Concert in 1911. Several thousand people attended, according to district records.

By 1912, Sinnissippi offered four tennis courts, another play area and, along the riverfront, sunken gardens and a wading pool. There were "comfort houses," rooms we call restrooms today.

The district's annual report states that thousands of people came to the park every weekend, and large companies and other organizations frequently held their summer picnics in Sinnissippi Park.

While Simmonds designed Sinnissippi, Commissioner Tinker oversaw the installation of gardens and greenery. He saved citizens countless dollars by donating his landscape expertise for as long as he served. In its first annual report, the board acknowledged its "great obligation to Mr. Tinker for his time spent and taste displayed in assisting in the work," in Sinnissippi Park.

Later, Tinker assisted in designing Fair Grounds and South parks, among others. His work included such creative projects as building shelters at Mandeville Park by suspending roofs from large trees. That project proved to be less than adequate over the long haul, but no one can fault Tinker's creative way of working with nature.

The board gratefully accepted his contributions. Commissioners paid Tinker $300 for his work at Black Hawk Park. But his designs, consultations and plantings at other parks were offered free of charge. Tinker enjoyed the work and wanted the Park District to be one of the best.

More than 20 golfers wait to tee off on the old first hole at Sinnissippi Golf Course, which opened in 1912.

Golf: 'Democratizing so Splendid a Game'

As the 20th Century opened, Americans were slowly gaining leisure time, and a game imported from northern Europe was all the rage. The game was golf.

In Rockford, it was an exclusive pastime. The only real course in town was at the Rockford Country Club, which was organized in 1899.

The Park Board, which was building playgrounds and ball fields for all, decided that golf fit into its mission of recreation for everyone. In a decision that changed the culture of the city, the district made plans to build a golf course in Sinnissippi Park.

> *"The need of democratizing so splendid a game."*
> – FRED CARPENTER'S ENDORSEMENT OF PUBLIC GOLF COURSES

The man who pushed for that golf course was not a golfer himself. He was Fred Carpenter, the first Park Board president. Carpenter enjoyed athletics and the outdoors, and he must have admired the game of golf. A newspaper article in 1918 reported that Carpenter's motivation for building a golf course was that "he felt the need of democratizing so splendid a game."

As I look back at this, I applaud Mr. Carpenter's choice of words and his sentiment. Rockford became one of the great golf cities in America. Tiger Woods never would have heard of us, much less visited here, if that were not true. No one has ever accused me of being a golfer (although I used to play the game), but I know this: The role of golf in this community might be second only to religion in its influence on families, friends and relationships.

Golf courses were still in short supply when the Park District formed. People who couldn't afford to join private clubs were out of luck. The first course in Illinois was built in 1892 in Downers Grove. The first public course in the nation opened in 1895 in New York City.

Sinnissippi became the first municipal course in the Rockford area. The board began construction of the nine-hole course in 1911 and planned to open it in the summer of 1912. It had an unexpected "preview day" in January when unseasonably high temperatures lured 25 golfers onto the unfinished links. They were intent on enjoying the weather, and their own public golf course, no matter the date or the fact that some holes weren't ready to be played.

Unfortunately, some local citizens were not welcome on Rockford's first courses. They were the African-Americans and people of certain religions. While no rule barred them from golfing at Sinnissippi, it was understood.

It was a shame, and it wasn't unusual. Tom Warren, who wrote "An Old Caddie Looks Back" about Rockford's golf heritage, recounts that "Persons of 'color' were typically not welcome on the courses of (Rockford) or on courses anywhere in the United States during that time."

Thomas Bendelow, a Scottish native who was called the "Johnny Appleseed of Golf Courses," designed the Sinnissippi course. He laid out hundreds of golf courses in the United States, including the nation's first municipal course in New York.

Bendelow was an ideal choice to design Rockford's first public golf course.

Thomas Bendelow designed the city's first two public golf courses, Sinnissippi and Ingersoll. (Photo courtesy of Stuart Bendelow Jr.)

These structures, which stand today in Blackhawk Park, were described as "Japanese covered piers" in the 1915 annual report.

He believed in keeping costs of municipal courses low with simplified upkeep. That way, he reasoned, cities would be more apt to build them and more people could enjoy them.[4]

At Rockford's first municipal course, the Park District specified that each golfer be given a bag and "at least three clubs, one of which shall be a putter." No high-heeled shoes were allowed, and no children under 15 could be on the course on Sundays, holidays or afternoons. A. J. Gillett received $70 a month as the first greens keeper of the course.

The board's belief in high standards of behavior extended to the golf course, too. When commissioners heard about "indecent and vulgar" language on the course, they went to the Sinnissippi Golf Club with a plan. The club selected six members and the board gave them "police authority" to reduce offensive talk.

Sinnissippi Golf Course produced early Park District partnerships. As told in the 1913 annual report by Superintendent Riis, "Many tournaments were held and the work of the Sinnissippi Golf Club, an organization made up from the players themselves, in conducting these matches is deserving of the highest praise." Riis also noted that the course was so popular, golfers sometimes had to be turned away on Sundays and holidays.

Now surrounded by homes, a cemetery and busy streets, the Sinnissippi links have marked their 100th birthday. A par 37, 3,230-yard course known for its hilly layout and tree-lined fairways, it is the oldest of five Rockford Park District golf courses and the one where many young golfers take their first swings. Among the golf enthusiasts who learned the sport at

Sinnissippi are Stuart Bendelow Sr., grandson of the course architect and historian of the senior Bendelow's achievements; Brad Benjamin, who became the first Rockfordian to play in the Masters Tournament; and Norris Aldeen, one of the best friends Rockford golfers ever had.

One Park District or Two?

In January 1910, with the Park District not yet a year old, the city made a significant decision. The City Council turned over to the Park District what had been called the city parks, the largest being the 24-acre Fair Grounds, and an assortment of small squares and triangles.

That decision wasn't made lightly. In May 1909, shortly after the Park District formed, the city decided it would have a park district of its own. The council passed an ordinance and appointed its own five-man park commission to take care of parks in the city.

Some aldermen objected, saying the city did not have the funds to maintain parks. Six months later, the majority of aldermen agreed that a city park commission was not a good idea, after all. They dissolved the city unit, acknowledging that the new township Park Board could do a better job of developing city parkland.

That solidified the Rockford Park District as the sole entity responsible for public parks and recreation throughout the city and township. Taxpayers did not have to worry about competing park districts, duplication of services or being taxed by two park agencies. That move, accomplished early on in Rockford, took decades in many other Illinois cities, including Chicago, which had 22 separate park districts until the early 1950s.

It is true that we also have a Winnebago County Forest Preserve District that taxes everyone, city residents included. The Forest Preserve District's mission is to preserve wild land and habitat. It does operate three golf courses and has picnic facilities but does not run programs, swim pools, ice rinks, athletic fields or the range of services of the Park District.

The "sand pile" in the front is the boys' playground at Fair Grounds Park in 1910. In the background is the girls' playground, without sand to get them dirty.

Fair Grounds Park for West Side

Another goal of the first Park Board was to create neighborhood parks throughout the city. Superintendent Riis agreed that parks were essential in all areas. Ideally, Riis believed, each home should be within walking distance of a neighborhood park.

After Sinnissippi, the board took on development of Fair Grounds Park on the west side. When the Winnebago County Fair moved to South Beloit for a few years and then, after World War I, to its current site in Pecatonica, the old fair grounds became city property.

The site was largely grass when the Park District took possession from the city. They named it what everyone called it, Fair Grounds Park. The board and Tinker envisioned it as a combination of play areas and beautiful gardens.

In 1910, they installed swings, seesaws, slides, rings, trapezes, sand "piles" and wading pools. For older children, the district built baseball diamonds, tennis courts and a running track. A concrete dam erected on Kent Creek provided a place to swim and wade in the summer and ice skate in the winter.

The southeast corner of Fair Grounds Park was converted into a sunken garden with a fountain and assortment of perennials. It became, the board believed, one of the city's most attractive havens of beauty. The board noted that it spent $1,000 on plants and shrubbery for Fair Grounds. With that amount in the early 1900s, certainly a lot of greenery could be purchased.

Fair Grounds was transformed from a place used by just a few people to a park

This romantic postcard photo shows Fair Grounds Park in the 19-teens.

The Dream Takes Shape • Late 1800s – 1928

Skaters enjoyed the ice provided by the Kent Creek dam at Fair Grounds Park in January 1914.

"of constant use by thousands of boys and girls, men and women," the Park District said in its first annual report.

"Many children came several miles from the country to avail themselves of the conditions for play which exist in this park, and many mothers have expressed themselves in a most touching manner to members of the board ... for the advantages offered by the park for their children, giving helpful amusement in the place of what had hitherto been harmful associations."

That Fair Grounds got major attention from the first Park Board is testament to its importance as a Rockford gathering place. Not only did it host county fairs from 1857 to 1902 but it heard speeches by Presidents Ulysses S. Grant and William Howard Taft, and served as home field for the well-known Forest City's baseball team of the National Association and minor league White Stockings of the Northwest League.

Development of Fair Grounds also illustrated a guideline the district has used throughout its history, that of balancing the number of facilities east and west of the river in order to serve citizens in all parts of the city.

Other parks in the original set from the city included Haight, Vogt, Northwestern, South East, Waterworks, Haskell, Sunset and Franz.

The district's first swimming facility was this pool of water, created by a dam in Kent Creek in Fair Grounds Park in 1914.

Wading pools were hugely popular. This photo was taken in 1913 at South East Park (now Keye-Mallquist) near 11th Street and 16th Avenue.

Also turned over to the Park District were 15 squares and triangles with a combined area of 35 acres.

The Park Board improved the properties as quickly as possible. Sunset Park, for example, once the site of the city's "pest house," (hospital for people with infectious diseases) was a priority because of the rapid growth on the west side of town. In 1909 – 1910, the district installed a baseball diamond, tennis courts and playground sets. Storekeepers on West State Street near the park expressed gratitude, saying the number of children hanging around their shops dwindled. Today Sunset Park is the playground for Lewis Lemon Elementary School. The Park District transferred ownership to the school district with the agreement that the park and school be open for recreational use year round. That arrangement was part of the People Who Care desegregation lawsuit of the 1990s.

The board, in 1910, looked at needs and possibilities of each of the smaller properties, developing some as play areas and others as places of beauty with gardens.

Then as now, the Park District welcomed citizen opinion and participation. Superintendent Riis reported on Park Associations formed in neighborhoods around each park, which "proved of great advantage in stopping bad practices."

'For Law and Order and Public Decency'

Listening to the public and responding have long been reasons for the Park District's success. Some of the earliest examples are land purchases.

The second piece of land the new Park Board bought, in March 1910, was five acres of Rockford Engine Works property at 126 Lane Street in south Rockford. The purchase was made to answer public requests.

The Rockford Police Department led the charge. Police believed the amount of time they spent dealing with mischievous children and vandals in that part of town would be greatly reduced if the youth had a neighborhood park.

The board agreed. South Park received

playground equipment, a baseball diamond believed to be the finest in northern Illinois, and a place for "soccer" football games by teams representing the Swedish and English clubs of the city.

The Park Board, consistent with its policy on neighborhood parks throughout the city, concluded its South Park investment was money well spent, according to this item from the first annual report:

"The necessity for a park in this location was shown by the great patronage given the park. Large families are the fashion in this part of town … and hitherto there has been absolutely no place for children to play … According to Officer Golden and records of the Police Department, this park has done more for law and order and public decency and the proper education of children than any other one thing which has been done in south Rockford."

The third major park purchase, also urged by citizens for some years, was Black Hawk Park, named for the Sauk Indian chief. With a second bond issuance in 1911 of $100,000, the board paid $46,000 for the 80 acres then known as Lathrop Woods.

In its first annual report, which reported the plan to buy the land, the board indicated it was responding to its "bosses," the citizens.

"It has long been the desire of the majority of the citizens of Rockford to have what is known as Lathrop Woods be devoted to park purposes…" the report states.

The citizens and board made a good choice. The land included woods, quarries

This 1911 photo shows Black Hawk Park, the second large property purchased by the board. It added 3,000 feet of riverfront to the public domain.

Boys pause to look at a photographer during a baseball game at South Park in 1910.

and 3,000 feet of riverfront. The first improvements there were shelter houses so picnickers could enjoy the groves of trees planted by former owner William Lathrop.

Slides, or chutes as they were called, were high, steep, and unsafe by today's standards in 1910, when these children frolicked at Fair Grounds Park.

Black Hawk Park became a "working" park. Part of it was used as a nursery to grow shrubs and trees destined for other parks. The quarry was a major money-saver. The cost of quarrying and crushing stone at Black Hawk was 50 cents a cubic yard, compared with 75 cents if the board purchased it, or $1.25 delivered. That saved the district thousands of dollars, the 1913 annual report indicated.

The First Museum

The district's lasting partnership with museums began in 1911 with Mandeville Park at Montague and Knowlton streets. Harriet Gilbert donated the family home to the district in honor of her parents, Michael and Elsie Corey Mandeville.

The Mandeville home became the Park District's first museum, a modest beginning to what has become a major contribution of the Park District to the community. The museum opened in 1915 with collections donated by more than 50 residents. Among them, according to the Register Gazette, were "a rare and valuable specimen of the carrier pigeon, Indian relics, arrowheads, pottery and bead work, a whistling swan, a Roman coin from 100 B.C., and Siamese curios in wood and ivory..."

THE DREAM TAKES SHAPE • LATE 1800S – 1928

The museum was operated by the Nature Study Club, setting an example for partnerships that exist between non-profit organizations, which run our museums today, and the Park District, which owns the property. The arrangement has worked well for both the district and citizens.

It's interesting that legislators back in 1893 saw the value of such partnerships. They passed a state law that said park districts could "erect and maintain within ... public parks, edifices to be used as museums for the collection and display of objects pertaining to natural history and the arts and sciences..." The law said fees of 25 cents for adults and 10 cents for children could be charged, but the museums had to be open free two days a week. Today, museums are required by law to offer periodic free days. The law also says school classes accompanied by a teacher must be admitted free of charge.

The Mandeville House, the first museum partner of the district, was in a "dilapidated and apparently hopeless" state before it was rebuilt by the district to this condition in 1914.

Today Mandeville Park, which once had the largest elm tree in the city, serves children attending Washington Academy public school, as well as the neighborhood. The home was razed in 1948 when the museum found larger and more suitable quarters elsewhere.

Campers lined up along the river in Black Hawk Park for 50 cents a night in the 1920s.

31

Workmen pose with their horses, machines and tools before starting work on Sunset Park in 1911.

Socialists Seek Control

Illinois law on park organization mandated that Park District elections be non-partisan, but politics dominated the campaign for commissioner in Rockford in 1913.

Socialists were a force in Rockford and other parts of the nation, especially Milwaukee, in the early 1900s. Often identified with labor causes, the party espoused support for the working man and believed that wealthy industrialists and many public office holders took advantage of the laboring class. The party had some support in Rockford. Two popular Rockford mayors of the first half of the 1900s, Herman Hallstrom and Henry C. Bloom, held Socialist philosophies although they ran on other party tickets at times.

The Socialists had opposed formation of the Park District and went for a voice on the board as soon as possible after the district was formed.

Socialist Napoleon Levasseur succeeded Fred Carpenter when his term was up in 1910. Carpenter stayed on as attorney for the board. The following year, another member of the Socialist Party, Dr. Alfred Olson, defeated George Roper by 19 votes.

In 1913 when another Socialist ran for the board, Faust put up a fight. Not only was it his seat that the Socialists wanted, but if they were successful, they would control the Park Board by a 3 – 2 majority.

That, Faust said, would be a calamity. He believed that if the Socialists won, they would hire only members of their party for Park District jobs. Faust got the newspapers to back him.

The Rockford Republic said on March 28, 1913, that while the two Socialists on the board had proved to be "able" commissioners, Faust deserved re-election. "He gives his time without pay to the public parks," the paper said, "and the growth of the park system is as much due to his work as to that of any other official on the board."

Just as the voters had agreed with Faust in creating a park district in 1909, they followed his lead again three years later. He defeated Socialist Oscar J. Johnson, proprietor of the Grand billiard and pool hall on Seventh Street, by a 2 to 1 margin, Faust receiving 3,338 votes to Johnson's 1,610.

That was as close as Park District candidates ever got to political parties. Candidates run non-partisan and, in almost all cases, their reputations are built on interests other than politics. Few voters even know what political party is favored by individual commissioners.

That has allowed the Park District to grow without the type of campaigning and conflict that partisanship brings to many public bodies.

Roots for Today's City of Gardens

The Park Board stirred up interest in beautification by showing how neglected pieces of land, large or small, could be transformed into community assets. In 1912, the Chamber of Commerce and Rockford Club took that theme to private properties with the first City Beautiful Contest to encourage homeowners to plant greenery and flowers around their houses. The Park District agreed to help.

Superintendent Riis said the primary purpose was to "interest the class of people who work in the shops and have little time to work about their homes, the class who can ill afford to hire their work done…"

He captured their interest, as shown by the 325 entries received in categories such as residential, window box, flower garden grown by any school child, factory property or fire stations, schoolyard showing greatest improvement, and vegetable garden by boy or girl in vacant lot. Winners received $10 for first place, $5 for second.

In its 1912 annual report, the Park

This photo shows the "before and after" appearance of the home of J. T. Miller at 2203 North St. It won a first place award in a city beautification contest in 1912.

District listed the contest winners and published before and after photos of the properties.

The early beautification contests ended after two years, but the seeds of competition were sown in Rockford. As the 21st Century opened some 90 years later, the Park District Foundation's City of Gardens, started with a $250,000 gift from Dan and Ruth Nicholas, enlisted the public once again in a campaign to spruce up the city. With the help of citizens, the city won several national awards for its beauty, tidiness, public spirit, heritage preservation, and conservation practices.

Park administration moved into the third floor of the old City Hall in 1911. The building still stands at Walnut and South First Street. (Register Star photo)

Lawsuit: 'Nervous Neurasthenia'

The Park Board called a special meeting in September 1914 to deal with a troublesome lawsuit. It seems that Mr. and Mrs. Harry Shores were resting on their bed on August 1 when a stump came crashing through the roof of their home and landed on the bed.

Minutes of the meeting don't specify, but presumably the flying hunk of wood came from a nearby park where workers were blowing up tree stumps.

A Dr. Culhane addressed the board and said Mrs. Shores was in a "nervous neurasthenic state." Neurasthenia was a term used at the time to describe a condition of fatigue, anxiety, headache, neuralgia and depression. It would take "some little time" for Mrs. Shore to recover, said the doctor. His fee to the couple, he said, would be around $25.

An attorney, D.D. Madden, asked the board for $500.

After some discussion, the board agreed, "if nothing better could be done," to pay the doctor and give the family $500.

Faust Stands Against Popular View

The board encountered what may have been its first controversy in 1911 when the National Guard asked to use Sinnissippi Park for an encampment.

It appears to be one of the rare times when the board, notably Faust, went against public sentiment.

Both Socialist Park Board members were against granting permission to the Guard and Faust sided with them. He said other cities that had let soldiers use public land reported they did not behave well and left a mess behind.

Businessmen brought in a petition with 500 signatures asking that the encampment be allowed and some powerful men, notably Mayor William Bennett and Catholic Bishop Peter James Muldoon, wrote letters in favor of the Guard.

Faust was not to be swayed. The Guard was denied 3 – 2, with Faust explaining that the parks could not be used for any purposes other than those prescribed in state law.

Setting Policy Day by Day

The district found its first "permanent" home in 1911 when it moved into space on the third floor of City Hall, corner of Walnut and South First Street. Before that, meetings were held in the offices of a commissioner or at a local bank. Commissioners no doubt felt quite at home when, in 1912, their City Hall space was provided with cuspidors (spittoons).

"Remember the Public, our friends, owns the Parks and always, under all circumstances, must be treated courteously,"
— ANNOUNCEMENT TO EMPLOYEES, 1913

The board got a surprise in 1912 when the city sent a bill for $400 for office rental. Commissioners assumed the space was free. After negotiations, they agreed to pay $200 a year.

The district's first encounter with severe weather came in July 1913 when a tornado hit the city. Winds damaged a number of parks, especially Sinnissippi where "many monarchs of the woods finally bowed to the forces of nature," wrote Riis.

The board set policy for staff as it went along. In June 1910, it voted to pay a surgeon's fee for two men injured on the job and give them half pay for the time they were incapacitated. In May 1911, it voted against a motion made by Socialist Commissioner Olson to give nine hours of pay for eight hours of work. In April 1912, a foreman was fired for "intemperance." In 1917, another foreman was given full pay for the two weeks he was off with a severe cold, but lost his vacation for that year. Also in 1917, the minimum wage for nine hours of work per day was set at $2.50. Daily pay had risen to $5 a day for some laborers by 1923, when everyone got a nickel-an-hour raise.

At least two parks could have had different names. Commissioner LeVasseur wanted Black Hawk Park to be named

Swim suits covered most of the body, as the children illustrated while playing in the South East Park (now Keye-Mallquist) wading pool in 1914.

Mauh Nah Tee See, after a legendary Indian princess. The Grand Army of the Republic asked that Fair Grounds Park be named after Col. T. G. Lawler, a Civil War veteran who became commander in chief of the G.A.R. The Park Board declined both suggestions.

It's interesting to see how the early Park Boards set standards and established procedures as issues arose. They started with a blank slate, after all, but made wise decisions, guided by their principles and fiscal conservatism.

'Behavior Above Reproach'

Likewise, the boards set conduct standards for everyone associated with the district. It was clear they expected behavior above reproach from both themselves and those who received paychecks from the Park District.

The board rules stated that when a member was talking, no one else could speak or walk between the speaker and the chairman.

Attorney Rew and Faust instructed board and staff members to attend strictly to duty and use proper judgment in their public affairs. Specifically, there was to be no swearing and no striking of another person.

"Remember the Public, our friends, owns the Parks and always, under all circumstances, must be treated courteously," employees were told in August 1913.

Patrons were expected to behave, too.

The board asked cyclists to stop speeding in Black Hawk and Sinnissippi parks after neighbors complained about the noise. A $25 reward was offered for information on who broke the flagpole in Fair Grounds Park.

In 1912, the board decreed it illegal for anyone to play games with cards or dice in any of the parks. Violators could be fined from $1 to $5. Alcohol was a far worse offense. Anyone caught with intoxicating drink in a park could be fined from $25 to $200.

This Factory League baseball game on a Saturday afternoon in 1914 drew a crowd to South East Park (now Keye-Mallquist).

Christmas Tree for the Public

The city enjoyed its first outdoor, community Christmas tree in 1913. The tree was at Montague House, an old stone building in South Park that the Rockford Woman's Club used as a community center for immigrant families. The center offered sports, music, art and education serving Italians, Lithuanians, Greeks, Germans, Irish, Jews, Swedes and, later, Poles and African-Americans.

In December 1913, the district's playground director, L.W. Thompson, wanted a large Christmas tree for the city, particularly the Montague House neighborhood. He felt a large tree in South Rockford would provide great joy for the immigrant families and especially, the children.

Thompson went to the Register-Gazette which promoted the idea with a story headlined, "L.W. Thompson of Montague House Proposes Outdoor Christmas Tree." The tree, the paper said, would be in front of Montague House in South Park.

Thompson hoped someone would donate a suitable tree. Some people contributed money, which he kept for gifts of candy, fruit and nuts for children. He got neighborhood kids to make paper chains and popcorn strings for decorations, and the Rockford Electric Co. offered to light the tree. A ceremony was planned on Christmas Eve.

John Andrews offered a 20-foot tree from his front yard on School Street. Thompson promptly sent five men to cut it down, load it on a wagon and haul it to Montague House. There, said the newspaper, on Dec. 22, "10 husky men and 100 or more willing youngsters" pulled ropes to hoist the tree in place. "A Christmas spirit is enveloping all of Rockford," said the paper.

On Christmas Eve, streets were

This community Christmas tree, erected with support from the Young Business Men's Association, was in Fair Grounds Park in 1921.

jammed as hundreds of people (one estimate said more than 1,000) came to see the tree lit up. Commissioner Robert Tinker was on hand, offering a "Merry Christmas" to one and all.

The Park District continues to erect outdoor Christmas trees. Some were at Fair Grounds and some were downtown, but the tree now is at Sinnissippi each year.

The tradition has gladdened the hearts

These girls were in a play festival in Sunset Park in 1913.

of thousands and thousands of children, and more than a few adults.

Tinker certainly enjoyed the spectacle on Christmas Eve in 1913. Before retiring that night, he wrote in his diary, "Another fine day … Rockford's first outdoor public tree at Montague House."

Excellent Early Rec Programs

The board kept fine-tuning its services for children. In the 1913 annual report, playground director L. W. Thompson reported that four young women were hired to supervise park activities for girls because they could be more effective than men in that role.

A few years later, the district employed Edith Sackett, a Wellesley College graduate who had completed a program in recreation at the Hull House in Chicago, the community center founded by Nobel Peace Prize winner Jane Addams.[5] Sackett's 1915 report to the board asked for shelter and wading pools to keep children cool on "torrid summer days" and for a fiddler or accordion player for folk dancing lessons.[6]

It is significant that the Park District, very early in its history, hired professional staff to conduct recreation programs for children. The money for playground programs no doubt came from corporate tax funds, generally reserved for land, facilities and maintenance. It would be almost 50 years before the Park District passed a separate recreation tax, which led to a wide range of programming in what became the golden age of public recreation.

Back in the early days, though, the district offered games and crafts including tennis, baseball, basketball, volleyball, football, soccer, quoits (throwing rings to land on a pole), field and track, gymnastics, circle and singing games, folk dancing, story telling and basketry.

Faust encouraged games that did not include "violent exercise" but competition flourished with a tennis tournament, baseball leagues, inter-park track and field meets, soccer and football games. The district presented drama festivals, too, and offered evening play hours when parents were invited. Total attendance for the summer children's programs topped 100,000.

By the summer of 1914, the district had opened a roque court (a game similar to croquet played on a hard surface) and lawn bowling green. Playground Director Thompson said baseball continued to be the most popular game, with city leagues taking advantage of the parks' ball diamonds. Tennis players crowded the courts all summer. Children received instruction in gymnastics and folk dancing.

Playground Director Thompson had one wish. Football was the chief sport in fall, he said, but soccer should be "encouraged in every way possible, as it is a much better game for the playgrounds than regular football."

By 1920, the district was paying a playground director along with five men and five women, each of whom supervised a playground from 10 a.m. to 9 p.m. while school was out.

The following year, the park and the school district formed a Department of Physical Activities and Recreation to ensure recreational programming year round, either in the parks or in school gymnasiums. Leo Lyons, who was known as "recreation director" for both the city and the schools, took charge. His report that summer made note of 70 school baseball teams; 48 school football teams; 950 youth in the annual track meet; boat excursions and a free movie day for children in summer programs; and an exhibition of handwork done by girls at the parks in Stewart's Dry Goods Store.

At the close of 1924, Lyons reported the gyms and school swim pools "were in almost constant use from the close of school at 3:30 in the afternoon until 10 or 11 o'clock at night." Basketball became the "king of winter sports," attracting such large crowds that games had to be moved out of the school gyms to the Inglaterra dance pavilion at 115 North Second St. (The Inglaterra, now demolished, later became the Ing roller-skating rink).

These collaborations marked the beginning of a long and productive relationship between the Park and School districts, which often worked to the benefit of taxpayers in the form on lower costs and better programs.

Lyons worked with the Outdoor Winter Sports Association to provide safe skating and coasting places for children. He also urged the district to inaugurate programs dealing with art, music and drama for children uninterested in sports.

Adults were not ignored. In 1910, Lyons organized the Rockford Industrial Athletic Association, an organization that became the oldest and largest group of its kind in

A church held its summer picnic in Blackhawk Park in 1916.

Developing the riverfront has been a topic in Rockford for well over 100 years. Here's a plan proposed by George Roper in 1909. In 1922, Park Board President E.W. Brown wrote of "a desire of mine to see a river drive" from State Street to Auburn and from Black Hawk Park to the Camp Grant bridge. Neither happened and, a century later, we're still talking about enhancing our riverfront.

the nation, according to a Register-Republic article in 1955. Original members were the Andrews Wire Co. and Rockford Mitten and Hosiery Co. There were no adult women's teams or co-ed teams in those days but adult men by the hundreds joined various teams. By 1913, the association split into the Factory and Commercial baseball leagues. Companies sponsoring teams included Free Sewing, Barber-Colman, Trahern Pump, Hess & Hopkins, Kurtz Action, Clark Manufacturing, Rockford Watch, Rockford Malleable, Busron's Knitting, Central Union Telegraph and Rockford Printers.

The Free Sewing team was cream of the league, primarily because of pitcher Hal Carlson and center fielder Fred Schulte. Carlson went on to play for the Pittsburgh Pirates, Philadelphia Phillies and Chicago Cubs. Schulte made the "Big Leagues" with the St. Louis Browns, Washington Senators and the Pirates. The league and its athletes grew to be so popular that, in 1940, baseball games were broadcast on WROK radio.

The Industrial Association has a long history. In 2011, it included more than 35 companies and 1,100 adults in softball, basketball, volleyball, trapshooting, riflery and darts.

Validating 'Forest City' Title

The city's tree population always interested the Park District, which planted different varieties each year in various parks. In the 1915 annual report,

the district reported on a tree census done by school children and "actuated by a desire to establish definitely and for all time to come the right to the appellation of Rockford, 'The Forest City.'"

The census counted 142,044 trees (excluding cemeteries, Browns Woods, and Sinnissippi and Black Hawk parks). That amounted to nearly three trees for every person in the city. Forty-five percent of them were elms, with box elder the next most predominant tree at 14 percent.

Today, there are an estimated 133,000 trees on city rights of way and in parks. That works out to less than one for every person. Most of the elms were wiped out 40 – 50 years ago. Maple is the overriding favorite, at least along streets, with ash in second place.

The Dream Takes Shape • Late 1800s – 1928

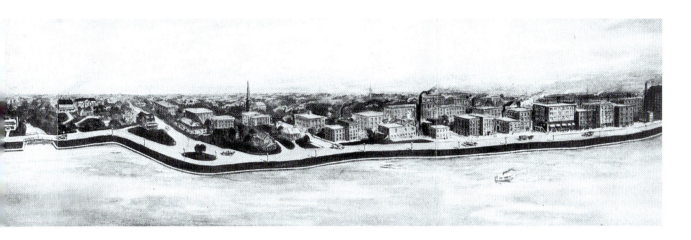

Music in the Parks

The first band concerts were held in Sinnissippi Park in 1911. They were extremely popular and the board soon scheduled concerts at Fair Grounds and Black Hawk parks, too.

Local military bands and Salvation Army bands performed often, but smaller groups played, too. Mr. Archie Short's Orchestra, for example, drew large crowds to Black Hawk Park on Sunday afternoons in the 1920s.

One band got a little carried away at a Labor Day concert in Black Hawk Park in 1917. The incident was so upsetting to the board that Emanuel Roos, captain of the Swedish Salvation Army band, was summoned to the next Park Board meeting September 18 to explain.

According to board minutes, "…the band refused to cease playing while famed attorney Clarence Darrow was addressing an audience in behalf of the workmen and after being told by President Faust to desist, they continued playing."

The minutes give no details on the "misunderstanding" that led to the band's behavior or on Darrow's appearance. They do state that the board did not find Roos' explanation entirely satisfactory but paid the band $25, anyway.

The Morning Star called the incident an "unfortunate interruption… that appeared to be of no particular significance other than unfortunate location of the speaker's stand and the music pavilion."

This Rockford band performed at some of the district's earliest park concerts.

Rockford Embraces Parks

By the thousands, people used the parks. "The capacities of the parks were taxed to their utmost" on July 4, 1914, Riis reported, adding that families and groups regularly used parks for picnics at all times of the day.

On any summer weekend, there were large park gatherings sponsored by local companies, churches, social or service clubs. Frequently, organizations came to the Park Board beforehand seeking permission to sell soft drinks and cigars. The list of organizations that were given approval in the summer of 1911 shows the diversity of Rockford citizens who were using the parks: South Park Lutheran Church, Skandinavians Socialist Sjick Kasson, Rockford Central Labor Union, African Methodist Episcopal Church, Carpenters and Joiners, Centennial Methodist Church, Forest City Lodge and Swedish Free Chorus.

The board made sure the parks were good neighbors. When the pastor of Third Presbyterian Church complained that baseball games at C. E. Brown Park on Sunday mornings disturbed services and encouraged children to miss Sunday school, the board closed the diamond until after 1:30 p.m. on that day. The board also turned down requests for dances on the Sabbath although dances generally were approved on other days of the week.

Still, people did not always get along. The board in 1918 noted that there was "friction" between the bands giving concerts and that the Italian band seemed to be composed "greatly of aliens." Since that apparently disturbed some people, the board canceled the Italian group's concerts.

We don't defend all the board actions throughout history; we report them to let you know what the world was like back then.

Partners in a Civic Vision

George Roper kept the parks on the front burner when he became chairman of the City Plan Commission in 1915. He had left the Park Board after serving just two years, but remained deeply interested in the well being of the parks and the city as a whole.

His role on the Plan Commission was to develop a comprehensive plan "for the improvement and extension of Rockford, Illinois."

Roper's group chose Myron Howard West, president of American Park Builders in Chicago, to formulate a plan for the city. The money for the study came from various sources, including the Park District, which contributed $1,000. Individual commissioners — former and current — wrote personal checks to help pay for the study. Among them

Riverfront land was prized by developers, as shown in this advertisement full of promises for lots in Loves Park.

The Dream Takes Shape • Late 1800s – 1928

Photos show the Beattie homestead with (from left) Anna and Mary I. Beattie. Levin Faust wrote in the 1920 annual report that the sisters' names will "shine like bright stars" among those "who made the world a better place to live in."

were Faust, Roper, Rew, Brown, Frank S. Horner, and F. L. Cleveland.

Adopted in 1918, the plan put significant emphasis on acquiring riverfront property for public recreation uses. "It is difficult to conceive a more beautiful river than the Rock," the Rockford Plan said. By 1918, it noted, "The city has encroached upon the river …" Still, West concluded, "Few waterways leading through cities have retained so much of their original beauty."

He proposed drives along both sides of the river, an idea Roper himself had pushed earlier. That part of the plan never came to be, but a bike/walking path now winds along the east side of the river from downtown Rockford 10 miles to Machesney Park. In 2011, work began on a shorter riverfront trail on the west bank.

"The Rockford Plan" was used as a guide for city growth for the next 50 years. The Park District's role in getting the plan written and keeping it alive illustrates again the civic vision and hopes of early Park Board commissioners.

Donors Helped Build Parks

The district bought land but it also received generous donations in its first two decades of existence.

By 1919, when the district was just 10 years old, it had more than doubled the initial acreage of 1909. Major acquisitions included the 150-acre Thomas G. Levings farm on the west side, a donation by the family.

Other major donors were the Winthrop Ingersoll family, which gave the district $50,000 for a west side golf course to honor their son, who died in World War I; and Mary I. and Anna Beattie, who provided both Beattie Playground off Rural Street and Beattie Park downtown, as well as a $30,000 endowment for upkeep of the historic downtown site.

World War I – "Duty to Save Money"

The district continued growing despite steering a very conservative course as war broke out in Europe. The United States, after struggling to remain neutral, was drawn into the conflict in 1917.

"Till the termination of the war," Faust said in his annual president's report, "we consider it a duty to save all money possible and not divert any funds from the channels that will strengthen the finances of our country and eventually win the war." The district steered clear of land purchases for the duration of the war.

As men went off to fight, there was a shortage of labor everywhere, including at the Park District. Riis reported the parks "were kept up as nearly normal as the labor conditions permitted."

Rockford was extremely important in the nation's preparation for war. In June 1917, it was chosen as Illinois' "cantonment" site.

Because of its railroads, electrical system, interurban rail service and other factors, including "wholesome conditions" in the city, the Department of War picked Rockford for a camp to train thousands of soldiers for battle. The 5,600-acre site south of the city was called Camp Grant.

Construction of the $13.5 million camp, complete with 12 miles of trenches for infantry training, may have been the largest and quickest project ever seen here. Work began immediately after the decision in June; the first soldiers arrived in September. As one observer said, it was as if the city doubled in size, almost overnight.

Press reports say 50 buildings went up each day. Miles of sewer and water pipe were installed, along with a water treatment plant, fire hydrants and three fire stations. An ice house to store 20 tons of ice and an incinerating plant were constructed. A depot big enough for 500 horses and other animals and a school for blacksmiths went up. Fifty telephone

Men from all over the country came to Camp Grant in Rockford to prepare for fighting in World War I.

Rockfordians lined the streets to show support as Camp Grant soldiers paraded before going overseas in World War I.

trunk lines were hung between Rockford, Camp Grant and Chicago. The Chicago, Burlington & Quincy Railroad built a station 400 feet in length and the Post Office built a branch office for the camp. A camp hospital was built.

By August, more than 8,000 civilian workers were employed at the camp along with several militia companies.

At any one time during World War I, Camp Grant housed 30,000 to 40,000 soldiers, many of whom relaxed, played sports and took in the city during their off-duty times. All told, the camp processed a million servicemen during the war.

Camp Grant gave Rockford a feeling of being a military town. The book "Sinnissippi Saga" reports that "hundreds of Army families moved to the city and soldiers were as numerous on streets as citizens."

The population jump of mostly young, single men put pressure on the city. The police force had to be expanded. Liquor violations increased. A soft drink stand was found to be a front for bootleggers. Laws were passed to prevent price gouging.

Organizations scrambled to keep the troops content. Mendelssohn Club, for example, transported its members and concert equipment to Camp Grant for performances. Once, it even got sleighs to plow through the snowdrifts for a show at the camp. Many shows and athletic events such as boxing matches were held in "Bell Bowl," a natural amphitheater on the camp near today's Chicago-Rockford Airport. And the Camp Grant military band entertained citizens with concerts at Fair Grounds and Beattie parks.

The saddest days were in the fall of 1918 when influenza took a heavy toll.

More than 300 Rockford citizens died and, in the close confines of Camp Grant, deaths reached more than 1,400. Every day, wagonloads of dead soldiers were hauled from the camp into temporary morgues.

War brings controversy and this war was no exception. Many people protested when, in May 1917, Congress passed the Selective Service Act ordering men between the ages of 21 and 30 to register for military service.

In Rockford, Socialist groups planned to meet in Black Hawk Park on June 3 for a "Big Repeal Conscription Law" rally. The board feared violence but allowed the meeting to take place. There was no trouble.

The Rockford Republic approved. In an editorial, it reminded that "it will be far better for America to accept the criticism of administration policies inevitable to a democracy … than to attempt to coerce unwilling action." Noting there was "of course, no disturbance," the editorial writer added, "the freedom of discussion has left the community on the whole much better satisfied than if this expression of what is acknowledged to be the feeling of a large number had been denied them."

But just days later, on June 11, the Park Board met in special session to consider an ordinance banning mass meetings in any parks unless the board gave its okay. Another proposal prohibited carrying banners or parading in any parks. Both ordinances were passed unanimously on July 3.

Lt. Clayton Ingersoll was killed during a plane crash in France in 1918.

Rockford wasn't the only city with folks who opposed the draft. During the first drawing nationwide, it was reported 50,000 men asked for exemptions and 250,000 just didn't register at all. The draft lasted only as long as the war.

Like other public entities, the Park District showed its support for the war. It increased the number of public concerts and used them to stir up patriotism, not only for the United States but also for our allies. There was a concert for France's Bastille Day and another in remembrance of the 1914 Battle of the Marne in France.

Soldiers were sent off to war with large parades and welcomed home the same way. On July 4, 1918, as 28,000 men paraded downtown on their way to deployments overseas, 100,000 local people lined the streets to cheer and salute.

A local newspaper collected quarters for "smoking kits for our boys," and devoted a page or more to Camp Grant news every day. The Park Board bought Liberty Bonds and Faust proposed a memorial park with trees planted in honor of local men serving overseas. But the memorial that would be remembered from this era is the one donated by the Winthrop Ingersoll family.

Remembering Soldier, Son

After losing their son, Lt. Clayton C. Ingersoll, in a military plane crash in France in 1918, the family presented the Park District with $50,000 for an 18-hole golf course and athletic field.

Land was purchased just south of West State Street and golf course architect Bendelow again was called to design the new course, some 6,400 yards in length.

Golfers were elated. They had been asking for a second municipal course almost since the first, Sinnissippi, had opened in 1912.

On September 2, 1922, the Ingersoll course officially opened, with a low-flying plane dropping flowers for Mr. and Mrs. Winthrop Ingersoll in a tribute to their son. Winthrop Ingersoll then drove the first ball and the course was in business.

Park District officials were proud of the course and its state-of-the-art watering system, which enabled one man to oversee the sprinkling of 18 greens at one time.

A golfer and his caddy on Ingersoll Golf Course, which opened in 1922.

'Ridiculously' Low Golf Fees

By 1925, golfers swarmed both Park District golf courses, prompting the hiring of a pro at Ingersoll. The following year, the district began charging golfers to use the courses.

Recreation Director Lyons explained why: "Golf is no longer a game for Scotchmen, those who have wealth, or those of old age, but is rapidly developing into a game played by men and women of all types, classes, nationality and financial circumstances. It is no uncommon sight at 6 o'clock in the morning or 5 o'clock in the afternoon to see a man in a blue shirt and overalls with hands and face smeared with grease on our golf courses playing one, two or three holes, depending upon the time at his disposal," Lyons wrote in the 1925 – 26 annual report.

Lyons said the fees were imposed with one object in mind, "that of supplying more golf facilities." Golfers complained at first but by the end of season, fees were no longer an issue, he said.

The fee, even by 1926 standards, was modest. Adult Park District residents paid $1 a year. Youth under 18 paid 50 cents and those under 15 could golf all year for 25 cents. Golfers who didn't live in the district were charged $1 a day.

That year, the golf courses collected $4,000 from in-district golfers and $3,500 from those who lived outside the district. After expenses were paid, the Park Board had $4,000 remaining, set aside for a third course.

The plan of charging "a ridiculously low price," would soon lead to better-operated and additional courses, Lyons predicted.

Rally organizers had to promise not to "criticise our Government's official actions…"

Constitutional Quandary

The ordinance passed in 1917 prohibiting carrying banners and holding mass meetings or parades in the parks was brought up for board discussion in 1924 by Commissioner Fay Lewis. He believed it was unconstitutional and asked for its repeal. Lewis also objected to an alternate ordinance proposed by Attorney Rew that would prohibit advocating the overthrowing of government by violent or unlawful means and the sale of books, pamphlets and any written material that advocated violence to reform or overthrow the government. The board passed the new ordinance with Lewis voting against it.

The board had been guarded about giving permission for mass meetings in parks. In 1919, Faust had brought a pamphlet from the Industrial Workers of the World (IWW) to a meeting and had the secretary read it. The document advocated free organization of trade unions, which seemed like a threat to manufacturers like Faust. He advised the board to use caution when considering permits for any speakers who wanted to talk about trade unions.

But Lewis was determined to have a rule that provided the freedom he believed the Constitution guaranteed. On July 15, 1924, he proposed that people who wanted to use the park for speeches agree to "respect the rules and ordinances governing the parks … and abide by the laws of the land, and duly respect the Constitutions" of Illinois and the United States. That permit form was approved and the matter resolved.

That brings two thoughts to mind. One, that Fay Lewis and I think a lot alike. Lewis, who operated a large tobacco distribution company and was respected as a businessman, also was a social reformer. He edited a book in 1903 decrying the horrible conditions in the Rockford jail. He joined the Anti-Capital Punishment Society, founded the local Humane Society, frequently hired paroled felons in his business, was a close friend of famed attorney Clarence Darrow and famed poet Edgar Lee Masters, who wrote part of his "Spoon River Anthology" while staying at Lewis' home in Rockford. And, of course, he was a commissioner and president on the Park Board.

Fay Lewis

The other thing Lewis' courageous action brought to mind was a request from the Nazis to meet in Sinnissippi Park in 1979. If Lewis hadn't carried the day with his ordinance about mass meetings, I wouldn't have been able to grant the Nazis' request. As it was, I had to, to uphold the Constitution just as Lewis had 55 years earlier.

Riis Earns National Respect

The first superintendent of the Park District, Paul Riis, put Rockford on the national map during his 17 years here.

Riis was highly respected by his peers, who elected him director of the American Institute of Park Executives and American Park Society from 1923 to 1926. That organization was a forerunner of today's National Recreation and Park Association.

> "The exterior growth of the city is still largely in the hands of the real estate operator."
> – PAUL RIIS

Riis also is responsible for bringing the headquarters of Park and Recreation magazine to Rockford. A friend had asked why the magazine could not be published here. Riis went to work on the idea, collecting $4,000 from local merchants to clear up a debt that hung over the publication. With that out of the way, the magazine was free to relocate from Minot, N. D., to Rockford in 1925. It is one example of the way the Rockford Park District, early on, made a name for itself on the national park and recreation scene and has continued to do so ever since.

The Institute held Riis in high regard. The September-October 1925 issue of the magazine contained a resolution about the national group's annual meeting at the Nelson Hotel in Rockford. It said in part:

"…we know that the great pleasure and profit in visiting this splendid city, in seeing its wonderful parks, its beautiful homes, its true hospitality … could not have been ours without the driving power, painstaking care and attention to detail of our respected fellow member and officer, Paul B. Riis. We as an organization have listened in delight to the encomiums that have been so justly showered upon him by all for his great achievement in the up building of the parks of Rockford and for this masterpiece convention…"

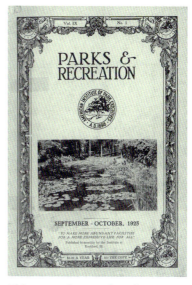

This 1925 issue of Parks and Recreation magazine referred to Rockford as a "splendid" city.

At the convention, delegates learned much about zoos and parks. A Cincinnati delegate, for example, spoke about the difficulties of keeping giraffes in captivity, noting there were only five giraffes in the United States at that time. They also heard presentations about horticultural topics and enjoyed a few less-serious events, including a review of a popular show at the public bathing pool in Beaumont, Texas, in which college freshmen and sophomore male students played the role of "burlesque bathing beauties."

Riis delivered opening comments, in which he noted the delegates would visit 22 of the Park District's 39 properties. He also boasted that the region had, two years earlier, started the County Forest Preserve to "supplement the demands for more open spaces, a demand more insistent perhaps because of the present day ease of individual transportation."

Riis also spoke frankly about what he saw as weaknesses in the district. "Unfortunately," he said, "no plans were ever made for a comprehensive park system. There are no parkways or boulevards linking its units … it simply grew … yet the somewhat haphazard building up of the park system has served the needs of Rockford admirably."

Riis lamented that the 1917 – 18 City Plan, the brainchild of early Park District commissioner George Roper, "sought to link and substantiate the existing system but failed to become an ordinance. In consequence, much idle land of that time has become irrevocably lost for all time through industrial development. The exterior growth of the city is still largely in the hands of the real estate operator."

Still, the Roper plan had helped, Riis said, by "neutralizing schemes of individuals or corporations and has focused attention upon the necessity of more comprehensive planning and building."

Riis leaves; 'Apparent Hasty Decision'

Riis' departure a few years later is a bit puzzling. On May 2, 1927, immediately after the board unanimously and routinely appointed Riis superintendent for another year, he stood up to announce that he was resigning as of June 1. According to the Rockford-Register, Riis gave no reason for his "apparently hasty decision," which was not expected. There was speculation that he was upset with the election of Adelbert R. Floberg, a bank cashier, as president of the board.

On June 7, the board tied 2-2 on a motion to accept Riis' resignation. Floberg then cast the deciding vote in favor of releasing Riis who, according to the newspaper, "sat silently watching the proceedings."

Just before the board adjourned, however, Riis rose and read a letter stating that he had fired Assistant Superintendent Arthur Reitsch May 18. The newspaper

Clarence Pedlow

account added that Riis "bitterly denounced his former aide and his letter was couched in terms that were anything but flattering to his ousted assistant."

Riis went to Pittsburgh where he became superintendent of the Allegheny County Park District. It was reported that Allegheny recruited him for a salary of $7,200 a year, a nice raise from the $5,000 he had earned here. He oversaw expansion of the Allegheny County system from 3,200 to 4,200 acres and turned it into the sixth largest park district in the United States. In 1932, he returned to Rockford where he did landscape work for local industrialist Howard Colman and helped famed conservationist Aldo Leopold of Wisconsin on groundbreaking deer food studies.

The Dream Takes Shape • Late 1800s – 1928

Clarence Pedlow Succeeds Riis

In facing what could have become a controversial personnel issue, the board avoided conflict with its choice of Clarence T. Pedlow as the district's second superintendent. Pedlow was as familiar with the district as anyone, having worked as an engineer and horticulturist almost since the district began. He had studied at Washington University and the Missouri Botanical Garden in St. Louis and Cornell College in Ithaca, N.Y., and had taught horticulture at North Carolina State College.

Speculation had been that the board would consider Reitsch, who had been fired by Riis, or County Forester T.G. Lindquist for the top executive post. But Pedlow was appointed June 14, the same day the board rehired Reitsch and put him in charge of Sinnissippi Park.

Swim Pools 'Neither Sanitary nor Practical'

The one area on which early Park Boards did not move quickly was swimming pools. It took 15 years before the board invested in a quality pool, after a number of less-than-successful attempts.

The first "pool," created with a dam on Kent Creek in Fair Grounds Park in 1910, was popular but problematic. So much silt flowed into the swimming hole that it became shallow. Pollution was evident. By 1916, the state said the water was too contaminated for swimmers.

The Park District's next "pool" was not a pool, either. It was an abandoned quarry south of Auburn Street between Horseman and Kilburn. The city gave it to the district in 1915. The district provided supervision and the quarry drew hundreds of bathers on hot summer days.

Because of intermittent contamination and other issues, however, the quarry was a problem. In 1918, the Park District closed and fenced it.

There was talk of putting pools in various parks but for years, nothing was done.

Faust devoted pages of space in two annual reports to his views of swim pools and his defense of the board for not rushing to build one. In the 1914 report, he said he had voted against spending $10,000 on a pool because he was convinced it would be "neither sanitary nor practical." Two years later, he asked the state to ban river pollution and wrote, "When the sewage nuisance is stopped,

The city gave the Park District this quarry in northwest Rockford in 1915, and it served swimmers until 1918, when it was closed because of contamination.

This mud-bottom pool at Fair Grounds Park was the first municipal pool in the city when it opened in 1924.

our river (the Rock) will be ideal for swimming and bathing purposes and this problem will be solved forever."

Rivers and creeks may have been the ideal swimming sites in Faust's native Sweden, but in the Rock River Valley in the early 1900s, with industry and population growing rapidly, that was not the case. Pollution was a problem, and drownings in the river were frequent during warm months. The Park Board recognized the Rock River's shortcomings when, in 1921, it budgeted $10,000 for a municipal pool. Construction started the following year at the north end of Fair Grounds Park at Acorn and Kilburn avenues. The pool, then known as a "tank" pool, had a mud bottom.

In early June 1924, final plans were made for operating the pool. The board said it would not charge swimmers, who were to supply their own suits. A couple of wringers were to be installed for wringing the water out of wet suits after swimming. Mixed bathing was not allowed, not even to allow men to teach their wives or girlfriends how to swim.

The pool was a huge success. In August, the board agreed to a request from night shift workers at Barber-Colman and Ingersoll to open the pool at 7:30 two mornings a week so they could get in a swim after work. (In those days, it was common for workers to use public pools as bathing facilities, particularly after long factory shifts).

By 1928, Park Superintendent C.T. Pedlow said the swim pool was the most popular feature of Fair Grounds Park. The district already had contracted to build a second pool to open in 1929 at Tenth Avenue Park.

Kissin' in the Parks

The Park District in 1928 authorized a motorcycle officer to control "the rough work of bullies" in the parks. Others using the parks, including lovers, would not be disturbed as long as their behavior was respectable, the board said.

> *"My fella always wants to do some kissin' before we go home…"*
> – LETTER FROM ANNIE BJORKLAND

That inspired a letter to the assistant chief of police, Homer Reid, from a young lady named Annie Bjorkland. As it was reported at the time, Annie wrote that she had seen the letter about "kissin' in the parks…" Then she asked, "Where is a young cupple going to make love if her folks won't let her bring her fella in the parlor and the movies won't let you do it there. My fella," said Annie, "always wants to do some kissin' before we go home and he can't park downtown nowhere."

"Did that mean," Annie asked, referring to the board's promise that lovers would not be bothered, "honest that the cops won't bother us none in the parks. Me and him will be at Harlem Park Friday night and probably out to Black Hawk Park about 11…We won't be bothered, will we?"

There are no arrest reports for Annie so apparently she and her amorous boyfriend found a suitable location for their smooching.

20 Years of Progress

The first park commissioners had pledged to put parks within the reach of everyone. By 1928, they could say they had kept their promise. It is doubtful even Faust envisioned the system of parks and programs put together in less than 20 years.

The district itself had grown with Guilford Township annexed to the Park District in the fall election of 1928, increasing its size by 36 square miles.

Summer playground programs for children attracted thousands of youngsters and the district served adults as well. By 1923-24, more than 660 men played basketball or baseball in leagues overseen by the Park District. A community that just 20 years prior had no public recreational outlets now had dozens.

Playground Director Leo Lyons wrote in that year's annual report that 1,257 children, on average, attended summer programs each day, and the schools, including Rockford Public and St. Thomas high schools, used the playgrounds every evening from the opening of school in September until after Thanksgiving. "With the public school gymnasiums using all

The roller coaster at the privately-owned Harlem Amusement Park was a great attraction in the late 1890s and early 1900s.

available time from early in October until late in March, one can readily see that the recreational facilities in Rockford are being used to their capacity," Lyons wrote.

The board had turned down an opportunity for entertainment. In 1927, owners of the Harlem Park Amusement Grounds offered to sell the westside riverfront attraction to the Park District.

Harlem Park had served the city well since 1891. With a wooden roller coaster that took riders 1,100 feet in 26 seconds, a 5,000-seat auditorium, dance pavilion, wharfs where riverboats docked, and other attractions, the 47-acre park has been called the "MetroCentre of its time." It thrived until 1927, done in partly by Park District facilities. Also competing with it was Central Park, an amusement center that featured newer, more thrilling rides.

Sellers of Harlem Park in 1927 did not name a price when they approached the Park Board, which felt the property was too costly for it to take on, anyway. The grounds were sold to developers in 1928. The site is the general area of the 2100 through 2500 blocks of Harlem Boulevard.

By 1928, there were three large public parks used for sizeable gatherings and sporting events, as well as individuals, and 16 neighborhood parks. They added up to 719 acres.

Sinnissippi remained heavily used for picnics by families and larger groups. The riverfront greenhouses, built in 1923, supplied nearly all plants for the parks. A rosarium, perennial garden and lagoon, built in 1922, attracted folks nearly every day. Superintendent Pedlow was largely responsible for the sunken gardens created along the river.

The district also took pride in attracting as many species of ducks as possible. The 1925 – 26 annual report notes that "interesting specimens of mute swan, Egyptian and Canadian geese and smaller waterfowl … have been an attraction and source of enjoyment." The editor of the national Parks and Recreation magazine, who had moved that publishing operation to Rockford, donated 75 wild ducks of 14 species to the Park District.

The district built a duck house next to the greenhouses as winter quarters for the birds and to "harden off" plants in the spring.

Black Hawk was more than a park. It was an overnight camp for tourists, at first free under Chamber of Commerce supervision. In 1928, the Park Board took it over and charged 50 cents a night per car. Four-thousand campers were registered that year. Black Hawk's shelter made the park a popular picnic and concert site.

Fair Grounds, the third large park, counted more than 46,000 swimmers in its pool in 1928. Fair Grounds was a busy park. Central High School used the track and hosted the Big Seven Conference meet in 1929. The park also had excellent facilities for lawn bowling, horseshoes, tennis and other sports.

'Rockford's 'White Elephant'

Black Hawk Park was perhaps most well-known for a zoo it housed from 1920 to 1923. Operated by a local Zoological Society, the zoo contained a Bengal tiger, a buffalo, monkeys and "Babe," an elephant donated by the Ringling Brothers Circus.

Babe brought crowds to the zoo but she literally ate the Zoological Society out of house and home. When the Park Board said it couldn't help pay for zoo operations, specifically, food for Babe, the zoo closed.

Babe remains a local legend. Back in the 1920s, however, there was a different sentiment, at least according to an article that appeared in the November — December 1925 issue of Parks and Recreation magazine, along with a picture

Rockford's one and only elephant was Babe. Unfortunately, she ate too much and was sold.

of Babe lumbering out of a grove of trees at Blackhawk Park.

The magazine noted that Babe was sold to the P.T. Barnum Company of Mexico. It added, "…her spirit still dwells in Rockford, not as an inspiration to further endeavors but as a solemn warning against any future attempt to establish a municipal zoo and as a fearsome example of what may befall if such an attempt be made."

If members of the American Association of Zoological Parks and Aquariums, at an annual meeting in Rockford, asked why there was no zoo, the magazine went on, "they found the universal answer to be 'Babe.'

"And there is no use to argue the question with the average Rockford citizen. He is as certain that a zoo is an institute of disaster and ruin as he is that the sun rises in the morning. For it should be known that Babe was Rockford's 'white elephant' and that she, or more properly, her appetite … created a condition in their fair city almost equal to the 'hard times' period of a Democratic administration."

When Babe arrived, the article reported, a "number of proud and public-spirited citizens immediately declared they would 'go good' for Babe's care and board. Little did they reckon on her

The zoo at Black Hawk Park had a Bengal tiger.

capacity for bales of tender hay and choice tidbits of succulent vegetables. Babe was fastidious, too, and required a valet to look after her trunk and keep her presentable and in good humor.

"But crowds went to Black Hawk Park by the thousands and the zoo began to grow. Rockford does not do things in small ways so the next addition was a royal Bengal tiger. Then a buffalo and a cage of monkeys were added. The crowds increased but so did the food bills.

"One by one, the aforesaid proud and public-spirited citizens lost their enthusiasm. They took their names from the list of Babe's supporters till but one man remained. He had faith that Babe would prove her worth, as well as the royal Bengal, the buffalo and the monkeys. But the enthusiasm of the others turned to indifference, and then changed into frank and open criticism. 'Why deprive poor widows and little, helpless children of bread and other necessities and maintain a big, healthy, elephant in lazy comfort?' Such was the cry of the critics.

"So Babe was disposed of, likewise the royal Bengal, the buffalo and the monkeys. Before writing this story, we interviewed the faithful, loyal citizen. He showed us the canceled checks that came from a big envelope marked 'municipal zoo.' There were many of them and some in three or four figures. He still believes in a zoo as a worthy, paying institution but the rest of Rockford doesn't.

"The citizen also told us a little of Babe's history. She came from a family of killers and her own son killed his keeper and had to be shot. But under the beneficent care at Black Hawk Park, Babe's temper mellowed and she became so tame that she would eat from the hand of the park superintendent without fear or sign of hostility.

"Of course," the all-knowing writer of the article concluded, "we know that Rockford began her zoo at the wrong end and that the moral of this little tale is that you must begin in a small way, develop your public interest, sympathy and support and expand in proportion. But Rockford has had her 'white elephant' on her hands and Rockford will not listen – even to our moral."

Parks 'Not an Expense but an Investment'

As the Rockford Park District concluded its first 20 years, it had changed the city, bringing a quality of life not previously afforded to working class families. What J. Horace McFarland, a key figure in creation of the National Park Service, wrote in 1925 was true in Rockford and throughout the nation:

"Look back to 1900, those of you who can," McFarland wrote in a letter to the editor of Parks and Recreation magazine. "You will remember that a park in America

The Dream Takes Shape • Late 1800s – 1928

in that year was a place in which the wealthy might drive, but on the sacred grass of which the common people dared not tread. Park expenditures were considerable for statuary and monstrosities of carpet-beds, but very little for playgrounds and recreational facilities.

"What does one find now after 25 years of education? ... the general knowledge that a well-placed, well-maintained park in any community is not an expense but an investment; that it serves as the most efficient means of promoting the public health and maintaining good order; that money wisely spent on parks is ... running parallel with the guarding of the milk supply and the provision of pure water in any forward-looking community."

Rockford's Park District already was moving beyond the basic function of maintaining parks. No one yet realized what strong partnerships would be forged by the district and local museums, but museum assets already were growing. Eighteen months after the death in 1924 of Commissioner Robert Tinker, his widow, Jessie, gave the Park District the land around their home in south Rockford and, in return for $150 a month for the remainder of her life, the Swiss Cottage upon her death.

Superintendent Riis recognized that the cottage was a treasure. In a newspaper article he wrote late in 1926, Riis said the "outstanding feature in growth" of the district the past year was Tinker park.

The home, Riis added, "reflected admirably the high degree of 'Uncle Robert's' artistic temperament and shall ever be a most fitting memorial to his kindly nature."

The tradition of families leaving property to the people via the Park District already was established. Thomas Goodsman Levings gave the district 135 acres of beautiful land on the southwest side in 1919. Opened for picnics in 1920, Levings Lake Park has the only swimming lake in the district and is thought by many to be the loveliest park. It is one of many

Fair Grounds Park became a sports and playground center and one of the loveliest spots in Rockford.

Photo was taken on "Hobo Day" in South East Park (now Keye-Mallquist) in Rockford in 1923.

parks — large and small — that are named for the families who generously turned them over to the Park District. The practice reflects the respect citizens had for the district and the careful way it handled both funds and properties. In the early days, it also signaled a growing recognition of the value of parks to a community's health and well-being.

As the Park District began year 20, its golf courses were crowded, even with resident fees raised to $3 a year for golfing at Sinnissippi or Ingersoll. Even though two new private courses — Mauh-Nah-Tee-See and what is today known as Forest Hills — had opened, golfers clamored for more. The Park District had purchased land for a third public course at 20th Street and Sandy Hollow.

The district owned or controlled 731 acres of land and the value of that property and the improvements upon them was nearly $3 million in 1928, according to an appraisal done by the Rockford Real Estate Board.

That year, the board collected $160,000 in taxes; $19,000 in sales at park concessions; and $14,000 in golf fees. It spent $67,000 on park improvements, including $31,000 on the soon-to-be-opened Sandy Hollow Golf Course, and another $54,000 on park maintenance. Other expenses included $3,450 for the superintendent's salary, $10,500 for playground staff; $4,000 for the greenhouse operation, and $3,800 for auto and motorcycle costs. "Because of vandalism and wanton destruction," the board said in its annual report, it was forced to hire a full time police officer.

The Park District had become a point of pride for the city, as much so, said Faust, as the School District was at the time.

He noted that the Park Board had at times been criticized as being too liberal with the public's dollars and at other times, charged with being too frugal.

When you looked at the value of parks compared to what had been paid for them, and the number of people using them, it was easy to defeat the argument that money had been wasted, he said.

He defended the Park Board's cautious spending with a personal note.

"The writer may be narrow on these points. Having fought for every inch of ground for economical independence himself, he will always have these defects of being economical with both his own and other people's money," Faust said.

That philosophy may explain why Faust was re-elected to the Park Board each year until his death in 1936.

The district's first two decades of success were no doubt inspired by commissioners and their refusal to accept mediocrity in facility, program or staff, and by the dedication of people they hired. That led to long tenures of service by superintendents, other employees and commissioners. In its first two decades, the board had only 14 board members. Some, such as Tinker and Faust, served until their deaths.

Seth B. Atwood Joins the Board

Before Faust died in 1936, another dreamer joined him on the board. While Faust was stumping for passage of the park referendum in 1909, this visionary was busy starting a vacuum machine company. But by the time he was named to the board in 1928, Seth B. Atwood had started a legacy of service that would match that of Levin Faust.

Although Levin Faust and Seth B. Atwood served eight years together on the Rockford Park Board, history did not record any conversations between them. That's unfortunate because each man was a business genius with inventive and entrepreneurial skills that took him to the top of the manufacturing scene in Rockford. Each also believed that success brought with it the responsibility to give back to the community. And each chose the Rockford park system as his way to do that.

Residents who today praise our park system usually don't realize the influence of these two men. One or both were board leaders for 51 of the district's first 100 years. And Atwood's son and grandson continued that support into the 21st Century.

Faust and Atwood cannot be given enough credit for their insistence on quality parks and programs. With their fellow commissioners and their choice of superintendents, they built a strong foundation indeed.

A community that did not understand the need for public parks as the 1900s dawned had wholeheartedly embraced them 20 years later.

As Faust wrote, if parks ceased to exist in Rockford, "I think we would have a revolution…"

---

1 Lee, called the father of recreation in the United States, had a major impact on the Rockford Park District. Allen Sapora, a professor of recreation at the University of Illinois in the 1950s, studied his work and did his doctoral thesis on Lee's findings. Sapora was a key figure in developments in the Rockford Park District and his teaching influenced important leaders in the Park District's modern era, among them former Executive Director Webbs Norman and Jim Brademas, former superintendent of recreation in the district as well as a U of I professor.

2 Park systems already in existence were Peoria, Springfield, Pekin, Winnetka, Riverdale, Clyde district of Cicero, Foss, Murphysboro, Urbana, East St. Louis and Highland Park.

3 Whirlpool and the Roper Pump Co. still make Roper brand products.

4 Bendelow and the park commissioners were pioneers in opening golf to the common man back in 1911. The concept spread, thanks in part to Albert G. Spalding, a native of Byron who employed Bendelow from 1895 to 1916 to design courses and promote golf. Spalding was a baseball pitcher of note who later made a fortune in the sporting goods business.

5 Addams was born in Stephenson County and graduated from Rockford Female Seminary, now Rockford College.

6 Sackett was the mother of John Howard, former president of Rockford College and founder of the Howard Center in Rockford.

GROWTH OF THE PARK DISTRICT 1909 – 1928

Parks acquired 1909 – 1928

1909: Sinnissippi Park, 1401 N. Second St., 126 acres

1909: Haskell Park, 450 N. Church, 2 acres

1910: Blinn Point Triangle, 101 N. Main, .22 acre*

1910: Boilvin Triangle, 1367 Boilvin Ave., .03 acre*

1910: Brown's Point Triangle, 541 Woodlawn, .11 acre*

1910: Crawford Triangle, North Rockton Ave. and North Winnebago St., .46 acre*

1910: Fair Grounds Park, 450 Kilburn Ave., 18 acres

1910: Haight Park, 451 Lafayette Ave., 2.5 acres

1910: Keye-Mallquist Park (formerly Southeast Park), 1702 11th St., 6 acres

1910: Kimball Triangle ROW[1], Fisher and Haskell Aves., .04 acre*

1910: South Park, 126 Lane St., 5.3 acres

1910: Spafford Triangle, 602 Walnut St., .25 acre*

1910: Sunset Park, 1993 Mulberry St. (now site of Lewis Lemon School), 6 acres

1910: Williams Parkway ROW, Williams Park between East State and First Ave., .36 acre*

1911: Black Hawk Park, 101 15th Ave., 108 acres

1911: Browns Hills Circle, 804 Brown Hills Court, .06 acre

1911: Carolina Triangle, Carolina Ave./Nebraska Ave., 02 acre*

1911: Mandeville Park, 650 Montague St., 3 acres

1914: Beattie Playground, 1251 Rural St. (moved from North Second because of road construction), 3.4 acres

1917: Franz Park, 3210 School St., 2 acres

1918: Beattie Park, 401 N. Main St., 3.3 acres

1918: Garfield Ave. Playground, 1028 Garfield Ave., 2.5 acres

1919: Brown Park, 2010 N. Main St., 5 acres

1919: Dennis School Playground, 730 Lincoln Park Blvd., 13 acres

1919: Hancock Triangle ROW, Post Ave., Auburn and Hancock Sts., .04 acre*

1919: Levings Park, 1420 S. Pierpont Ave., 135 acres

1919: Oxford St. Triangle, Ellis Ave., Oxford and Clinton Sts., .05 acre*

1919: River Park, on west bank of river, north of Auburn to point where residences begin, .7 acre

1919: Westgate Parkway ROW, center right-of-way on Westgate south of Broadway to Oregon/Minnesota, .17 acre*

1920: Churchill Park, 2002 7th Ave., 13 acres

1920: Easton Parkway ROW, 1 acre*

1920: Ingersoll Memorial Park and Golf Course, 101 Daisyfield Road, 154 acres

1920: Ohio Triangle, 2002 Ohio Parkway, .11 acre*

1924: South Horace Park, 871 South Horace Ave., 4 acres

1925: Auburn St. Triangle, Auburn and Harlem Blvd., .01 acre+

1925: Bennett Triangle, 1206 North Ave., .08 acre

1926: Tenth Ave. Playground, 825 Tenth Ave., 10 acres

1926: Tinker Swiss Cottage Museum, 411 Kent St., 9 acres

1927: Andrews Memorial Park, 850 N. Central Ave., 4.2 acres

1927: Nelson Park, 1421 Nelson Blvd., 1.7 acres

1927: Oxford Park, 2420 Oxford, 4.5 acres**

1928: Franklin Parkway ROW, Franklin Place, .2 acre*

1928: Harmon Playfield, 1924 East Gate Parkway, 5.6 acres

1928: Huffman Blvd. Parkway ROW, 2200 Huffman Blvd., .65 acre*

1928: Sandy Hollow Golf Course, 2670 Sandy Hollow Road, 122 acres

Owned by the city and controlled by the Park District
** *Leased*
[1] *Right of Way*

THE COMMISSIONERS OF THE ERA 1909 – 1928

Levin Faust *Robert Tinker* *Fred Carpenter* *George D. Roper* *Henry W. Williams*

LEVIN FAUST
On board 1909 – 1936; president 1911 – 1920
Created what became Borg-Warner Co.; co-founded National Lock; re-organized Rockford Drilling Co. (Rockford Clutch). Served on boards of 19 companies. Helped found SwedishAmerican Hospital and Swedish American Bank (now Harris). Died in 1936 while still on Park Board at 73 years of age.

ROBERT H. TINKER
On board 1909 – 1924
Mayor in 1875. His Swiss Cottage was first home in city electrified in 1882. Convinced Illinois Central Railroad to route tracks through city. President, Chicago-Rockford Northwestern Railroad Co. Affiliated with Rockford Twist and Bit, Rockford Oatmeal Co., Rockford Steel and Bolt, and West End Street Co.

FRED C. CARPENTER
On board 1909 – 1910, first president 1909
Influential member of Rockford Club, which spearheaded campaign to create Park District. After term, remained active in Park District and served as attorney. Board held first meeting in his law office.

GEORGE D. ROPER
On board 1909 – 1911
Well-known for efficient and tireless leadership given to the Rockford Plan, adopted by Rockford City Plan Commission in March 1918. Document influences much discussion in public sector to this day. Started Roper Co. which made gas stoves and other appliances. Roper brand still manufactured.

HENRY W. WILLIAMS
On board 1909 – 1917; president 1910
Insurance executive, key in founding what today is Williams Manny Insurance Co. Retired from board in 1917 after serving nine years.

Continued next page

Napoleon Levasseur   *Dr. Alfred Olsen*   *Frank L. Cleveland*   *Frank S. Horner*   *Edward W. Brown*

NAPOLEON LEVASSEUR
On board 1910 – 1915

First Socialist on board. Brought interests of Rockford's Socialist Movement to board with little impact. Pushed for higher wages for workers.

DR. O. ALFRED OLSON
On board 1911 – 1916

Physician and Socialist who later started Communist Labor Party in Rockford. Arrested in Communist raid in city in 1920. Charges dropped.

FRANK L. CLEVELAND
On board 1915 – 1928

Native of Winnebago County. Business career in finance, banking and insurance. Served until death in 1928.

FRANK S. HORNER
On board 1916 – 1927; president 1925 – 1926

Established Horner Printing Company and operated it until 1905. Created Horner and Horner real estate business in 1915. Upon his death, was cited for "four decades (as) one of the builders of the city" by Morning Star.

EDWARD W. BROWN
On board 1917 – 1925; president 1921 – 1924

Mayor of city from 1895 to 1901. Early and staunch proponent of buying Rood Woods for Sinnissippi Park. Father and other family members owned controlling interest in Brown Building.

THE DREAM TAKES SHAPE • LATE 1800s – 1928

Fay Lewis   *Adelbert R. Floberg*   *Harry B. Andrews*   *Seth B. Atwood*

FAY LEWIS
On board 1924 – 1947; president 1937 – 1942
  Largest wholesale distributor (Fay Lewis and Brothers Co.) of tobacco in Midwest, outside city of Chicago. Personal friend of Clarence Darrow and Edgar Lee Masters, who portrayed him as "Lewis Fay" in "Spoon River Anthology."

ADELBERT R. FLOBERG
On board 1925 – 1937; president 1927 – 1937
  Brief but distinguished career with Manufacturers National Bank, where he became vice-president. Organized several manufacturing enterprises. President of Exel Manufacturing at the time of his death at age 53.

HARRY B. ANDREWS
On board 1927 – 1941
  Cited as quiet moving spirit on Park Board. Made motion to buy Colton tract, later linked to become Anna Page Park. Family donated Andrews Park, given as memorial to his father.

SETH B. ATWOOD
On board 1928 – 1960; president 1942 – 1960
  Founded Atwood Vacuum Machine Co.; invested in banks, savings and loan associations, real estate and hotels. Dedicated environmentalist and major force in growth of Park District. Made large donations to district and Forest Preserve. Longest length of service as commissioner with 32 years, last 18 as president.

PROFILE OF THE PARK DISTRICT 1909 – 1928

Year:	1910	1928
Statistic:		
Population	48,405	91,750
Number of Parks/ Properties	15	45
Park District Acreage	159.47	731.35
Total Budget	$140,343.49[1]	$177,063.00
Property Tax Revenue	$35,999.00	$160,142.00
Per Capita Expenditure from Taxes	$0.74	$1.74
Median Family Income	Not available	Not available
Estimated Total User Visits	Not available	Not available

[1] 1910 budget covered 18 months instead of 12 months.

CHAPTER 2
The Dream Grows
1929 – 1944

People need park services whether times are good or bad.

Atwood takes over leadership

When Seth B. Atwood came on the board in 1928, he brought values and a philosophy that were a close match to those of Faust. The two believed that the area's nicest pieces of woodland and riverbank ought to be used as public parks, and that a city's quality of life suffered greatly if parks were not part of the landscape. Atwood had been fortunate, he once told a newspaper reporter, to have a mother who introduced him at an early age to botany, geology and, even, the mysteries and majesty of storms. His interest in and love for nature never left him.

His involvement in the Park District began in 1924. It was his turn to speak at the Rotary Club's weekly meeting and his wife, Helen, suggested he talk about the local parks. She helped him with research and Atwood came up with a speech so impressive that he was asked to repeat it for other civic groups.

No doubt, park officials heard it, too. Four years later, they tapped Atwood to fill a vacant position on the Park Board. He accepted and went on to serve 32 years, from 1928 to 1960. For the last 18 years, he was president.

Atwood's time on the board spanned huge growth and challenges. The community and the Park District survived the Great Depression and World War II. The Atwood years saw a third golf course opened and major parks added, among them Anna Page, Alpine, Sand Park, Searls and Martin. Sinnissippi Park grew and the district got deeper into the world of art, museums and, even, airports.

Atwood, who thought there were too few parks, made it his personal business to add more. He gave the Park District a 332-acre piece of land near New Milford known as the Atwood Park, home to

Opposite: There may not be a prettier picture in the Rockford Park District than the sun setting over Levings Lake on the southwest part of the city. Levings Park was the first large donation to the district, a gift of 135 acres from the Thomas Goodsman Levings family in 1919. (Photo by David Scott)

Right: Seth B. Atwood

Building a Lasting Dream

This photo of the Park Board is from the late 1930s. From left are Harry B. Andrews, Seth B. Atwood, President Fay Lewis, Harry O. Swanson and Dr. Robert F. Schleicher.

the Atwood Environmnetal Center where more than 250,000 school children have been introduced to the wonders of wildlife, woods and water. Atwood also donated 350 acres to the County Forest Preserve, some of which were kept as a nature preserve and some of which became a golf course.

In an interview with a fellow Rotarian when he was 90, Atwood explained the reasons for his gifts. As a college student, he said, he felt he should make a career with a YMCA or Boys Club. "Then," he said, "I realized that I wasn't really fitted for it and made a promise to myself that if I could be successful, I would make it up from my business and personal effort … instead of going into YMCA work, I would earn some money and help that way."

He had a feeling, he said, that God gave him success in his business ventures so he could keep his promise.

Seth was retired from the board by the time I came to Rockford but we became friends. I was privileged to spend time with him. He was principled and highly energetic, a problem-solver with an incredible determination. His doctors, he told me once, had told him he should be dead by now. "I can't die, Webbs," he said. "I've got too much to do." He was always on the move. I think he must have slept with one eye open because he always had a new idea to try out."

'Children…play with all their might'

Seth Atwood came into a Park District that valued the younger generation. In its first annual report covering May 1909 to December 1910, the board boasted that it had installed four playgrounds where "children are welcome to come at any time and play with all their might." The report went on to estimate that 15,000 children, and almost as many adults, visited the sites in the summer of 1910.

With organized play the following summer, the district put children on the top of its priority list by inaugurating supervised summer activities. The only limitation? Programs were acceptable only if they responded to the hearts and minds of citizens and were affordable. That was the hallmark of Park District operations from the get-go, as set down by Faust, Atwood and others.

The Rockford School District, too, was a leader in recreation for youngsters. In 1930, the federal government took note of how Rockford cared for its children when it reported the city was one of just 71 in the nation and five in the state that provided supervision of school playgrounds.

> *"Instead of going into YMCA work, I would earn some money and help out that way."*
> — SETH B. ATWOOD

While the government saw school playgrounds as an essential part of a school's equipment, only half the nation's high schools had athletic fields, the report said.

Rockford was given credit for having 13 teachers of physical education to deal with its enrollment of 13,560 students.

Depression and Recreation

The Great Depression hit Rockford hard. Park services were needed more than ever.

In his book about golf in Rockford and Beloit, author Tom Warren reveals that the low-cost game of golf brought his parents together. His mother introduced his dad to golf in the 1930s, when a golf game was a cheap date. They fell in love with each other and golf, which led to son Tom and his love for the links.

"Inexpensive equipment plus modest greens fees meant that golf in Depression-era Rockford was not just for rich people," Warren wrote. "White folks like my parents, irrespective of their fragile financial status, could take up the game and play it all the time. They knew that golf was waiting there for all the people, and proudly affirmed that anyone can play golf in Rockford no matter what their wealth or income."

Well, anybody who was white and Christian. Sadly, that's how it was then.

The citizens were dealing with less income. So was the Park District. Like the people, the board concentrated on surviving. In 1931, the board decided against concerts in the parks. It canceled annual banquets and stopped printing annual reports.

> "Park use increased by a third in 1932 and, because of more people out of work, will go up again in 1933."
> – SUPERINTENDENT CLARENCE PEDLOW

The next year, park staffers took a 10 percent reduction in pay; they wouldn't see a raise for nearly five years.

The board set up a $2,000 revolving emergency relief payroll fund from which men would be paid 30 cents an hour for up to 16 hours a week, for a grand total of $4.80 a week. The Illinois Emergency Relief Commission reimbursed the district.

The district raised tomato and cabbage seedlings and gave them to the Rockford Community Fund for distribution to needy families in 1932.

Parks Superintendent Clarence Pedlow told newspaper reporters that use of the

Clarence Warren gets ready to hit a golf ball off a tee held in the teeth of his son, Tom, in this 1950s photo. Tom Warren wrote about Rockford as a golf town in "An Old Caddie Looks Back."

parks had increased by a third in the summer of 1932 and, because of people out of work, he expected it to go up again in '33. Yet, he said, the park budget had to be cut by $35,000. The new budget, Pedlow said, covered only fixed expenditures and operating expenses, all of which were pared.

The 1933 – 34 budget was approved at $106,000. That was enough for average monthly spending of $8,800, just $1,500 more than the district spent in its first year of existence 24 years earlier. But in '33, the district was tending almost five times as much acreage in parks, golf courses and pools.

The tax levy, which had reached $170,000 in 1927, was down to $88,000 in 1933. It stayed at or near that level until 1940, when jobs reappeared as the nation geared up to fight World War II.

The board stayed true to its anti-gambling stance, turning down the idea, in 1932, of putting slot machines in golf clubhouses to make money. Apparently, some people believed then, as they do today, that legalized and taxed gambling is a legitimate way for government to collect money.

It appears golfers had no money to play the slots, anyway. The board was having trouble collecting the $3 annual fee from golfers who paid on the installment plan, and the privilege of paying piecemeal was dropped in 1932. The board also rejected a move to raise golf fees to provide money for jobs programs.

Levings Park once was the farm of Thomas G. Levings with Kent Creek running through it. The park changed dramatically starting in 1935 when federal Work Progress Administration crews built a dam and excavated a large area for Levings Lake. This boat house was built by work crews hired by the federal government to give people work during the Depression.

Mum shows were held at Park District greenhouses from 1927 through 2007. At the first one, 5,000 people came to see the colorful flowers on opening day. The most recent show in '07 featured 3,000 plants and drew about 1,000 people.

During the lean years, the district continued to operate the pools and playground programs. In 1938, when the area was still deep in the Depression, the Morning Star reported in June that adult attendance at local parks was up by 1,300 from the previous year, to 5,398. The reasons: unemployed people looking for something to do, and the district's expanded programming that included ping pong, deck tennis, badminton, shuffleboard, baseball and volleyball.

When children and youth were included in the count, 17,267 people took part in organized activities during the second week of June, the newspaper said. Attendance was highest at Fair Grounds with 1,220 adults and 2,070 children.

I believe the Park Board's experience during the Great Depression illustrates exactly why park services are vital when people are struggling financially. They need free and inexpensive recreation. But what many people don't realize is that the opposite also is true. When the economy is flourishing and people are upbeat, they look to the parks for family fun and recreation. There is never a time when parks are not a necessary part of any healthy, balanced community.

The board opened its pocketbook a little bit in 1934 when it approved a celebratory banquet to mark the 25th anniversary of the district. Held at Sandy Hollow clubhouse, the event included talks by founders Levin Faust, who was still a commissioner at the time, and former Mayor E.W. Brown. A newspaper photo shows Commissioner Atwood sitting next to Faust, surrounded by Commissioners A.R. Floberg and Fay Lewis and board attorney A.V. Essington.

Above: The 10th Avenue Pool was an above-ground structure that could accommodate 1,000 swimmers.
Right: It was the first pool bathhouse in the city with separate locker rooms for men/boys and women/girls.

WPA helps out

The Works Progress Administration (WPA), one of the alphabet soup programs of President Franklin Roosevelt's administration, was a tremendous boon to this area and all of America. Started in 1935 to employ people, the federal program concentrated on public projects that would have long term value, things like roads, bridges and parks. The Rockford Park District got much from the WPA: bridges, shelters, paths, benches, fireplaces and roads in Alpine and Ingersoll parks, along with lake excavation, a bathhouse, shelters and roads in Levings Park.

At Levings, a WPA crew of 175 workers built a dam on the Kent Creek and excavated a 35-acre lake in 1935. The laborers moved 64,000 cubic feet of dirt, about two-thirds of it by hand. By the winter of 1935, skaters in the city had a nice, big lake on which to try out their blades.

WPA crews also added fireplaces, playgrounds and more picnic spots at Levings Park.

In 1939, the board used WPA money to reinstate band concerts in the parks. The program was repeated in 1940, when the parks hosted 25 WPA concerts, costing the Park Board $2 each.

And the WPA got involved in programming, offering 14 play areas in 1938 that attracted 12,072 users.

WPA funds dried up in the early 1940s, when industry mobilized to provide supplies for World War II. By June 1943, the WPA was folded because civilian employment was sky high.

10TH Ave. Pool goes co-ed

The second pool in the Park District, at the 10th Avenue Park, opened in July 1929 to the big news that mixed bathing would be allowed. That meant boys and girls, men and women, at the same time. It was possible because the pool had separate locker rooms for men

The Dream Grows • 1929 – 1944

and women, a total of 150 dressing stalls, a first in the Park District. Because Fair Grounds Pool did not have separate dressing rooms, it did not offer mixed swimming.

Some rules didn't change. Smoking was not allowed inside the pool enclosure. Swimmers were to exit the area immediately after leaving the water and dressing. Women were not to wear tank suits. (Tank suits were similar to a dance leotard, one piece with legs ending just above the knee and with a sleeveless top). It was felt they emphasized the shape of the body too much. Swimsuits with more foundation at the top and with skirts were preferred.

The 10th Avenue Pool, an above-ground, concrete structure, was one of just 200 such pools in the nation. Built for $35,000, it was 171 by 100 feet, big enough for 1,000 swimmers at a time. Although 85 percent of it was considered shallow, there were lifeguards. With a circulating chlorinator system, the pool cleaned the water every 14 hours.

Alas, much like the first swimming "pool" in Kent Creek and the popular but short-lived Quarry swimming hole experiences, the 10th Avenue Pool had problems. Illinois winters damaged the exposed concrete walls with frequent freeze and thaw cycles, just as the weather contributes to potholes in roadways. By 1975, a study showed the pool was losing 30,000 gallons of water per day and needed costly repairs. It was closed in 1976 and demolished.

By that time, Alpine and Sand Park pools both were in operation.

Air Mail via the Parks

Because the Illinois statute governing park districts gave them authority to operate airports, a group of citizens led by the Chamber of Commerce turned to the Park Board in 1930. They asked the district to build and maintain an airport for the region. After some discussion, the board decided to follow its traditional

Aviation pioneer Fred Machesney worked with the Park Board and the Chamber of Commerce to set up an airport in what is today Machesney Park. (Truman Lander photo)

approach of asking voters what they thought.

On April 1, 1930, voters gave their answer in a referendum. No: 10,327; Yes: 4,117. The overwhelming defeat didn't stop the Chamber or aviation pioneer Fred Machesney from efforts to get an airport. They saw the Park Board as their best hope because of the way state law was written and continued to urge the board to get into the airport business. That, said the Chamber, would ensure that the city would have air mail service and allow the introduction of passenger service.

In 1931, Machesney and the Chamber came up with a plan involving the Park District, the city and Central Illinois Electric and Gas Co. The district leased the 160-acre airport site (currently the Machesney Park Mall) from Machesney but recovered its money by charging Machesney for lighting, which the district installed. That agreement lasted until around 1950 but air mail was discontinued, at least temporarily, in July 1934, a casualty of the Great Depression.

Superintendent's shocking death

A shocked board heard the news on July 23, 1934, that Superintendent Pedlow, just 39 years of age, had died. Fighting intestinal flu for less than a week, he succumbed to pneumonia. Pedlow's friends believed work stress killed him. He had not taken time to recover from an appendectomy several months earlier, his friends told the Register-Republic.

"Reserved, quiet, highly efficient, invariably considerate, he brought to public service qualities all too seldom found," the newspaper said.

Parks Superintendent Earl F. Elliot (left) and board President Seth B. Atwood led the district through sparse times and periods of great growth.

A month later, the board named Earl F. Elliot the new superintendent. He had been with the Park District six years as an engineer and landscape architect and would serve as head of the district for 34 more years. Elliot and Commissioner Seth B. Atwood were of the same mind when it came to acquiring and developing parks. Under Elliot, the park system would more than triple in size.

Moving HQ to North Main

After 22 years downtown (15 in the old City Hall building at 126 S. First St. that today is an apartment building and seven in the Fire Department building across the street at 407 Walnut), the board began looking for a new site for administrative offices in 1934. Considered were the News Tower at 99 E. State St.

Clarence Pedlow

The Dream Grows • 1929 – 1944

and the Electric Building on Chestnut St. The board chose the News Tower with rent of $720 a year.

When the newspaper company raised the rent to $1,200 a year in 1937, the Park Board balked and told Elliot to get an architect to sketch a building to be located in Sinnissippi Park.

The next move, however, was to the Fletcher Barnes home at 813 North Main Street, which the board bought that summer for $12,500. The Park District took over the first floor and talked of remodeling the second floor and attic for a natural history museum.

Rockford Grows as Golf City

The Park Board learned from the beginning that it was important to geographically balance its facilities so all parts of the district had access to recreation. Thus, the district's third golf course, Sandy Hollow, was located in the southeast sector.

Termed the "sportiest public links in the city" by the Rockford Republic when it opened on July 4, 1929, Sandy Hollow was an 18-hole course, 6,320 yards long with a par of 71. The 124-acre site was purchased for slightly more than $200 an acre.

These autos are antiques now but when Sandy Hollow Golf Course opened, they were state of the art. This is the clubhouse at Rockford's third public course, opened in 1929.

Construction began in 1928 and the clubhouse was built in 1930-31 for $25,000.

"Crowds Storm New Course and Celebrate Holiday with Golf," said the newspaper headline when Sandy Hollow opened. The story read:

"Thousands of brogue-shod golfers and golfing fans thronged the ceremonies which opened Rockford's third municipal golf course, Sandy Hollow, and witnessed the initial drive ... After a brief speech in which he presented the course ... to the citizens, A. R. Floberg, president of the Park Board, stepped to the first hole tee and banged out a two-hundred-yard drive which scampered merrily down the fairway. Following him, Levin Faust sent another ball in hot pursuit. Immediately after, Seth Atwood, a member of the Park Board, E.N. Erickson, president of the Rockford Parks Clubs, and Frank Seaver, president of the Ingersoll Golf Club, joined Floberg in the first foursome to play the 18 holes."

The story described the course as beautiful and sporting but "built in a very tricky fashion, offering abundant trouble for the average fan who just can't escape the rough."

Charles D. Wagstaff, who also designed the Mauh-Nah-Tee-See Country Club course in Rockford and helped redesign the Rockford Country Club course, designed Sandy Hollow. The Park District's third course served the city well. It would be nearly 40 years before a fourth municipal course was added in 1968.

In the meantime, the three courses and the district's maintenance and management of them drew acclaim. In April 1937, William G. Robinson of the National Recreation Association visited the city and issued this compliment: "I do not know when I have seen in a city your size as fine a park system as you have. I admire very much the facilities and the way in which they are kept. The distribution has also been carefully done and planning for the future seems to be equally well thought out.

"Then, too, I do not know of any place in any state in the union where you can play golf as cheaply as you have provided it in your municipal system in Rockford. Your $3 a year for a season ticket is providing a service that no other city, to my knowledge, has thus far been able to do."

Two years later, a Register-Republic editorial repeated Robinson's view: "The

> *"I do not know when I have seen in a city your size as fine a park system as you have. I admire very much the facilities and the way in which they are kept."*
> – WILLIAM G. ROBINSON, NATIONAL RECREATION ASSOCIATION, 1937

Milt Mahlburg guided Burpee Museum of Natural History for more than 40 years.

This stately home at 813 N. Main St. was headquarters of the Park District from 1939 to 1971. Burpee Museum of Natural History used the upper floors during that period and the entire building when Park District offices moved. The building now houses administrative offices for Burpee.

golf bargain made available by intelligent, well-directed operation of these courses is appreciated here. It is almost incredible to golfers from other centers who learn that the cost of a day's sport in their cities would provide a season ticket for Rockford's municipal courses."

Parks and Museums

Rockford's current world-class museums struggled early in their histories, searching for decades for permanent quarters. Supporters shared a passion for art and natural history and stubbornly persisted in their quest for permanent facilities.

The beginnings of today's the Rockford Art Museum and Burpee Museum of Natural History back to 1888, when the Rockford Sketch Club was formed, and to 1915, when the Nature Study Society was organized. They became the Rockford Art Association and the Rockford Natural History Association. Each group had collections it wanted to share with the public but no place to do so.

The Park District was just two years old when it got into the museum business through a gift from the Mandeville family. They donated their home, what is now Mandeville Park on Montague Road. Included were three acres of land, a house and a collection of items that grew as local citizens donated exhibits.

The Park District had neither staff nor expertise in running a museum. The Nature Study club came to the rescue and opened the collection to public viewing at the Mandeville home starting in 1915. In 1916, an addition was built to house the mineral specimens and Indian artifacts collected by Dr. E.C. Dunn. In 1919, a furnace was installed and, in 1921, electric lights.

The early mingling of art and natural history evolved into today's Rockford Art Museum and the Burpee Museum of Natural History. In 1929, the Art Association laid out a proposal to build a natural history museum in Sinnissippi Park. The Park Board said if the association raised the money for the building, it would raise the museum tax to help in the operation. Neither happened, however.

Both the natural history and art groups moved to North Main Street in the 1930s in arrangements that were the basis for what has developed today.

The arts group got space in what was called the Manny Mansion at 737 N. Main St. in 1936. The building had narrowly escaped being turned into a WPA armory when it was purchased by Harry Burpee in 1936. His first thought was to use the building as a funeral home, but a number of prominent citizens objected.

Instead, he established the Harry and Della Burpee Art Gallery Association for the operation of a civic art center with the art association as a partner. The gallery opened in 1936. John R. Salter, an exhibiting artist at the Art Institute of Chicago, was named gallery director in 1938. A two-story addition was completed in 1939.

Meanwhile, the Mandeville/Nature Society collection was growing into what was called the Burpee Natural History/Rockford Art Association collection. The exhibits, said the Star, were a "center of attraction for knowledge-seeking citizens."

That consolidated collection found its home in the upper two floors of the mansion at 813 N. Main St. The building

This building at 737 N. Main St., once known as the Manny Mansion, is part of the Burpee Museum of Natural History. The Burpee is connected to the museum/arts complex known as the Riverfront Museum Center.

A typical exhibit in the old Burpee Museum of Natural History.

The Burpee Trust and Art Association worked with the Park District to create the Natural History Museum, which today carries the Burpee family name.

The two museums were next door to each other in two well-known Victorian homes, the Art Museum in the Manny Mansion and the Natural History Museum and Park District in the Barnes Mansion. Both of these handsome buildings still stand solidly today.

Rich woodworking craftsmanship is evident in this photo of Tinker Swiss Cottage. The curved board at right is the railing of a circular staircase that leads upstairs to the library.

was the headquarters of the Park District, which maintained offices on the first floor.

The Museum of Natural History opened in 1942. Exhibits included collections from the Mandeville house and items donated by the Beattie sisters which had been displayed at the Rockford Public Library. Dr. Robert Velie donated a collection of nearly every bird in North America displayed in backgrounds typical of their habitats. Other exhibits included 55,000 different types of seashells, a geological collection of 6,000 specimens, and more than 1,000 reptiles, flowers and plants.

Self-taught naturalist Milt Mahlburg was the first curator, serving until 1986. Mahlburg's ornithological expertise was known and respected nationwide as he guided the new museum for more than 40 years.

Mrs. Jessie Tinker requested that a group of citizens separate from the Park District board be selected to preserve her unique home and its contents. Upon her death in 1942, Mayor Henry Bloom chaired a board that took on that responsibility. The photo shows how the cottage was built on a steep bluff on Kent Creek.

A few years after the art and natural history museums found homes on North Main, the unique Tinker Swiss Cottage joined the Park District's museum family. Built by founding Park District Commissioner Robert Tinker, the home had been given to the district two years after Tinker's death in 1924. There were stipulations, however, that his widow, Jessie, would be allowed to spend the rest of her life there and receive an annual stipend of $1,800.

That she did, until her death in 1942. Her dream of preserving the picturesque cottage as a museum was not achieved until Mayor C. Henry Bloom and a group of residents formed a Tinker Swiss Cottage organization, which later evolved into the Tinker Museum board. The Tinker Museum opened in 1943. In the past 40 years, it has been painstakingly restored, outbuildings and grounds included.

Furniture and valuable art were included in the gift of the Tinker Swiss Cottage to the Park District.

World War II

Rockford came out of the Depression the way the rest of the nation did, aided greatly by the need for equipment and supplies to fight World War II.

The city also was fortunate to have metal and tool and die factories, including the Atwood plants. They were heavy into automobile parts and when that industry slowly revived in the late 1930s, so did Rockford.

The city got a bonus economic boost because of Camp Grant, a leftover from World War I that had been used as a National Guard training center and quarters for Civilian Conservation Corps (CCC) workers. The camp again became a major military post in the fall of 1940 when, more than a year before Pearl Harbor, the government put up 365 new barracks and other buildings. It was clear that many believed the United States could not avoid getting into the war that was raging in Europe.

When the Japanese bombed Pearl Harbor, the war hit home. Those new barracks filled with soldiers as Camp Grant became the largest Army reception center in the nation. Later, the camp became a Prisoner of War facility and housed some 2,500 German soldiers.

As the war came, many of Rockford's manufacturers converted to making military materials. With so many men going into service, there were factory jobs aplenty for those who stayed behind, and for women.

Life changed. There were shortages of gasoline and rubber; those commodities were diverted to the war machine. Families needed ration coupons to buy sugar, meat, butter and canned goods. Civil defense drills occurred routinely. Children collected tin foil from gum wrappers and cigarette packs for scrap drives.

The U.S. government urged Americans to grow their own food in "Victory Gardens" and the Park District supported the effort by sponsoring contests for the best vegetable gardens. By 1943, Park staffer George Pedlow (no known relation to Clarence) was inspecting 220 registered Victory Gardens competing for $500 worth of War Bonds. The government issued instructions on canning and preserving food.

Ration coupons from World War II.

The Park District sent season golf passes to the USO for men in the armed forces. The board announced that pension benefits would be honored for employees who went to war but returned to work within 40 days of getting out of the service.

After the war, the district indicated it would help provide temporary housing for returning servicemen and suggested two parks — Churchill and Huffman Playground — as suitable. Nothing, however, came of the discussion.

If building materials were not being used in the war effort, they were nearly impossible to obtain and so the Park District took on no major building projects during the war years.

Anna R. Page Park is one of the district's most beautiful parks.

Most New Parks Were Gifts

In the tight budget years of 1940 through 1953, the district acquired 290 acres in 10 sites, most of them gifts. Among them were Highland Playground, Charles Woodward Martin Memorial Park, Searls Memorial Park, South Henrietta Avenue Playground, Sabrooke Playground and Sand Park.

The U.S. Navy asked, in 1947, to use a part of Black Hawk Park to construct an armory. Permission was granted. The armory building is no longer used by the military. It has been rented to a number of groups, most recently to train industrial employees.

The Park District found it had to say "no" sometimes. When the Rockford Industrial Athletic Association wanted more horseshoe courts for its 16 teams, the board said fine, if the group "solved the problem of construction" itself. When the Yacht Club asked to use a spot in Sinnissippi to dock boats, the board said OK if the club installed the docks and controlled the noise.

Camp Grant Becomes Airport, Park

The end of World War II meant the end of Rockford's importance as a military center. Built originally to train World War I soldiers, the camp was permanently closed in 1946. Some barracks were converted into makeshift apartments for returning veterans and their families. By the late 1940s, many of the buildings were torn down, with veterans getting the first chance to buy usable lumber to build their own homes.

Later, the Park District would get a piece of Camp Grant, thanks to the generosity of Seth B. Atwood. He gave us a check for $15, 818.87, which covered the cost of appraising and buying the 321-acre rifle range at the camp. The Rockford Airport Authority, which had been given more than 1,000 acres by the federal government to build an airport on Camp Grant land, gave us a 61-acre quarry site so we had a new 382-acre park that we developed for environmental education. It's called Atwood Park and is a gift that continues giving to area children in the form of fun and valuable environmental education.

The airport, of course, is known as Chicago Rockford International Airport.

Westside Park Gems

The Park District had purchased its first major parks, Sinnissippi and Black Hawk. In the following decades, however, gifts of land created parks bigger than the first two.

The donations are evidence that citizens continued to value their Park District. People with the means to make major gifts believed the district would care for the land and use it for the benefit of the community as a whole. The Park District had earned the trust of the community.

In 1943, following the death of Thomas Goodsman Levings' widow, the district received title to the 123 acres of Levings land that had been leased to the district for $1 a month since 1919. Thomas Levings was Rockford Township's highway commissioner from 1886 until his death. The park, at 1420 S. Pierpont Street was primarily used as a picnic spot until Depression work crews built a dam and a lake. The park became a major draw for summer and winter recreation.

The northwest side gained two large parks during this era. In 1929, the board had purchased 120 acres known as the

This is Searls Park from the air. The park is home to a BMX track, softball diamonds, soccer fields and the district's first dog park.

Colton tract west of Springfield Road, halfway between Auburn and the Trask Bridge. The nearly treeless property cost $23,400 and was seen as a future golf course.

The plan changed when Anna R. Page donated 80 acres just northwest of the Colton land. Her donation was, according to Superintendent Elliot, "much natural forest, with a heavy growth of wild flowers and many beauty spots. The north branch of Kent Creek flows through ... to add natural attractiveness."

Anna Page gave the land on condition it be used as a "conservation park, a forest and field refuge, a sanctuary for birds and wildlife, and growth of wild flowers, forest trees and shrubs."

The Park Board combined the two pieces of land into the Anna R. Page Conservation Forest. The park once was known for a toboggan run but Frisbee golfing, fishing in Kent Creek, picnicking and family fun are its uses today.

A second large west side park started as a 14-acre tract of woodland along Safford Road donated to the district by Emily J. Searls in 1943. She gave the land in memory of her husband, John F. Searls, and her uncle who homesteaded the site. Emily Searls asked that the park be dedicated to children and recreation. The site contained a beautiful stand of hickory and oak trees. A year later, when Mrs. Searls died, she gifted the Park District with another 150 acres adjacent to the 14 acres. About half was cleared, and half was wooded with Kent Creek running through it.

The parks today serve as nature preserves, as well as park sites, with heavily-used recreational facilities.

New Needs as War Ends

The war had not yet ended when, in 1944, the Park Board began talking about meeting the post-war needs of the community. As men came home from the service, they would need recreational opportunities beyond what was then available. It also was taken for granted the veterans would start families and a booming generation of kids would need more space and services than the Park District then had resources to serve.

Under the leadership of the ever-steady and progressive Seth B. Atwood and Earl F. Elliot and the guidance of a new group of dreamers who came from Academia, the growing demands were met in what became the golden era of Park District recreation programs.

Alpine Park glistens on a winter day. The 55-acre park was purchased for $13,000 for two parcels in 1937 and 1942. It was needed to relieve summer weekend congestion at Sinnissippi and Black Hawk parks.

THE DREAM GROWS • 1929 – 1944

GROWTH OF THE PARK DISTRICT 1929 – 1944

Parks acquired 1929 – 1944

1929: Anna Page Park, 3102 Springfield Ave. 943 acres (includes more than 600 acres of dry dam area leased from city)

1929: Calvin Park Blvd., Welty Parkway, 5.5 acres

1929: Ken-Rock Park, 2930 Bildahl St., 6.3 acres

1930: Collins Playground, 1406 River Bluff Blvd., 2 acres

1930: Dahlquist Park, 3251 Oak Grove Ave., 16 acres

1930: Oaklawn/Princeton Circle, Rome Ct. and Oaklawn Ave., .42 acre

1931: Harlem Blvd. ROW[1], between North Main/John St. and Auburn, 1.7 acre*

1933: Bradley Triangle, Bradley/Crest roads, .1 acre

1933: John Nelson Park, 950 Seminary St., 4 acres

1937: Alpine Park, 950 S. Alpine Road, 55 acres

1937: Home which housed Park District administration until 1971 and today is part of Burpee Museum, 813 N. Main St., 3.5 acres

1937: Talcott-Page Memorial Park, 1128 Russell Ave., 24 acres

1937: 22nd Ave. Parkway, 22nd Ave between Kishwaukee and 7th Sts., .7 acre

1938: Hall Memorial Park (undeveloped), Euclid Ave. and Linden St., 40 acres

1939: Huffman Playground, 2302 Huffman Blvd., 9 acres

1940: Highland Playground, 3011 Rural St., 2.6 acres

1941: Sand Park: 1041 Riverside Blvd., 42 acres

1943: Searls Memorial Park, 4950 Safford Road., 289 acres

1943: Williams Sports Field, 1701 Huffman Blvd., 2 acres

Owned by the city and controlled by the Park District

[1] *Right of Way*

PROFILE OF THE PARK DISTRICT 1929 – 1945

Year: Statistic:	1910	1928	1945
Population	48,405	91,750	113,410
Number of Parks/Properties	15	45	65
Park District Acreage	159.47	731.35	2,361.26
Total Budget	$140,343.49[1]	$177,063.00	$150,412.00
Property Tax Revenue	$35,999.00	$160,142.00	$122,837.00
Per Capita Expenditure from Taxes	$0.74	$1.74	$1.08
Median Family Income	Not available	Not available	Not available
Estimated Total User Visits	Not available	Not available	Not available

[1] *1910 budget covered 18 months instead of 12 months.*

THE COMMISSIONERS OF THE ERA 1929 – 1944

Levin Faust

Seth B. Atwood

Fay Lewis

Adelbert R. Floberg

Harry B. Andrews

LEVIN FAUST
On board 1909 – 1936; president 1911 – 1920
Created what became Borg-Warner Co.; co-founded National Lock; re-organized Rockford Drilling Co. (Rockford Clutch). Served on boards of 19 companies. Helped found SwedishAmerican Hospital and Swedish American Bank (now Harris). Died in 1936, still on Park Board at 73 years of age.

SETH B. ATWOOD
On board 1928 – 1960; president 1942 – 1960
Founded Atwood Vacuum Machine Co.; invested in banks, savings and loan associations, real estate and hotels. Dedicated environmentalist and major force in growth of Park District. Made large donations to district and Forest Preserve. Longest length of service as commissioner with 32 years, last 18 as president.

FAY LEWIS
On board 1924 – 1947; president 1937 – 1942
Largest wholesale distributor (Fay Lewis and Brothers Co.) of tobacco in Midwest, outside city of Chicago. Personal friend of Clarence Darrow and Edgar Lee Masters, who portrayed him as "Lewis Fay" in "Spoon River Anthology."

ADELBERT R. FLOBERG
1925 – 1937; president 1927 – 1937
Brief but distinguished career with Manufacturers National Bank, where he became vice-president. Organized several manufacturing enterprises. President of Exel Manufacturing at the time of his death at 53.

HARRY B. ANDREWS
On board 1927 – 1941
Cited as quiet moving spirit on Park Board. Made motion to buy Colton tract, later linked to become Anna Page Park. Family donated Andrews Park, given as a memorial to his father.

THE DREAM GROWS • 1929 – 1944

Harry O. Swanson   *Howard C. Gregory*   *Dr. Robert F. Schleicher*   *Edwin W. Carlson, Sr.*   *O. G. Nelson*

HARRY O. SWANSON
On board 1937 – 1942
Appointed to fill out term of friend and business associate Levin Faust. Faust was president of Elco Tool and Screw Co. and Swanson was secretary, treasurer and manager. Later elected to board and served until his death.

HOWARD C. GREGORY
On board 1937 – 1939
Appointed to fill term made vacant by the death of A. R. Floberg. Secretary of the J.L. Clark Manufacturing Company. His widow, Coffey Gregory, donated family home to Park District in 1980; it became the Rockford Arboretum at 1875 North Mulford Road.

DR. ROBERT F. SCHLEICHER
On board 1939 – 1962
Rockford optometrist. Resigned Park Board post in 1962 to accept appointment to Greater Rockford Airport Authority Board of Commissioners. Appointment made by twin brother Ben Schleicher, then 4-term mayor of Rockford.

EDWIN W. CARLSON, SR.
On board 1941 – 1955
President of David Carlson Roofing Co., which his father founded. Six-year member of Fire and Police Commission, trustee of SwedishAmerican Hospital, director of American National Bank and Trust.

O.G. NELSON
On board 1942 – 1952
Appointed to the Park Board to fill term of the late Harry O. Swanson. President of National Mirror Works and, later, chairman of the board of Sundstrand Machine Tool Company. Resigned from Park Board in 1952 because of failing health.

CHAPTER 3
The Dream Seeks A New Level
1945 – 1971

Returning WWII veterans were catalyst for great changes in society, park districts.

Better Life for Children

The nation relished the peace and prosperity that followed World War II. Some felt America was invincible. We had defeated the greatest war powers in the world and now were rich enough and compassionate enough to help rebuild their nations. When you think about it, that was heady stuff.

Families of the day, millions of them with a veteran as the breadwinner, were determined to put the Depression and war behind them. Many men who would not have dreamed of going to college took advantage of the GI Bill to do just that. They started business and professional careers and bought homes. They expected to give their children a better start in life than they had experienced, and they wanted something better for themselves than the struggles their parents had endured.

A 1950 Associated Press article predicted that recreation and travel would lead the growth in family expenditures. People would have more free time because of technical advances in household chores. A 35-hour work week was on the horizon, with even a 20-hour work week possible, experts said.

Opposite: Is there a local family that hasn't taken toddlers to the Sinnissippi Lagoon to see the swans, ducks or geese?

Right: Earl F. Elliot, standing, was an excellent choice to lead the district through a period of great growth after World War II. James Brademas, seated, came on board in 1956 to add year-round recreational programming to traditional Park District operations.

It was inevitable that business would grow with the population, which expanded at a brisk pace until the 1960s. Locally, the city's population was at 93,000 in 1950, and the big boom was still to come with more Baby Boom infants. The exodus of people from rural areas to cities continued as machines replaced manual labor.

Rockford became Illinois' fastest-growing city, known as the state's "Second City," below only Chicago in population. That nickname applied until Aurora took over the distinction in 2003.

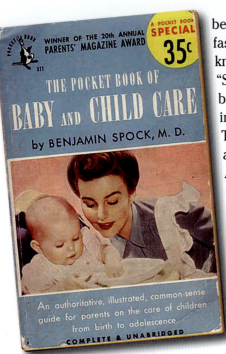

Post World War II was a time of transition. Many people expected the women, who had been welcomed into the work force during the war, to return exclusively to homemaking roles. Some did, others refused to give up their new-found independence. People of color, who had made their share of sacrifices during the war, began to demand equal rights. Children were raised in a way many oldsters thought lenient, thanks to Dr. Benjamin Spock, who revolutionized child-rearing with his 1946 book, "Baby and Child Care."

Television dramatically changed our way of living, damaging family relationships and friendships, in my view.

Society's transitions created a challenge for the Park District. Veterans and their families demanded more park and recreational services. Meeting those needs led to an expansion of the traditional role of parks, a transition that was not without pain. It also led, however, to a golden age of parks and recreation, one that was nowhere more apparent than here in the Rockford Park District.

Not Our Job to Hold Dances

To serve the growing number of growing families, the Park District needed more revenue. Soldiers with young children who were buying cars and homes had little money for entertainment. They looked to the Park District for recreation, just as their parents had during the Depression.

Moreover, their concept of recreation had grown. Returning GIs had suffered through combat but they also had enjoyed recreational facilities and programming designed to keep them physically and mentally fit. They came home with a new appreciation for organized recreation.

In Rockford, they came home to a Park Board that was very progressive by traditional standards but still firmly entrenched in the belief that, outside of summer children's programs, a park district's primary job was to build and maintain parks. Period.

Atwood made clear that arranging dances was not in the Park District's job description.

Consider this exchange between the Rockford Square Dance Association and the Park Board in May 1943. The dancers brought a petition with 146 signatures to the board, asking for public square dancing events in the parks.

Board President Atwood replied that the

The Dream Seeks A New Level • 1945 – 1971

These greenhouses, opened in 1960, cost $58,000 and were used for floral exhibits until 2009 when they were torn down to make way for the Nicholas Conservatory. These greenhouses were the second built by the district. They replaced greenhouses built in 1914.

Park District only had authority to provide and maintain parks, playgrounds and athletic facilities. He made clear that arranging dances was not in the district's job description.

He did leave the door open a crack by asking Park Superintendent Elliot to see whether the board could do anything for the dancers. But the subject never returned, at least not in official board minutes. Elliot, one of the best "parks men" around, didn't want to move toward tax-supported recreation, either.

The Park Board had maintained some recreation programs since its beginning. Those were primarily summer playground activities and sports events for children. They cost the district about $33,000 a year during the 1940s. That was between 20 and 30 percent of the taxes collected, and it squeezed the remainder of the budget, needed for park maintenance.

Park commissioners knew they could not continue to maintain and add parks to meet the growing demand if they spent up to a third of tax revenue on recreation. Sooner or later, something had to go or taxes had to be raised.

In 1945, the board discussed holding a tax referendum to fund recreational programming. Support came from the Rockford Community Fund (forerunner of United Way) and the Rockford Council of Social Agencies. But with no support from the public or the media, the idea was scuttled. Better to back off than to see a referendum go down to defeat.

The following year, in 1946, the district incurred a $12,000 deficit as it again provided children's recreation programs from general tax funds.

'Cheaper to Keep Children Out of Jail'

As 1947 began, the board decided it had no choice but to go for a referendum. It put a question on the ballot April 1 for a recreation tax of 3 cents per $100 of valuation.

The timing couldn't have been worse, and not just because the election was on April Fool's Day. Tax hikes also were being sought for the police department (7.5 cents) firefighting services (10 cents) and library (8 cents). And there was a fifth referendum question which aggravated voters and would have taken change out of their pockets. The city was asking for permission to install parking meters. The post-war growth had all governmental units scrambling to catch up.

Proponents of "yes" votes explained their views at a Rockford Woman's Club meeting on March 27, 1947. Ernest Westerg of the Library Board said the library had "19th Century funding for 20th Century youth." Fire Chief Wayne Swanson said the department had not added a man since 1920 but the city had grown from 60,000 to almost 100,000 people. Police Chief Folke Bengston said the eight officers hired since 1936 couldn't cover the 339 acres added to the city in that time.

George R. Fridly, recreation supervisor for the Park District, appealed for higher taxes to benefit children.

"It's cheaper to keep our children out of jail by giving them a supervised play program than it is to care for them when they get into trouble," he said. "We have a 10-week summer recreational program

The fountain in the old greenhouse was donated by Mrs. Edwin W. Carlson in honor of her husband, who was a commissioner from 1941 to 1955.

when we should have a year-round program."

Complicating the arguments for and against taxes was a new state law calling for 100 percent assessment of property. Arthur Logan of the Civic League, which was against all the referendums, told the gathering the way to raise more tax money was to lower the rates but go with the 100 percent assessment.

Newspapers were of little help to the Park District this time. The Register-Republic urged "no" votes on all the ballots, saying taxes would go up anyway because of the assessment change. The Morning Star was kinder. It recommended "no" votes on police, fire and library tax hikes until the new assessment system was in place and its impact could be seen.

> *"We have a 10-week recreation program when we should have a year-round program."*
> – GEORGE R. FRIDLY, PARK DISTRICT RECREATION SUPERVISOR

But the Star gave a thumb's up to the Park District request, arguing that "one of the wonders of the park world" is that the Park Board has delivered so much on so little revenue.

As April 1 approached, eight printing firms were hired to put out 407,780 ballots, a record for a local election. Each Rockford voter would receive what the Register-Republic called a "bundle of ballots," eight different pieces of paper. One ballot was for a police magistrate and 10 city aldermanic positions; one for 12 township offices; one for two Park Board openings; one for each of the tax referendums; and one for the parking meter question.

No, No, No and No

"Voters in 'No' Mood for Taxes," said the Republic in its April 2 edition. All four referendums failed by "thumping" majorities.

The Park District fared best, losing by a margin of 2.5 to 1. The fire and police taxes went down 5 to 1 and the library and parking meter proposals, 3 to 1.

Later that week, the Star chided voters for rejecting the park tax request. Headlined "We Still Need It," the editorial said the tax increase would have cost each person in the district about 90 cents a year. Compare that, the Star suggested, to what a person spends on ball park admission, circuses, golf balls or picture shows. Turning down the tax increase simply created "unfinished business, which we shall be compelled to take care of at a future date," the paper warned.

The Star was right. The district's shortage of revenue and the city's need for a public recreation program would reappear.

The 1947 referendum defeat started a radical reduction in Park District services. The summer program was limited to small children only, and summer park concerts were eliminated.

> *We Still Need It "…unfinished business, which we shall be compelled to take care of at some future date."*
> – MORNING STAR, 1947

'A Modest Plea'

Four years later, the Park Board went back to voters to raise its tax from 3.6 cents per $100 to 6 cents. It would be part of the general levy, not set aside for recreation as in the '47 referendum.

Newspapers lauded the proposal.

It was, said the Star, "one of the most modest pleas ever put before our electorate, particularly when we consider the immense job that the Park District is doing in providing recreational facilities, pleasant environment and actual civic beauty ... We have felt that the request is actually too small ... But no public body should be punished for its modesty and its efficiency..."

> 'No public body should be punished for its modesty and efficiency ...'
> – MORNING STAR

Park officials pointed out that the babies born after the war were reaching school age and new neighborhoods were being developed without parks because the district could not afford to buy land.

Voters apparently were not in a good mood when they went to the polls April 3, 1951. Not only did they defeat the park tax increase by a margin of 2 to 1, they ousted five incumbent city aldermen.

That prompted the Park Board to stop all recreational programs. For the first and only time since 1910, there were no organized park activities for children in the summer of 1951. The board also ended maintenance of the sunken gardens at Sinnissippi Park, stopped using the greenhouse, imposed fees on the Rockford Lawn Bowling Club, and told users of the Churchill Park baseball diamond they could turn on the lights only if they paid for them.

That action was taken on April 26, 1951.

The Great Sinnissippi Plant Raid

Four months later, on Labor Day, to be exact, there was a strange public reaction to the decision to close the greenhouse and reduce garden care. A rumor began — who knows why it happened on Labor Day, but it spread quickly. People were free to haul off plants from the sunken gardens at Sinnissippi, or so neighbor told neighbor.

Police were called at 5:00 p.m. September 3 and told that cars and trucks at Sinnissippi were being loaded up with plants, bushes and, even, trees. One officer arrived to see a "throng" of citizens digging up everything from geraniums to six-foot evergreens. The Star said there were hundreds of thieving gardeners, many with shovels, spades, boxes and baskets.

The officer called for help and more police arrived to send the crowd home, but only after flower beds were ruined and many small evergreens and dozens of rose bushes were taken. No one was arrested.

Superintendent Elliot warned that the plants were not free. The gardens where annuals had been grown would be planted with grass, he said, but the district intended to continue the perennial and rose bush gardens.

Gardeners got the message and Sinnissippi Park survived. There still could be some rose bushes, trees or shrubs in private yards that were taken from Sinnissippi that crazy Labor Day some 60 years ago.

Boys Club Playground Recreation Association

Norris Aldeen	William Hockstad
William H. Barnes Jr.	William W. Jones
Dr. Joseph C. Cleveland	Leslie Lofdahl
Morris D. Davis	Ray Lotzer
Earl F. Elliot	

Rockford Boys Club Provides Leadership

By 1952, staff and board members of the Rockford Boys Club saw that the community needed recreation far

THE DREAM SEEKS A NEW LEVEL • 1945 – 1971

Charles K. Brightbill *Allen Sapora*

beyond what private and volunteer organizations could provide. The club formed the Rockford Boys Club Playground Association in the spring of 1953. Its mission was to promote recreation so that a comprehensive, year round program could be established. The need for recreation, the group believed, would only intensify.

Boys Club leaders and those who agreed with them knew that change would be difficult. They came up with a new strategy, bringing in "heavy hitters" from the world of academia, where park management was being wed to recreational programming. They didn't have to go far because two of the brightest stars in this new field were right in the state at the University of Illinois in Champaign.

56,000 in Pilot Program

The new bright stars were Professors Charles K. Brightbill and Allen Sapora of the University of Illinois. They had planted a seed in the minds of several Boys Club staff members who took U of I classes in public recreation.

Both Harold Callihan, head of the Boys Club, and Don Ellis, assistant Club director, believed the professorial duo could help Rockford. They shared their impressions with their board and, in 1953, a Boys Club committee sent a formal request to Brightbill and Sapora. The committee also invited the Park District to join the experts, and the board responded by appointing Superintendent Earl F. Elliot to represent the district.

Brightbill, Sapora and Jim Brademas, one of their students, first visited the city in the fall of 1953 to meet with Boys Club leaders. When Sapora suggested they try for a referendum, he was told it had little chance of passage. Sapora then suggested they do some groundwork by holding a pilot program that would show people the value of a well-organized, professionally-led recreation program.

Sapora also mentioned doing a study

Playground leaders work with boys on the fundamentals of baseball during the summer pilot program of 1955.

Pat Albee in a "frontier" dress leads the Loves Park contingent to an all-city Playday in the 1955 summer program.

to compare Rockford recreational facilities and opportunities with the state and nation. That was put on the back burner as the group focused on a summer pilot program.

The Boys Club Playground Association took charge. They chose four sites for eight weeks of programming in the summer of 1954. The association raised $7,000 from Ingersoll Milling and Machine, the Tebala Shrine Temple and American Cabinet Hardware Corp. Sapora and Brightbill recommended Brademas to lead the program. He got the job and hired professionally trained supervisors for each of the parks — Sunset, Fair Grounds, Southeast End, and Beattie Playground. Neighborhood councils were formed and from them came neighborhood volunteers to help.

Attendance at the 1954 program was pegged at close to 56,000. That meant about 1,400 participants each day, averaging 350 at each park. The games, sports, pet shows, bike parades, family nights, crafts, dancing, movies and other activities were extremely popular and the public wanted more. Thirty neighborhoods came to the Boys Club that fall and winter asking for similar programs.

The Boys Club association couldn't satisfy everyone, but it made plans for six full-time and four part-time programs in the summer of '55, this time collecting $17,000 in donations from the Rolling Green Garden Club and these industries: Ingersoll, American Cabinet, Greenlee Brothers, Barber-Colman, J. L. Clark, W.A. Whitney, Sundstrand Tool and Woodward Governor. Attendance that summer doubled the previous year, reaching 118,774. Media coverage was extensive. The pilot programs gained strong public support.

> *"You mean we can play here and do all this stuff free for nothin'?"*
> – CHILD'S QUESTION IN 1954 PILOT SUMMER PLAYGROUND PROGRAM

The Boys Club knew it could not fulfill its own mission and continue the summer programs, much less meet the future recreational needs of the city. While the Park District was deeply involved in the pilot programs, it could not take them over with the revenue at hand.

My Summer of Great Learning

It was time for Sapora's study: a comprehensive look at the players in the field of recreation, what they were doing and could do in the future, and which was best equipped to operate a year-round recreation program.

This is where I come into the picture. Sapora agreed to do a survey for $1,500 and living expenses while he spent the summer of 1955 in Rockford. I was his student at the U of I, and was already in Rockford working for Brademas at Sunset Park. I was fortunate to share an apartment with Dr. Sapora.

It was a summer of great learning for me. I got hands-on experience with children at Sunset Park and enhanced my understanding of citizens through the survey work.

The best part of those summer days was around 9:30 at night when Sapora and I got home from survey work. He'd have some pretzels and a beer and we'd talk for an hour or so about what he had been doing, how, and why. His cardinal rule was always to involve citizens. There is no such thing as an unimportant problem to the person who has it, he believed. A successful park district was one that

Staff of the 1955 program included your author (at left), next to U of I football star Wally Vernasco. Seated in light shirt is Jim Brademas. Jim Hostey is the fellow in the jacket.

Al Sapora could enthrall any crowd, including 1,000 kids outdoors on a sweltering afternoon in 1955.

listened to what people wanted and then set up the structure through which they could achieve it.

I admired the persuasive and intelligent way Dr. Sapora approached people and won their trust. He showed me what professionalism was in the recreation business.

A Stubborn Donkey and the Genius of Sapora

Sapora met and captivated thousands of people that summer. When it came to selling his message, there wasn't a crowd or a task he wouldn't take on with enthusiasm.

He proved that one 90-degree August day when he popped in at Fair Grounds Park around noon to see how the All-City Play Day was going. It had been a morning of challenges for Brademas, the other playground supervisors, and me.

We had some 900 kids to feed and entertain for the entire day. A noted city chef from Jacks or Better restaurant was on hand to make a special lunch of beef stew. That was all fine and good until someone remembered that it was Friday and Catholic kids wouldn't eat meat on Friday. An emergency meeting was held and the menu was quickly expanded to include fish stew. But we had nothing to serve it in. Somebody came up with a thousand aluminum pie tins. But they would be too hot for the kids to hold. Someone else came up with a couple stacks of old newspapers the kids could use as pot holders.

Happily for Brademas and the rest of us, Sapora stayed for lunch. And, happily, he was still there when the afternoon's entertainment was to start. Mrs. Ceil Nelson and her trained donkey were to perform.

The trouble was, the donkey wasn't happy. Remember, temperatures were in the 90s. The beast was hot, tired and obstinate. It sat on its haunches and there it stayed, despite entreaties and demands from Mrs. Nelson, and the looks of "what do we do now?" on the faces of Brademas and the rest of us. We had nearly a thousand restless kids who had been promised entertainment after lunch.

Sapora saved the day. He calmly walked on stage and reached for the microphone, which Brademas gratefully handed over. Sapora then captivated the kids with 45 minutes of stories and games. The donkey was forgotten.

When Dr. Sapora was through, he took a $5 bill from his pocket and said it belonged to the child who could pick up the most newspapers and other debris blowing around. To this day, I've never seen a park cleaned so fast by so many at so little cost.

> *Al Sapora used this quote from John Muir in his recreation survey: "Everybody needs beauty as well as bread, Places to play in, and pray in, Where nature may heal and cheer And give strength To body and soul alike…"*

The Dream Seeks A New Level • 1945 – 1971

Al Sapora (right) explains how he's canvassing the city for the recreational study. From left, in nifty bowties, are Parks Superintendent Earl F. Elliot and Russ Foval of the Decatur Recreation Department.

'Cannot Afford Not to Have Recreation'

As he worked on his survey, Sapora assessed private non-profits and public agencies involved in recreation. He talked with hundreds of people, in playgrounds, in formal meetings, on the street or in restaurants, wherever someone was willing to discuss the role and value of public recreation.

Among his findings:

- Rockford public school enrollment was 20,500 in 1955, up from 12,000 just 12 years earlier.
- There were more than twice as many kindergarten students (1,955) in fall 1954 than high school seniors (820). Clearly, the demand for recreation and sports opportunities for children would more than double in the near future.
- After analyzing the programs of every private agency — the YWCA and YMCA, Boys Club, Scouts, Booker Washington, St. Elizabeth and Ken-Rock centers, neighborhood organizations and others — Sapora reported those groups were stretched thin trying to fill the demands for recreation and meet their missions, too. The Boys Club, for example, was not doing one-on-one work with youth because of expanding needs for group recreation. There weren't enough volunteers for the Boy and Girl Scouts to answer requests for new troops.

Ironically, Sapora pointed out, the school and park districts each had outstanding recreational facilities. The Park District's were underused because of no supervised programming. The schools were underused because they were closed when school was out.

Local non-profit agencies spent $336,000 on recreation services in 1954. If you think that's a lot, Sapora said, consider that local residents spent $600,000 on movies that year, not to mention hundreds of thousands of dollars on other forms of commercial recreation.

Perhaps the most convincing part of Sapora's research showed that other Illinois cities — Peoria, Springfield, Decatur, Evanston, Joliet, Aurora, Moline, Skokie and Pekin — all had recreation taxes. Rockford raised not a penny in taxes for recreation. Evanston led the group with a tax that brought in more than $300,000 annually. Peoria had 11 full-time recreation leaders and 37 part-timers; Joliet had two full-time and 30 part-timers. Rockford had none.

> **Sapora made five general recommendations:**
>
> **1:** The Park District should be the major provider of public recreation services in the area.
>
> **2:** The community should establish a Recreation Coordinating Council.
>
> **3:** Recreation programs must contain a wide variety of activities so everyone could get involved.
>
> **4:** The Park District should ask voters to levy a 5-cent tax per $100 of valuation to operate a recreation program.
>
> **5:** The program should be carried out by trained recreation personnel.

"Rockford can afford public recreation services," Sapora wrote. "As a matter of fact, Rockford cannot afford not to have public recreation services."

Parks enhance a community, Sapora said. Similarly, recreational programming raises the quality of life by strengthening families, reducing accidents and crime, and improving community solidarity, he summarized.

> **Advisory Committee for Sapora's Study**
>
> Ray Lotzer
> Leslie Lofdahl
> Gerard Verstynen
> H.A. Noreen
> Morris D. Davis
> John Fortin
> Mrs. Ronald Steffa
>
> Jack Mellon
> Richard Willis
> Joe Sinkiawic
> Mrs. Alex Welsh
> Mrs. Rudy Asprooth
> Emmett Folgate
> Donald Trout

Atwood Stance "Crucial"

Sapora presented the report five nights before Christmas in 1955 at a meeting at the Faust Hotel attended by the Park Board, Boys Club Association, Community Welfare Council and others. When Park Board President Atwood rose to speak, Sapora might have held his breath. Atwood was on record as believing that park districts existed to build and maintain parks, not to run recreation programs.

I had driven up from Champaign with Sapora that night and was at the meeting. On our way up, we nearly landed in the ditch because he was reading his mail while he drove. Fortunately, he decided to let me drive so he could concentrate on things important to him. Driving clearly was not among them.

At the meeting, Atwood repeated his belief that park construction and maintenance were the sole functions of park districts. Sapora simmered. He was tempted to stand up and challenge Atwood but was restrained by his friend, City-County Planner Richard "Rusty" Arms, who warned that a public confrontation might destroy any chance of success.

The Dream Seeks A New Level • 1945 – 1971

Sapora soon was glad he held his tongue. Atwood surprised everyone when he reported that he had taken the survey to New York and showed it to George Butler, the highly-respected head of the National Recreation Association. Butler, according to a research paper later done by Paul Elmer, "was amazed at the small cost ($1,500) of the study, considered it a model for other cities, and told Atwood the Park District 'would be crazy' if it did not follow Sapora's recommendations."

In a stunning announcement, Atwood said he would end his opposition to a recreation tax. Further, he said, the Park District should go to voters with a proposal at the next election.

While Atwood did not endorse the tax, his change of position to neutral was, as Elmer said, a "crucial event" in the campaign to pass the tax. Had Atwood been against it, such a referendum might not even have gone to the public until after he left the board in 1960.

The Park Board set April 10, 1956, as the date for a referendum on a 4-cent per hundred recreation tax. It would cost the owner of a $10,000 home $4 a year and raise $197,000 for the Park District. It was left to the Boys Club Playground group, with Sapora's help, to develop a campaign that would educate and win over voters.

> *"Planning for recreation, like planning for other community services, cannot be done in a vacuum — it must be accomplished as an integral part of the overall comprehensive plan for Rockford."*
> *– AL SAPORA IN HIS 1955 RECREATION SURVEY*

'Best Possible Investment'

Proponents laid out a strategy that called for a speakers' bureau and 32 neighborhood groups, with volunteers going door-to-door. Those who didn't answer their door got a telephone call. Brochures were distributed showing a picture of smiling, active children with professional leaders in a park next to a photo of an empty park.

In a development reminiscent of the creation of the Park District, businessmen became powerful allies. A group charged with raising money for publicity and brochures included Morris D. Davis, shrine potentate of Tebala Temple and president of Davis Store Fixtures; Richard Wills of Williams-Manny Insurance; Walter Colman of Barber-Colman; Robert Gaylord of Ingersoll Milling and Machine; Norris Aldeen of Amerock and Irl Martin of Woodward Governor. Like Faust, Tinker and Roper before them, these businessmen realized that a recreation program would make Rockford a nicer place to live. That, in turn, would lead to a stable labor force and a brighter economy.

> *"Atwood, a very astute and pragmatic man, realized that even though the (recreation) concept differed from his own ideas, he could not stand in the way of public progress."*
> *FROM PAUL ELMER'S "HISTORY OF THE 1956 RECREATION TAX AND THE SUBSEQUENT DEVELOPMENT OF RECREATION IN THE ROCKFORD PARK DISTRICT"*

Seth B. Atwood

Population of the Rockford Park District grew from 127,000 in 1950 to 134,000 in 1952 to 143,000 in 1955.
From Sapora's 1955 Recreation Survey

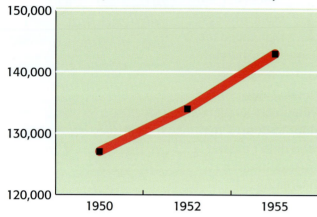

The 1956 campaign for the Park District tax was unlike the efforts in 1947 and 1951. This time, everyone understood the summer programs because the news media had covered them in 1954 and 1955 with dozens of stories and photos. Churches backed the wholesome, family-oriented programs the Park District provided. In addition, Sapora had convinced athletic organizations and other agencies that Park District programs would stir greater interest in recreation and benefit them instead of compete with them.

Endorsements came from Sheriff Leonard A. Friberg; Police Chief Thomas P. Boustead; Probate Judge Seely P. Forbes, County Judge Fred J. Kullberg; Raymond J. Froehlich, president of the Rockford Federation of Labor and Federation of Teachers; and others. Both judges said a recreation program would cut down on juvenile delinquency. Hugo Borgnis, Jaycee president and later, president of the Boys Club, supported the referendum and said his service club could no longer handle the summer sports program it sponsored for teenagers.

Organizations that urged yes votes included the labor groups CIO and AFL, Boy Scouts, Chamber of Commerce, Welfare Council, and Ken-Rock Center. Proponents appealed to citizen pride with claims that Rockford was the only city of its size in the nation that did not have a year-round recreation program.

Youth took to the streets in a downtown rally a week before the election. More than 300 teenagers marched in a torch-light parade organized by the Rockford Youth Council.

After the police-escorted parade, a number of speakers, including members of the 1955 and 1956 state championship basketball teams from West High School, urged voters to say yes to the referendum.

Both newspapers covered the

Teens who demonstrated in favor of the recreation tax carried signs with these messages.

Help Rockford and Help your Kids

$1 Million of Recreation for $3

campaign in detail and strongly endorsed passage. "A supervised public recreation program, utilizing the already excellent park and playground facilities, would be the best possible investment," said the Register Republic. "It would make the community attractive to people, play an important part in public health, prevent needless expenditures caused by accidents in the streets, crime and delinquency, and strengthen family life and community solidarity." Radio and TV outlets also supported passing the referendum.

As winter turned to spring, it was time to see if Rockford was ready to move its park district into the recreation era.

> "Shall the Rockford Park District be authorized and empowered to levy and collect a tax of .04 percent for the purpose of recreational programs…"
> –BALLOT QUESTION IN APRIL 1956

'Yes' by 5,000 Votes

The night of April 10, 1956, election officials counted 17,941 votes for the recreation tax, and 12,874 against.

Supporters celebrated at the Rockford Boys Club. Ever-conservative Seth Atwood, president of the ever-conservative Park Board, thanked voters and promised they would get more than they paid for.

"It is our opinion," he said, "that through proper use of these funds, we may provide healthful, worthwhile activities for our young people that in the long run will save the taxpayers more money than they will contribute for this work."

Aware of the historic vote, Atwood added "We approach this task entrusted to us with humility and will do our best to justify the confidence placed in us."

Reached at his home in Champaign, Sapora told the Register-Republic that he was "highly pleased."

"That's wonderful, my gosh, I think that's just wonderful," he said. "The people of Rockford really have taken a tremendous interest in the program."

Thanks to him, indeed they had. That's why I was so proud to help dedicate Sapora Playworld, the indoor playground at the Carlson Ice Arena, in 1998. I was thrilled and humbled to have Dr. Sapora back in the Rockford Park District and to host a ceremony in his honor. A playground is the perfect way to pay tribute to his legacy. His ability to lead and teach in that informal learning environment was extraordinary.

I have had the opportunity to help design and build hundreds of playgrounds, and each time one was dedicated, I said a prayer of thanks to Dr. Sapora. Thousands of Rockford kids of all ages have had their lives enriched due to his vision, passion and commitment to the Rockford Park District. His mentor, playground pioneer Joseph Lee, would be pleased.

Dr. Sapora died in 2004.

> Recreation Tax: Yes by 5,067 votes. Change to Council-Manager city government: No by 3,505 votes. Winners included John B. Anderson as Winnebago County state's attorney.
> – RESULTS OF APRIL 1956 ELECTION

'Dream Come True' Job

After the successful referendum, I was fortunate to be hired by the Park Board to direct the 1956 summer program. The Register-Republic quoted me

From left, Paul Douglass, chairman of the advisory committee of the National Recreation Association and keynote speaker at the November 1958 conference of the Illinois Park and Recreation Associations in Rockford; Jim Brademas and Seth B. Atwood.

correctly in a headline, stating it was a "dream come true." It was the summer between my junior and senior years at college. This was not only a job I would enjoy, but it was significant work and excellent preparation for a career.

That was the first summer of the new recreation tax. We had programs at 20 playgrounds. The 47 playground directors got three days of training and parents in each neighborhood stepped up to help. We expanded the athletic program and stressed safety, as well as fun and exercise.

More than 6,300 youngsters signed up and, by the end of summer, attendance passed the 209,000 mark. We got adults involved with square dancing and social dancing, sometimes hiring bands and holding dances in parking lots or tennis courts. We had family nights with movies and talent shows at all supervised playgrounds. Teenagers enjoyed an overnight campout. We did tours of local attractions, held golf clinics, introduced drama and baton twirling and formed playground bands. We did our best to get the Park District's recreation program off to a rousing start.

No More 'There's Nothing to do'

When I returned to college that fall, my classmate and colleague Jim Brademas was hired as the Park District's first year-round, tax-supported recreation director. Brademas, who had a master's degree in recreation, had spent the previous year teaching in Greece on a Fulbright Scholarship. He was destined to

The Dream Seeks A New Level • 1945 – 1971

raise public recreation in Rockford to a new level.

Brademas knew the city, having directed the summer pilot programs in '54 and '55. The Park Board gave him a budget of $207,000 and he established a year-round program that quickly became one of the best in the nation. It set a standard that has served the Park District well for more than 50 years. I view Jim's era as the "golden age of public recreation" in Rockford.

Brademas hired a superior staff. Among the recreation employees were Rockford native and Rockford College grad Charles Fiduccia; U of I grad and former Boys Club leader Don Ellis; University of Wisconsin grad Helen Pederson, who had experience with the YWCA; Freeport native and future Harlem Globetrotter McKinley "Deacon" Davis; former Boys Club program director Walt Buttimer; and Frank Lupton, who later taught at Western Illinois University for 22 years and served as department head for six years. Lupton became a nationally-respected leader in the field of environmental education.

An editorial in the Rockford Register expressed pleasant surprise at the 1956 winter recreation schedule Brademas and his staff put together in a matter of weeks. Soon, the newspaper predicted, locals would no longer complain, "There's nothing to do in Rockford."

Earl F. Elliot (right) welcomes Jim Brademas and his wife, Than, after Jim was hired as the Park District's first year-round recreation director. Standing in the back is yours truly, who was leaving in the fall of 1956 to return to school.

Winter programs included square dancing, social dancing for teens, folk dancing, ice skating, basketball, art and writing contests, downhill skiing in Twin Sisters Park, and Rec nights on Fridays in junior high schools.

Some programs were easy to start. Others were not. When Brademas approached schools about weekend recreation nights for students, he heard tired old excuses: There was enough for kids to do. Schools were booked. The Park District should concentrate on summer events.

But Brademas was not a man to give up. He persuaded the principal of the city's newest junior high, Jefferson, to allow Rec nights after an assistant principal agreed to supervise.

The program was a great success and, soon, six other schools asked to be included. The events featured table tennis, billiards and other games in the hallways. Teens swam in the pools, played basketball and volleyball in the gym, danced in a large class room, watched movies in the auditorium, and snacked in the cafeteria. It was a dream night for young teens. In 1959, an estimated 3,200 junior high students regularly attended Rec nights.

Saturday mornings, Brademas opened elementary schools to adults, who responded in similar numbers. The idea was to have something for everyone, so the district started basketball leagues for people under 6 feet 1 and for those ages 28 and older, and offered slow-pitch softball for those who could no longer compete in fast-pitch.

When Sapora returned in 1957 to address summer playground staffers, he praised the tremendous progress.

"Rockford has a bright future in recreation," he said. "I am especially pleased with the adult interest; it's the only way a sound and lasting program can be built."

Twin Sisters Park once had a tow rope for skiers.

"Sad Sacks" from Andrews Park line up for a picture.

The Score 'is Not Going to Matter'

In the summer of 1957, the district adopted a new philosophy for youth sports.

"Every boy will get a chance to play when the boys' baseball program gets underway next week at every main park and playground in the Rockford Park District," a newspaper story explained.

"The program will be strictly to teach boys to play ball — and it's not going to matter if the scores winds up 1 to 0 or 100 to 2, says Jim Brademas…"

The story quoted Don Ellis, who said the hundreds of boys who had watched from the sidelines in the past would now get a chance to learn and play the game.

That approach didn't sit well with some old-timers, who felt it amounted to pampering. At least a dozen letters to the editor on the subject were published.

"I am very much worried that the children of Rockford are being taught just

Nig Holiday (far right) stands next to his wife in this photo taken at a square dance. Nig was the best square dance caller I ever heard. We'd get more than 1,000 people at dances he called, held in places like the Sears parking lot on North Main. The woman in the center is Pat Albee.

Rec program kids got a break from sports and active games to exercise their minds in games like Checkers.

is routine in sports programs for younger children today but, in the 1950s, during the Cold War, it seemed un-American to some.

Other innovations under Brademas included a toboggan run at Atwood Park, better sledding and ice skating sites, lighted ball fields, classes in such things as bike safety and fly casting, and "how to" programs for neighborhood councils

Some kinks had to be ironed out. A headline in the Morning Star on Dec. 31, 1957, announced that Rockford's first ski tow had gone into operation at Twin Sisters Park. A story the following day reported that a 10-year-old boy was rescued after his jacket got tangled in the rope. Brademas promised extra precautions until a safety device could be installed.

to play and not to win," said one writer… "Communism has no spirit of competition. Is this what we want?" asked another. And from a third, "If youngsters learn early the important lesson that there are winners and losers in every give-and-take situation, then we'll have fewer mollycoddles to turn delinquent when they can't get their own way as teenagers."

To Brademas, and to letter writers who agreed with him, winning was less important than teaching children how to play sports and be good sports. Under Brademas, scores and league standings for children's teams were not publicized. That practice

Look at the size of this summer rec program crowd checking out, for one thing, a watermelon eating contest.

The Dream Seeks A New Level • 1945 – 1971

These boys are all smiles as they get archery instructions from Parks staffer Charles Fiduccia.

'Moral Dangers' to 12-Year-Olds

Environmental education became one of the strengths of the Park District under Brademas and Lupton. One of the Park District's most successful programs, and one that placed it in the forefront of environmental education nationally, started with a gift from Commissioner Atwood.

As I mentioned before, most Camp Grant land went for the Chicago-Rockford Airport when the government decided to dispose of the property. The Park District got 312 acres, land that had been used as the rifle range, thanks to Atwood who in 1956 gave the Park District a check for $15,818.87 to pay for it.

Atwood, perhaps the most committed environmentalist ever to serve on the Park Board, loved the outdoors. Half of the pleasures in his life, he once said, came through outdoor recreation and nature. He wanted to introduce city children to those pleasures through his gift of land and, later, donations to the Forest Preserve.

Named Atwood Park, the site is bisected by the Kishwaukee River. Atwood and park officials realized it was a valuable educational tool, especially after the Chicago-Rockford Airport contributed a 20-acre quarry in 1957. The board built a 220-foot swinging suspension bridge across the river in '59.

Frank Lupton, who was working on his master's degree at the U of I, drew up a proposal to develop Atwood Park into a major outdoor recreational center to include an environmental education building equipped with classrooms, kitchen and sleeping quarters for 80 students. Brademas, who loved the

She's the winner. We say that because she blew a bubble and balanced a hula hoop at the same time.

concept and so did Atwood. The board OK'd the $135,000 lodge, which was completed in 1960.

Controversy was sparked when Register-Republic Associate Editor Rex Karney learned of plans to take boys and girls to camp at the same time. Karney was a friend of Communist-hunting Sen. Joseph McCarthy of Wisconsin and felt having boys and girls sleep overnight in the same building was dangerous. It would, he said, present "moral dangers" to "curious 12-year-olds." The fact that boys and girls would sleep in separate rooms with adult supervision at all hours didn't pacify him. Karney also charged it was another example of the government taking over the role of parents.

Karney had support from a handful of letter-to-the-editor writers. One called the field trips "school-sponsored co-ed slumber parties" and another said the new "fancy recreation program was spending money in the wrong places." But there also were letters from people who supported outdoor education, including a woman who noted people are less likely to destroy the environment if they understand the natural world.

> *"Communism has no spirit of competition. Is this what we want?"*
> –FROM LETTER TO THE EDITOR

The programs served children from ages 6 through junior high. Offerings included day camps, overnights and week-long sessions. A former sixth-grade teacher, Lupton offered his expertise to Rockford teachers looking to expand environmental instruction. The overnight program for fifth or sixth grade students still operates some 50 years later.

Parents got involved as volunteers. Some were recruited by way of the evening programs for parents that were part of Atwood camping experiences.

Lupton responded to parents' enthusiasm by forming the Rockford Family Campers Association. It met once a month year round. Summer meetings were camping trips within a 100-mile radius of Rockford.

Seth B. Atwood showed his lighter side as he tried out a slide at the opening of the Kiddie Korral at Harmon Park in 1958. The Kiwanis Club helped equip the new playground.

The Dream Seeks A New Level • 1945 – 1971

A few Rockford folks worried that this lodge at Atwood Park would lead to trouble when the park and school districts began overnight trips for sixth graders.

Atwood remains a busy place for environmental education. More than 400,000 people have taken part in Atwood programs. That includes more than 50,000 school children who have come with their classes and spent at least one night at Atwood and 72,000 children in summer camps, many of which include overnights. For many children, these experiences at Atwood are their most memorable elementary school experience.

Atwood's staff also reaches another 10,000 children each year with programs at the park and around the community. The Atwood Environmental Center was a model for many communities and remains one of the best in the country.

Parks and Recreation Collide

Many early leaders of the recreation program went on to share what they learned in Rockford success through similar programs in cities across the nation. Brademas was among them.

Parks staffer Steve Hakes takes a group of children through the woods at Atwood Park. The chance to explore the outdoors became especially important after 1950, when television started us on a march toward relying on technology for work and play.

Frank Lupton in recent photo

He, sadly, left the district in anger and frustration in 1960 because of long-standing disagreements with Park District Superintendent Elliot.

Paul Elmer, who wrote a thesis on Rockford's recreation program, explained the issue in his paper: "The great speed with which programs were developed and implemented (under Brademas) amazed Earl Elliot, and the limelight cast upon the Recreation Department caused him to feel that the 'tail was wagging the dog.'"

Prior to hiring Brademas, Elliot had been the single professional guiding the Park District, wrote Elmer. At that time, Elliot had been managing the district for as long as Brademas had lived. The elder man was devoted to the mission of a traditional park system — buying land and turning it into parks. He might well have felt that young Brademas was a "runaway locomotive."

In 1960, Elliot could take it no more. He told Brademas there would be no new recreation programs. He implied that Brademas would be paid but he expected nothing from him. He didn't even want to see him.

Brademas resigned.

He was not shy about airing his problems with Elliot. The director had forbidden him to meet with the Park Board, said Brademas, who also was frustrated when Elliot took 10 percent of the recreation tax revenue for park maintenance.

I knew both of these men, and I do not want you to get the idea that this was all a personality conflict, or two huge egos clashing. More accurately, it was a painful but expected part of the transformation from traditionally-managed park districts, which built and maintained parks, to park districts that gave equal priority to the recreational needs of residents.

Elliot was standing up for a philosophy he had been taught and believed was right; Brademas was doing the same. Both men

> *"Fancy recreation programs is spending money in the wrong places."*
> – FROM LETTER TO THE EDITOR

> *"The four-year tenure of Jim Brademas as superintendent of recreation must be characterized as dynamic … (Brademas and staff) gave the public what was expected, and more. The credibility of public recreation grew tremendously…"*
> FROM PAUL ELMER'S "HISTORY OF THE 1956 RECREATION TAX AND THE SUBSEQUENT DEVELOPMENT OF RECREATION IN THE ROCKFORD PARK DISTRICT"

The Dream Seeks a New Level • 1945 – 1971

Jim Brademas   *Earl F. Elliot*

contributed much to success of the Rockford Park District and their influence continues today.

Brademas worked in the business world before returning to the U of I at age 46 to earn a doctorate. He then taught in the U of I Department of Recreation, Sport and Tourism for 25 years, frequently relying on his experiences in Rockford to make classroom topics relevant.

Brademas and Lupton, both now retired, remain in touch with colleagues and friends they made in Rockford almost 60 years ago. The work they did has an impact every day on staff and programs in the Park District and, more importantly, on children.

Brademas was replaced by Chuck Fiduccia, the son of an alderman and County Board member. Fiduccia, wrote Elmer, "understood the political realities of a community whose power structure was very conservative, which included the Park Board and Earl Elliot." The "runaway train" slowed down and drew less attention though it continued steady growth. Fiduccia and Elliot developed a cordial working relationship.

The recreation program continues as a

In recent years, one of the most popular Sinnissippi Music Shell shows is that of the Phantom Regiment Drum and Bugle Corps. A. Reyner Eastman, a local architect and a student of Frank Lloyd Wright, designed the music shell.

strong and vital part of the Park District today. With a budget of $15 million from tax revenue and fees, it includes a wide-ranging group of programs and facilities. Among them are Magic Waters, Sportscores, summer playground programs, Music in the Park, Atwood environmental education, snow sculptures, Lockwood Park, swimming pools, golf courses, figure skating classes, the Forest City Queen, and many more.

There are still people who say there is nothing to do in Rockford but they are people who either have never seen a Park District activity guide or who have never gotten off their couches.

$20 Monthly Raises

Finances may have dominated the headlines for the Rockford Park District during the 1940s and '50s but there were plenty of other things going on.

Labor relations became an issue. In December 1946, Superintendent Elliot informed the board that park employees had formed a union affiliated with the American Federation of Labor (AFL). They presented no demands initially but returned more than a year later with requests. Local 104, Chapter 6 of the AFL, State, County and Municipal Employees, asked for $40 monthly raises for all salaried men. In addition, they wanted sick leave not to exceed 10 working days a year, accumulative up to 30 days. The board thought about it and returned in two weeks, on April 28, 1948, to give each staffer a monthly raise of $20 and to accept the union recommendation on sick days.

Board minutes don't make any mention of the union thereafter. A court ruling in March of 1950 disallowed city workers from joining unions. While that ruling had no lasting impact, it may have ended the short life of that Park District local.

The board continued to deal with salary issues, in its own time and at what it considered fair pay. Some years, employees got $10 monthly increases. Other years they got nothing but the following year might get a $25 raise.

Music Shell has Frank Lloyd Wright Connection

Music always was a popular attraction at Rockford parks, but it took 40-some years to get a permanent place for bands and entertainers to perform.

The Civic Symphony Orchestra campaigned for a music shell and held a

Trumpet star Chuck Mangione was among a slate of well-known musicians who played at the Music Shell in the late 1970s.

The Dream Seeks A New Level • 1945 – 1971

The Park District observed Arbor Day with school programs, such as this one at Conklin School, and tree give-aways. Many such programs were done with the help of our devoted environmental educator Jan Lindenmier, who developed the district's Let's Go See program.

two-day music festival in 1948 to launch the project. In October 1949, the Rockford Lions Club coordinated donations and marked $5,000 of its own for the structure. Plans were made to build a music shell in Sinnissippi Park.

Local architect A. Reyner Eastman contributed a design for the music shell. He had studied under Frank Lloyd Wright and had designed the Mendelssohn Club, Henrietta and Westview schools, and the YMCA Log Lodge. Local firms donated most of the materials and the shell was ready for musicians and audiences by June of 1950.

The music shell has been remodeled a number of times and remains in use for frequent band concerts and children's programs every summer.

A host of regional and local entertainers have performed there, the most popular of them in recent years being the Phantom Regiment Drum and Bugle Corps, an award-winning, nationally-acclaimed corps of musicians from around the nation. Other acts that pack the place year after year are the Decatur Park District Singers and Johnie Faren, a Rockford drummer who has performed around the nation and in Europe.

In the late 1970s, the district got an anonymous gift that was large enough to bring in headliners of the day, including Jose Feliciano, Lou Rawls, Melba Moore, Gladys Knight and the Pips, Roberta Flack, the Mills Brothers and Chuck Mangionne. Some drew audiences of 10,000 or more. Beyond entertainers, the most distinguished guest the music shell ever hosted might well have been Frank Lloyd Wright, who was invited by architect Reyner and symphony director Arthur Zack.

Bloom School has just one of the playgrounds built jointly by the Park and School Districts to serve students and children who live in the area.

Wright attended a concert on August 11, 1955, at age 85. He had spent the day in a meeting at the Faust Hotel where he complained about the "uncooperative" mayor and city council in Madison, Wis., who would not back his plan for a $4 million civic center on Lake Monona.[1] Wright also spoke at the concert, where he told the audience, "Your city is like a jewel in a beautiful setting."

'Devious Methods' Denounced

It was big news in the fall of 1949 when several aldermen objected to the Park Board's intention to buy land to extend Sinnissippi Park northward along the Rock River. Ald. Lewis B. Lundberg and Milton Lundstrom appeared before the Park Board to say the money could be better spent on recreational facilities.

Park Board President Atwood informed them the district was fulfilling long-range plans to expand the riverfront park. He promised the Park Board would make every effort to comply with all "worthy requests" from taxpayers but made it clear this was not one of them.

Atwood also rebuked the aldermen for "misrepresenting the facts." The board had set aside $4,000, not $12,000 as was reported. He told the two they should have talked to the Park Board before going public at a City Council meeting. Official minutes add that he "strongly denounced the strategy of one public organization attempting to tear another down by such devious methods."

'The Forest City' Loses Elms

The Rockford area lost its battle with Dutch elm disease. Today, as it faces the similarly-dangerous emerald ash beetle, it still mourns the loss of stately elms that had grown to glorious canopies over many city streets.

Dutch elm disease appeared here in the mid-1940s, but it wasn't until almost 10 years later that the potential damage was acknowledged.

The Park District removed diseased trees as soon as possible, taking down more than a thousand trees between 1957 and 1961. The district also found funds to plant a tree for every one taken down. As the new trees grew, the parks and golf courses regained their beauty.

Overall, Rockford was not as fortunate. City crews could not keep up with spraying trees that might be saved and taking down those that were doomed. In both 1958 and '59, voters defeated tax increases for the Forestry Department.

When it was too late to save the elms, citizens approved a five-mill tax rate in 1962. It was only to last five years and was only to be used to remove dead elm trees.

The total loss in the city was estimated at 60,000 elms, most of them never replaced. A full-scale replacement program never was undertaken, although the Park District and other organizations through the years have made saplings available to residents and neighborhood groups.

Today, the city faces the loss of ash trees, which make up nearly 20 percent of its street trees. I hope we do better saving and/or replacing our ash trees than we did our elms. Unfortunately, public funds are stretched thin and attempts to reforest the city by public and private groups have not been successful on any large scale.

Ironically, on July 1, 1961, in the midst of losing the Dutch elm battle, the city of Rockford received copyright control of the title, "Forest City."

> *Ironically, on July 1, 1961, in the midst of losing the Dutch elm battle, the city of Rockford received copyright control of the title, "Forest City."*

One Playground for School, Neighborhood

In the 1950s, after years of wrangling between the School District and the Park District, the beginnings of a sane agreement regarding school playgrounds was worked out.

The major disagreement revolved around the old Henrietta Park at 200 N. Johnston Ave. which today is the site of a Head Start program. The school district owned the land but had let the Park District install a playground on it in 1931. When the School District in 1942 asked for the land back to build a school, neighbors and aldermen fought for their playground. The solution was for the Park District to buy land for a new playground on South Henrietta Street, about seven blocks from the school. Henrietta School then was constructed on the Johnston site.

The Park District and School District worked out better arrangements in future school construction. In 1954, the two entities agreed on a plan to build playgrounds adjacent to elementary schools. The School District would sell the Park District, at cost, three to five acres of land for a park adjacent to a school. The Park District would install a playground and, sometimes, sports fields, and maintain them for the school and neighborhood.

The agreement, which may have been the first such partnership in the nation, illustrates the progressive and conservative nature of the Park and School boards. Everyone agreed it made sense and saved money to build one playground to serve both neighborhood and school. At the same time, many other communities were decades away from having two public agencies come together to better serve everyone.

Since that time, the Park District has built playgrounds at more than 40 public elementary schools.

Nothing to Lose in Open Meetings

For decades, the Park Board had been able to conduct meetings any way it wanted to. Citizens were welcome only if they had business, and then they still had to get permission.

Not that open meetings were an issue. Most meetings were held in the mornings, when few people could have attended. Few citizens questioned the board's procedures or their right to hear what the board said or did.

Illinois adopted its first Open Meetings Act in 1957, but things changed slowly. When Elliot banned Brademas from attending board meetings in the late 1950s, Brademas felt he had no choice but to resign. These days, such an order would be challenged publicly, with media alerted or, possibly, leading the charge.

But open meetings weren't the practice then.

LEFT: The riverfront in Loves Park has always attracted crowds, as shown in this postcard photo from the early 1900s of the spot where the riverboat docked.

ABOVE: The picture of cars parked at the Martin Park area is circa 1950.

Parks 'Essential in Day-to-Day Living'

In part to fulfill its commitment to schools, the Park Board in 1954 approved issuing $600,000 in bonds. It was a significant move because it was only the third such borrowing in Park District history, the first two having been done back in 1910 and 1911.

The $600,000 was to be used to buy and develop 13 additional park and playground sites as well as improve roads in existing sites. The new parks were Twin Sisters, Marsh School, Loves Park Playground, Summerdale Playground, Pierpont Playground, Ridge Avenue Playground, Bloom School, Riverdahl School, Barbour School, Rolling Green Playground, Alpine Park, Lathrop Tract and Guilford Road Playground.

The borrowing raised eyebrows but the Morning Star called it a foresighted move. The Park District acted while land still was available in neighborhoods that were rapidly being filled with new homes, the newspaper said.

Parks, the Star added, would only become more important in the second half of the 20th Century: "The task of the Park District in our decade must revolve chiefly around provision of playground and recreational facilities suitable to our new scheme of living, in which parks are not for occasional picnics or outings but are an essential facility in day-to-day living in an increasingly urban society."

The Park District was willing to partner with any agency that shared its goal of bettering the community. It was a no-brainer, therefore, when the Boy Scouts asked permission to build its headquarters in Churchill Park. Construction took place in 1960 and the Blackhawk Area Council still operates from there. As of this writing, the Boy Scouts and Girl Scouts of Northern Illinois are jointly buying an existing building to use as a combined service center.

Valuable Riverfront Donated

In the 1950s, the district acquired two more valuable pieces of riverfront property, both in Loves Park. Both have become well-used parks with functions beyond picnicking.

Loves Park citizens formed the Parkside Citizens Committee in 1945 to convince the city of Rockford and the Park District to use a river shore site at 5600 Park Ridge Road as a landfill. Five years later, after the landfill had been compacted and filled according to environmental regulations, the committee gave the eight-acre site to the Park District and asked that it be developed. The Park District complied, helped by a 1957 gift of $25,000 from the Charitable Trust of the Woodward Governor Co. for a shelter house. The park also was renamed Charles Woodward Martin Memorial Park in honor of the son of Mr. and Mrs. Irl Martin. Charles was 13 when he died in 1945 following an illness. Irl Martin was president of Woodward Governor.

The Charitable Trust of Woodward Governor donated more land in later years, until Martin Park was 15 acres and

> *"The task of the Park District in our decade must revolve chiefly around provision of playground and recreational facilities suitable to our new scheme of living, in which parks are not for occasional picnics or outings but are an essential facility in day-to-day living in an increasingly urban society."*
> *– Morning Star*

Our local Ski Broncs water skiing team has brought national attention and national shows to Shorewood Park in Loves Park.

reached north to Riverside Boulevard. The popular park was the site of Loves Park's Young at Heart festival for 29 years until the fest moved to the City Hall site in 2001.

Hundreds of kids got the sand for their sandboxes at Martin Park through a program that ran for 20 years, until the early 2000s. Free sand was made available each spring by Rockford Blacktop, Rockford Sand and Gravel and labor organizations.

'Important' Purchase

Loves Park got another sizeable riverfront park in 1958, when the district bought 39 acres along the river south of Martin Park. Purchase of the wooded tract of land was "one of the most important moves the Park Board has made," said board president Seth B. Atwood. "It is the last sizeable piece of property near the downtown area with the great advantage of river frontage.

"The community is fortunate to have this wonderful park for its future use and enjoyment."

The land, which had 1,500 feet of river frontage, cost $58,000. It was named Shorewood Park by 11-year-old Marcia Wallace, who won a TV set in a naming contest that drew 700 entries.

The park features picnic and playground facilities, boat launches and a paved path. It is most well known today as home of the Loves Park Ski Broncs, the local water skiing troop that has won national and regional acclaim. The Broncs, organized in 1967, use Shorewood as their base, putting on free shows Wednesday and Friday nights in summer. The group also has brought state and national water ski tournaments to Shorewood Park.

'They Feel this is Their Place'

Any good park district knows its neighborhoods well and serves each according to its needs. The Rockford Park District demonstrated that in 1956 when it accepted responsibility for the Washington Park Community Center on the city's far west end.

The Rockford Community Trust funded the $45,000 center with donations from groups around the city, including Junior League and the West End Business and Professional Men's Association. Built on Park District land, the center opened in 1958 to serve 3,000 people, about 900 of them children. Most of the families struggled on low incomes in one of

The Dream Seeks A New Level • 1945 – 1971

the most poverty-stricken areas of town.

The Park District got the center off to a successful start by hiring two experienced leaders as directors, Deacon Davis, a Freeport, Iowa and national basketball star who had worked in Freeport's and Rockford's summer recreational programs; and Norman Flachs, who had directed Montague House in south Rockford, as well as centers in New York and Minnesota.

The community center opened in 1958 to neighborhood school children and their families. It had a gym and meeting rooms, and homework help, charm school for teenage girls, movies, athletics, dances for teens, family events and adult classes. In its first week, attendance reached over 1,000.

Mrs. Adell Ingram (left) and Mrs. Loreen Denny were invaluable mentors to the girls who came to Washington Park Community Center.

Three years into the center's operation, it seemed to have made a big difference, according to a story in the Star in September 1959. The Washington Park neighborhood, said the Star, formerly had 14 youths a year committed to the Illinois Youth Commission. That was half the total from Winnebago County. By 1959, just one or two teens from Washington Park found themselves in that kind of trouble each year.

Neighborhood adults such as Mrs. Loreen Denny and Mrs. Tom Ingram gave the center strong support.

The photo, dated 1981, shows one of Washington Park's football teams. The center offers academic, recreational and neighborhood programs.

McKinley "Deacon" Davis (center) teaching a proper baseball swing.

They and their friends held classes in cooking, clothes-making and proper social behaviors. Their parental attitudes and skills had a significant impact on neighborhood youth.

Through the years, the center and its programs have been remodeled and expanded. Both are strong parts of the neighborhood yet today. The Park District's partnerships there broadened further when the Winnebago County Housing Authority built single-family homes under the Hope VI program. Today, both agencies offer a variety of services to all citizens in the area.

The impact of such a facility was no surprise to Deacon Davis. Early in Washington Park Community Center's operation, he explained why crime in the neighborhood had gone down. The kids and teens, Davis said, "have a feeling of being part of something — they feel this is their place."

> *"They feel this is their place."*
> – BASKETBALL GREAT AND YOUTH COUNSELOR DEACON DAVIS EXPLAINING WHY JUVENILE DELINQUENCY DECLINED IN WASHINGTON PARK AREA AFTER THE COMMUNITY CENTER OPENED.

Happy 50th Birthday!

The Park District celebrated its 50th anniversary in 1959 with a pageant in Beyer Stadium featuring 600 children from the summer recreation program in a lantern parade, youth ballet and Indian dancing, along with speeches from Park District officials.

At age 50, the district served a population of 150,000 and a land area of 92 square miles. A newspaper story noted the district had beautiful gardens; an art gallery; 55 softball and 19 baseball diamonds, three of them lighted; two lighted basketball courts under construction; two swim pools; a log cabin at Blackhawk Park; boating ramp; three camps; a band shell; three golf courses; horseshoe pitching courts; ice skating at 19 sites; lawn bowling green; natural history museum; 14 shuffleboard courts; junior ski jump; 26 tennis courts; and 17 wading pools.

The district's 1959 budget was $830,000, with $264,000 for the recreation program. The district collected $112,000 in fees, including $97,000 from golfers and $12,000 from swimmers. That year, it levied about $720,000 in taxes, or about $4.80 per capita. Expenses included not only park maintenance and recreation but also debt retirement and pension plans for employees.

> *"Run around your own parks and have fun in them."*
> – BOARD PRESIDENT SETH B. ATWOOD AT 50TH ANNIVERSARY CELEBRATION OF PARK DISTRICT

Swim Pools Not a Priority

Swimming pools were a difficult issue for the Park District for decades. The board's early attempts to provide swimming in Kent Creek at Fair Grounds

THE DREAM SEEKS A NEW LEVEL • 1945 – 1971

> **Survey Results**
>
> When 683 adults were asked how to improve aquatic facilities in 1957, the top five answers were:
> - Better use of school facilities in summer and evening hours.
> - Develop rivers, creeks and lakes.
> - Control pollution of streams.
> - More ice skating facilities.
> - Build indoor-outdoor type swim pool.
>
> Source: Robert Cryer's thesis study on aquatic facilities and needs in Rockford Park District

Park and later, a quarry site south of Auburn Street, were unsuccessful because of safety and health issues.

Some early commissioners felt swimmers should use local rivers and creeks. Others felt swimmers could join private clubs or use the pools in public schools.

The district built Fair Grounds pool in 1924 and the 10th Avenue Pool in 1929, and felt that was adequate. Despite continued requests for more pools, the matter was not a priority for the Park Board.

At a meeting on Saturday afternoon in September 1958, the board took action on several issues citizens had been clamoring for. It OK'd bonds of $750,000 for a lighted baseball diamond in Black Hawk Park and other projects. The borrowing did not need voter approval.

At the same meeting, it scheduled November 4th referendums on borrowing $1.15 million for a golf course, three swimming pools and an artificial, indoor ice rink. The action was a response to what some members of the public wanted, not to what the Park Board wanted.

Board President Atwood issued a statement that the questions would be on the ballot "because of requests from various people and groups.

"We are, however, leaving the question up to the public whether they want to increase their taxes for these purposes," he said. "The Park Board will be glad to carry out their wishes."

The Morning Star noted that people had been asking for more swim pools for many years and, in Loves Park, a group had organized to campaign for a pool. Similarly, the district's three golf courses were crowded, with 25,000 more rounds played in 1958 than the previous year.

Although the Park Board remained neutral, the referendum got support. A citizens group formed to urge a yes vote. City golf star Charles O. Lindgren was chairman. The Register-Republic told voters to say yes to the pools and golf course but no to the indoor ice rink. "Ice skating is at its best in neighborhood parks and playgrounds," the newspaper said. The Morning Star newspaper said the cost to the average family for the ice rink, pools and golf course would be only 65 cents a year, and that the golf and skating facility would pay for themselves.

That fall, an exhaustive study by U of I graduate student Robert Cryer on community aquatic facilities in Rockford was completed. Cryer, who used the 175-page report as his master's thesis, cited a survey of local people who listed swimming, and then fishing, ice skating and motor boating, as their favorite aquatic pastimes. Cryer recommended five new pools, three immediately and two later.

The Register-Republic told voters to say yes to the pools and golf course but no to the indoor ice rink.

Most people disagreed. On Election Day, all three proposals were defeated, 3 to 1 for the ice rink and golf course and 2 to 1 for the pools.

Golfer Lindgren said his group would try another way to get the facilities because they were needed. The Loves Park group vowed to find a way to build a pool on its own. As for the Park Board, Atwood said "the voters showed they don't want to pay for new facilities now."

If he thought the matter was closed, he was wrong. The issue of swim pools resurfaced every time the district made a large expenditure for anything else.

Atwood Retires After 32 Years

As the district went into its 51st year, a key board member retired. Seth B. Atwood, a commissioner for 32 of the 51 years the Park Board had existed, and board president for 18 years, left in March of 1960 to have more time for personal activities. He presented the board with a three-page list of what he called "carry over park ideas."

In the opinion of this writer, Seth B. Atwood's service to the Park District and community cannot be overstated. His son, Seth G. Atwood, and grandson, Bruce Atwood, have carried on the tradition.

The title of this Bob Dylan album. "The Times They are a-Changin'" told the the state of the nation in the 1960s.

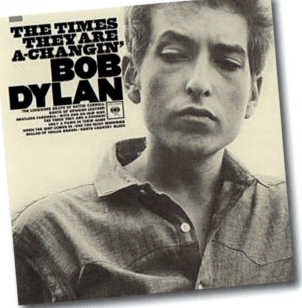

Times Were Changing

As 1960 dawned and the Park District began the second half of its first century, big changes were sweeping the nation. Rockford was not immune.

President John F. Kennedy was assassinated in 1963; 11 years later, President Richard M. Nixon resigned in

This headline from the Loves Park Post in September 1961 reflects the times. The story is about a marijuana crop two men had planted on Park District land.

disgrace. Hippies were rejecting their parents' fashions and ways of life, preferring long hair, "free love" and communal living. Illegal drug use mushroomed. The nation was split between those who supported our fighting in Vietnam and those who did not.

Seventy-million Baby Boomers became teenagers and injected a youthful attitude into popular culture. The teens locked onto Elvis and the Beatles, despite oldsters' warnings that the music was immoral. So many teens were entering colleges that emergency living quarters were set up. Black Americans demanded equal rights and did not back down in the face of fire hoses, police with billy clubs or the assassination of civil rights leader, Dr. Martin Luther King Jr. A new way of life was emerging or, as influential singer-songwriter Bob Dylan proclaimed in 1964, "The Times, They Are A Changin'."

The Dream Seeks A New Level • 1945 – 1971

One of the best places to be in summer is Sand Park Pool in Loves Park, opened in 1969.

'The Love In' Raided

Societal problems show up in all public entities. Park districts are not immune.

In September 1961, Rockford police arrested two men for possession of marijuana. To the great surprise of the Park District, they said they got the marijuana from six acres of land owned by the district at Springfield Avenue and Kent Creek. The police recovered about 8 pounds of marijuana, worth about $760 in that form and enough marijuana to have made 7,000 cigarettes. Police said the "high quality weed" was on its way to Chicago to be sold to a drug syndicate. Before they got out of town, however, the two men got into an accident when one drove their car into the Central Park Tap on Auburn Street. Police destroyed the six-acre crop.

In 1968, the district banned heroin, marijuana, and other substances "designed to induce excitement, exhilaration, drowsiness or other abnormal or unusual conduct or behavior" from parks. Alcohol, of course, had always been banned.

Just in time. The following year, police arrested eight people, including three 14-year-old girls, after a raid on a party in Aldeen Park on the "city's far east side," said the Star.

According to the newspaper, police had the park under surveillance for several weeks. The park had a reputation among "hippies" as the place to get illegal drugs and had become known as "The Love In."

Five young men were charged with possession of marijuana and the girls were turned over to juvenile authorities. Police confiscated three marijuana cigarettes, a bottle of pills, a bottle of wine, and a revolver.

One man tried to escape but was caught in a telephone booth. Police returned to the park later that night. As they began checking vehicles for city stickers, lights over license plates and other such violations, a crowd of about 150 youth left quickly, some driving over private lawns to elude police.

No 'Beatle' Hair Cuts

Some oldsters didn't like long hair on boys, either. In 1966, the Park District said boys wearing hair longer than "average athletic style" must wear bathing caps in pools. This meant no "Beatle" or "Rolling Stone" haircuts.

Those going more for the Elvis look, using tonic to hold ducktails in place, would be required to shampoo before swimming because the grease was clogging filtration systems.

> *"Officials reported very few boys with extra long hair show up to swim."*
> – MORNING STAR

A follow-up newspaper story the following year said long hair wasn't a problem. The Star surmised that maybe long-haired guys didn't swim.

"Officials reported very few boys with extra long hair show up to swim," the paper said. One boy with a Beatle cut was sent home for a swim cap; he never returned.

'Biggest Bargain' in Town

Realtor John B. Whitehead sounded a bit like Levin Faust when he addressed several hundred members of the Park and Recreation associations at their annual meeting in Rockford in 1964. As Faust had done decades earlier, Whitehead called parks and recreation a bargain for John Q. Public.

The cost averaged out to $4.40 a person, or $12.49 a year to the person who owned a $165,000 home, said Whitehead, past president of the Rockford Board of Realtors. Since most homes at the time were hardly worth $165,000, the average price was half that or less.

John B. Whitehead

"It's the biggest bargain in the community," Whitehead said. "Look at the cost of country clubs."

He advocated beautifying the river bank downtown and building a path along the river. "It can be done cheaply and it will boost property values…" the Realtor said (a path was opened in 1977).

Whitehead's interest in parks didn't go unnoticed. Six years later, he was named to the board and served from 1970 to 1983, four years as president.

'14,000 Reasons' to Build Pools

When the board decided in 1964 to build Elliot Golf Course and Park and borrow $1.8 million for that project and other parks and expansions, the subject of pools came up big time.

Many residents had been lobbying for additional swimming pools for decades. The last pool, 10th Avenue, was built in 1929 and was crumbling. People complained that the district continued building golf courses, but would not make pools a priority.

The Dream Seeks A New Level • 1945 – 1971

The issue went public on Oct. 26, 1964, when Ald. Hugh Deery asked the Rockford City Council to sponsor a plaque for the Park District to recognize its foresight in preserving green space. Deery wished to commend those who had created parks for this and future generations.

His motion was twice called for a vote but received only scattered mumbles. Deery was frustrated. "I didn't know honoring a citizen was such a momentous job," he complained.

Ald. Edolo "Zeke" Giorgi said he wouldn't support the plaque because the Park Board had built only one public swim pool in 30 years. Other aldermen voiced objections, leading Deery to exclaim in frustration, "Why don't we just make the town into one big dump?"

A newspaper editorial explained the issues.

"There is keen resentment of the fact that the board, without reference to the public, has just sold improvement bonds totaling $1.8 million," the paper said.

"When parents of the district asked that more swimming pools be provided, the request was placed on the ballot and defeated. When a completely unnecessary golf course was wanted, the trustees did not hesitate to create the debt."

The editorial contended that residents' wishes were being ignored.

In July 1965, the Park Board had carried out its Elliot Golf Course plan by issuing $1.8 million in bonds. The money also would be used to improve 10 parks and create three new ones.

Loves Park folks wanted a pool so desperately they explored numerous ways of getting one, including having the city build it. None of the plans worked but the issue was constantly in the news in the small city.

Finally, in May 1967, the Park Board got around to swimming pools. It unanimously passed a resolution for the sale of $1.17 million in bonds to build two new swim

Alpine Pool and Sand Park Pool each cost $300,000 in 1969. More than 30 years later, the pool in Fair Grounds Park (shown here), built in 1924, cost more than $1 million to renovate. The Fair Grounds Pool is named after James Lesley Harkins, who died there in a tragic accident in 1996.

More than 3,000 children take swimming lessons at Park District pools each summer.

pools (Alpine Park and Sand Park), three baseball diamonds, roads, bathrooms and other facilities.

The Star reported the borrowing would raise the district's debt to one-half of one percent of valuation, which is the limit set by the state. Some observers pointed out that was not a good situation. But the board had heard enough about swim pools and wanted to get the project done.

"It is necessary and in the public interest to improve and equip park facilities at this time," said a board resolution, "even though there is a lack of funds."

Some Rockford folks complained that one pool would be in Loves Park. The board reminded them that Loves Park was part of the Park District, and that the location would serve north Rockford, too.

Alpine Park made sense because the population was steadily and quickly moving east, the board said.

The Register Republic was partly satisfied. It's too bad the district put the pool projects off for so long it could no longer afford three pools, said the newspaper, referring to requests for a facility in south Rockford.

There were more delays. The board didn't negotiate the sale of bonds until December. In July 1968, more than a year after the decision to build the pools, specifications for construction were not complete.

"Now the target date is next year — 40 years after the opening" of the 10th Avenue pool in 1929, the Star complained.

The Register Republic was impatient, too. In July 1968, it noted that 14,000 people had used school swimming pools during the first week they were opened that summer. "The park commissioners now have 14,000 reasons why they should get on with the job. Do they need more?" it asked.

In September, when bids came in $300,000 over budget, the newspaper had little sympathy for the Park District's plight.

"…public patience is wearing thin," it said. "The deadline of June 1969 for the opening of the two new pools has been established. It must be kept if the park commissioners are to keep their word with the public."

The original concept of three separate pools at each site — wading, swimming and diving — was scuttled in favor of combined swimming and diving. Each pool ended up costing nearly $300,000. They did open, as promised, in June 1969, with fees for an afternoon or evening of 35 cents for children under 16 and 75 cents for adults. Morning swims were free.

The last obstacle to opening the pools was the weather. The day before Alpine was to open, the city's high temperature was 67 degrees. A photo cutline of the pool in the Register-Republic said it was set to open June 9, "barring complications (like ice, maybe?)."

> *"The park commissioners now have 14,000 reasons why they should get on with the job. Do they need more?"*
> *–Register Republic*

Pools Attract 50,000 More Swimmers

The high temperature on June 9, 1969, was only 70 degrees. Still, by mid-afternoon 445 swimmers had used the new Alpine Pool. The situation was much the same the following day at Sand Park, where police and the City of Loves Park hurriedly lowered the speed limit and put in crosswalks on Riverside Boulevard once they saw how many children were walking to the pool.

The new pools were heated, a big attraction on days when temperatures were barely summer-like. By July 19, when the pools had been open about 40 days, Alpine had recorded 28,955 swimmers and Sand Park, 25,786. Fair Grounds and 10th Avenue had 5,583 and 11,515 respectively.

The following numbers illustrate how hungry residents were for more swim pools. By mid-July 1968, 22,000 swimmers had used the Park District pools. By the same time in 1969, that number was 72,000 — an increase of 50,000 despite cooler temperatures!

Capacities at the pools were: Alpine, 543; Sand Park, 543; Fair Grounds, 574; and 10th Avenue, 910.

As for the board, once it got into the swimming mode, it kept going, with a discussion of improving Fair Grounds Pool at its July meeting that summer. In fall, bids were approved for a $248,000 renovation of the west side pool.

Popularity of the pools did not diminish once the newness wore off. Two years later, swimmers lined up at Alpine Pool shortly after 7 a.m. on June 13, the day pools opened — at 9 a.m. Four-hundred people came through Alpine's gate by 9:15 a.m.

Surely, one reason the pools were so

> *By mid-July 1968, 22,000 swimmers had used the Park District pools. By the same time in 1969, that number was 72,000 — an increase of 50,000 despite cooler temperatures!*

well used is that they were life-guarded. Newspapers of that era were full of stories about drownings. Between June 5 and June 14 in 1971, seven local people — six of them children — drowned. The sites were an abandoned gravel pit, the Rock River, a residential swim pool, Windsor Lake and Lake Louise.

All Park District pools were overseen by lifeguards and swim lessons were offered.

Three pools (10th Avenue is gone) continue to serve the district, with nearly 108,000 swimmers and more than 3,000 children in swim lessons each summer. Many Rockford kids who have learned to swim in the past 40 years have done so at one of the pools. The Park District provides reasonably-priced lessons, starting in the toddler wading pool and going through junior lifeguarding classes. The pools have provided fun and exercise and, no doubt, have saved lives through lessons and providing a safe place to swim.

Parks Soften on Rock 'n Roll

Part of the 1960s social revolution centered on music and that, too, became an issue in the Rockford Park District.

Rock 'n' roll was a huge hit with the younger set but was regarded as noise and sometimes as sinful by older citizens. In 1970 when promoters tried to stage a rock concert in Sinnissippi Park, the board turned them down because it would cost $700 to hire extra police the Park Board deemed necessary.

The following year, a Mother's Day rock music concert took place with about 5,000 attendees, most under age 25, said

> *FACT OF THE DAY:* Among the information reported by the Star May 19, 1971, about the rock concert: *"Almost no one but police were wearing socks."*

This early '80s rock concert at Page Park drew thousands of young people.

the Star, which ran a huge picture and headline on Page 1 the following day. Police, both uniformed and undercover, reported the only problem was a shortage of parking. After the concert, many people from the audience roamed the park with plastic bags picking up litter, the paper said.

The powers-that-be were so impressed with behavior at that concert that, two days later, the board allocated $5,000 for summer music programs, with $1,000 of it for 10 rock or folk-rock concerts if someone would match the amount. It seems Rockford was beginning to soften its stance on rock 'n roll.

"Although rock is a relatively new form of music, we have to recognize it as being a part of society," said Bert Gibson, president of the Rockford Concert Band.

A few days later, the local chapter of the American Federation of Musicians said it would provide $6,500 for concerts.

This being the era of the controversial Vietnam War, peace movement, hippies, draft-dodgers and flag-burners, the board elders felt they needed to reinforce pride in America. Commissioner Gilmore Landstrom thought every concert should end with a patriotic song.

"Let's send them home thinking of America and what a great country it is," he said.

"Frankly, I don't know how the Star Spangled Banner would sound on a guitar," Commissioner Gerald Wernick responded, "but I'll go up there on the stage and sing it myself if all else fails."

Apparently Wernick had missed the screeching version of the National Anthem by Jimi Hendrix on his electric guitar at Woodstock in 1969, two years earlier.

Elliot a 'Championship Course'

Earl F. Elliot got the surprise of his life the evening of September 24, 1964, while attending a banquet of the Illinois Association of Park Districts and the Illinois Recreation Association in the Faust Hotel.

Reuben A. Aldeen, president of the Park Board, took the floor to announce that the new 220-acre park and golf course being developed off Lyford Road would be named after Elliot.

Elliot, four years from retiring at the time, had been in the district 36 years and had been director 30 years. He was visibly moved as he stood to acknowledge a standing ovation from the crowd. In impromptu remarks, he honored the park boards he had worked under, adding, "with such commissioners, you can't help but be a success."

The Elliot Golf Course opened in 1968. Golfers were thrilled with the course, which was designed by Lawrence Packard of LaGrange, regarded as one of the top golf course architects in the nation. But they didn't like the fees. Nearly 600 golfers signed a petition complaining that Elliot fees were higher than at other courses in the district.

The district responded that higher charges were justified because Elliot was a

---

Bands at the May 9, 1971 rock concert at Sinnissippi

- *Forest City Sound*
- *New Moderia*
- *Cross*
- *Zander Walker*
- *Flight*
- *Fuse*

"Although rock is a relatively new form of music, we have to recognize it as being part of society."

– MORNING STAR QUOTE OF BERT GIBSON, PRESIDENT OF ROCKFORD CONCERT BAND, IN 1971

The clubhouse at Elliot Golf Course, which opened in 1968.

championship course. The Elliot fees were $2 a round on weekdays and $3 on weekends. Rates at Sandy Hollow and Ingersoll, the other two 18-hole courses in the district, were $1.50 on weekdays and $2 on weekends.

Elliot was the first course for the Park District with watered fairways. On other courses, only the greens were watered, not the fairways.

The Register Republic hailed the golf course but also called it overdue. When construction contracts were awarded in 1965, the newspaper noted it had been 35 years since a golf course was built. "Over the years, the rapid growth of population and of the number of golfers has put a heavy strain on the three public courses," the editorial said.

The 220-acre Elliot site, which includes a park, cost the district $188,000. Developing the course and grading the rest of the site for park use cost $432,700.

Women golfers enjoying the Elliot course.

'Parks Man' Retires

After Director Elliot suffered a heart attack in 1960, he returned and ran the Park District for eight more years. In October 1968, Elliot retired after 40 years with the Park District. He had started as an engineer in 1928 and become director six years later, after the unexpected death of Clarence Pedlow. When he retired, he was just the third superintendent of the district in its then 59-year-history.

Retired Superintendent Earl F. Elliot (left) is pictured with your author in the old greenhouse. Elliot supported the Park District any way he could, even after he retired, and was always a friend and mentor to me.

In his 34 years as superintendent, the Park District grew from 719 acres to 2,651, including the east side park and golf course in his name. Much of this time, Elliot had worked with Seth Atwood as board president. The two had concentrated on building parks to serve the city's growth in acreage and population.

Elliot was the old-fashioned "parks man." Buying land and developing parks was his strength and his mission. He had never believed that park districts needed to offer programmed recreation, thus the difficulty in the 1950s with Brademas and others. But Elliot loved the community and the Park District and devoted his life to both. Without his achievements, the district would not have been equipped to enter the era of recreation.

Elliot died in Rockford in 1984, at age 80. Until his death, his heart remained with the Park District as a loyal supporter of the projects and programs we took on.

Robert Milne succeeded Elliot in 1968. The board had hired Milne as assistant superintendent in 1960 when Elliot had his heart attack, expecting Elliot to train Milne as his successor. Milne came from Champaign, where he had been general manager of the Park District for two years. Under his direction, 12 neighborhood parks and four major park-school playground areas were developed in Champaign. He resigned the Champaign Parks job to organize the Family Camping Association of America.

Slow Acceptance of Money from the Feds

Conservative Rockford didn't have much trust in big government, and that included the United States federal government. The money that Uncle Sam was willing to dole out came with too many strings attached, many Rockford folks believed.

The Rockford Park District generally shared that view. It steered clear of federal dollars until 1969, when then-Executive Director Milne advised the board to look into seeking a federal grant from HUD to buy land owned by the county at River Bluff Nursing Home.

The subject of taking federal funds had almost been off limits. In September 1964, when the state Association of Park Districts and Recreation Association met in Rockford, a speaker said the federal government had $6 million for Illinois communities to use for park land. The speaker stressed that the grants were "administered at the local level by local people."

The Park District didn't go for the money and the idea was dropped for another five years.

When the notion resurfaced in 1969, the board asked Milne for a public rationalization. He did so, explaining that the district would carefully evaluate the pros and cons of federal funds and would commit itself only if the grant would clearly benefit local taxpayers.

"The board," Milne said, "is in the process of investigating the possibility of using federal funds for the purpose of offsetting the tax budget, which is becoming increasingly larger." In other words, money from Washington, D.C., could help reduce local tax bills.

The board promised to consider each federal fund application separately, and then agreed to ask the feds for money for the land at River Bluff, later renamed Veterans Memorial Park and then Sportscore One. In August 1970, U.S. Rep. John B. Anderson informed park officials they had received $68,697 from HUD to pay half the purchase price of 67 acres of land adjacent to the county's River Bluff Nursing Home to construct Veterans Memorial Park. State funds helped build a boat launch and shelter house, as well as a field for model airplane enthusiasts.

Since Milne nudged the board into that initial federal grant, federal funds have helped the district out on many projects. Some of the big ones were $225,000 for the Riverside pedestrian bridge, $250,000 for the Tinker Cottage Museum suspension bridge, $172,000 for machines to groom snowmobile trails, and $750,000 for expanding Sportscore One. The feds also helped with smaller items such as $1,850

The Children's Farm, later named Lockwood Park, opened in 1970. (Photo by Leah Shackleford)

The Dream Seeks A New Level • 1945 – 1971

These cages, used when the Children's Farm opened, don't meet our standards of humane treatment of animals today and were disposed of years ago.

for bulletproof vests for district police officers and $2,500 for planting a prairie at Midway Village.

The truth is, the state and federal governments have been a great help to us. Grants from each of them enabled us to complete a lot of projects we would not have started alone.

'A Mix of Fair, Zoo and Grandpa's Farm'

Back in 1954, the district had invested $31,000 in a 115-acre site in northwest Rockford. In 1968, the board took Milne's recommendation to develop the site, known then as Quarry Hill Park (now Lockwood Park), into a children's farm.

Milne wanted the farm to represent the county's agricultural heritage so children, especially those raised in the city, would understand the importance of local agriculture and enjoy personal contact with farm animals.

The Children's Farm opened in July 1970 with remodeled buildings, fencing, a new covered bridge, and more than 200 birds and animals. The Register Star called it "a mix of a county fair, small-scale zoo and your grandfather's farm." On display were domestic animals like cows, mules, horses, ducks, chickens and turkeys, and wild critters like mountain goats, deer,

A boy meets a goat at the Children's Farm in this 1972 photo.

pheasants, foxes, raccoons, peacocks and a great-horned owl. Visitors could ride on a horse-drawn wagon, pet some of the smaller, tame animals and, if they arrived around 6 p.m., watch the cows being milked.

The community loved the idea of a Children's Farm. Officials said 2,500 visited each week that summer. They enjoyed wagon and pony rides at fees of 20 to 50 cents.

To get the farm up and running, donations had come in from a dozen or more local businesses. One paid the cost of the covered bridge, another gave $6,000 for a team of Clydesdale horses, another donated the henhouse, incubator and hatchery, the most popular display at the farm. Donors included D.J. Stewart and Co., Amerock Corp., American National Bank and Trust Co., Mallquist Butter and Egg Co., Elco Industries, B and F Hi-Line Construction, Commonwealth Edison, Allabaugh Well Co., Comstock Feed and Equipment, Coca Cola Bottling Co. and the Association of Independent Insurance Agents of Rockford.

A controversy sprang up when Milne refused to waive the 25-cent admission fee for a group of children from a Head Start class. Milne realized how much it would cost to maintain the farm and believed he couldn't afford to make exceptions. The community cried for compassion for the low-income kids. In true Rockford style, residents made donations to Head Start, and the preschoolers got to see the animals.

Caring for the animals was a big job. The owl needed raw meat, mixed with fur or feathers once a week to clean its digestive tract. Pheasants and turkeys needed medicated food and the turkeys' water had to be treated. The cows needed milking twice a day. Six horses, three burros and 20 ponies were curried and brushed each morning before the park opened. There were 22 farm "hands" that first summer, many of them part-timers.

The district tried to keep maintenance costs down by "farming out" the cows and chickens in the winter. Farmers who boarded them were reimbursed for food and got to keep the milk and eggs.

Other animals stayed at the farm, which offered wagon and sleigh rides in winter to keep visitors coming.

But the farm cost more to operate than it brought in from admissions. Deficits in its first three years of operation ranged from $47,000 to $58,000. It was obvious that somewhere down the line, the Park Board would have to revisit the value, the operation and the cost of the Children's Farm.

Year In, Year Out

Not every issue generated controversy or headlines. Here are some happenings, largely taken for granted, that illustrate life in the Park District and the community in the 1960s.

In 1963, the district successfully fought a proposal to build apartments next to Sinnissippi, south of Auburn, on the east bank of the Rock River. That land since has become property of the Park District.

That same year, Michael Meehan, planning director of the City-County Planning Commission, recommended the addition of 24 parks and playgrounds and the expansion of 15 parks and nine playgrounds. To keep pace with population, the district would have to double its size from 2,345 acres in 1963 to 4,600 acres by 1985, Meehan said.

This was the first and only administrative headquarters the district built from scratch. Offices were in this Sinnissippi Park building from 1971 until 1994. The William Charles Co. now leases the building from the district.

City newspapers and the district sponsored a snowman contest for children in 1965. The kids got creative. Entries included Peter Cottontail's cousin; a Beatle snowman with a guitar and a mop for hair; a dinosaur; a polar bear; and various dogs. Winners got savings bonds.

That year, the district started holding school recreation nights for children with disabilities. And the Loves Park Lions Club said it would finance construction of two tennis courts and a basketball court at Sand Park.

In 1969, the board incurred the anger of past President Seth B. Atwood by voting to demolish the historic stone shelter built in 1911 in Sinnissippi Park. Cost of repairing the shelter was estimated at $15,000. The board decided to use the site for a new administration building, instead.

Golf prices in 1969
Season pass: $20
Weekdays: $1.25
Weekends: $1.75

Atwood was not happy at seeing the shelter come down. It was one of the prettiest picnic sites in the city with its elevated view of the river. Atwood felt that was being taken away from the people. He thought the new office should be built at the park's main entrance, thus preserving the shelter. But the board went ahead with its plan. Staff moved into the Sinnissippi headquarters in May 1971.

Golf season passes went from $15 to $20 in 1969. Daily fees were $1.25 weekdays and $1.75 Saturdays, Sundays and holidays, still among the least expensive in Midwest.

It took years before a path was built but in 1970, the district started examining the feasibility of putting cinder jogging paths throughout the district. The era of fitness had begun, though a path would not be built for seven years.

'Nothing to Lose' With Open Meetings

According to writer Lowell Hamilton, who compiled a partial history of the Park District, "Park Board meetings were best described as closed" before the 1960s.

In his history, Hamilton wrote that "If a person wanted to attend a Park Board meeting … permission of the board was required and your business with the board had to be stated beforehand. After your business was concluded, you were expected to leave the meeting."

A decade later, it was still difficult for citizens to follow Park Board action at meetings. In a story in the Loves Park Post in May 1971, then new Park Commissioner Gerald Wernick complained about the way officers were elected. He charged that the Park Board regularly met Friday mornings ahead of the regular Tuesday meetings to discuss the Tuesday agenda. The Post said even the press didn't know about the Friday meetings.

When the district moved into its new Sinnissippi Park headquarters, the board decided to change meeting times, too. The board had met at 8:30 a.m. on the second Tuesday of each month. Commissioners changed it to 7 p.m. on the same day.

The board said it made sense to hold meetings at times more convenient for citizens now that there was enough space to accommodate spectators.

Wernick wasn't through fighting closed

> *"The board has nothing to lose by opening its meetings … It will lead to better public understanding of the issues."*
> COVE HOOVER, PUBLISHER OF ROCKFORD NEWSPAPERS

Gerald Wernick

meetings. In 1972, he filed suit against three commissioners who met at a private home and took a vote. The meeting took place during an employee strike and an emergency situation arose. Wernick was not available, unfortunately. He claimed the vote should have been taken at an open meeting with notice given beforehand.

The lawsuit got media attention. Rockford Newspapers Publisher Cove Hoover was quoted in a story urging commissioners to end their practice of "private" meetings.

"The board has nothing to lose by opening its meetings within all areas prescribed by law," Hoover said. "It will lead to better public understanding of the issues."

After months of headlines about the lawsuit, park commissioners promised to follow the law. In November 1973, Wernick announced he was dropping the suit because the open meeting law was being followed.

An Abrupt Change at the Top

Robert Milne, who became district executive in 1968, might never have been comfortable as director of the Park District. Commissioners believed Elliot had trained him for the job before Elliot retired in 1968, but that was not true.

Elliot was used to doing things himself. He had clued Milne in on precious few of his methods of running the district and handling the board. In fact, Milne had limited responsibility and authority from the time he was hired by the board until Elliot retired.

Milne came under fire in a series of newspaper articles that began in November 1970 and continued in January 1971. The stories criticized the way finances were handled in the district. One complaint was that the district paid for Milne's membership at Forest Hills Country Club and the Rotary Club. Board President Reuben Aldeen felt Milne should join those groups, but the newspaper saw it as a waste of money.

The paper also accused Milne of awarding no-bid contracts and letting district money sit in non-interest bearing accounts.

I believe much of the criticism was instigated by Wernick, who was seeking a Park Board seat in the spring of '71. For his part, Milne was largely carrying on policies the district had followed for decades.

The board promptly — in February 1971 — committed itself to competitive bidding, named a finance committee to watch expenditures, and appointed a treasurer outside of the board. Milne had been treasurer, too.

Milne also repaid the board $149 for Rotary Club luncheons.

But an election was coming up in spring and the news accounts and board changes provided plenty of fodder for candidates. That spring, there were seven candidates for two board seats.

"The normally sedate, uncontested Park Board election is a spirited contest this year as five challengers try to unseat the two incumbents…" said the Register-Star.

Incumbents were Harley "Moon" Mullins and John B. Whitehead. Challengers were Gerald Wernick, Hugh Deery, Frank Manarchy, Walter Ryan and Eugene Sjostrom.

At one point, Mullins got himself into trouble by calling a local radio talk show which was featuring Whitehead and Wenick. Mullins gave a fictitious name and adopted a Southern accent while he praised the Park Board. Wernick

Robert Milne

immediately recognized Mullins' voice while on the air and said so. Mullins admitted his mistake a day later.

Voters kept Whitehead but defeated Mullins and put Wernick on the board. That livened things up considerably for the Park District — and spelled the end for Milne.

Wernick questioned many procedures that had been taken for granted and picked topics that made good headlines. He said the district was supposed to be environmentally conscientious and should stop burning its garbage. He questioned the way money from golfers was handled at golf course clubhouses.

He was right. Clubhouse staff kept money in cigar boxes instead of cash registers. We changed that the following year, for the protection of all involved.

At a meeting Sept. 14, 1971, Wernick set up the scenario for Milne's exit. First he questioned how the district had handled a bid — not by public advertising but by contacting firms it felt were qualified to bid.

Wernick went on to attack Milne. Reading from a prepared statement, he asked a series of questions that were critical of Milne's job performance. He said the district needed a strong leader respected by the community and park staff and then asked for a vote of confidence on Milne.

"What will it take for men personally embarrassed, publicly compromised, to correct this ill?" Wernick concluded.

Aldeen was upset. He accused Wernick of using the issues as campaign fodder and said it was not "ethical or businesslike to bring up personnel matters at public meetings."

That ended the Milne discussion for the evening. Wernick won one battle when Whitehead successfully urged the board to open bidding on the issue raised by Wernick.

A month later, at the board's Oct. 12 meeting, Whitehead read Milne's resignation. Wernick moved to accept it.

Milne issued a statement to the press and public.

"I don't feel that any human being has to take the constant criticism that has been leveled over the past six to eight months at one of the finest park districts in the country, especially when he was attempting to do the most honest job possible for the public," Milne said.

Less than two weeks later, Park Board President Reuben Aldeen stepped down after 16 years on the board. Aldeen, who had donated $47,500 for the land that became Aldeen Park on North Alpine, said he wanted to slow down and play more golf.

Aldeen had been criticized by Wernick for spending time in Florida during the winter.

Wernick brought about some positive changes in the Park District. I'm not saying forcing Milne out was one of them, and I didn't agree with Wernick on a number of things. But he was right about open meetings, bidding, and proper handling of money.

> *"I don't feel any human being has to take the constant criticism … especially when he was attempting to do the most honest job possible…"*
> – ROBERT MILNE
> AS HE ANNOUNCED HIS RESIGNATION AS EXECUTIVE DIRECTOR IN 1971

Where I Re-Enter the Story

With Milne gone, the board named Commissioner Joseph Bean as board president and interim director. The district began to search for a new leader. That's where I, your retired director, historian and humble author, re-enter this story. Remember, I knew the district and some of the players from my college summers when I worked for the district in 1955 and 1956. That was the era when the recreation tax was approved by voters, in the administration of Earl F. Elliot.

The district had endured turmoil under Milne, and more issues loomed. We were about to undergo the first and only labor strike in district history. Following that, we undertook a multi-year reorganization of district policies, practices and procedures, with the aim of rebuilding confidence in a system that had lost public trust. Of course I'm biased but, in my opinion, this is when it really gets interesting. Please read on.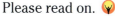

Webbs Norman

The Rockford Arboretum at 1875 N. Mulford Road is one of the loveliest spots in town. The 6.5 acres were donated by Florence "Coffy" Gregory in memory of her parents, Louisa and Andrew Coffman, in 1979. The site contains maples more than 250 years old and a 300-year-old oak with a diameter exceeding 52 inches.

[1] Wright's civic center, called Monona Terrace, finally was built in 1997, 38 years after his death. It cost more than $60 million.

GROWTH OF THE PARK DISTRICT 1945 – 1971

Parks acquired 1945 – 1971

1945: Martin Memorial Park,
5600 Park Ridge Road., 15 acres

1947: Wantz Memorial Park,
602 E. Riverside Blvd., 5.6 acres

1948: Sabrooke Playground,
2900 Kishwaukee St., 13 acres*

1949: The Oaks Park, 4249 North Main.,
1.8 acres

1950: South Henrietta Ave. Park,
527 S. Henrietta Ave., 2.4 acres

1953: Twenty-fifth St. Playground,
2100 25th St., 6 acres

1954: Lockwood Park and Children's Farm (formerly Quarry Hills Park),
5201 Safford Road, 143 acres

1954: Loves Park Playground,
5101 Louisa St., 14 acres

1954: Marsh School Playground,
2100 Edgebrook Drive, 8 acres

1954: Ridge Ave. Playground,
3317 Ridge Ave., 2.5 acres

1954: Summerdale Playground,
2815 Overdene Ave., 7 acres

1954: Washington Park Community Center (formerly Concord Commons),
3617 Delaware St., 15.7 acres

1955: Barbour School Playground,
1506 Clover Ave., 3 acres*

1955: Bloom School Playground,
2901 Pelham Road, 4 acres

1955: Riverby Park, east bank of river between Auburn and Illinois St.,
3 acres

1955: Riverdahl School Playground/ Don Schmid Athletic Fields,
871 Sandy Hollow Road, 22 acres*

1955: Rolling Green School Playground,
3621 West Gate Parkway, 8 acres

1955: Twin Sister Hills Park,
3001 Harney Ct., 23.5 acres

1956: Atwood Park, 2685 New Milford Road, 326 acres

1957: Liberty Park, 1555 Morgan St.,
10 acres

1958: Shorewood Park, 235 Evelyn Ave.,
35 acres

1961: Conklin School Playground,
3000 Halsted Rd., 5 acres*

1961: Lathrop School Playground,
2600 Clover Ave., 5 acres

1961: Maud Johnson School Playground,
3800 Rural St., 3 acres

1962: Earl F. Elliot Park and Golf Course,
888 S. Lyford Rd., 230 acres

1963: Belden St. Playground,
2337 Belden St., 6 acres

1963: Vandercook School Playground,
5929 Darlene Dr., 8.4 acres

1964: Guilford Center School Playground,
1824 Guilford, 20 acres

1965: Aldeen Park, 623 N. Alpine,
104 acres

1965: Brookview School Playground,
1788 Madron Rd., 12 acres

1965: Mariposa Drive Playground,
2175 Arnold Ave., 6 acres

1966: Froberg School Playground,
4551 20th St., 9.7 acres, partially leased

1967: Alpine Meadows Playground,
4880 Marjoram Ct., 17 acres, partially leased

1967: Forest Hills View Playground,
4015 Pepper Drive, 9.7 acres

1968: Atwood Park Estates Playground,
Haverson Dr. and Rockview Rd.,
18 acres

1968: Gregory School Playground,
4820 Carol Ct., 7 acres

1968: Sawyer Road Playground,
2249 Sawyer Road, 7 acres

1969: Veterans Memorial Park (Sportscore One), 1288 Elmwood Road, 151 acres

1971: Kennedy Haight School Playground, 4590 N. Rockton.,
12.3 acres

1971: Swan Hillman School Playground,
3701 Greendale Dr., 17.7 acres

1971: Water Works Park, 1130 Preston St.,
1 acre*

* Leased

THE COMMISSIONERS OF THE ERA 1945 – 1971

Seth B. Atwood

Fay Lewis

Dr. Robert F. Schleicher

Edwin W. Carlson, Sr.

O.G. Nelson

SETH B. ATWOOD
On board 1928 – 1960; president 1942 – 1960
Founded Atwood Vacuum Machine Co.; invested in banks, savings and loan associations, real estate and hotels. Dedicated environmentalist and major force in growth of Park District. Made large donations to district and Forest Preserve. Longest length of service as commissioner with 32 years, last 18 as president.

FAY LEWIS
On board 1924 – 1947; president 1937 – 1942
Largest wholesale distributor (Fay Lewis and Brothers Co.) of tobacco in Midwest, outside city of Chicago. Personal friend of Clarence Darrow and Edgar Lee Masters, who portrayed him as "Lewis Fay" in "Spoon River Anthology."

DR. ROBERT F. SCHLEICHER
On board 1939 – 1962
Rockford optometrist. Resigned Park Board post in 1962 to accept appointment to Greater Rockford Airport Authority Board of Commissioners. Appointment made by twin brother Ben Schleicher, then 4-term mayor of Rockford.

PROFILE OF THE PARK DISTRICT 1945 – 1971

Year:	1910	1928	1945	1971
Statistic:				
Population	48,405	91,750	113,410	160,460
Number of Parks/ Properties	15	45	65	109
Park District Acreage	159.47	731.35	2,361.26	3,570.27
Total Budget	$140,343.49[1]	$177,063.00	$150,412.00	$2,965,929.00
Property Tax Revenue	$35,999.00	$160,142.00	$122,837.00	$2,197,237.00
Per Capita Expenditure from Taxes	$0.74	$1.74	$1.08	$13.69
Median Family Income	Not available	Not available	Not available	$13,249.00
Estimated Total User Visits	Not available	Not available	Not available	1,500,000

[1] 1910 budget covered 18 months instead of 12 months.

Continued next page

Raymond F. Dahlquist *Francis H. Colehour* *Reuben A. Aldeen* *Joseph Bean* *Gilmore J. Landstrom*

EDWIN W. CARLSON SR.
On board 1941 – 1955
President of David Carlson Roofing Co., which his father founded. Six-year member of Fire and Police Commission, trustee of SwedishAmerican Hospital, director of American National Bank and Trust.

O.G. NELSON
On board 1942 – 1952
President of National Mirror Works and, later, chairman of the board of Sundstrand Machine Tool Company. Resigned from Park Board in 1952 because of failing health.

RAYMOND F. DAHLQUIST
On board 1947 – 1970
President of Rockford Figure Skating Club. Daughters Lois and Joyce became city's first professional ice skaters. Sought to improve district's winter sports facilities. Valley Park at 3300 East State St. renamed Dahlqiust Park in his honor.

FRANCIS H. COLEHOUR
On board 1952 – 1964
Campaigned on promise to restore flowers in Sinnisssippi Park Sunken Gardens, a vow he fulfilled. Colehour had insurance business. Served as president of Men's Garden Club of Rockford.

REUBEN A. ALDEEN
On board 1955 – 1971; president 1960 – 1971
With his brother, founded Amerock Corporation. In 1966, donated $17,500 to district for puchase of Memorial Forest on N. Alpine Road, which was renamed Reuben A. Aldeen Park. Led planning and design for former Park District administration building in Sinnissippi Park.

JOSEPH BEAN
On board 1960 – 1973; president 1971 – 1973
Named acting director of the district in December 1971 following departure of executive director Robert Milne. Led district until Webbs Norman took over as director in March 1972. Owned and operated Bean Shoe Service in Rockford and Beloit. After retirement, operated shoe stores at Gunite Foundry and Chrysler Corporation on a part-time basis.

Harley W. Mullins   *John B. Whitehead*   *Gerald Wernick*   *Edwin W. Carlson, Jr.*

GILMORE J. LANDSTROM
On board 1962 – 1973

"Gilly" served as district treasurer. Managed Rockford Union Foundry, which became part of Sundstrand Machine Tool Company. Was a director of Sundstrand Machine Tool. Financial vice president and secretary of Sundstrand to his retirement in 1963. Landstrom Road Tract named Gilmore Landstrom Park in 1975 in his honor.

HARLEY W. "MOON" MULLINS
On board 1964 – 1971

President of Williams-Manny Insurance Company. In 1979, became president of district's Park Foundation. Helped organize television station WCEE (now WIFR 23). Governor of Rotary International's Northern Illinois district. Advocate for Children's Farm. Pebble Creek Park named Mullins-Pebble Creek Park to honor Harley and Vera Mullins in 1983.

JOHN B. WHITEHEAD
On board 1970 – 1983; president 1973 – 1977

President of J.B. and Loren L. Whitehead Inc. Realtors. Served on civic organizations, including City-County Planning Commission, Rockford College board and Rockford Goodwill Industries. Credited for leadership in creating Sportscore One.

GERALD WERNICK
On board 1971 – 1979

Ran unsuccessfully for Park Board in 1963 but won election in 1971 on campaign promise "to change many of the policies of the present board." Professional photographer. Promoted open discussion of Park District business; board adopted his suggestion to hold evening meetings. Resigned for business reasons in 1979.

EDWIN W. CARLSON JR.
On board 1971 – 1990; president 1987 – 1988

Son of earlier board member Edwin Carlson Sr. Ran family business, Carlson Roofing Co. Built Little League baseball fields at 900 S. Pierpont Ave. Donated fields to district in 1975. Major player in bringing professional baseball to town with renovation of Marinelli Field, and to district's acquisition of Magic Waters. Wife Vi instrumental in establishing Midway Village Museum.

A Special Tribute to Bob Greene
Principal, Haskell Elementary School, 1971 – 1986

Bob Greene, a very passionate and foresighted educator, was the driving force behind the development of Terry Lee Wells Memorial Park. It took only one call from him to convince me the project was vitally important to the success of Haskell students.

After talking with Bob, I visited with the planning chief for the City of Rockford and found a very different attitude toward the project and the School District. During that meeting, I called Dr. Robert Salisbury, superintendent of the School District, introduced myself and shared with him my interest in the Haskell playground project. He invited us to come to his office. We did, and within 20 minutes, we had an agreement including the city of Rockford, federal government, Park District and School District.

The rest is history. But what is less known is the role Principal Bob Greene played in keeping alive the need for the playground and his persistent pushing for its completion.

I truly believe the project would not have happened without his insight and determination. Bob passed away on Oct. 8, 2011, but his ability and dedication will live on for generations to come in the creative learning environment he designed, planned, fought for, and achieved.

CHAPTER 4
The Dream Reaches Out
1972 – 2006

Park District staff gives best service to public by working effectively with one another.

Setting the Scene

When I arrived in 1972, the city's unstoppable east-side growth pattern was well underway. The Northwest Tollway had opened in 1958, and it ran seven miles east of what were then the city limits. Manufacturers, hospitals and Rockford College had moved out of populated areas of the city to green fields where it was cheaper to put up new buildings. Some industries had outlived their prime, including the furniture and farm equipment factories that once were among the foundation of Rockford commerce.

Retail was moving, too. When I got here, construction was underway on CherryVale Mall in Cherry Valley, which seemed like quite a drive from the central city back then.

Still, there was optimism. With a population of 147,370, Rockford had passed Peoria as the second largest city in the state. Many factories had prospered, giving employees a comparatively high level of disposable income, more than half of it coming from manufacturing plants. Workers made machine tools, heavy machinery, automotive and aerospace parts, fasteners, cabinet hardware and packaging devices. Families with a wage earner at one of the city's larger

OPPOSITE: These children are enjoying Terry Lee Wells Memorial Park at Haskell School. Of all the playground projects we did, this is my favorite. It was critically needed, it was a catalyst for big improvements at the school, and while we faced some setbacks in getting it done, we had great cooperation from a number of sources.

RIGHT: Webbs in his office shortly after coming to the Park District in 1972. (Register Star photo)

Building a Lasting Dream

> *...Rockford had more parks, churches, color televisions, privately-owned homes and millionaires per capita than any other city...*
> — CHAMBER OF COMMERCE

manufacturers felt they had a good standard of living. Since the early part of the 1900s, one generation had followed another into the factories after high school, and many joined the labor market before graduation. College was seen as something for the upper middle class or very determined young scholars. A large part of Rockford simply did not see a need for formal education after high school. That view became tradition in many highly industrialized cities.

The Chamber of Commerce boasted that Rockford had more parks, churches, color televisions, privately-owned homes and millionaires per capita than any other city in the United States.

Coming Back to Rockford

I became the chief dreamer in the Rockford Park District in March 1972. Or, I should say, the chief in charge of making other people's dreams happen. My dream was to lead a park district that responded to the needs and desires of the people it served. After you read about what we achieved, I hope you'll deem us successful.

I had been in Rockford before, to work in the pilot playground program in the summer of 1955 and, in the summer of 1956, to manage the first summer recreation program funded by the newly-passed recreation tax. Having grown up 90 miles away in the small town of Morrison (population 3,300), I knew a little about Rockford. I remember coming to

If I had a nickel for each wedding photo taken at Sinnissippi, I'd be a wealthy fellow. (Photo by Dusan Djuric)

Painting the dam in Aldeen Park is a tradition, although now that we require permits and certain kinds of paint, we don't see as many works of art, unfortunately. The Unofficial Bears Fan Club celebrated the Superbowl with this artistic statement in 1986.

"the big city" with my dad when he came to attend union meetings.

After getting my bachelor's degree in secondary education in 1957, I explored two career options – teaching and recreation. I spent a year in Milwaukee as an intern in the public school system because the town was known as the "City of the Lighted Schoolhouse," meaning the schools were open to citizens for recreation and adult education when classes ended. I wanted to see how that concept worked. I earned $240 a month as an intern there, working 2:00 – 10:00 p.m., and mopped floors in a neighborhood tavern in the early-morning hours to make enough to live on. I learned a lot from both jobs.

I got a master's degree in parks and recreation in 1960 and still was thinking of how to mesh that degree with my education credentials into one career. I tried that for a year in Charleston, Ill., where I was director of parks and recreation half time and a teacher of eighth-grade English the other half. I quickly found out each was a full-time job.

So I made a choice. I picked parks and recreation. I probably would have stayed in teaching if park systems simply built and maintained parks. But recreational programming had become the new focus. That intrigued me. Recreation — what we choose to do in our leisure time for personal enjoyment — is a big part of life but one we too often take for granted. I was convinced quality recreational offerings could have enormous impact on the health and well-being of children and adults and, thus, the quality of life in any community.

I worked in the Moline, Westchester and Oak Park park districts until 1969, when I quit to start a consulting firm to help park systems with

> *"The district, the park and recreation profession in general and other institutions were heading toward a global political and economic transition."*
> – AUTHOR WEBBS NORMAN

internal operations and long-range plans. I moved my family to Niles and was making a good living with my business when I heard, in late fall of 1971, that the Rockford park director's job was going to be open.

I sent a letter to the board president, Joe Bean, indicating my interest. Three or four months later, on a Sunday afternoon, I got a call from the Rockford Park Board secretary asking if I'd come for an interview the next day at 9 a.m. I said no, but I could come later in the week. We made an appointment for Thursday.

I believe in preparation. I came to Rockford the afternoon of the day I got the call. For three days I learned all I could about Rockford and the Park District. I went to the library and read newspapers, I drove around town, I talked to former employees of the Park District, Chamber of Commerce officials and others. I reviewed Park Board minutes and newspaper accounts, and toured as many of the parks as I could.

I already knew that the Park District had a good reputation in the community and strong support from the business sector. Remember, I had worked here in the

> ### What I Saw in Rockford in 1972
> - *Low unemployment, which would end too soon.*
> - *44,000 students in School District.*
> - *Recent dismissal/forced retirement of heads of park and school systems.*
> - *Minority community felt left out of Park District and other parts of life in Rockford; west-siders felt east side got favorable treatment from local government.*
> - *Citizens did not trust big government; media did not trust any government.*
> - *No local agreement on what effective public governance was.*
> - *Growing fear of using parks because of crime.*
> - *Local unions organizing in public sector.*

summers of 1955 and '56. The citizens, I believed, were open to change if they were given the facts and time to consider them.

I also believed something many people in Rockford had not yet become aware of: The district, the park and recreation profession in general and other institutions were heading toward a global political and economic transition. The profession, I believed, had to change in order to maintain its leadership role.

Here are some observations I made about the city at that time:

- Unemployment was very low — 2.5 percent in 1972. Some plants couldn't find enough employees to take on additional contracts. Ten years later, Rockford led the nation in unemployment.
- The Rockford School District had 44,000 students. Superintendent Thomas Shaheen had just been dismissed and Robert Salisbury hired. They headed what is now a long list of superintendents whose tenures end after two or three years because of conflicts with one or more segments of the School District. In 2009, enrollment was 26,000.

Parks are one of the best places in town to take pictures.

- The minority community felt that the Park District was dominated by white males and its work force did not adequately represent the minority population here. The Park District board would soon pass a policy of paying wages and benefits that were competitive to similar work performed in the marketplace. Similarly, the district's work force would need to reflect the composition of the community's population.

- The citizens did not trust big government and resisted asking for federal grants because of fears of strings attached. The Park District could have received thousands of federal tax dollars for land acquisition, facility construction and unique recreational programming, money that had been paid to the federal government by citizens of the district. It was like we were refusing our own money.

- Local media, it seemed to me, had an adversarial approach to all tax-supported agencies. Newspapers printed the names of all public employees who earned $20,000 or more and frequently wrote about how ineffective many public workers were. Interestingly, none of the newspapers offered an editorial policy stating their definition of successful work performance in the public sector. I have always thought it unfair to judge anyone's performance using unwritten and unknown criteria. It still is.

- There was no local standard of what effective public governance looked like. Efforts to do long-range planning were generally met critically. Cooperation between private, public and non-profit agencies was very limited. That would soon change, thanks to cooperation from Mayor Bob McGaw; Pete Perrecone, chairman of the County Board; Robert Salisbury, superintendent of the Rockford School District; Ed Kelly, superintendent of Harlem Public

This is me (far right, standing) with the board that hired me. Standing from left are John Whitehead, Ed Carlson and Gerald Wernick. Seated from left are Gilbert Landstrom and Joe Bean. The photo was taken in 1973.

Skateboarders are welcome to use parks made for them at Washington Park Community Rec Center, Flodin Boys and Girls Club and Harlem Community Center.

Schools; Jon Olson, executive director of the Tri-County Planning Commission; Supervisor Helvig "Sory" Sorensen of Rockford Township; and Dr. Karl Jacobs, president of Rock Valley College. All these men, and many others, were ready to cooperate for the common good.

- There was a growing fear of using parks. Media coverage of drug use and violent behavior had frightened families. A Park District survey found that over 50 percent of adults and students felt unsafe in their own city parks. That trend continued until the district established its own police department two years later.
- Local unions were beginning to organize in the public sector, including city workers and police. Park District employees would attempt to organize a few weeks after I started work.

That was the community. I also gathered what information I could about the internal workings of the district and concluded the following:

- The tax rate of 22 cents per $100 of assessed valuation was considerably lower than in many districts throughout the state.
- The school and park districts had both recently dismissed their CEOs for various poor decisions, covered extensively by the media. It seemed to me that each leader received, in effect, a 20-year sentence for, at most, a six-month crime.
- West-siders felt their part of town had to compete with the east side, and that the east side generally got more favorable treatment from governmental agencies. It is fair to say that the location of I-90 on the far east side assured long-term divisiveness between the east and west sides of this community.
- The transition between passive use of urban parks to centers of organized activities was obvious. That transition, which accelerated after World War II and grew exponentially after the recreation tax passed in 1956, had a negative impact on district staff. It resulted in a growing split between workers engaged in park maintenance

and those putting on recreational programs. There was a competitive work environment rather than a cooperative one. The upshot was internal conflict and lower productivity. The challenge was clear.

- Park District staffers were concerned about who would be their new boss. They wanted the board to appoint someone already on staff, and eight employees had applied for the job. Those feelings were deep, and the board's decision to hire an outsider (me) would lead to considerable strife in the months ahead.
- The Park District did not have a clearly stated purpose and mission, or a well-designed program to meet growing citizen needs. Many local groups were seeking expanded or new facilities or services, and their requests were not being responded to in a timely manner.

A Latin group performs at one of the Sunday local music events at Levings Lake Park. Talent contests and gospel, blues, soul and jazz concerts are held summer Sundays at Levings.

- I believed the district had outgrown its level of funding. I based that on the deferred maintenance I observed in park roads, tennis courts, etc. It seemed to me more parks were needed to serve the growing population. Issues that had to be addressed were the tradition of keeping fees at rock bottom, a reluctance to increase taxes and the continued reluctance to seek federal funds.
- Frankly, I came to the conclusion that most people, those inside as well as outside of the district, were uncomfortable talking about the real issues we faced. Instead of confronting problems, they complained about the symptoms. If I were hired, that situation would prove to be the most difficult I had to address, but also, the most important.

The Rockford Rotary Clubs placed this sundial in the Sinnissippi Rose Garden in 2000.

> "March 27 was my start date, 63 years to the day since Rockford citizens had voted to start a Park District in 1909."
> – AUTHOR WEBBS NORMAN

Getting the Job

With all that in my mind after three days in Rockford, I met the board on a Thursday for what was supposed to be a one-hour interview. Instead, our session went all day and through dinner at the Faust Hotel that night. I wanted the commissioners to know my past experience was compatible with their current challenges. I shared slide shows of where I'd worked and what we had done. I talked about how the commissioners and their director and staff needed to clearly define the purpose of the Park District and develop shared values and objectives. They were most interested in how the board could connect and interact with all the special interest groups and employees. It was a marvelous day.

I drove home to Niles that night and waited. They called in about 10 days and asked if I could bring my wife to meet the board the following day. I did, they offered me the job and I accepted.

March 27 was my start date, 63 years to the day since Rockford citizens had voted to start a Park District in 1909.

First Day was Eye-Opener

I started my first day in a meeting with board president and acting district director Joe Bean. We spent two hours going through a stack of files that was two feet high. They contained citizen project ideas and requests the board wanted me to look at, organize and recommend plans for action. Among them were an artificial ice rink, a local history museum, tennis courts and other concepts that would become reality in the future.

After talking with Joe, I went to greet a couple of guys I knew from when I was here in the '50s, Chuck Fiduccia, superintendent of recreation, and his assistant, and Vince Provenzano. I knew what a good job Chuck had done when he succeeded Jim Brademas as head of the recreation program. Chuck understood how to get things done in the culture that was in place. When Chuck saw me, he stood up, put out his hand and said, "Norman, if you think I'm going to work as hard for you as I did for Brademas, you're crazy." He said it with a smile but I knew he was serious. And I didn't blame him. You had to run 24/7 just to stay even with Brademas.

> "I required everyone in management to have a home phone number listed in the book. I believe public employees in service agencies need to be accessible to the public."
> – AUTHOR WEBBS NORMAN

I talked to the full-time employees that day — there were about 110 — and had them fill out a 10-question survey. When I got to my motel room that evening, I read them. Dear me, I thought. Things are a lot hotter here than I realized.

There was a lack of planning and cooperation within the district, with considerable conflict and competition between and among the maintenance and recreation staffs. The maintenance people thought recreation people caused trouble for them and vice versa. There were a lot of strong personalities.

There was a lack of internal communication and communication with citizens, and no system to deal with either of those issues. There was no system to train and develop employees.

I saw that there was no clear-cut mission and an ineffective organizational structure in which people didn't have the skill level needed to keep pace with the growth and complexities of services. For example, we didn't have a chief financial officer. It took me 90 days to get a financial report.

The way I saw it, we needed to define the purpose and mission of the park district and the board's relationship with the director and staff. Without that, it was difficult to assess whether the organizational structure, the programs and the people on the staff could be effective.

I went to the board and recommended we hire consultants to analyze our organizational structure, as well as someone who could help us develop a compensation system that was fair and consistent. We lacked a competent CFO, and I found we had 13 different pay grades for mowing grass, depending on location and supervisor.

The board put me off. There was a reluctance to go outside for advice, just as there was to ask the feds for money. Meanwhile, the seeds of confusion within the district were growing.

I went ahead initiating what changes I could. I required everyone in management to have a home phone number listed in the phone book. I believe public employees in a service agency need to be accessible to the public. I started training programs to make sure everyone had the skills they needed. We established maintenance standards for the playgrounds and parks and held staff accountable for them. Crews that had gotten used to lazing around for hours at a time were reminded that they were paid for eight hours of work.

Standfield Beach at Levings Park is one of our nicest places for water fun. It was named for Joe Standfield, maintenance foreman for the district (shown in inset photo) who died in a tragic accident at the lake in 1990. Standfield was working at midnight, trying to adjust a valve to lower the level of the lake so it would not destroy new sand that had just been laid down on the beach.

First Big Challenge: Maintenance Strike

In retrospect, we were dealing with too many issues in too short a time. I had not given our employees sufficient time to get to know me before making changes.

Some management people decided they had to stop me. I heard through the grapevine that they had agreed, "We've got to get Norman out of here."

Things hit the fan just over three months into my tenure. Bill Bailey, who was in charge of the maintenance department, came to see me one morning in early July and said, "By the way, the men met last night and decided to join the International Teamsters." I said, "Well, they have the right to join whatever they want."

Bailey and his men then told the board they would withdraw their union request if the board would send me back to Chicago and appoint Bailey in my place.

Apparently, the board had no intention of dismissing me. The third week in July, our maintenance staff and three of our four full-time policemen went on strike. The leaders of the strike told their people it wouldn't last more than three days, and the board then would fire me and increase their pay by 50 cents an hour. They thought the board would get rid of me in a hurry given their work stoppage.

> *"Park employees out of line."*
> — MORNING STAR
> EDITORIAL HEADLINE
>
> *"Park Board's Hate of Unions Put Above Welfare of Public."*
> — LABOR NEWS
> EDITORIAL HEADLINE

The strike began July 26. It went on for five weeks, and I was still here. The longer the strike lasted, the more I met with people who had things to share with me, primarily about management people who had organized the strike. What they told me helped me understand what misinformation was being fed to the striking workers and also enlightened me about some questionable practices within the district.

The board did not back down. Commissioners did not believe union members ought to be controlling the Park District. We negotiated nearly every day for weeks, but we got nowhere.

The strikers picketed Park District offices and several other facilities. We kept parks and golf courses open as long as we could. Supervisory staff fed the animals at the Children's Farm and our recreation staff crossed picket lines to keep summer programs going.

One worker stayed on strike just one day, but 50 regular employees and about 120 seasonal workers remained off the job. Charles Gagliano, head of the Teamsters local, insisted publicly that the issues were union recognition and pay but it was well known what they wanted was to get rid of me.

After about a week, we had to close the Children's Farm. The Men's City Golf Tournament, a popular and long tradition, was cancelled. We had to close the golf courses and they were closed for seven weeks.

The pressure on our working staff was enormous. We kept things going as best we could.

The majority of our citizens backed the board. They could not visualize having the Teamsters in charge of their Park District. The Morning Star headlined an editorial "Park employees out of line."

"…they are making a demand which is not in their province — the replacement of a park director who is answerable only to the board," the paper said. "Hiring of supervisory personnel is the sole responsibility of the Park Board."

That same day, the Park District published a letter in the newspaper signed by all five commissioners. "We have decided to invest $589 in advertising to present to you an account of our efforts to date to settle an unfortunate and unnecessary walkout on the part of your Park District's maintenance staff," said the letter, which occupied nearly a full page of the paper. It laid out the district's pay proposal and how it would handle dismissals, layoffs and disciplinary actions. The board acknowledged it had fallen behind in pay but said 5% raises in '71 and an additional 5.5% in '72 would quickly bring salaries up to par. No more could be done, said the board, unless it raised taxes, raised fees or cut services.

That day, the district shut down the golf courses. We couldn't scrape up the manpower to mow them.

Newspaper coverage of the strike was intense. A photo showed uncollected garbage in Anna Page Park.

A headline warned that strikers would be replaced. The union said it would step up harassment of non-striking employees.

> *Picket lines expected at every park "by the time the sun comes up." Union organizer Charles Gagliano*
> *– MORNING STAR, JULY 27, 1972*

Bluntly-worded sign at Sandy Hollow Golf Course tells the story . . . City courses remain closed because of maintenance workers' strike

Union slogans — "Teamsters All the Way" — were plastered on park district signs.

> Park pickets ask ouster of Norman "Pickets paraded in front of the district administration building with signs demanding Norman's replacement."
> – Morning Star, August 1, 1972

backed the Park Board. Other labor groups, including the teachers' union, supported the Teamsters, often reluctantly.

The board didn't budge. Commissioners said they were elected to run a park district, not a union.

Some of the people who kept working had their cars spray painted or tires damaged. Fences were cut at the Children's Farm. We needed police protection to pick up garbage at parks. Gagliano was hauled away in a police car after he punched me in the jaw at the beginning of a board meeting.

> "The strike and resulting poor playing conditions at park district golf courses have forced postponement of the city's men's tournament."
> – Morning Star, August 2, 1972

Rumors were rampant, inspiring newspaper Publisher Cove Hoover to run a lengthy column asking people to tone down the rhetoric.

"The parks are a great asset, the result of a lot of hard work by many of Rockford's best citizens," Hoover concluded. "Left alone, free from meddlers, the Park Board and its employees will work things out."

We did work things out, after a 35-day strike. Workers started to return one by one and, on Aug. 30, all but four came back. Many said they could no longer live on the Teamsters' strike benefit

A newspaper analysis maintained that the "once happy park 'family' fell apart" when I came aboard. I believe it was falling apart before then.

The Labor News backed the union, once running a story headlined, "Park Board's Hate of Unions Put Above Welfare of Public." The daily newspapers

of $25 a week. We gave our employees a 5 percent raise but did not recognize the Teamsters union. We welcomed them back and worked hard to get things running smoothly. Bailey resigned as park superintendent. As I said then, his departure was "mutually advantageous for all concerned."

Sandy Hollow had 340 golfers the day the course reopened. That was two weeks after the strike ended because it took two weeks to get golf courses back in shape. The grass had grown high enough to constitute a nice crop of hay.

> "…there was only one way to handle this, and that was to make good things come from it."
> – AUTHOR
> WEBBS NORMAN

As the strike ended, I had put in five months as head of the Park District. Talk about baptism by fire. But there was only one way to handle this, and that was to make good things come from it.

It was clear my initial instincts had been right — we had to deal with the internal part of the park system before we could tackle external services.

The strike had shown that employees could not do their jobs well unless their colleagues in the system were doing the same. With that understanding, we now had the opportunity to come together and agree on fundamental issues.

Laying the Foundation

The first consultant I hired after the strike was Don Hart, a Rockford businessman I admired. I asked him to teach us how to talk to each other, how to listen, and what to talk about. Until we learned that, we would not have trust and respect among ourselves, much less those we served. And without that, we could accomplish nothing of significance.

Don Hart came every Wednesday morning for three hours, for eight weeks, as we started to build our system from the inside out. If you think of it as a wheel, staff had to form a strong hub and programs grew from there.

> "The level of trust and respect we earned from citizens became and remained a fundamental guideline for our performance."
> – AUTHOR
> WEBBS NORMAN

The first weeks were difficult but, as time went on, people began to discuss the things most important to them. At the end of eight weeks, the staff voted to keep Don on for another eight weeks.

What came out of that was a realization that has guided the Park District ever since. The staff decided that the most important thing to them was to develop relationships based on trust and respect, both internally and with the citizens. The level of trust and respect we earned from citizens became and remained a fundamental guideline for our performance evaluations.[1]

We called the program Management by Values. As you will note, it still is in effect.

Once everyone understood the importance of trust and respect, staffers were happy to respond to a citizen with,

"How can I help you?" They became cooperative, creative and flexible and realized the importance of doing things right the first time. It came down to things as simple as mowing the grass. If you were mowing near a picnic table full of people and blew rocks at them, you weren't earning respect. It was all about human relationships and customer service.

Those basic understandings about respect and job performance were the heart of how we came together. We developed a team that agreed on a common goal for the common good.

The words on a plaque in Sinnissippi Park recognize the great contribution Prof. Kizilbash made to our district, employees and programs.

> A Loving Tribute
> To
> Professor Askabi H. Kizilbash
> Northern Illlinois University
> 1971 – 2004
> This scarlet oak tree is planted in recognition, admiration and honor of Professor Kizilbash, who during his 20 years of service to the Rockford Park District (1984 – 2004), raised our desire and ability to better understand, organize and serve the park and recreation needs of all citizens. His talent, knowledge and skills elevated the insights, involvement and inspirations of board and staff alike, allowing the district to move to the forefront of the park and recreation profession.
> "Cary" will always be remembered as a master teacher, loyal mentor, and true friend of all district team members.
> From
> The Men and Women
> Of the
> Rockford Park District
> Oct., 1, 2005

We learned that to be successful, we must share a mission that enabled us to function as a competent and dedicated team of servants. That became the hallmark of our Park District staff and service and remains so 40 years later.

We also hired a firm to analyze our organizational structure and present an objective viewpoint. And we started to fix a compensation system that was not fair or consistent. We looked at pay for similar work performed within our marketplace, both the public and private sectors. For most of our staff, we defined the marketplace area as within 15 miles of the city. That's the area from which we hired people and, if they left us for another job, it was usually within that area, too.

Pay scales were scrutinized. We looked at comparable jobs and pay, both union and non-union, in 36 companies and agencies. We covered work from maintenance and office duties to management, and set our pay scale based on the average paid by those 36 employers. We updated that every year and followed it.

It all was done openly. The board appointed a compensation committee of outside experts from the private and public sectors to tell us what the marketplace was doing and what the district needed to do to stay competitive.

We also had to develop an effective way to communicate both within the district and externally. Without that, we did not do a good job of planning or cooperating with each other. And we risked being the last to know about problems. The district could not afford to be in that situation.

Regular staff meetings were held at all levels of the work force and we started a monthly newsletter. We set up feedback and support systems. For my first two years on the job, I spent most of my time in meetings inside and outside of the Park

This is one of my favorite pictures of the Sinnissippi Gardens, an aerial view looking south. Greenhouses in this photo have been replaced by the new Nicholas Conservatory.

District dealing with these fundamental and vital issues.

We worked hard to create an environment where the board, the employees and the citizens could connect with one another. We needed them to see the common ground in their roles, responsibilities and needs.

One of the most effective tools we developed was a Citizen Information Form. Whenever a resident called with a concern or request, the person taking the call filled out a form and sent it to me. I assigned it to the appropriate staffer who was to get details on the issue and respond to the citizen within 48 hours.

There was initial resistance to that but as employees saw the results, they supported it. It solved problems when they were small and resulted in the trust and respect our staff was seeking.

Employees came to agree that our role was to help people fill their recreational needs. Indeed, we believed that there was no such thing as an unimportant problem to those who had it. All citizen comments were welcome. We could not always do what they asked, but we could explain why. That's how we established trust and respect, both internally and externally.

A big need was the development of an effective training and development program for all employees. It covered not only on the tools and technology people needed to do their jobs but the changes taking place in society and how they affected our jobs. That last part is fundamental in any staff development because society is always changing.

We set aside 15 percent of an employee's time for training. That's how fast things were changing in our world, everything from the rules on handling chemicals and fertilizers to new philosophies on personal health, safety and recreation.

Our staff development philosophy broadened into a program that helped other agencies in town and provided more expertise for our people. It all started one winter day with a photo on the front page of a local newspaper of six CETA (Comprehensive Employment and Training Act) workers on State Street near the bridge following a snowstorm. Three had shovels. The other three did not. The photo was intended to make a laughing stock of government employees.

The next day I called the heads of the sanitary district, the city, Rock Valley College, the county, Rockford and Harlem school districts and Rockford Township for a coffee session. Our topic was related to that photo: Why do we allow ourselves to be put in a position like this which draws so much criticism?

We talked about the needs for training all our staffs. Out of that grew a really great inter-agency training program. Each agency put in $5,000 and we set up an advisory group to plan programs on everything from grounds maintenance to typing. Eighty-eight percent of our staff took part in one or more sessions and it greatly improved our employee skill levels. Other agencies also benefitted.

The interagency training program ran for three years; then had to be cancelled because some of our partners ran out of money. It was a true bargain while we did it.

It took about 18 months before our Park District was functioning as it should. Then we built on those internal strengths that now were part of our system. We planned and worked together. We celebrated achievements and people who made special efforts. We were a team committed to building the best urban park system of any city our size in North America. Our level of service had to be the highest, because we agreed that we would be judged by the citizens, the people who paid our salaries and deserved our best.

One more thought: The strike allowed me to get acquainted with virtually all local union leaders, leading to cooperative relationships ever since. Without exception, the labor unions have been and continue to be wonderful partners.

The Dahlquist sisters and their dad, Ray, formed the Rockford Figure Skating Club which got Park Board permission to flood the Black Hawk Pavilion for winter skating. Here it is decorated for a show.

Skaters Want Year-Round Ice

One of the files I inherited contained letters and pleas people had been submitting for a decade for an indoor ice skating arena. An artificial ice rink, they called it back then. Figure skaters and hockey players had been leading this campaign for 11 years.

They wanted to expand their skills and felt they could not in the limited outdoor season. The Wagon Wheel, a Rockton resort that had a big indoor rink and was the training home of Rockford Olympic sweetheart Janet Lynn, couldn't handle all the people who wanted to skate.

Before we get into building the Ice House, let me tell you about Rockford's long history in ice skating. The district had always maintained outdoor rinks and, in the early 1940s, gave permission to ice skaters to flood the shelter house at Black Hawk Park for an ice rink.

That idea came to the district via the Dahlquist family, specifically dad Ray and daughters Joyce and Lois. The girls had fallen in love with skating when they were about 7 and 9. Their dad took them to Chicago to see Sonja Henie, the great Norwegian actress and figure skater, at the old Chicago Stadium on Madison Street.

The girls were impressed, to say the least. They did not rest until their dad answered their pleas for figure skates — he spent 25 cents on a pair of clamp-on skates they had seen in a second-hand store on Broadway as they walked to

Lois (left) and Joyce Dahlquist, now Lois Woodworth and Joyce Lundstrom, were regional ice skating stars in the 1940s.

Turner School. The skates didn't fit right so they tied them on with old neckties. They took turns skating on a frozen mud puddle in a vacant lot next door to their apartment. There was no one to teach them skating moves so they got a book from the library.

When dad Ray saw how much they enjoyed the sport, each girl got a pair of white figure skates for Christmas. Then Ray flooded the entire vacant lot and it became a neighborhood rink. The kids put up discarded Christmas trees around the edge for a windbreak after the holidays.

The sisters were part of a circle of young people who loved to skate. As Lois Dahlquist Woodworth recalled many years later, "we would call each other when one of us discovered some good outdoor ice, and arrange to meet and skate together.

Skating and hockey were always popular things to do when the Sinnissippi Park lagoon ice was suitable for skating. (Photo by Gedeon Trias)

Sometimes we would set up a card table in the middle of Levings Lake with a hand-cranked portable phonograph to provide music. Or we would meet on the Rock River or Sinnissippi Lagoon, wherever the ice was best. When skating on the Rock River, we would chop a hole in the ice and lower a bucket so water could be poured on the rink to make a fresh, smooth surface. We brought our own scrapers to shovel the ice every day. You might say we were obsessed with skating."

One day in the early 1940s, the Dahlquists were picnicking in the Blackhawk Park Pavilion on a hot summer day when they observed that the building was cool, even when the weather was stifling. They had been looking for a building large enough for an ice rink and this was it. It had no posts to interfere with skating and was all stone, with a cement floor.

The Park District gave them permission to flood the pavilion, and the Dahlquists got it done, with help from others skaters and their families. According to Lois, "The rink was flooded every night. Since the hose would freeze, at first we would run it down a very steep hill behind the rink to drain it. This kept us all in shape. How can work be so much fun? Then we got the bright idea to put it down a manhole about seven feet deep. Someone had to crawl down to get the hose. That solved the problem."

Ray Dahlquist[2] was the backbone of the group. He took on the job of spraying the rink after skating, often late at night to take advantage of the coldest temperatures.

The group installed a pot-bellied stove and a record player so they could skate to music (the old 78s). On Sunday nights, they had potluck suppers. They purchased sheet metal and sliding doors to enclose the pavilion, the better to preserve the ice. The building became a giant icebox. Some years they skated until Easter.

The family organized the Rockford Ice Skating Club in 1946. Anyone could join. Dues were $3 for kids and $5 for adults. If you couldn't afford skates, someone would buy them for you.

The club held benefit ice shows, with parents making costumes that Joyce had designed and kids skating routines that Lois had choreographed. Music for the shows was recorded by transferring parts of records to a "wire recorder." They took the shows on the road to Beloit and Freeport.

Volunteers made the shows special: electricians, lighting experts, costume designers, seamstresses, stage decorators and builders, and a real radio announcer as emcee. It was, as Lois says, "a special place and time with a special group of people."

She and Joyce made a regional name for themselves in skating, twice being invited to perform at the Sun-Times All Star Ice Show in the same Chicago Stadium where they had admired Sonja Henie.

In 1957 – 58, the Rockford Figure Skating Club had a membership of 138 skaters using the Black Hawk Pavilion. But they lost their ice when the board, after hearing from a disgruntled citizen that a "private" club was using a public facility, told them to move.

The Dahlquists pointed out their club was open to anyone who wanted to skate, but the board's decision stood. In 1959, the club disbanded and, just four years later, the pavilion at Black Hawk Park burned down.

Building Riverview Ice House

Since that time, local figure and hockey skaters had been lobbying the Park District to build an artificial ice rink. During my first months here, I found their names and requests in the ice rink file that Commissioner Bean gave me. I pulled the names of 30 people and called them together. They agreed to work with us and turned out to be one of the best committees I ever partnered with. They were competent, open, honest and knowledgeable.

Led by Alden Orput and Howard Walgren, the committee wasted no time, breaking into subgroups to look at various aspects of the project. They came back to the board with a report while the strike was still going on. Their conclusion: It would be feasible to construct an artificial ice rink. The $1 million to $2 million needed could be raised through a bond issue, with the debt paid by user fees.

This committee did its due diligence. Of all their conclusions, only one was off. That one concerned the cost of heating

Our first Zamboni, courtesy of First National Bank and Trust.

and cooling. Like all of us, they failed to foresee the energy crisis that would hit the nation in the late 1970s.

Of course, there were critics, people who believed ice skating facilities ought to be constructed by private interests, not a park district. But we had tremendous support from citizens.

In June 1973, I informed the board that staff had reviewed the report and agreed with the committee. We presented three recommendations:
- Use $200,000 from the Capital Improvement Fund and borrow $900,000 through revenue bonds.
- Have the rink ready to open by September 1974.
- Build the rink on a 13-acre site on the far east side, at Elliot Park next to Elliot Golf Course.

The Park Board agreed and so voted. That might have been the start of a smooth, on-time, non-controversial project but for another good idea that made things much more complex.

Jon Olson, head of the tri-county planning commission, stopped by my office late one Wednesday afternoon and asked if we had considered building the ice rink on old city yard site downtown. It soon would be available, he said.

Jon ticked off the reasons a downtown site was better than the far east side: Its central location was convenient for east- and west-siders. It would help rejuvenate downtown. It could be tied in with a civic center, which planners thought would be built just south of it.

This aerial view of Riverview Ice House shows how the old city yards changed into a boat dock, ice house, a place for the Forest City Queen and, later, a trolley station.

Young hockey players at Riverview Ice House.

I called Alderman John Holub and told him Jon Olson had just given me some good reasons to move the ice house downtown to the public works site. I asked him what he thought of Jon's reasoning. Holub told me he would talk to his fellow aldermen the following night.

He caucused the GOP members of the council and they all loved the idea.

Then he sauntered over to the News Tower and shared the idea, unbeknownst to me and, more importantly, the Park District Board and the advisory committee.

Friday morning, there was a huge headline on the front page: "Park District relocates ice rink." You can imagine how I felt and how I knew my board members would feel about such an "announcement" being made in the newspaper when they had no knowledge of what was going on.

I called John Holub and asked what he was doing. He was happy, all excited about the story. You could tell he wasn't working with a board, like I was. Well, I then contacted all my board members and the committee and explained exactly what happened. Happily, I wasn't fired.

Then we got back to work. The Park Board and committee agreed the downtown site was better. We told the city we would build the ice house and a marina on the site and the city promised to give us their property and $200,000 because the site was in poor condition for construction.

But that was just the beginning. We should have looked deeper into the complexities of this piece of land. That wouldn't have changed our minds but it might have prevented some misunderstandings.

As we began relocating the businesses

Congressman John B. Anderson spoke at the dedication of Riverview Ice House on July 4, 1975. We can't name everyone in the photo but we recognize (behind Anderson) Joe Marino, Tim Simms and John B. Whitehead. Joseph Bean is the gentleman in a white jacket to Anderson's right, and next to him are architects Hans H. Simmon and Charles E. Boettcher. In the back row behind Bean is Harley "Moon" Mullins, former commissioner; Wally Halvorson, former executive of the Rockford Chamber of Commerce; Frank St.Angel, former School Board and County Board member; Howard Bell of First National Bank and Trust, and others. The front row (from left) includes Commissioners Gerald Wernick, Ed Carlson, Jo Baker and Alden Orput, Mayor Bob McGaw and Ald. Lee Shervey.

that were on the site, we ran over budget — by about a quarter of a million dollars. The over-runs were to dig out old garbage on the site and replace it with crushed rock to create suitable soil conditions. The city and Park District shared those costs.

There were frequent stories and slanted editorials in newspapers taking us to task for, supposedly, doing a poor job of planning the ice house project. When we attempted to share the cost overrun with the city, one columnist accused us of trying to "con" the city into bailing us out. An editorial in January 1975 called the project a "boondoggle" and suggested work on the ice house stop immediately before it sends the "city and park district into bankruptcy." One newspaper story referred to the rink as a project "conceived in controversy and born in pessimism." I think they were reacting from the popular but erroneous notion that park districts should not build ice rinks. They were criticizing us editorially without considering all the facts.

Happily, Park District and city staff didn't panic and calmly worked through the difficulties. What people didn't acknowledge is that the project cost more than estimated because we were no longer dealing with just an ice house on the Elliot Park site. Instead, we developed a riverfront park and built boating facilities, besides an ice house. The rink actually cost less than anticipated. The so-called overruns were costs for the land we needed. The city and Park District ended up sharing those costs.

In addition to the rink, the site was designed to share parking facilities with the proposed metrocentre, at that time proposed to be built just south of the ice facility.

First National Bank and Trust Co. President Howard Bell arranged for the bank to give us $12,000 for our first Zamboni, a large machine which smooths and polishes the ice. The bank held a contest to name it and "The Buck" won.

The final cost — $3.2 million — was well worth it. We had a top-notch facility. With the help of local landscape architect John R. Cook, who has been invaluable to the Park District for many years, we constructed a building with a tremendous insulation value, priceless when you're heating along the river in the winter and cooling to a comfortable level in summer. We used earth berms nearly halfway up the building. It was, as John says, a building ahead of its time in design. Our architects were Charles E. Boettcher and Hans H. Simmon.

The Grand Opening

The Riverview Ice House opened July 4, 1975, with Congressman John B. Anderson speaking at a short dedication. He gave a great speech, as he did 25 years later when we celebrated our anniversary. The first two skaters were 15-year-old James Beattie and 9-year-old Patricia Hennigan, winners of the Name the Rink contest. One had suggested the name "Ice House," the other "Riverview." Honorable mention honors went to people who had suggested "The Cooler" and "Dinky Rink," names we used for the large rink and the smaller, studio rink.

There was free skating that weekend, and more than 1,000 people tried the ice each day. Curiosity about this "artificial" ice rink lasted a while. After six months, the rink had counted 35,000 visitors. About 10,000 were curious folk who came during open houses but 25,000 were people who paid admission in order to skate.

Riverview was operating 90 hours a week with 40 different rink programs and lessons to 450 skaters. Jim Murphy, who managed a local retail store called H20 Sports, reported that hockey and ice skates were selling year round.

We set priorities for ice time: First, public skating, then instruction for children in figure skating and hockey; then rentals to ice rink groups, and then rentals to others.

The ice house hosted such events as a game between the U.S. Olympic hockey team and the University of Illinois Chicago Circle, and games with the always-strong University of Wisconsin hockey team.

Riverview Ice House remains one of the district's most popular facilities and has hosted millions of skaters, including 105,000 in 2009. It continues going strong, even though the district now operates a second ice house in Loves Park.

Through the years, the Ice House has been responsible for its share of headlines.

> *The first two skaters were 15-year-old James Beattie and 9-year-old Patricia Hennigan, winners of the Name the Rink contest. One had suggested the name "Ice House," the other "Riverview."*

Locals became familiar with the sports of broomball and curling at the rinks. Rockford's Janet Lynn, Olympic bronze medalist and five-time U.S. Ladies figure skating champion, keynoted the 25th anniversary banquet in 2000, the year we renamed the main rink after her.

Skating champions routinely appeared at Riverview for public shows. Among them were Sandy Lenz of Rockford, who skated in the 1980 Winter Olympics, Olympic skaters Caryn Kadavy, Brian Boitano, Scott Hamilton, Peter Oppegard and Jill Watson, Dorothy Hamill, Jason Dungeon, Yuka Sato, David and Jimmie Santee, Sandy Lenz, Kath Malmberg, and others.

The Ice House for years was the site of the American Lung Association's "Let's Put Smoking on Ice" fund raiser featuring local celebrity skaters, regardless of whether they knew how to skate.

In 2004, the Park District closed the rink over summer to save money. That move backfired when the district let the ventilation system run but turned off the dehumidifiers. The result was mold in the carpets and ceiling tiles. The cleanup cost $300,000, three times the savings from closing the rinks.

There were many who sang the praises of the Ice House. Carol Riler wrote an essay for the Register Star in 1986 in which she said her family moved to Rockford so their daughter could train at the Ice House.

Aerial photo shows the 14 tennis courts at Guilford High. In the foreground is Swanson stadium; ball fields at right and school at left facing Spring Creek Road.

She listed the reasons they loved Rockford, including these offered by the Park District: "a summer stroll in Sinnissippi Park … ice skating by a gazebo covered with snow … a spring ride on the trolley or riverboat …"

Of course, one change always leads to others. After the Ice House was built, the Park District gradually stopped flooding neighborhood parks to provide outdoor rinks in cold weather months. The outdoor rinks were expensive to create and maintain because you had to flood them at night when the temperatures were down. And they didn't get that much use because warm daytime weather could melt the ice, and frequently did. But a lot of folks fondly remember those outdoor rinks.

Ribbon cutting at Guilford Tennis Center in 1974.

Schools our Tennis Partner

Early on in my time here, we also looked at requests for tennis courts. The School District needed better facilities for its teams, and the community needed more courts for adults and youth who wanted to play tennis for fun and recreation. Dick Bernardi, who was then president of the Northern Illinois Tennis Association, and a group of citizens had been lobbying for additional tennis courts for several years. Tennis fans were just asking to be treated like golfers, who by then had four courses on which to enjoy their sport, Bernardi said.

The board appointed a committee to look at both school and citizen needs. It brought in a plan for new courts at Auburn and Guilford high schools. We followed up in 1973 by putting in 14 courts at Guilford and six at Auburn, the number being determined by the demand. We lighted the courts at Guilford for night play.

The project went smoothly because it built on agreements between the parks and schools that had been in effect from early on and were broadened under Jim Brademas' tenure as recreation director. Both courts still serve students and citizens.

The Park District had built its first tennis courts 60 years earlier as part of the early development of Sinnissippi Park. Since then, courts were routinely installed in many neighborhood parks as they were developed.

Like golf, tennis was a sport of affluent folks who belonged to country clubs and tennis clubs when it first was introduced to this country in the 1870s. Park districts opened tennis to everyone by building tennis courts in public parks. Some tennis histories say the courts in St. Louis, built in 1911 and thereafter, were among the first public tennis sites in the nation. If so, Rockford was right there with them. By our hundredth birthday, we maintained more than 90 tennis courts.

Quick Work to Help Booker Washington

One tennis project I remember well began with a phone call on a Friday night from Oscar Blackwell, who directed the Booker Washington Community Center. Oscar said he needed $250,000 from the Park District. I responded, "Do you want it in cash or a cashier's check?"

Seriously, Booker Washington was embarking on an expansion program and needed $250,000 locally to get a matching grant from the federal government. The community center had just 20 days to put together the local funding or it would lose the federal grant.

The Park Board said we could use money set aside for a swimming pool in southwest Rockford, but only if our citizens agreed. We immediately scheduled public meetings in southwest neighborhoods and heard strong support for the Booker Washington proposal. So that's how the money was invested.

Because of our partnership with Booker, the city and feds, the center received $550,000 from the federal government. The project involved clearing nearby homes and creating a nicer environment for both Booker and the nearby Tinker Swiss Cottage. The final project included a new social services center for Booker Washington, as well as lighted tennis and basketball courts and a playground.

Photos show Booker Washington Center before (top) and after portrait murals were painted on the southwest side community center. The Park District helped Booker Washington acquire land and complete several projects, including tennis courts and a playground.

Bringing History to Life at Midway Village

One of the great developments during my first years here was the start of the Midway Village Museum.

Midway Village wouldn't be here without farsighted folks with interests in local history who agreed, some 40 years ago, to merge three historical societies — Swedish, Rockford and Harlem — into something called Rockford Museum Association.

That move was inspired by the Park District when the groups first came to the board in the late 1960s and asked for help. Get together, merge your resources and decide what you would like to do, the Park Board had said.

The Dream Reaches Out • 1972 – 2006

In 1972, my first year here, John Nelson, Carl Severin and Carl Linde came to see me one Saturday morning. They explained their dream of a local history museum. On the back of a brown paper bag, they had a sketch of a museum and historical village and they were excited.

I can still remember Mr. Severin telling me, "This will never cost the Park District more than $25,000." Of course, Midway has grown beyond all of our early dreams, and way beyond his cost estimate.

At the time, the museum consisted of 16 acres of land off Guilford Road promised to them by the Severin family. Their proposal to us was: Would the Park District construct and maintain exterior facilities such as a parking lot and road if the museum association gave us ownership of the land and buildings?

We were happy to help, but we couldn't afford it. If the museum tax were raised, however, from 1.5 cents per hundred to 3 cents, we could make it work. That we did, by getting the state Legislature to approve the increase. Then the Park Board gave the nod to working with the association to build the museum.

Groundbreaking took place Oct. 1, 1972, with Gov. and Mrs. Richard B. Ogilvie and Congressman John B. Anderson bringing greetings from President Richard M. Nixon. Others in attendance were B.G. Jarnstedt, the Swedish consul general, and

A 1900s era street at Midway Village with buildings preserved from 100 or more years ago. (Photo by David Cooper)

The Old Millhouse signals the entrance to Midway Village Museum at 6799 Guilford Road.

Rockford Airplane.

That's the plane local aviation pioneer Bert "Fish" Hassell crashed in Greenland in 1928 when he was trying to establish a northern air route to Europe. The route later became routine for airlines. "Fish" and his mechanic survived the crash and returned to Rockford many years before The Greater Rockford was recovered, restored and installed in the Hassell Aviation Wing of Midway Village Museum.

Construction, I should say reconstruction, of Midway Village began in 1974. The village, which represents a typical rural town in northern Illinois at the end of the 19th Century, now has 26 historical structures. Included are a general store, hardware store, print shop, blacksmith shop, school, town hall, police station and jail, plumbing shop, bank, hospital, hotel, fire station, church, barber

Midway often has "interpreters" in period dress guiding visitors through the village.

members of the museum board including president Allan Mallquist. Most exciting was the promise that here, local history would come alive as something youngsters and adults could see, hear and touch.

With ground broken for a $125,000 building of 10,000 square feet, the museum was on its way. Today, the museum has more than 52,000 square feet of space and houses an Industrial Gallery, Exhibition Hall, Aviation Gallery, Education Gallery, and Old Doll House Museum with more than 104,000 pieces in the collections.

Among the most popular exhibits are those featuring the famous Sock Monkeys; the Rockford Peaches[1] baseball team, which played professional ball in Beyer Park from 1943 to 1954; and The Greater

The Dream Reaches Out • 1972 – 2006

The Greater Rockford airplane, with which local aviation pioneer Bert "Fish" Hassell made history, is on display at Midway Village Museum.

shop, law office, two barns and four farm houses. Landscaping and gardens are as they would have been in the late 1800s and early 1900s.

The village is a place where history comes alive. School children take field trips that include a day in the Midway one-room schoolhouse. Youngsters attend summer camps at Midway. The "village" hosts a Chautauqua weekend each summer, with entertainment and culture such as people enjoyed in the early 1900s, before radio and television came along and isolated us at home.

What we learned when we got into museums was that they needed land for expansion. We looked at museums around the nation and found that Park Districts that partnered with museums had the role of acquiring land for future growth and development. In 1979, we looked at 70 acres adjacent to the museum, where the walking path and the Vietnam memorial are now. The land was already platted but we didn't want to let it slip away. The Park District did not have the money then, but the land had to be purchased or it would turn into another subdivision. We went to the County Board and the Forest Preserve Board. They, through the leadership of Frank St. Angel, chairman of the County Board, and Bob Millard, chairman of the Forest Preserve, bought the property. Frank called a special meeting and explained the project and the vote to buy passed easily. Ten years later, we bought the land back. That was one of the greatest examples I've ever seen of cooperation between governmental units helping each other fulfill their missions.

It's easy to imagine you are living in the early 1900s while walking the streets at Midway Village Museum.

Midway Village Museum today has a 137-acre site and is a major tourist draw. With nearly 90,000 visitors a year, the museum illustrates beautifully the Park District's role in helping others make dreams come true. When that happens, we all benefit. Alone, neither the Park District nor the local historical societies could have put together the success that Midway Village is today.

A Gift Horse with Bite?

When I got here and had a look at Sand Park, I cringed. There was nothing wrong with the swim pool. But health conditions around the pool were not good.

The problem was, Sand Park was being used as a municipal waste disposal site and the garbage was not being compacted and covered like it should have been. That brought rodents. I quickly learned that the stench was so bad, people who worked across the street at Barber Colman were getting sick.

Within hours of seeing the pool and meeting with executives of Barber Colman, we told the hauler he could no longer dump there. I recommended to commissioners we close the dumping operation, at least until we had an analysis done.

The dumping had been going on since the mid-1950s. Allowing the park to be used for waste had seemed like a good idea to the Park Board, which got the 41-acre site for $1 in 1941. It had been a gravel pit and wasn't suitable for anything until it was filled. So when Loves Park suggested dumping its waste there, the Park Board thought it was a good way to make the site useable.

A few years later, after the site was filled to grade and the pool was open, operators suggested piling the trash into a 70-foot high "mountain" which could be used for sledding. It seemed like another great idea, so the Park Board went for it.

In 1969, Sand Park Pool opened. All the waste was taken out from under the pool and a layer of crushed rock put in before the pool was built. That insured a safe foundation for the pool, but did not insure that rats would stay away. And they didn't.

In 1972 we hired a firm to do 18 test borings around the "mountain," then 35 feet high. Results from 17 of them did not meet standards. The "mountain" project never re-opened and no more garbage was dumped there. The mountain remains today, slowly sinking every year.

The state told us that since we owned the site, it was our responsibility to put a layer of dirt on the site and, when we couldn't get the landfill operators to do that, the Park District went ahead and did the job.

As the years went on, it became obvious that the landfill site had not been properly operated. The trash was supposed to have been crushed, packed and covered daily to provide a firm base. But we had frequent problems with parts of the site sinking and garbage protruding.

And a problem arose with a municipal well Loves Park had near the site. In the early 1990s, it was found to be contaminated and the city closed the well. Your first thought might be that the Sand Park site was the source of the contamination, but studies proved that not to be true. The contaminating agent had never even been dumped at Sand Park.

In the summer of 2010, the Park District and city of Loves Park helped pay to hook up 39 nearby homes to city water, shutting down their private wells. We had no proof there were any problems with the well water but we did not want to take any chances.

So here we are, 70 years since this $1 "gift horse." The pool is perfectly safe, but we still are dealing with the garbage buried around it. The state has asked for another covering of clay and top soil, a project that would cost us millions of dollars. The Park District has its own environmental experts, and negotiations with the state are continuing.

We can say that to our knowledge, since the dumping was stopped in 1972, no one has gotten sick because of what is buried in Sand Park. We have done all we can to continue that record and will continue to do so.

'Can You Do Better?'

I'll never forget the day I met Miriam "Miggie" Perrone. Miggie, described in a local newspaper article as "animated, articulate, interested, interesting,

Miriam Perrone

humorous, entertaining, volcanic, deft, seemingly daft." To that description, I would add, always a passionate advocate for the rights of the disadvantaged.

That fit my first impression of Miggie. I met her shortly after I started work here. I overheard someone delivering a verbal beating to Chuck Fiduccia, who was in charge of our recreational programs, and I went to see what was going on. There was Miggie, although I didn't know her yet. She had Chuck pinned against the wall.

Miggie had taken her developmentally disabled son to the Park District's program for special kids and found it insulting. She was there to tell us so. Having the kids make birdhouses out of popsicle sticks and letting them sit in a sandbox didn't cut it, she told Chuck in no uncertain terms. I interrupted just as she was declaring that as a taxpayer, she was demanding better programs for disabled children.

I immediately saw Miggie's passion and quickly learned that she knew what she was talking about. She knew a lot more about programming for disabled children than I did. She probably knew more than anyone in the Park District on that subject. Finally, I said to her, "Do you think you could run this program better?"

Of course, she could. You're hired, I said. After the formality of making her part of the staff, she took over. The program, named Camp Sunshine, grew quickly. Parents and children loved it. The staff who worked for Miggie initially didn't know what to make of her. As they saw how she related to the kids, they became

Miggie Perrone understood that children with disabilities need to have fun and be challenged, just like all children.

Mig taught our staff and kids the circle concept as a way to keep the children involved and learning.

as excited as she was. People from around the nation started asking questions about our program.

Miggie says she started with four goals:

1: Campers (the disabled kids) and staff would have fun by consistently interacting;

2: The arts — dance, drama, music and visual arts — would be the tools to implement consistent exchange between campers and staff;

3: The arts would encourage campers to develop self-confidence and self-expression, while demanding discipline and giving each camper a lasting memory of achievement; and

4: Parents, educators, business leaders, community activists, medical personnel and the artistic community would be involved.

Camp Sunshine succeeded beyond our dreams. I should say, beyond the dreams of the Park District. I don't suppose it surprised Miggie that children reacted in ways their parents had never observed before. They took part, they learned, and they had a great time. We constantly heard comments like this, from the relative of a little boy diagnosed with autism and/or emotional and mental impairment: "He is a different child this summer – easier and happier at home – and eager to come to camp in the morning."

The program put Rockford and the Park District on the map nationally as a progressive community that offered the best it could to all its citizens. Miggie took a group to New York City where they performed at the Institute of Rehabilitation for Dr. Howard Rusk, a renowned figure in the field of medical assistance for handicapped people. She spoke at sessions around the country, showing other cities how to conduct similar arts camps. A story in the Denver Post called the Rockford Park District program a "nationally outstanding example of what can be done for … handicapped children … through the creative use of theater and fine arts."

At a program Miggie gave in New Orleans, Jean Kennedy Smith was in the audience. Smith, the sister of the late President Kennedy, was a catalyst for better programming for handicapped children and told Miggie in a letter she was deeply impressed by the Rockford program. Later, Camp Sunshine was named one of nine national models by the National Committee, Arts for the Handicapped, which was headed by Smith.

A Camp Sunshine counselor and child.

> "I ask you not to brand a child with a label but instead nurture him or her in an environment that is challenging."
> – MIGGIE PERRONE

It is no exaggeration to say that Camp Sunshine inspired and improved programs for tens of thousands of handicapped children and youth across the nation. Secondarily, as Miggie says, it was an "effective catalyst that made the arts more visible. All segments of the population in Rockford in 1973 began to value the arts as an integral part of their lives."

It shows, once again, that you never know what spinoffs you might create once you put together a positive program. It's a fact of life and one that frequently makes me appreciate the wonders of our world. Some of Miggie's staff, teens she hired because of their interest in children and the arts, have gone on to great careers. Among them are Marin Mazzie and Joe Mantello, big names in the New York theater world; and area recording artist and children's entertainer Jim Gill.

Camp Sunshine continued to expand. In the 1980s, programs for teens were added. In 1989, the Rockford and Freeport park districts formed the Northlands Association for Special Recreation, which enabled them to levy a tax used exclusively for programs for handicapped citizens (Belvidere joined them in 1991).

Miggie left Rockford in the mid-1980s, but not before changing the lives of so many individuals and their families. Before she left, Miggie wrote a letter to the editor that appeared in the Register Star: "I want to implore the community of Rockford to give all children a chance to interact with other children," she wrote. "I ask you not to brand a child with a label but instead nurture him or her in an environment that is challenging."

The Rockford Park District takes that to heart in its programming, which operates year round, serving people of all ages. With passage of the Americans With Disabilities Act of 1991, it focused on the then-new concept of inclusion rather than segregation. Adapted sports programs such as the Junior Chariots wheelchair basketball program were added, and the district partnered with public schools to offer leisure education and after-school programs.

In 2011, the Park District offered more than 40 programs to citizens with disabilities plus inclusional services, where we give support to people with disabilities to take part in all our activities. There are 20 partnerships with community organizations that enhance the quality of programs to serve people with disabilities in a community setting with their non-disabled peers. Among our offerings in adapted sports are golf, Paralympic sports such as boccia, swimming, archery, cycling, sled hockey, wheelchair softball, track and field, wheelchair basketball and power soccer. Therapeutic programs include gymnastics, dance, art and music lessons, social clubs, after school and summer camps. Those serve 500 individuals who each visit the Park District about 20 times a year.

These are programs where the benefits to participants and their families are exhilarating to observe. The services are offered nowhere else locally and they mean so much to the participants and their families. Staff are impacted almost as much. The young people we hire for seasonal programs in this field find their whole perspective changed after working with disabled kids for a summer.

That's what I love about this business. It changes people's lives. I firmly believe that hiring students, training them and providing their first service-oriented work experience is one of the most valuable services we provide.

Trailside Centre in Lockwood Park is used for the equestrian program as well as snowmobilers.

Snowmobilers enjoy winter on trails at Lockwood, Searls and Page parks.

Horses and Snowmobiles

Snowmobiles went on the mass market in the 1960s and became a popular new form of winter recreation in snow climates like ours. Snowmobilers began asking for permission to use parks and, in January 1967, the board gave the OK for snowmobiles in Searls, Blackhawk and Atwood parks.

Pressure for trails grew. Snowmobile sales peaked at 2 million nationally from 1970 to 1973 and that was reflected locally. Over the years, the district opened more land to snowmobilers and, in 1973, built a 7-mile trail in Quarry Hills (now Lockwood Park), Page and Searls parks for the sport. The district opened the cookhouse and restrooms for use by the snowmobilers and invited them to picnic if they so chose.

We were happy to cooperate, although many people found snowmobiles a noisy infringement on their enjoyment of parks. Snowmobilers certainly needed public help if they were to have trails of any length. We found that with rules, respect and enforcement, parks could be used by snowmobilers.

That continues today, and snowmobiling has proven to be an economic driver. There are about 40,000 snowmobiles in Illinois, most of them in the northern counties like ours. The average snowmobiler rides 1,402 miles a year and spends $4,000 each year on related recreation. Lockwood Park and adjacent Page Park offer 15 miles of multi-use trails for snowmobilers and others. The parks are the hub of a 300-mile trail system that serves three counties. The district also continues to be a major provider of snowmobile safety courses.

Now Come the Horses

In 1976, the district got an $89,000 state grant for snowmobile facilities. That, strangely enough, was the beginning of the Park District's equestrian program.

Horseback riders were after us for trails and other facilities. Atty. Chuck Thomas even brought horses out to Quarry Hill Park so the board and I could ride and see what potential the park had as an equestrian center.

We wanted to accommodate both groups and came up a way to kill two birds with one stone, that is, fund two programs with one investment. The state would give us money to build a center for snowmobiling and to develop trails. We figured we could use the building and the trails for horses, too. The state agreed and with that first grant of nearly $90,000, we built Trailside Centre in what was then known as the Children's Farm.

It opened on April 16, 1977, to the great joy of horse riding enthusiasts. We had 15 horses initially and offered them for rides on 14 miles of trails in Quarry Hills, Searls and Page parks.

Later, from 1983 to 1997, Trailside Center provided the animals and trails for the Blackhawk Valley Riding Club, which uses horseback riding as physical therapy for people with disabilities. More than 50 children and adults improved their balance and coordination, not to mention self esteem, through horseback riding at the farm in that program. That service is now offered at the Bergmann Centre in Poplar Grove.

The Lockwood Connection

We continued to have trouble, financially, sustaining the Children's Farm. Attendance from 1978 to 1979 went down by 10,000 — to 26,295. We brought in new animals and scheduled more special events but couldn't break even, partly because of poor weather.

Lockwood Park offers horse riding lessons and trail rides.

Building a Lasting Dream

In the 1980s, the Children's Farm got a champion. James E. Lockwood, who had generously given to other causes including a park in Racine that bears his name, loved the combination of children and animals. He offered us $300,000 to expand and improve the farm.

Unfortunately, not all of Lockwood's ideas were things the Park District could do. We could not afford to maintain some of the exotic animals he wanted us to keep at the farm. We renamed the park in his honor — Lockwood Park — but neither his dream nor his gift to the Park District were ever realized.

In 1986, we laid out a plan to make Lockwood Park into a year-round Family Fun Center, modeled roughly on Bay Beach Park in Green Bay, Wis. We planned rides, a creative play center, Old McDonald farm, games, shelter and picnic areas. We never came up with the funds for that, although it's possible it still will happen someday.

By 2004, we had "carried" the Children's Farm as long as we could, I believed. We had hoped to pass a referendum to increase our recreation tax in April 2003, but voters soundly rejected it. That fall, we presented a list of potential budget cuts, including the elimination of all animals at Lockwood, which meant no more children's farm, no more horses and no more horseback riding.

Well, we no more than laid that possibility out when we heard from Lockwood supporters that they wouldn't stand for it. What's more, they asked what they could do to keep Lockwood's animal tradition going. We said we needed money and volunteer labor.

The group of people, recruited by longtime Lockwood volunteer George Franklin and his wife, Tanya, immediately responded. They called themselves Friends of Lockwood and indeed they were. The first year, they raised $10,000 for us. They sold coupon books, held dozens of bake sales, put on a dance at Midway Village and talked money off everyone they could. They were an enthusiastic and determined group.

Horses provide wagon rides at Lockwood Park, too.

The covered bridge (center) leads to the playground in this bird's eye view of Lockwood Park and the Children's Farm.

They also gave us more than 2,000 hours of volunteer work that year. And this was not easy work. It was such things as putting up fences, cutting new trails out of the brush, painting buildings and spreading mulch.

Some of their ideas were brilliant. They found animal owners who would let us keep a few sheep, goats, pigs, rabbits and chickens in the summer as long as we would feed and care for them. They found a veterinarian who treated the animals for no charge. Then in fall, owners took the animals back so we didn't have to look after them all winter. That means our Children's Farm, a very popular attraction, continued to operate.

Friends of Lockwood continue to help us out. The group has raised nearly $100,000 for Lockwood Park, including $40,000 from the late Harry Espenscheid.

Lockwood Park still has about a dozen animals for children to get acquainted with during the summer months, a playground, picnic spots and lots of room to run. We board around 20 horses and have nearly 40 of our own. The park gets about 130,000 visitors each year, putting it among the top 10 attractions in the city.

The farm remains one of the district's most popular parks, and former Executive Director Milne deserves credit for initiating its development. For the past several years, the park has been under the leadership of Deb Ackerman who, along

Families form a long line at Lockwood Park while waiting for the signal to let youngsters hunt for thousands of plastic Easter eggs filled with goodies. In the photo at right, they're off.

Learning to Say 'No, thank you'

We can't leave the subject of the Children's Farm without relating a hard lesson we learned out there: Be careful of what "gift" animals you accept.

with assistant Linda Wise and dedicated staff and volunteers, has brought new life and expanded programs to the thousands of people who use the park each year.

Lockwood has hosted some of the district's most popular special events, including haunted hayrides at Halloween and Easter egg hunts. Many were done with the help of The Undertaker (aka Steve Hilton), who brought prizes and organized games for the kids. In 2005, he put Searls Park in the Guinness Book of World Records when he organized what was then the world's largest Easter egg hunt of 1,500 kids looking for 292,686 plastic eggs filled with goodies.

Friends of Lockwood Park remains one of our most valuable allies. Those volunteers have made a consistent positive impact on programming and facilities at Lockwood Park.

As soon as the farm opened, people started offering to bring us all kinds of animals. For example, D.L. wrote a letter to the newspaper saying she had found a baby skunk wandering the streets six weeks earlier, had taken it home, fed it with a bottle, and tamed it. She wondered if a veterinarian would be willing to "deodorize" the animal so it could be displayed at the Children's Farm. The newspaper, quoting a veterinarian, advised her to immediately turn the skunk out of the house, adding it would be able to fend for itself as long as humans left it alone.

The Children's Farm did accept some animals, including peacocks and Havana rabbits. And it took in the girl rabbit named Peter in 1970 when her owners wrote this letter to Bob Milne:

"Do you have a rabbit for the children's farm? My brother and I have one we would like to share with other boys and girls. It is a pretty mama rabbit but her name is Peter because we first thought she was a boy. Peter is white and has black spots down the back. Love, Lori and Scott Solberg."

In fact, Milne told the newspaper that the farm appreciated "donations of this kind."

Three years later, the farm had all the donated animals it could handle. I believe we were feeding more than 50 rabbits at one time. After Easter, families swamped us with chicks and bunnies their children had received.

Superintendent of special park facilities Clarence Hicks announced in May 1973 the farm would no longer "accept unwanted animals indiscriminately and freely." They would be welcome, he said, only if the farm has space, quarantine facilities and the donor gives $5 for food and medical care.

Would that we had followed that policy a month later when a family offered to give us a pony named Snowball. The donors said they convinced their 8-year-old son to part with the animal so other children could enjoy her, too.

Now, maybe Snowball was docile with that family, but she wasn't friendly to our farm staff, kicking one while he was cleaning her stall. She had a nasty disposition. There was no way could we put that pony out for children to pet.

At the time, we didn't keep track of animal donors. There had been so many of them. We shouldn't have accepted Snowball because we already had too many horses. But there we were, with a pony that wasn't Children's Farm material. So we did what was customary at the time. We sold her, along with two old, blind horses, to a processing plant.

Then the family brought their little boy back to visit Snowball, who was no longer there. Their next stop might have been the newspaper office because on June 8, 1973, this headline appeared in the Morning Star: "How do you explain pony now 'dogfood?'"

The story included our profuse apologies for the way the donation was handled. Poor Jerry Burnam, Children's Farm director, felt terrible.

"I wasn't aware that they would have wanted the pony back … I don't remember who I got what pony, rabbit or duck from. I'm not callous. I'm just trying to do my job and keep my inventory at the right level," he explained.

The district agreed to donate $31, Snowball's sale price, to the Animal Rehabilitation Foundation. And we put a strict policy in place about donated animals.

Headline in Morning Star June 8, 1973

Fishing in 10th Avenue Pool

The Park District never was afraid to try something new. In late September 1973, after the Tenth Avenue Pool had been closed for a month and the chlorine had dissipated, the water was fit for fish. Our plan was to stock it with rainbow trout and charge 50 cents a person to enter a fishing derby at the pool. No fishing license was required, and anglers could take up to three fish a piece. No casting was permitted.

I had done this when I was in Oak Park with great success. The kids loved it.

Here, we ran into delays. The weather turned warm and the pool water was too warm for rainbow trout when the derby was initially scheduled September 29 – 30. We postponed it to the following weekend, when the same thing happened.

Finally, on October 27 – 28, we turned loose 150 pounds of rainbow trout — average length 11 – 12 inches — into the pool. But we had rain and cold weather, and not many fishermen or women that weekend. They didn't catch nearly all the fish. So we set fishing hours for a couple more weekends.

We still had leftover trout. Finally, we donated them to people who wanted them.

The idea had been that we would hold the derby each year as a fall sporting event. But after finding out it wasn't that simple, we never repeated it.

But we did open Alpine Pool to dogs years later. In 2005 and 2006, we hosted "Poochapoolooza." Pet owners were invited to bring their dogs for a swim. It was a great success but the Health Department saw some potential problems so we stopped.

Winters Took a Toll on 10th Avenue Pool

The 10th Avenue swimming pool, a concrete, above-ground behemoth which could handle 1,000 swimmers at a time, outlived its usefulness. Opened in 1929, it had taken 40 years of Illinois winters by the 1970s and was deteriorating rapidly. A study in '75 showed it was losing 30,000 gallons of water each day.

By 1976, we were picking up children from schools and neighborhood centers during the summers and giving them free bus rides to pools. So closing 10th Avenue didn't deny people the chance to swim, even if they had no transportation on their own.

But there were objections to closing the pool. A group called the Near East Rockford Cluster of Churches said young people in that neighborhood needed more recreation, not less. I told them we'd provide lighted basketball and tennis courts, which would cost us far less than the $50,000 we'd have to spend to run the pool for 10 – 12 weeks each summer.

> *It cost $25,000 to build 10th Avenue Pool in 1929. In 1976, it cost $25,000 to take it down.*

I recommended closing the pool as part of a list of budget reductions. The summer of '75, we'd had a $40,000 swim pool deficit, largely because of 10th Avenue. The pool was used less each summer since Alpine and Sand Park opened in 1969. I couldn't see throwing money away on a 50-year-old pool that was crumbling.

We were told, if the pool closed, we'd get petitions signed by hundreds of people but we never did. We did hear from members of the Churches group. One called the pool

The Dream Reaches Out • 1972 – 2006

More than 5,000 people attended the Black Family Reunion in Rockford in 2011. The three-day event, with Saturday and Sunday at Levings Park, has been held here each year since 1992. Sponsored by the National Council of Negro Women, the reunion is a multi-cultural, family-focused event open to everyone. In the photo above right is the Washington family, recipients of the 2011 Family of the Year award. Members are (from left) the Rev. Dr. James E. Washington of St. Paul Church of God in Christ; his wife, Vanessa; their granddaughter, Miss Penix; his sister, Jackie Pullins; his brother, Dr. Charles M. Washington; and Charles' wife, Minnie Washington.

---

a "decaying pit of doom" but said if it went, a new pool should be built.

I sympathized but the facts were: (1) we couldn't afford to maintain that pool or repair it at cost of $270,000; (2) we could not afford to build a new one; and (3) the days of neighborhood pools were over. The economical way to provide swimming facilities was through pools that served a larger area.

In April 1976, the board voted to demolish the 10th Avenue pool. We built lighted tennis courts on the site as soon as we could and put a baseball diamond and more playground equipment at the 10th Avenue Park.

Interestingly, it had cost $25,000 to build the pool in 1929, and it cost about that much to take it down in 1976.

Rockford's First Rec Path

One of the earliest visions of park commissioners was a path or roadway along the Rock River. George Roper talked about it as the district was formed in 1909. He revisited the idea in the Rockford Plan of 1918, in which experts suggested an esplanade along part of the Rock River with shop frontage, and a "system of boulevards ... designed with the idea of being restricted to the use of pleasure vehicles ... to connect the larger park units."

Superintendent Elliot, in his 34 years as director of the Park District, had suggested a walking path more than once. The idea was pooh-poohed. No one would use a path, people said.

Bikers and joggers enjoy the path along the Rock River in Sinnissippi Park. So do folks who like to sit, rest and watch the river..

Early in the '70s, Commissioner Jo Baker started talking about a bike path in the city. She brought us pictures of a path in Wichita, Kan. At a parks conference in Washington, D.C., she rented three bikes and talked parks staffer Dave Wiemer and me to go biking along the Potomac (Had I known how much my body would ache the next morning, I might not have gone. But I did and the rest, as you will read, is history).

Jo's promotion of a bike/jogging path was a reflection of what was going on throughout the nation regarding physical fitness. A 1953 report in the Journal of American Association of Health, Physical Education and Recreation had declared that Americans were becoming soft. The affluent lifestyle of the 20th Century had made life so easy that adults and children were "rapidly losing muscle tone," the authors wrote.

President Eisenhower said he was shocked and called a national conference on physical fitness to spotlight the issue. His successor, John Kennedy, took up the cause with public awareness campaigns and physical fitness tests for school children. Kids of the '60s worked out in school gyms to "Chicken Fat," written by Meredith Wilson ("The Music Man"). The lyrics included:

"Push up, Every Morning, Push up, Starting low.

"Once more on the rise, Nuts to the flabby guys!

"Go, you chicken fat, go away..."

The drive to fitness — and finally, to the fact that health is primarily the responsibility of each individual and not his doctor — slowly became part of the American culture. Even the comic strip

"Peanuts" got into fitness. The surgeon general warned against smoking and each cigarette pack reminded that the habit "may be hazardous to your health."

> *"Once more on the rise, Nuts to the flabby guys! Go, you chicken fat, go away…"*
> – LYRICS FROM "CHICKEN FAT" FITNESS SONG

Jogging, once practiced only by a few so-called health fanatics, was picked up by middle Americans who saw it as a natural, inexpensive activity they could practice anywhere and anytime. They began hitting sidewalks, streets, school tracks and parks in a quest to stay fit and trim. Running marathons became a part of American culture. Title IX mandating equal opportunities for women in sports became law in 1972 and inspired young and old females to take up sports and fitness activities.

Bicycling, for the most part, was still looked upon as a mode of transportation or fun for children, but Jo saw beyond that. She educated us on the health benefits of biking and believed that any park district worth its salt would provide safe places for citizens to exercise, whether they preferred jogging, biking, running or walking.

The Park District had always worked to protect the riverbank, hoping eventually to control more of it for public use. In 1963, for example, we successfully opposed a plan to build apartment houses adjacent to our property just south of the Auburn Street cloverleaf. As then Supt. Earl Elliot said, "We don't want people to drive over the cloverleaf and see the roofs of houses. This would kill our park …" Through the years, the district acquired land, including railroad right-of-way,

A sign invites activity in June but the district's oldest rec path is busy year round.

Building A Lasting Dream

Thanks to Joe Marino and Project First Rate, as well as the support of local businesses and organizations, the Holiday Festival of Lights has made driving through Sinnissippi Park a family tradition.

along the river whenever possible.

In the '70s, the bike/walking path became reality. Jo chaired the district's Greater Rockford Bicycle Committee which surveyed bikers about why and where they biked. Bicyclists were few in number, but they insisted the reason was there were not many safe places to ride. They called for a network of paths. The Blackhawk Bike Club was eager for a trail. In the meantime they requested, and received, exclusive use of other parks, such as Levings, on certain Saturdays. Exclusive use meant only bikes or pedestrians on the roads, no motor vehicles.

The Morning Star informed us in 1973 that the "bicycle has come into its own in Rockford..." estimating that there were 110,000 bikes in the city and that two-thirds of new bikes were sold to adults.

By 1975, we had a plan for a bike/walking path along the east side of the river, from the YMCA to Martin Park in Loves Park. It would be done in stages. We called it the Bicentennial Bicycle and Pedestrian Path and planned to open it in 1976. The Jaycees raised $4,000 for a bridge over Spring Creek, the stream, and we planned a pass under busy Spring Creek, the road.

Key planners to get this done included Bill Graham and David Wiemer of the Park District, local landscaper John R. Cook and Rick Strader, who was with the city of Loves Park. I'm not sure Rick helped or hurt us but he drew attention by titling his path plan "Pedal Your Ass All Over Town." That's exactly what some of our detractors feared would happen if we built the path!

As usual, the project was not going to be easy. The district needed to obtain riverfront properties north of the YMCA, and we encountered three owners who refused to sell. They were Ed McCanna, Robert Nauert and Hugh Deery. We had appraisals done for the strips of land we needed, and they came to $15,000 to $19,000 each. We offered those amounts but were turned down. The owners believed they would lose property value by selling us riverfront. We argued the opposite, that a well-designed and maintained path along the river would improve their view of the river and the value of their homes.

It seemed the issue would go to court. We couldn't give in and neither would they. Then I invited Hugh Deery to a meeting. I had never met him and thought we should talk face to face.

He came to our offices one very cold day. The weather was so bad, it was the only day I ever closed the Park District. We sat down in the board room and chatted a little bit about our backgrounds. It turned out we had mutual friends, people I knew from my home town in Morrison who also were customers he called on.

When we got down to business, we discussed the lighting, the design and the security planned for the path. He saw that we had plans to prevent the things he feared. He withdrew his opposition and, shortly afterward, his neighbors did, too. That saved us all from going to court and enabled us to get moving on the bike path. Hugh Deery and I became friends.

The path opened in 1977. Controversy over it has long since subsided from memory. These days, try and find someone who has not enjoyed what we commonly call the "bike path" along the river, although it hosts at least as many joggers and walkers as cyclists. By 1986, we had to widen the path from 8 to 10 feet, reroute it slightly, and improve the shoulders and bridges so it could accommodate everyone. By 1996, 600,000 people were using the path each year, and the stretch in Sinnissippi Park was the favored site of local charitable walks.

Today, the 10-mile paved path — the Rock River Recreation Path, officially — is the granddaddy of the region's path system. You can start at Davis Park downtown and walk, jog or bike to Sportscore One and then on through Loves Park and Machesney Park on the Bauer Memorial Path. Along the way, you'll pass some of the nicest scenery in town.

Today's challenge to the park district and our municipal partners is to keep up with the public demand for walking/biking trails. The Park District has built a 1.4-mile path in Cherry Valley, the 3-mile Mel Anderson Memorial Path along Kent Creek in northwest Rockford, and shorter paths in our neighborhood parks. We've also partnered to help build the Charles Street Community Path, Perryville Path and Willow Creek Path. The majority of citizens now realize that bike/walking paths are part of the quality of life many citizens have come to expect.

I can't end this section without giving Jo Baker credit for getting this started. Jo was deeply involved in many worthy projects, first as a board member, from 1973 to 1981, and then as a planner and administrator on our staff until 1992. She was one of the most enthusiastic and energetic people I ever knew at either job. Sometimes, I had to try

> *"The bicycle has come into its own in Rockford..." estimating that there were 110,000 bikes in the city and that two-thirds of new bikes were sold to adults.*
> *–Morning Star, 1973*

to slow her down. I never had that "problem" with any other employee. Jo was the first woman on the Park Board and later, when I hired her, one of the first woman administrators on staff, which raised eyebrows of some male employees. She overcame all of that and was instrumental in our progress and many projects, including the Riverfront Museum Park, Sportscore One and the holiday lights display in Sinnissippi Park coordinated by another great friend of the Park District, Mr. 4th of July, Joe Marino.

The YMCA and the Path

In some cities, local YMCA organizations openly compete with park districts over attracting people to their programs. That hasn't been true in Rockford, to the benefit of all of us.

When we put the bike path in, the Y could have seen it as competition to the programs and facilities at the downtown facility. Instead the agency recognized, correctly, that the bike path would bring more people into its neighborhood and encourage Y membership growth.

Haskell School kids check out their new playground on Sept. 17, 1976. The man directing children in the tan jacket at left is Principal Bob Greene.

The Dream Reaches Out • 1972 – 2006

Mayor Bob McGaw speaks at dedication of the Terry Lee Wells Memorial Playground at Haskell School.

As Wray Howard, who came to the Y in 1974 and retired as CEO in 2011, puts it, "You couldn't have asked for a better deal all the way around." The Park District let the Y expand parking on our land because we both knew we'd need more space for users of the path and the Y. People who used the path discovered the programs and facilities of the Y and membership increased. What's better than an invigorating walk, run or ride along the river, then a shower at the Y before returning home?

It worked so well we duplicated the idea at the Y's newer Northeast Branch. And through the years, we shared staff, expertise and other things with the Y, which enabled us both to build stronger programs.

Among the things we've collaborated on through the years are after-school programs, summer day camps, child care, "Hot Nights … Summer in the City" for teens, mentoring, Senior Olympics, Corporate Cup, as well as statewide advocating for youth initiatives.

The Y, by the way, has a history that eclipses that of the Park District. It started in Rockford in 1876 and built its first facility, at State and Madison, in 1888. Levin Faust had been in this country just a year when that happened. He wouldn't get the Park District going until 21 more years had passed.

A Love Story of Children and a Park

Proponents of a new playground at Haskell School had been lobbying the Park District even before I came to town. In one memorable meeting in October 1971, 25 citizens came to a Park

This outdoor seating area was an important part of the program and playground at Haskell School.

Board meeting to ask that a Haskell playground be made the district's No. 1 priority. Among the 25 was Third Ward Ald. David Ingrassia who brought word that the City Council wanted the Park Board to "reorder its priorities."

After the meeting, Park Board President Reuben Aldeen asked Ingrassia to take a message back to City Hall.

"Give our loveliest love to the City Council and ask them to tell us what priority we should cut out," Aldeen dictated. Haskell wasn't the only school "screaming" for a playground and the Park District "couldn't provide them all anymore than we could fly," he added.

But Haskell School had no playground space at all. Its principal, Robert E. Greene, had 500 active kids and no place to send them for recess, or to hold the then-popular physical fitness tests for children. We got busy looking for ways to get this done and, in early 1973, formed an agreement with the School District and city of Rockford to each spend $110,000 for a block of land west of the school.

There was some opposition. Some feared the Park District would be expected to build a park at each school. But my view was that Park District involvement was justified because there were no neighborhood parks in the area. I agreed with Principal Greene that this was becoming a critical problem for those school children and their families.

Our hopes took a hit a month later when HUD told us it wouldn't give us funding for the playground. But we didn't give up and neither did Greene or our congressman, U.S. Rep. John B. Anderson.

The following year, we received $450,000, thanks in large part to Anderson and his staff. Added to pledges from us, the School District and the city of Rockford, the fund was enough to buy 18 homes and three businesses around the school, relocate the families and demolish the buildings.

Before the park was complete, the Park Board responded to a letter signed by 750 Haskell School neighbors to name the playground after Terry Lee Wells, a 6-year-old who had been killed when his bicycle collided with a truck in June 1974. The petition showed that Terry Lee was a most unusual little boy.

> *"This little boy was loved by all the neighbors and he was always talking of the things he would do for people...he loved people, parks and school."*
> – SAID OF 6-YEAR-OLD TERRY LEE WELLS

"We loved him so dearly and he never did anything wrong. He would help the janitors of Haskell School pick up the garbage on the lawn," the letter said. "He would help neighbors with little odds and ends. He would talk with teachers on their way home from a hard day of work. This little boy was loved by all the neighbors and he was always talking of the things he would do for people...he loved people, parks and school."

The playground was completed in 1976 and was a key part of a turnaround for Haskell.

"We've rebuilt the image of the school..." said Greene at the time. "The park is the most visible thing but I think the real thing is the attitude of the students ... I've seen a tremendous change in student attitude."

Thirty-four years later, Greene still believed the park had a direct impact on Haskell student achievement, which climbed out of the cellar toward national averages in the years Greene led the school after we installed the playground.

"They cleared out two blocks of deteriorating housing — we had had a house of prostitution across the street from the school — and gave us open space, a baseball diamond, a playground. It was a totally different atmosphere and made a big difference in the achievements of the kids," he said a few months before his death in October 2011.

The students looked upon the park as their own, he added. "One year we were putting flowers around the school and someone came by and commented, 'That's a waste of time, those flowers will be trashed.' A 12-year-old neighbor boy who was helping us was insulted. 'It's not a waste of time,' he said.

"Well, that year we had the most beautiful show of flowers you've ever seen. Word got out that if you messed with the flower beds, you had to deal with the kids," Greene said.

To this day, this project remains one of my favorites. The long term impact of this park and playground on kids and their families is tremendous. It's something that is taken for granted today but was a real challenge at the time.

Sun Singer Energizes District

The Park District logo, used on our news releases, signs and other public documents, was once a picnic table under a tree. It had been used for decades, although we couldn't establish just when it had been adopted.

Around 1975, some of us got to thinking there was something missing in that logo. The only living things on the symbol were the trees and the grass, and the grass looked shaggy. There was no wildlife, not even a bird. Most important, where were the people?

We believed a logo of the Park District should symbolize people enjoying the outdoors, with a feeling of vitality, exuberance and optimism. So we put together a committee of staffers Bill Graham and Dave Wiemer, and Commissioners Jo Baker, Jerry Wernick and Alden Orput. We got Gene Holmberg of Design Center, a local graphic arts firm, to help design a new logo.

He gave us two choices: a pine tree in a circle, and a sun singer, in two circles. The two circles were in bright red and yellow tones, representing the sun, the source of energy for all living things on Earth.

We picked the latter. Several committee folk strenuously objected to even considering a logo that did not have a person in it.

The logo we selected represents the reason the Park District exists — people. The figure, celebrating life with arms outstretched, is a Sun Singer, a modernized version of a Native American symbol.

We sent it back to the artist once. The earlier figure, we thought, held his arms as if he were being held up by a bandit. The revised design showed the arms in a more welcoming and relaxed position. The board adopted the new logo on Aug. 12, 1975.

It was a cutting-edge piece of artwork, especially coming after the staid picnic table logo. Did it go too far?

Commissioner Baker said she was sure it was the perfect logo after park

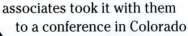

(Top) The old Park District logo. (Below) The Sun Singer.

associates took it with them to a conference in Colorado Springs. One night, as she was waiting for an elevator dressed in jeans with a belt buckle depicting the Sun Singer, a person came running over to her, shouting, "You're from Rockford, Illinois." He had recognized the logo.

I have always found the Sun Singer logo inspiring. As my friend Jo Baker says, it had a lot to do with propelling our minds forward.

As Jo put it, "The recreational facilities that came about, the programs we offered, the way we looked at ourselves, and the way we felt about our work — all improved with the emergence of the Sun Singer. Suddenly, all things were possible. It was like going from the industrial age to the information age."

Gene Holmberg says the Park District got a good deal on the logo, since his firm was doing work for us anyway. We certainly did. The logo has stood for 35 years and readily identifies the Park District to just about everyone.

I want to recognize Commissioner Harris Agnew, who encouraged us to use the Sun Singer logo as much as possible on buildings, vehicles, equipment and every publication and brochure we produced. Thanks to Harris' efforts, most citizens recognize the Park District logo.

I like it so much, every time I see Gene and his lovely wife Joyce, our former state senator, I give Gene a kiss. Like they say, no good deed goes unpunished.

Scandals and Tragedies

I'd be lying if I didn't own up to the scandals that hit the Park District through the years. Like any organization, we occasionally had to deal with behavior that didn't measure up to standards.

One of the worst examples came to my attention on Christmas Eve 1975. I was home and getting ready to take my family to church when the phone rang. It was Lt. Gene Coots of the Sheriff's Department. He asked if I was sitting down and suggested I do so.

He then told me they had arrested two summer workers at Sand Park Pool and charged them with sexual crimes involving minors. What was worse, the two had made sexual films after hours at Sand Park Pool. One was a lifeguard, the other was the pool manager who had been a teacher in a local district.

Another man was charged with grand theft for stealing money from pool revenues.

The legal system took care of them. Our job was to do everything possible to make sure we didn't employ people like this again. We started screening police records of job applicants and took more time checking out references. We made sure no one would go unnoticed if they returned to a Park District facility after hours unless they had a valid reason. We also tightened our cash control policies.

The newspapers had a field day with the story, which coincided with a similar investigation involving workers at a local mental health facility. I was sad about it, but I believe that society's ills are sooner or later reflected in its institutions, especially those as open and public as a park system or school district. Our job is to prevent wrongdoing as much as possible, to be on the alert for it, and act immediately if we suspect it.

We also dealt in the 1970s with illegalities in the Comprehensive Employment Training Act (CETA) program. The Park District was supervising and assigning 100 of the CETA workers in Rockford. One of our employees noticed some strange things going on: Equipment and materials were disappearing. Workers were sent, with CETA equipment and on CETA time, to jobs at private concerns. I worked with our employee to get details and went to the FBI with them.

Shortly thereafter, the director of the program left town. Authorities found him two years later somewhere down South and he went to prison. We fired a couple dozen CETA workers who had been involved.

Like I said, you're not going to keep the bad eggs from invading your turf every now and then. A responsible agency responds by stopping wrongdoing when it's discovered. And you must put in place policies to prevent a repeat or similar problems.

We had tragedies, too. Over 100 years, our parks have been the scene of murders, overdoses, drownings and other traumatic events. In each case, we did all we could for the families of the victims and, of course, looked for ways to prevent future crimes or accidents. You cannot prevent them all, but you must try.

> *"Society's ills are sooner or later reflected in its institutions, especially those as open and public as a park system or school district. Our job is to prevent wrongdoing ... and act immediately if we suspect it."*
> – AUTHOR WEBBS NORMAN

> *"Like any large organization, we occasionally had to deal with behavior that didn't measure up to standards."*
> – AUTHOR WEBBS NORMAN

Call them Rangers or Police, We Need Them

Early on, the Park Board strived to make the parks as safe as possible. Police alarm boxes were installed at Sinnissippi and Fair Grounds parks in 1911. In 1914, the board offered a $25 reward for the apprehension of miscreants who broke a flagpole at Fair Grounds. That same year, the board began talking about establishing a Park District police force.

Although most citizens had great respect for their parks, board minutes and annual reports tell of problems from time to time. In 1918, "Dr. Boswell and Miss Marsh" suggested patrols at the large parks since "there appears to be more or less immorality going on." The board's response was to close all parks after 10:30 p.m. with fines of $2 to $10 for violators. The board also voted to have Fair Grounds, Sinnissippi and Black Hawk policed for a few hours each evening.

When things went wrong, the board hired part-time or temporary officers to straighten things out. When gambling and crap shooting was reported in South Park in 1919, the board OK'd spending $30 on police to arrest the offenders. In 1928, it

The first Park policeman on wheels rode a motorcycle and was hired in 1928 to stop bullying in parks.

engaged a full-time motorcycle officer after bullying was reported in the parks.

That officer stayed with the Park District for more than 20 years, and was joined by another in the late 1940s or early 1950s. One officer patrolled parks on the west side and one on the east side. A 1964 newspaper article noted that both Park District police squad cars had Park ID on the doors and the police got new blue uniforms. The article added the police were going to spend more time monitoring small neighborhood parks, which had become targets of vandals.

Joe Brown joined the Park District police in 1970, giving us three officers. That year, at Park District request, the City Council gave the 215 city police officers authority to enforce Park District laws. Previously, only Park District officers had jurisdiction in local parks.

In 1974, two years after I arrived, a disturbance at Page Park convinced me we needed a more professional police presence. On Saturday afternoon, April 27, the park was crowded as usual. It had become a hang-out for young people, some of whom were bringing alcohol and other drugs with them. That afternoon, park police asked for help from county sheriff's deputies because of the number of people drinking and misbehaving. A deputy who responded was surrounded by a threatening crowd and assaulted by two people while he was making an arrest.

Page wasn't the only park with problems. For a time, Levings Lake Park was a hangout for troublemakers. They frightened citizens away. We took that on with increased police patrols in 1973. In one week, I recall, we sent 100 Levings arrests through the court system. It worked and Levings today is as safe and serene as any park.

But, to get back to the Page Park brouhaha, that incident was it for me. Keeping the parks safe was our first job. And by "keeping parks safe," I didn't mean handling trouble after it started. I meant preventing trouble from getting a start. In reality, we must do both.

To do that, I recommended a separate Park District Police Department, a professional unit with officers trained not only in police techniques but in the philosophy of a Park District dedicated to the recreational needs of citizens. I wanted officers with all the authority of police but who would be looked upon as helpful and who would arrest only as a last resort.

I also wanted our own police because they had to be on duty the times people were out in the parks having fun. We couldn't be sure there would be enough off-duty city police available when we needed them.

We discovered that a state law allowing park districts to levy a tax for police units was about to be changed. If we acted quickly, we could be grandfathered into the old law, which gave us a small amount of tax money to use for building a department. That we did.

Our "new" police department went into service in January 1975. By June 1976, we had seven officers, with two more in training. The force, which would have nine full-timers, patrolled 105 parks and playground areas, including Riverview Ice

In 1918, "Dr. Boswell and Miss Marsh" suggested patrols at the large parks since "there appears to be more or less immorality going on."

"Keeping the parks safe was our first job. If we couldn't do that, why have parks?"
– AUTHOR WEBBS NORMAN

John Royster (left) with the Park District Police Department works on a bicycle safety event with a Rockford City police officer.

House, our museums and swim pools.

Like municipal police, they ran into just about everything. In March 1977, Cpl. David Mace was checking Twin Sisters Park when he spotted a parked car there after the park had closed. He investigated and found two people inside, unconscious. Mace called for help and started resuscitation, saving the lives of the two, who had been overcome by carbon monoxide.

Our officers once found a man who was shooting ducks and squirrels in Martin Park. They apprehended tree rustlers who were naïve and/or nervy enough to cut down live trees. They talked people out of fights or broke up the fisticuffs, kept order at gatherings with thousands of people, and patrolled our parks with a sharp eye for trouble, as well as assisting citizens.

In January 1987, we drastically changed our Police Department, going from 10 to four full-time officers and from 36 to 58 part-time personnel. Our goal was to schedule police hours to better cover the parks during the summer and for special events. We also needed to reduce costs; we had overspent the police budget. With this system, we could hire twice as many part-time officers who would carry guns and have full police powers, and up to 60 lower-paid officers who would be uniformed but would not carry weapons.

We also stopped calling our officers "police" and instead referred to them as "rangers." We believed that title more accurately described what we wanted from them. They were enforcers, yes, with all the powers of police, but their role was that of "host" first and "enforcer" second. After all, they came into contact with as many or more members of the public than any other employee of the district. We wanted people to feel comfortable going to them with any question or concern about the Park District, not just those involving laws and lawbreakers.

The changes worked OK but our need for security kept increasing and we had to add people. In the next 18 months, we added Magic Waters, the Mel Anderson Recreation Path, several new parks, and professional baseball at Marinelli Stadium.

The "Ranger" title lasted until 1997, when the force went back to being called "police officers." Former Chief Jerry Venable recommended the change. "The public doesn't always know what the word ranger means in terms of authority," he said, especially those members of the public who encounter rangers in less than friendly circumstances.

"We were getting no respect from the wrong-doers," Venable said. "Even though we wore uniforms and had weapons, the bad guys didn't see us in the same way as they viewed police officers. They would say, 'You're just a Ranger.'"

In 2009, the department handled 3,282 calls, an average of nine each day. The greatest number — 647 — were to check out suspicious vehicles.

In my opinion, the Park District could not provide safe parks, facilities and services without a full-time professional trained force of officers.

Nazis vs. Communists in Sinnissippi

In the summer of 1979, I was called upon to do something that sickened me. I had to sign the permit allowing the National Socialist White People's Party, a Nazi group from Virginia, to hold a rally in Sinnissippi Park.

We had consulted attorneys and knew we could not deny the permit without violating the U.S. Constitution. The right to peaceful assembly and free speech applies to everyone, no matter how distasteful their message.

The rally was held Sept. 15 at the Band Shell. Nineteen Nazis attended; most were from Chicago or Milwaukee. I don't know that anyone attended to support them, but about 35 members of the Progressive Labor Party showed up with signs of protest. The Progressives, who described themselves as Communists and said they advocated violent tactics, outshouted the Nazi speakers and threw rocks, eggs, sticks and tomatoes at the Nazis.

Police were on hand and 11 people

The Register Star, along with other media outlets, agreed to give minimal coverage to the Nazi rally, resulting in low attendance and preventing a potential major confrontation. Church leaders joined the Park District in making the request to media. This story appeared on the bottom of the Star's local page, underneath reports on the county budget and Greenwich Village Art Fair.

were arrested. More than half were members of the Labor Party. The Nazis left quietly, with no arrests in their ranks.

About 200 people attended, many of them out of curiosity. A Guilford High School teacher passed out yellow cloth triangles to remind people of how the Nazis had treated Jews. A young man played spirituals and jazz on his trumpet.

Meanwhile, 200 people gathered at Levings Lake that afternoon to picnic. Organized by the Rockford chapter of the NAACP, that event drew about 40 percent white and 60 percent black residents to celebrate fellowship and freedom.

Men's Garden Club Helps Out

Our 75th anniversary year, 1984, was a banner year for the riverfront portion of Sinnissippi Park. It got a new look with a Floral Clock and an overdue upgrade of the rose garden.

The 32-foot diameter clock was donated by the Atwood Co., which coincidentally started business in 1909, the same year the Park District began. The Atwoods also donated the timepiece from an old clock renovated at The Time Museum, a splendid collection of historical clocks at the Clock Tower that, unfortunately, no longer is in Rockford.

The Sinnissippi Floral Clock, one of seven in the nation, gets a new face every spring.

The Dream Reaches Out • 1972 – 2006

The Men's Garden Club tended the Sinnissippi rose garden for years and are building an endowment fund for its upkeep. Pictured are (from left) Darrel Rhodes, Wally Hobart, Wilbur Groskreutz, Bill Hanson, Chuck Boyer, Bob Newell, Reinhold Johnson, Don Foster, Russell Dollman, Lee Fetzer, Jo Baker of the Park District, Dick Beck, Jim Tracy, Earl Samuelson and Richard Odahl.

We are told our Floral Clock is one of only seven in the nation. Its hour hand is 11 feet long and the minute hand is seven feet. Each year, it gets a different backdrop of colorful annuals.

The rose garden, first planted in Sinnissippi in 1924, has been popular with citizens ever since. The WPA excavated the garden in 1935 to lay rocks, covered by straw and black dirt. In 1946, a newspaper reported there were 8,870 bushes in the garden, described as a "fairyland of roses." But the Park District found it hard to keep up with this demanding plant and, by the 1970s, the rose garden had deteriorated and the All-America Rose Society withdrew accreditation.

Our friends in the Men's Garden Club came to the rescue. One of their goals was to help others beautify the community, and they surely carried that out in Sinnissippi. In the summers of 1983 – 84, they discarded all but 30 of the hardiest plants in the rose garden. Then they talked rose companies into giving us 2,090 new bushes, valued at $14,000.

Club members also brought in yards and yards of peat moss and dirt to get the soil in shape, and installed more than 1,000 feet of steel edging. Their work got us back in the good graces of the Rose Society which granted probationary accreditation to the garden.

The district continued to work with the garden club on the rose garden. In 1985, we installed drainage culverts and, while we were at it, the foundation for what became a bridal gazebo.

In 1987, the district and the club were proud to host the Men's Garden Club of America's national convention. Of course, our visitors toured and admired the rose garden, enjoyed a seven-course meal, along with the music of a 17-piece orchestra. A display of fireworks topped the evening, which many thought was the best convention ever.

The partnership continued. In all, the

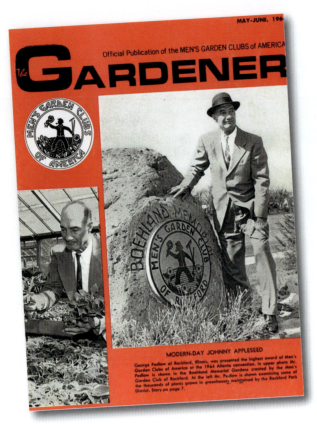

George Pedlow of the Park District and the Men's Garden Club was pictured on the cover of the national organization's magazine after the club installed the Gustav J. Boehland Memorial in Sinnissippi Garden in 1964.

They brought their national convention here again in 1963 and 1987, providing national exposure for the Park District and the city. In a way, the club was a forerunner for the Convention and Visitors Bureau and City of Gardens in terms of beautification and spreading the word about Rockford.

The Men's Garden Club has since become the Rockford Area Gardeners of America, and now includes women as members.

Forest City Queen Rules the Rock

I first started thinking about operating an excursion boat when ComEd lowered the Rock River to repair the dam. You could see smokestacks sticking up through the water near the YMCA coffee shop. That was the remains of the old Illinois passenger steamer, I was told, the excursion boat that burned in 1924 and was towed out into the river to sink. In its heyday, the boat, rechristened as the City of Rockford, carried 50,000 passengers a year.

I also learned about other local passenger boats of the past and started asking about them. It was amazing how few people had ever seen Rockford from the Rock River. Why not get a boat going again, I thought.

My first idea was to get the private sector to operate a boat, but I couldn't stir up any interest. So we at the Park District decided to do it. We got a pontoon boat and put 20 chairs on it and offered 30-minute rides. We docked near Riverview Ice House downtown on the east side of the river.

Thanks to First National Bank and its president, Howard Bell, and North Towne National Bank, people could ride free. The banks paid and the people loved it.

Very soon the banks saw the popularity of the riverboat and the value of the program. In 1979, they gave us a $47,000 grant and we ordered the Forest

club raised more than $50,000 for a perpetual care fund for the rose garden that has grown to more than $100,000. The expertise of club members with roses showed when, in 1995, 2001 and 2006, we received awards for outstanding maintenance from All-America Rose Selections.

The Men's Garden Club sold petunias to raise money and spent a lot of it helping the Park District. In the 1950s, they planted trees native to Illinois along the east side of the road in Sinnissippi. In 1963 – 64, they installed the Gustav J. Boehland Memorial in Sinnissippi in honor of a long time member of the club. They were involved in landscaping the Beattie Park Esplanade on the Rock River and helped us at both Tinker Swiss Cottage and Midway Village.

City Queen. The boat, which cost us $26,000, carried 46 passengers and docked at the Ice House. The remainder of the grant was used for its maintenance for the first five years.

The new Forest City Queen, 45 feet long and large enough for 49 passengers, was the sixth excursion boat on the river in Rockford, and the second run by the Park District. It was preceded by our 20-passenger boat and by boats dating back to the 1800s named the Illinois (City of Rockford), the Queen, May Lee, and the Arrow.

Commissioner Fleur Wright and staff member David Wiemer, we renamed it the Rockford Park District Foundation. We also reconfigured the board to include more community members. That gave us more connections with citizens.

So much of what we enjoy is possible because, from the beginning, citizens have given us millions and millions of dollars worth of land, funds, stocks, in-kind gifts, volunteer expertise, and more. In fact, 40 percent of the more than 4,650 acres we own were donated to us.

Thousands of people see Rockford and Loves Park from the river each summer during narrated cruises on the Forest City Queen.

Foundation Supports Parks

The Park District always has enjoyed extraordinary generosity from our citizens. In 1979, a foundation was formed to make it easier for people to name the Park District as a recipient of land or other gifts. It was called the Rockland Park Foundation and district board members served as trustees.

In 1993, thanks to the leadership of

Think of our Park District without Aldeen or the Ingersoll golf courses, Aldeen Park, Page Park, Levings Lake Park, Beattie Park and Playground, Carlson Ice Arena, the wondrous, new Nicholas Conservatory, and more. That's us without generous, supportive citizens. We can never thank them enough.

The first Foundation director, Mary Dinges, and the first board president, Dan Nicholas, built the Foundation into a modern and efficient organization.

The Rockford Park District Foundation encourages and processes citizen gifts to the district. The foundation also supports the City of Gardens, which leads the way in beautifying the city. For example, it hangs nearly 200 flower baskets each spring, with the help of donors and volunteers.

Dinges was succeeded by Elaine Harrington, who led the foundation during its task of raising $13 million for the Nicholas Conservatory. Current Foundation director is Stacie Talbert, who also is CFO of the Park District.

The Foundation became a leader in beautification with the City of Gardens, funded with a gift from Dan and Ruth Nicholas. The City of Gardens was first led by Judy Shields, who started a hanging basket program that brightens streets downtown, on the North End and in Midtown. Under the leadership of Ruth Miller, who succeeded Shields, the City of Gardens led three campaigns to beautify our community in national and international contests sponsored by the America in Bloom organization.

In the national contests of 2005 and 2007, Rockford took first place for its population division. More important, citizens were enthusiastic about getting involved and did yeoman's work on their own properties and in their own neighborhoods. The contests truly changed the city and winning changed some attitudes.

Ruth Miller went on to become the first manager of the Nicholas Conservatory, which will serve as the center of City of Gardens programming.

BMX Track Lauded Nationally

I suspect that most citizens are not aware there is a BMX racing track in Searls Park. But the racers know. Here is a report from the Web site bmxnow.com, about the Midwest Nationals held in Searls in the summer of 2010:

"'The Rock,' as it is lovingly called, is one of those must-attend races each year. A geographically-desirable location (close to both Chicago and Milwaukee's airports), as well as a masterfully-groomed facility which is constantly and meticulously maintained by track operators Jake and Candy Karau, plus the 60-acre park that the track sits in, all are ingredients in making the annual Midwest Nationals a deliciously-spicy BMX soup."

The article went on to mention the home nations — yes, I said nations — of some of the racers. They came from South Africa, New Zealand, Australia and, of course, all over the United States.

The internationally known track was opened in 1977 as a community service project of the Rockford Jaycees. Some believe it was the first BMX track in the Midwest.

Six years later, Jake and Candy Karau took over its operation after their son took up BMX racing. The Karaus have given their hearts, souls, sweat, toil and free time to the track for 30 years. As a result, Rockford has acquired a national reputation for its BMX track and the Rockford BMX Club has flourished.

The 1,200-foot track is in the shape of an M, with three banked corners and multiple dirt obstacles each biker has to negotiate. Together with the Park District and the BMX Club, the Karaus have spearheaded the installation of a special surface that resists erosion, along with fencing, lighting, concession stands and a storage building.

The track hosts 25,000 people each season, with racers ranging in age from 4 to over 60s. Karau tells me about 85 percent are folks from the Rock River Valley. They usually come with their families. This is not a sport where you can drop your child off and run errands or, even, sit on the bleachers. You are the coach, the equipment manager and, for young kids, the logistics expert who makes sure your child is lined up and ready to go on time. Afterward, parents are campfire builders and cooks as families spend the weekend in their RVs at Searls during a race event.

The national race each year attracts 5,000 people. Karau and his club are justifiably proud that Rockford has hosted a

Bikers take off in a World Cup race held at Searls.

Dedicated volunteers maintain and operate the track, which attracts 25,000 racers, family members and spectators each summer.

national each year since 1986. Not another city in the nation can say that. It has happened because of the Karaus and their volunteers, the care that has gone into the great track at Searls, the professionalism of the racing protocol, and the hospitality of Rockford folks.

The club also hosted the Rockford World Cup in 1998. In 2002, the track was ranked as one of the nation's top 10 BMX tracks by Transworld BMX Magazine.

The Little Trolley That (Almost) Couldn't

In 1983, we added another ride, this one on rails. We got $165,000 in federal revenue sharing money through Rockford Township for a trolley station we put on the south end of the Ice House parking lot. The Rockford Rotary Club donated $50,000 toward our $66,000 trolley, which was a replica of a turn-of-the-century, open trolley car. It was powered by a Volkswagon engine that ran on propane. The 28-foot trolley was the first in the city since 1936, when trolley service stopped and bus service began.

We gave the trolley the number, 36, to mark that bit of history. We ran it from the Ice House parking lot up Madison Street and along the river to Auburn Street, and back again, on Chicago and Northwestern railroad tracks.

The trolley gave us some problems early on. First we discovered the carriage was too low to clear the Madison Street portion of the railroad track if we filled all 44 seats. The builder had made the carriage two inches lower than we had specified. We compensated by installing bigger wheels to raise the trolley. We looked all over the continent and finally

Trolley No. 36 struggled at the beginning but she has motored along the tracks in Sinnissippi Park each summer for nearly 30 years. (Dennis Eksten photo)

Rockford Township directed federal revenue sharing to the Park District for the trolley station, which also sells tickets to the Forest City Queen.

found a Canadian firm that could make what we needed — 24-inch wheels. The builder paid for them.

The trolley started running in early September 1983. People loved it; we had almost 400 people one Sunday. Just like folks on the Forest City Queen loved waving at boaters and people on shore, the trolley riders took to waving at bikers, joggers and picnickers along the bike path.

Among our early riders were Jim and Sharon Hess. They didn't get there early enough to get tickets one weekend, but vowed to return. Jim explained to a newspaper reporter what the trolley meant to them.

"Thank goodness for the Park District," he said. "At least there's something still alive in Rockford. With this recession and so many people out of work, we needed something like this."

We had another setback on September 8, when the front axle on the trolley broke. Rockfordians came to the rescue. Four Hamilton-Sundstrand engineers redesigned the axles to withstand the stress of the 44-seat oak trolley. Said one engineer, Don Stefanelli, "Compared to the normal things we do, it was fun." He and his volunteer crew — including Bill Puskac, Bob Mezey and Dallas Augustine — were usually involved in federal projects like the B-1 bomber as staffers in Sundstrand's Aviation Division.

Their pay for working over their lunch hours and after work? The men asked for a free ride on the repaired trolley.

They got it.

People loved the novelty of the trolley. Newspaper clips show entire wedding parties taking a ride on the street car. It was a busy operation during the summer of 1984, until trouble hit us again.

We learned that the trolley had a used engine, not a new one like it should have. But the big problem was its drive system broke down and we needed to replace wheels, hubs, axles and gear cases. This time it was out of service for a year and a half. By the time we got it back, in early 1986, we discovered the city had partially paved over the tracks under the Jefferson Street viaduct. We fixed that in no time and then, guess what? We discovered yet another problem with the brakes.

Local volunteers again came to the rescue, this time Engineers from Gunite Division of Kelsey Hayes Co. Led by Bill Shinn, they designed a brake system that could handle the weight of the trolley. You think that fixed things? Of course not. We found the trolley didn't have enough clearance for a conduit used to carry wires from one end to the other. Our friendly Gunite engineers solved that problem for us, too, and we learned how to run and maintain our little Trolley No. 36, the only one like it in the world.

> *People loved the novelty of the trolley. Newspaper clips show entire wedding parties taking a ride on the street car.*

It nearly did in our deputy director, Bill Graham, though. The trolley had been his baby from the beginning. He designed it, he had visions of its popularity, and he never lost his enthusiasm through the axle and wheel and brake issues. I kept reminding him that these things weren't problems, they were just opportunities. Bill took my teasing in stride and hung in there. When we were looking for him, we'd joke, "Look under the trolley." And sometimes we'd find him there, wrench in hand. By March 1986, when we still were struggling to get No. 36 back on track, Bill had retired but continued to work for us as a consultant. His job still focused on the trolley. He would get "that turkey" running, he told the Register Star, "if it's the last thing I ever do, and it well may be."

I am happy to report that he and our competent staff and expert local engineering volunteers did get the trolley going, and Bill Graham survived, too.

In the summer of 1987, the Peoria Journal Star sent a reporter and photographer to do a story on our trolley, which had just turned its first profit by accommodating 10,681 riders in the summer of 1986. We knew it was a popular attraction — 85 percent of the riders were local. Peoria came to see how we did it.

The most recent trolley problem was a fire that nearly destroyed the car in July 2007. The trolley was repaired in Arlington, Wash., in the summer of 2008. The cost of $217,000 was covered by insurance.

Saving Money on Insurance

In the early 1980s, we faced an insurance problem shared by park agencies across Illinois. Premiums for our property, liability and workers' compensation insurance were skyrocketing. Some park districts were desperately looking for new carriers after having their policies canceled.

Here in Rockford, we had sought a solution by meeting with other

> *Ten districts joined us when, in 1984, we formed the Park District Risk Management Agency, or PDRMA.*

governmental units to talk about jointly buying insurance and, we hoped, getting a discount. But insurance companies told us our functions were too dissimilar to be covered by one program.

So we tried another tack. Don Elliot, our chief financial officer at the time, contacted other park districts in the state about starting our own insurance program. Ten districts joined us when, in 1984, we formed the Park District Risk Management Agency, or PDRMA.

The agency was a great success. Today

The Dream Reaches Out • 1972 – 2006

A trip to Discovery Center the Riverfront Museum Park is extra special on warm days when children step outside to romp on this made-to-order science playground. When built in 1991, it was the first such play area designed by the well-known Robert Leathers firm.

it serves more than 150 park districts, forest preserves and recreation associations. Over the years, PDRMA has saved tens of millions of dollars in commercial insurance costs. The agency is governed by its members, who believe in controlling costs and promoting health and safety so as to prevent losses.

I am proud that staffers here in the Rockford Park District initiated forming PDRMA. To me, it illustrates our attitude of facing a problem, looking at a myriad of proposed answers, and seeking partners who can add to the solution. It's the same way we faced other challenges but this particular one had a cost-cutting benefit for many park agencies in Illinois. It's one more way in which the Rockford Park District is a leader beyond its borders.

Wooden Playworks a Big Hit

When people walked into my office, there was no telling what the result might be. One day in the mid-1980s, two women involved in Spectrum School stopped by. Spectrum is a private school, then located at Guilford and Mulford roads. Sandy Scott and Diane Fitzgerald wanted a playground for Spectrum and they had an idea that was new to Rockford.

On a trip to Florida, Sandy had seen an unusual playground in Sarasota made to the specifications of the children who played on it. She learned it was designed by playground architect Robert Leathers of Ithaca, N.Y.

Another dream was born. By the time

Sandy and Diane came to see me, they knew all about the Leathers firm, which has a mission of designing "Unique Playgrounds, Imagined by Children, Built by Community."

Sandy and Diane learned how to raise money and came up with the $50,000 we needed. Leathers came to Spectrum and asked the kids what they wanted in the playground. Then he and his firm did the design, and we solicited volunteers for a five-day building project in May 1988.

More than a thousand people came to help as we built the 24,000-square-foot playground with its mammoth sand box, upside-down house, mirror maze, bucking bronco, balance beam, slides, phone system, yacht and cars, periscope and more. Forty percent of it was accessible to children in wheelchairs.

The finished product, which we were told was worth more than $300,000, was a huge hit, both for the Spectrum students and people in the community. As one parent said, "Every time I come here, it's packed." It quickly became known as the "wooden park" because most of the material was wood.

It wasn't long before we were working with Leathers again to build a similar playground in Liberty Park on Rockford's west side. Children, this time at Washington, Nashold and Barbour schools, were interviewed about their playground dreams. Lutheran churches led the campaign, Spectrum leaders helped, and teacher Don Kriechbaum and Park District staffer Gloria Cardenas Cudia co-chaired the project. A campaign was launched to raise a million pennies for $10,000 toward the $60,000 project. Half the cost came from a community development grant from

The Getaway, a Leathers playground in Black Hawk Park, was built in 1992 at the request of teens who asked for a wooden playground their size. The Youth Recreation Council raised $200,000 for the project.

Project Playworks I, built at the corner of Guilford and Mulford, was moved to Harlem Community Center in 1996. It was the first "wooden playground" in the Park District.

the city and the rest was donated.

The park, called Playworks II, was built by more than a thousand volunteers in May 1990. It was as big a hit as the first one. The first summer it opened, the county restricted parking near the park to safeguard children running to and from cars and the playground.

Our third Leathers project was a "first," an outdoor science playground for Discovery Center along the Rock River in the then-new Riverfront Museum Center. The multi-level science playground fits right in with the children's museum's hands-on philosophy. We built it in 1991 in partnership with the Junior League of Rockford and, of course, hundreds of volunteers.

There's more to our Leathers playground story. This part is my favorite.

We had been getting complaints from neighbors about teens hanging out at Project Playworks I at Mulford/Guilford. Then the land it was on was sold and there were fears it would be demolished. Instead, it was moved to the Harlem Community Center in 1996 where it continues to delight children.

The complaints gave us an opportunity, however. That opportunity was discovered by a group of 21 teens from nine area high schools who joined our Youth Recreation Council. We regularly met with them to talk about recreation and other issues. They came up with the idea of a playground for them, built to their size and with activities and "hang-out" havens they would enjoy.

We started developing it in 1990, using the same protocol that we did with the children's Playworks. Leathers himself came to talk with students at Jefferson and Auburn high schools about the design. He was impressed with their ideas and promised that, when the teen playground was built, people would come away saying, "Man, that was awesome."

Never have I seen a group of teens as enthusiastic and constructive as the kids on this council. They raised $200,000 for what was to be named the Getaway. Along with hundreds of their friends, both adult and youth, young people from all nine schools were there — some of the schools bused them — to help erect the first teen playground in the nation in Blackhawk Park in 1992.

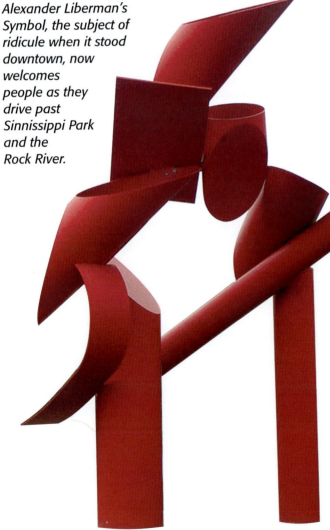

Alexander Liberman's Symbol, the subject of ridicule when it stood downtown, now welcomes people as they drive past Sinnissippi Park and the Rock River.

We continued to look to the teens for programming ideas for the Getaway, which became the site of organized activities — music, games, theater, etc. — that the teens selected. With its stage and dance floor, maze, obstacle course, teen-size swings, treehouse and other features, the Getaway continues to attract teens for informal fun as well as programs we run in the summer.

Anytime I get discouraged about the state of today's youth, I remember the dynamic force of this group of teens. They helped the Park District better serve the community and gained valuable personal experience in the process.

A final note: I mentioned that Gloria Cudia co-chaired the fund raising committee for Playworks II. Gloria was an important person to the Park District for many years. She became the first minority member of the Park Board with her appointment in 1990 to succeed Ed Carlson. The board selected her from 23 candidates.

After her term, in 1993, she joined us as a staff member and worked until 2011. Gloria's dedication, inventiveness and ties to the Hispanic population served the district and the community well.

Parks and Outdoor Art a Natural Combination

By the early 70s, Rockford was ready to add public art to its list of city assets. Funds raised by the "Beattie Is" committee, spearheaded by Robert Funderberg, made the purchase of the first sculpture possible. "Cape Variations," by John Henry, was installed in 1973 and stands today in the northwest corner of Beattie Park

The 12-foot Rockmen Guardians, by Therese Agnew, appear to protect the city from any invaders who come by way of the Rock River. The Guardians were a gift from John and Linda Anderson and the Art in the Parks Committee.

Local artist Gene Horvath added to the collection in 1974 by gifting "Sinnissippi River Crab" for the riverfront in Sinnissippi Park.

The district took a more aggressive position on public art when, in 1979, Deputy Director of Park Services Bill Graham suggested a "sculpture garden program" that would make space available along the recreational path from the YMCA to north of Auburn Street. So we were ready when the city decided, in 1984, to move Rockford's most stunning and yet most notorious piece of art, "Symbol," out of downtown.

"Symbol" had been funded through the National Endowment for the Arts (NEA), which worked with the Rockford Council for the Arts and Sciences (predecessor to the Rockford Area Arts Council) to erect a sculpture at the intersection of State and Wyman Streets. An artist and sculptor of some renown, Alexander Liberman, was picked to create a sculpture for Rockford.

He came up with a 47-foot, bright orange composition made from discarded tank drums, boiler heads, giant pipes and steel beams. Liberman saw the pieces as architectural models for everything from grain silos to Greek temples and medieval cathedrals. "To me, it symbolizes an uplifting spiritual feeling and, I hope a sense of exhilaration and of stimulation … if people react badly, fine, at least they react," he said.

Well, Rockford reacted badly from the day "Symbol" was unveiled in 1978. Local folks blamed the sculpture for the new traffic pattern downtown because streets were closed and "Symbol" was set on part of the now-demolished downtown mall.

In 1985, when the city decided to

Suspended Motion is a striking park sculpture by local artist Gene Horvath and donated by Bengt and Mary Kuller.

remove part of the mall, "Symbol" was relegated to the river bank, in pieces. We decided to give it a home and looked at various sites. The best seemed to be Sinnissippi Park, on the east bank of the river just south of Auburn Street.

Symbol seems to please most everyone in its new home, where the river, the grass and the sky are its backdrops. It's amazing how much it seemed to change, and the public perception of it certainly changed, once we found the right spot for it.

In 1990 and 1991, we acquired more art with a Rockford identity, a set of four 12-foot high granite figures entitled "Rockmen Guardians" commissioned and donated by John and Linda Anderson and the Arts in the Park Committee. Terese Agnew is the sculptor. The "Rockmen" stand along the path at Sinnissippi.

Richard A. (Dick) Behr and the Art in the Parks Committee added to the collection with two totemic sculptures created by Robert N. McCauley, artist and art professor at Rockford College.

"Inlet Markers" was added at the confluence of the Rock River and Spring Creek in 1990.

In September 1991, a statue of a man with a camera called "Sight Seeing" was dedicated at its first site along the river by the Rockford Public Library. The realistic statue by J. Seward Johnson Jr., commissioned by the Arts in the Park Committee, fooled more than one passer-by. Unfortunately, it has been vandalized more than once and is being moved to a more secure site near the Nicholas Conservatory.

Arthur W. Anderson conceived the idea of a memorial to honor veterans who served in the five wars of the 20th century. You will read about that imposing set of sculptures elsewhere in this book.

The Rockford Rotary Clubs placed a Rotary Sundial in the Rose Garden in 2000. It was designed and constructed by Rotarian Sofus Sorensen.

In the past 10 years, the following pieces of art were placed:

- 2003: Angel of Hope by Ortho Fairbanks, renamed "The Christmas Box Angel," Marino Park (formerly Waterside Park).
- 2005: "Flame," originally dedicated to Mexico by artist Leonardo Nierman, was gifted by the government of Mexico to us. A stainless steel sculpture 23 feet high, it was installed along the river north of the Auburn Street bridge.
- 2005: Local sculptor Gene Horvath's "Suspended Motion" was relocated to the Sinnissippi riverfront near the greenhouse. It was commissioned and donated by Bengt and Mary Kuller.
- 2009: "Sinnissippi Guardian" by Chicago artist Terry Karpowicz of Chicago is placed on the east side of North Second Street to overlook the Nicholas Conservatory and Gardens.

The conservatory features these works:
- "Sight Seeing," the camera man we talked about earlier
- "Dancers" by O.V. (Verne) Shaffer, a donation from CherryValley Mall/CBL Properties
- "Anemotive Kinetic," a sculpture by artist Robert Mangold and a gift from Tom and Darlene Furst.
- "Wild Flower," a 16-foot, colorful, aluminum sculpture in the fountain by Chicago native Jerry Peart.

Art will also be an important part of the inside of the Conservatory. When you visit, please pause to scan the 142-foot historical mural titled "Rock River Influences" by Bill Hueg and see the Rock River and its tributaries on the terrazzo floor designed by Linda Beaumont and titled "River Within." The floor was laid by Northern Illinois Terrazzo and Tile Co. Also note the sculptures from the Berengo Collection donated by the Joseph and Sharyn Castrogiovanni family. Made of Murano glass, they are described as "totems of the river" and were created by noted international artists Juan Ripolles, Silvio Vigiaturo and Christoph Kiefhaber.

As one observer noted, many cities envy the public art we have been trusted to display along the river. We hope the collection will grow in the future. We know that art, like recreation, is a vital part of quality of life for a city and its citizens.

Other sculptures in our properties include the "The Big Chair" by Jim Julin; "Inland Passage" by Michael Dunbar; "Prairie Till" by Mike Baur; "Twin Fin, Too" by Bruce White; "World of Information" by Josh Garber; and "The Juggler" by David Foster at the Rockford Art Museum; and "Founders" by Gene Horvath near the Park District headquarters in the 300 block of South Main.

The city is graced by sculptures elsewhere around town, including the Rock Valley and Rockford College campuses, Memorial Hall, Keeling-Puri Peace Plaza along North Perryville Road; and other locations.

"Flame", by Leonardo Nierman, a gift from the government of Mexico, stands north of the Auburn Street bridge.

Parks, Courts Partner to Help Kids

In 1979, Judge Harris Agnew came to see me. Harris was building a distinguished career which included 22 years as a circuit judge and 17 years as chief judge of the 17th Circuit by the time he retired in 1996.

Harris wanted to take advantage of a new law passed by the '79 Legislature that allowed courts to set up public service work programs with public bodies for juvenile offenders. Up until then, he told me, judges had two choices with these adolescent boys and girls — either give them probation, often seen as a "slap on the wrist," or incarcerate them. The work program seemed to him to be a valuable intermediate option that could change lives.

> *"How many juvenile court judges arrive at the critical moment without an answer to their most nagging question …*
> *'What am I going to do with you?'*
> *Harris Agnew … decided to fill that silence — and that quandary…"*
> – ROCKFORD REGISTER STAR EDITORIAL, 1981

The problem was, probation officers and the court system could not afford to staff such a program.

Harris and I agreed the opportunity was too important to pass up. I promised support of the Park District, and he went to his service organization, Rock Valley Kiwanis. Together, we put together a weekend work program at parks for juveniles supervised by two volunteer Kiwanians and Park staffers.

The program was successful and remains so today. It works with about 350 youth each year, and fewer than 10 percent of them return to the court system afterward. Working with Kiwanians and our staff, they learn not only work skills but the importance of punctuality, accountability, and self-respect.

Park staffers handle the program now, but through the years it received invaluable assistance from the Rock Valley Heritage Kiwanis, Kiwanis Club of Rockford, Golden K Kiwanis, Alpine Kiwanis, Notre Dame Club, Phi Delta Kappa and VietNow. These adults impressed the young people, not only with their mentoring but just the fact they took time out of their weekends to spend with kids who were strangers to them.

Harris says he knows of no similar program that has lasted this long. And, based on the troubles in the world today, he adds, "it is needed now more than ever."

Respecting the Mounds

When the Park District accepted a gift of 3.4 acres in downtown Rockford from Mary and Anna Beattie in 1921, the Beattie sisters stipulated that the site be a "place of rest and relaxation…

"…Said park shall not be used as a public playground for noisy or boisterous sports, or for other uses which might tend to disturb or annoy the peace and quiet of those seeking relaxation or rest therein, or of the surrounding neighborhood."

The Beatties also expressed "earnest" hope that "the mounds and the native trees now peculiar to the premises be not destroyed but rather preserved and maintained … they also hope that roads or driveways shall not be constructed or laid out through the premises…"

In 1924, we put a gazebo on the site near the river. That still stands, along with the Naval Memorial installed in 1972. We installed a boat dock in 1977. The rest of the park was grass, which we mowed and maintained.

Indian dancers perform at the Honor the Mounds gathering in Beattie Park each summer.

We turned down several requests from the city to use part of the park for a road.

In 1973, we let the Rockford Arts Council use the park for the first "Beattie Is …" arts festival. As the festival grew each year, we began to hear from people who were concerned about the mounds.

David Van Pernis headed the next door Indian Terrace Neighborhood Association. He and his group had done research showing some of the mounds to be around 1,500 years old. Two are thought to be burial mounds. One is linear and the other is an effigy mound in the shape of a turtle. Others had been destroyed by nearby construction during the years. Besides their sacred history, the mounds are valuable because the turtle is the only effigy mound in Illinois on public land.

Van Pernis and others were concerned that continued trampling would destroy what was left of the mounds. And indeed, "Beattie is…." did leave the park in sad shape. In June of 1988, we started pumping water out of the river to water the grass after a six-week dry spell and the beating it took from 150,000 people walking on it during the art festival.

Van Pernis also questioned how we thought we were living up to the agreement we had made with the Beattie sisters. Since 1921, he noted, 40 trees were gone, a bike path was built over one of the mounds, the rest had been eroded and the park was not restful, especially during festivals.

In 1975 we put up a bronze plaque commemorating the mounds but it wasn't enough. Finally, in January 1989, the Park Board voted to deny holding any new festivals in Beattie Park, to allow temporary structures such as tents to be erected only on park areas away from the mounds, and to ban scheduled sports events and motorized vehicles except for maintenance

The Burpee Museum of Natural History can trace its origins and relationship to the Park District back to 1911. Of course, the family trees of its stars, dinosaurs Jane and Homer, go back much further than that.

equipment. We gave the "Beattie Is …" festival one more year to use the park and then asked them to find another site.

The art festival did find another site. And in 1995, we found a reason to permit a new festival to use the park. The Honor the Mounds Gathering has been held each summer since then. It's an all-day event in which native Americans and others enjoy drumming, dances, speakers and living history events in Beattie Park, where they respect the mounds and honor the people who built them.

Museums Live and Work Together

In the 1980s we got deeply involved in projects that led to a marked improvement in quality of life for our citizens and made us a destination for people from out of town. We developed a unique relationship to the Rockford Area Convention and Visitors Bureau to promote local attractions, including museums, sports facilities and a water park.

Not to boast, but I would judge this effort a success. I believe we made a positive difference in this community.

First, the museums. The Park District was just two years old when the Mandeville family donated their home in what is now Mandeville Park on Montague Road. Included in the gift were rare and valuable specimens of Indian relics and other items. You have read about how that collection and others evolved into the Burpee Museum of Natural History. During the same time, people who loved art were collecting and trying to establish a museum.

Both the natural history and art groups moved to North Main Street in the 1930s in arrangements that were the basis for what has developed today.

That setup worked for 30-some years.

It changed in 1971 when the Park District moved into new headquarters in Sinnissippi Park and contemplated selling the 813 N. Main building. Happily, that idea was put aside and the building instead was turned over to the Burpee Museum of Natural History, which had been on the upper floors and now expanded to the ground floor.

Both the Art Museum and Burpee Museum began the most exciting chapters of their existences in 1985, when the Sears Corporation offered to donate its store at 711 N. Main St. to the Rockford Art Association. The property transfer was completed in February 1986 but the art museum did not move into the old store. Instead, the Art Association ordered a study of how to best use the building and

The skeleton of Jane the dinosaur was buried for 66 million years until she was unearthed by Burpee Museum staff and volunteers. Lew Crampton was the director of Burpee at the time; he was succeeded by Alan Brown. (Photo by Dave Monk)

Burpee Museum's exhibit of a prehistoric forest contains lots of surprises.

the cost of turning it into a museum.

When it was determined the art museum did not need the 130,000 square feet of space in the building, there was talk of using the building as a home for various arts and science organizations. The association recruited the Discovery Center children's museum, Rockford Symphony Orchestra, Rockford Dance Company, Northern Public Radio and the Rockford Film Projects/Storefront Cinema. All those organizations came to the Park District for help in developing an arts/science building.

We said we'd get involved under four conditions: The Art Association had to pay off its debt; $1.7 million must be raised to renovate the building; the museum tax fund must go up from 3 to 7 cents; and a governance structure must be worked out by the agencies that would make their home in the old Sears.

This deal wasn't easy – it seems big, worthwhile projects never are. A capital campaign drive with a goal of $1.7 million was started. Led by then-Sundstrand CEO Harry C. Stonecipher and community arts activist Sally Funderberg, it had a great start with a lead gift of $1 million from Sundstrand and a $500,000 gift from Harry and Joan Stonecipher. But cost estimates on renovating the building went up and up. The drive continued and, in the end, $5.5 million was raised, including $900,000 from the Park District and $300,000 from the state's Build Illinois fund.

The Sears store, while a great space and location, had to be redone extensively to accommodate offices for arts organizations and facilities for art exhibits, a dance company, a children's museum, radio broadcasting facilities and a small movie theater. There were special concerns. For example, the air conditioning system had to be just right to preserve the art pieces that would be stored and/or displayed.

The other challenge was having the organizations come together with a system of managing the building. They had all been separate; getting them to live under the same basic rules was not as easy as it might sound. Jo Baker was instrumental in the success of that, as were the heads of the arts groups themselves. When everything was said and done, they all realized their organizations would flourish if they shared overhead costs and presented an impressive museum/arts front to the community.

Children love playing in the hands-on Discovery Center in Riverfront Museum Center. Don't tell them, but they're learning, too.

In February 1991, the Riverfront Museum Park opened. In the next 18 months, the nation's first community-built outdoor science park opened in conjunction with Discovery Center and an outdoor gallery, the Ahlstrand Sculpture Garden, was established.

The Park District is the proud owner of the building and the proud landlord of these organizations. They have done much to entertain, educate and inspire the community. Here is a brief picture of our partner museums:

- The Rockford Art Museum, which began as a small local arts group in 1913, operates one of the largest gallery spaces in Illinois and has frequently been named a Partner in Excellence of the Illinois Arts Council. Two galleries feature contemporary exhibits of regional and national art. Another devotes more than 5,000 square feet of space to the museum's permanent collection, with artwork rotated in and out from the 1,600 pieces. There's also a collection of contemporary art glass.
- Burpee Natural History Museum won international acclaim for its work in paleontology. The "star" is Jane, a teenage dinosaur uncovered by staff and volunteers in Montana. The dinosaur is named Jane in honor of the wife of Robert Solem. The Solems donated more than $3.5 million to Burpee for its expansion and dinosaur digs.
- Discovery Center Museum is a children's museum started by the Rockford Junior League and Rockford Arts Council in 1980. It has become one of the best in the nation. When parents want a few hours in which they don't have to be telling children "don't touch," they take them to Discovery Center, which has more than 200 "hands-on" exhibits. It's a grand place where children have fun as they learn,

Who doesn't like to play in the water? At Discovery Center, learning is spelled f-u-n.

and parents can stand back and enjoy. It also features the first community-built outdoor science park in the nation, designed by renowned Ithaca, N.Y. architect Robert Leathers and sponsored by the Junior League, the Park District and Discovery Center. Hundreds of volunteers helped build the science playground over 12 days in the summer of 1991.
- Rockford Symphony Orchestra and Rockford Area Youth Symphony Orchestra (RSO and RAYSO) have their offices, music library, box office and classrooms in Riverfront. RSO, which performs at Coronado Performing Arts Center, was named Illinois' Orchestra of the Year in 2007, thanks to its dynamic conductor, Steven Larsen.
- The Rockford Dance Company matches the excellence of the symphony. Its

The Rockford Art Museum has a section for traveling exhibits as well as a permanent collection, rotated on display, that includes 1,500 pieces representing modern and contemporary American art, American Masters from 1830-1940, photography, contemporary glass, and outsider art.

dancers make up the resident dance company for the Coronado. The company also provides top-notch dance instruction. Studios in Riverfront are equipped with two-way mirrors so visitors can see rehearsals, props, costume storage and offices.

- Northern Public Radio is the umbrella organization for the broadcasting services of Northern Illinois Studios. Affiliated with Northern Illinois University, stations WNIU 89.5 FM and WNIJ 90.5/105.7 are joined with Northern Illinois Radio Information Service, a closed-circuit radio channel for visually impaired people.

The final partner in this building, Storefront Cinema, which specialized in classic and alternative movies, closed in 2003.

We have two other museum partners we're equally proud of:

- Tinker Swiss Cottage, the magnificent home built in 1865 by Park District founder Robert Tinker. Perched on the edge of a limestone bluff overlooking Kent Creek on the city's southwest side, the home is filled with original furnishings, artwork, diaries and household items. The property includes a suspension bridge high across the creek, a three-story barn and gardens modeled after the originals maintained by the Tinkers.
- Midway Village and Museum Center, the 137-acre complex on the city's east side that contains a museum plus a village of reconstructed local buildings around 100 years old. It's chock full of local history and fun for families and attracts folks from near and far.

I hope readers appreciate this fine "family" of museums. All have rich and long histories. All were kept alive during lean years by people who had a passion for art, local and natural history, and who never quit on their dreams. Rockford boasts a group of museums that would make towns twice our size proud. I am thrilled the Rockford Park District could play a role in giving them the wherewithal and encouragement to grow.

Bright Lights and Sportscores

We all learned a new word, and sound — remember the vuvuzelas[3] — in 2010 when we watched the World Cup soccer playoffs on television. You didn't watch? Well, more people did than watched the Yankees beat the Phillies the fall before in baseball's World Series.

Some of those viewers grew up playing soccer in Rockford, at schools and neighborhood parks and, especially, in Sportscores One and Two.

We opened the first Sportscore in Veterans Memorial Park along North Main in 1983. The complex contained eight soccer fields and eight lighted softball diamonds. It was our first large soccer facility, built in response to requests from local teams that had a limited number of fields on which to play. Later, a growing number of professionals who came from England also asked for soccer fields. They had grown up with soccer the way American kids follow baseball and football. A fall 1983 adult soccer tournament attracted 750 players, double the number of a year before.

Soccer was growing as a youth sport, too. A local soccer organization doubled its membership — to 2,400 kids — between 1980 and 1982.

We were serving our local players, but had not yet thought of maximizing the use

This is an aerial view of Sportscore One, which includes eight lighted softball diamonds, eight regulation soccer fields and nine practice fields, concessions, playgrounds, locker facilities, boat ramps and a recreation path.

Girls play softball in this photo from Sportscore One.

new job was to increase the tourism dollars spent here.

Working with local sports groups and national organizations, they made Rockford a center of regional soccer play. After Bob and his turf expert, Steve Roser, were through, Sportscore One was one of the best fields in the nation. Wendy and Bob spread the word to athletic organizations around the Midwest and, before long, motel chains were building near the Interstate to accommodate, in part, the athletes and their families who were coming here weekends. Another person who was instrumental in bringing in tournaments was Brenda Paulson of the U.S. Softball Association.

A man from Granite City expressed what many people told us about Sportscore and our city. He wrote a letter to the editor of the Register Star thanking Rockford for its hospitality when his family

of our facilities by bringing teams in from elsewhere.

Enter Wendy Perks Fisher, who had worked for us as a teacher putting on plays with Camp Sunshine kids in our showmobile. Wendy went on to head the National Committee: Arts for the Handicapped in Washington, D.C., before coming back to her hometown as director of the Rockford Area Convention and Visitors Bureau in 1986.

Wendy paid a visit to Sportscore One one weekend and asked Bob Papich, the fields' manager, why no one was there. Papich replied that the fields were busy Mondays through Fridays, but on the weekends, all the players were at out-of-town tournaments.

Click! Why not have tournaments here? Wendy and Bob were the perfect duo to start this (soccer) ball rolling. Bob knew there were local youth who were excellent soccer players who couldn't afford the travel for out-of-town games. And Wendy's

Future soccer stars go after the ball.

This is an aerial view of Sportscore Two. The complex includes 19 regulation soccer fields and 14 practice fields outdoors, five sand volleyball courts and the Indoor Sports Center containing three multi-sport surfaces. Among the games played here are soccer, rugby, football, volleyball, golf, softball, basketball, wiffle ball, dodgeball, ultimate Frisbee, adapted sports and wheelchair sports.

brought his son for a soccer tryout.

"The sports complex is extremely impressive, and the people of Rockford who had the foresight to build a complex of this magnitude should be commended," he wrote.

Well, sir, he ought to see us now.

Weekend softball and soccer tournaments became the norm at Sportscore One. The United Watermelon Tournament, started in 1984, was bringing in 2,000 athletes from 152 teams by 1993. We had earned a reputation that enabled us to get tournaments like the American Softball Association girls national championship in 1995 with 70 teams.

Once quiet on weekends, Sportscore One now saw activity from dawn to dusk. "Every weekend in August will be a busy one" at Sportscore, said a newspaper article in 1993. A sports columnist wrote that our "overflow" facility, a private field called Wedgbury, was as "overflowed" as Sportscore, which had to create makeshift fields and start games at 8 a.m. for some tournaments.

As we entered the new century, we started planning for Sportscore Two. We needed it if we were to serve the growing local numbers of athletes and continue to bring in the weekend tournaments that, by now, had a significant impact on tourism dollars spent here. We picked a site near the Interstate and Riverside Boulevard. Local business and civic leaders raised almost $2 million for the project. Our state lawmakers — Chuck Jefferson, Dave Winters, Ron Wait, Dave Syverson and Brad Burzynski — nabbed another half-million through the Legislature's Member Initiatives Program.

In 2001, we broke ground on Sportscore Two, a 150-acre site which would have 20 professional soccer fields, a neighborhood park and playground, and walking paths. By 2005, it had earned the distinction of being the Soccer Complex of the Year for parks, a title conferred by the Sports Turf Managers Association.

An unplanned and huge enhancement to Sportscore Two came along in 2001 when owners of the Wedgbury Sports Complex, next door to our new soccer fields, offered to sell. They asked us to pay off the remaining $2.5 million mortgage and the Indoor Sports Center with its Skybox restaurant and three indoor multi-sport fields and 40 acres would be ours. The complex was valued at $4 million. We borrowed the money and are paying it back with Sportscore Two revenue. The offer was too good to pass up, and the resulting sports complex is one of the best in the Midwest.

So we have the 105-acre Sportscore One on North Main, with eight lighted softball diamonds, eight regulation soccer fields, nine soccer fields in the Atwood Soccer Center, locker facilities, playgrounds, concessions, boat ramps and a red path. It has more than 1 million visitors each year.

And, Sportscore Two, a 124-acre site with 19 regulation soccer fields, 14 practice fields, five sand volleyball courts, and three multi-sport fields indoors. The

Volleyball and other activities are played on this hard court in the Indoor Sports Center.

The Atwood family donated funds for this soccer center at Sportscore One.

complex hosts players for soccer, rugby, volleyball, basketball, wiffle ball, dodgeball, ultimate Frisbee, adapted and wheelchair sports and golf. During an average season, more than 4,000 soccer teams play at Sportscore Two.

Wedgbury Stadium seats 2,000 spectators for soccer, football and rugby games.

And those motels we talked about when we started in on this Sportscore topic? Let's just say if you want a room during the summer months, book early.

Tourism now brings in about $300 million to the Rock River Valley each year, supporting 3,000 jobs. The Rockford Area Convention and Visitors Bureau (RACVB) reported 7.7 million visitors at 40 sites and attractions in 2010.

Leading the list were our Sportscores and Indoor Sports Center, credited with attracting 2.5 million people.

Other major entertainment/recreation draws are Rock Cut State Park, the BMO Harris Bank Center (you may still think of it as the MetroCentre), Riverview and Carlson ice houses, Magic Waters, golf courses, Rockford Riverhawks, Discovery Center, Lockwood Park Trailside Center, Volcano Falls Adventure Park, Anderson Japanese Gardens, Klehm Arboretum, Coronado and Starlight theaters, Burpee Museum of Natural History, Midway Village, the Rockford Art Museum, Tinker Swiss Cottage, Coco Key, the Rockford Speedway, and others. The Park District has a strong connection to more than half a dozen of those attractions. If you've been paying attention, you know which ones.

This chapter can't end without a word about the relationship between the Park District and the Convention and Visitors Bureau. Wendy and I collaborated closely on many, many projects. We shared some common goals and worked to bring our staffs together to achieve them. Our philosophy was that if the RACVB needed help, our people responded immediately, and vice versa.

While tourism isn't the primary responsibility of the Park District, tourism did enable us to provide better recreational facilities to local taxpayers at less cost. As Wendy said, we were not promoting just recreation or just tourism, we were building community.

One more word about Sportscore One. We had a big problem up there when we first opened with the lights on our softball fields. Neighbors across the river complained that they couldn't block out the light, even to sleep. One resident said he could sit in his living room at 10:00 at night and read the newspaper without turning a light on.

That issue went to the courts. We found the best lighting expert in the country and finally, we worked it out to most everyone's satisfaction. It required a new lighting system and a modified operational schedule imposed by the court, which remains in effect. It's an example of the varied education you get working in the fascinating field of public recreation.

Inspirations in ice

In January 2011, Rockford hosted the 25th annual Illinois Snow Sculpture Competition with nine adult teams and 14 high school groups creating works of art at Sinnissippi Park. As the sculptures were completed Saturday morning, January 22, carloads of sightseers and dozens of walkers wended their way through the park to see the art pieces before blowing snow or a hot sun took a toll on them.

That tradition began during the winter of 1985 – 86 when local businessmen Denny Johnson and Brian Hampton were "up north" in Eagle River, Wis., on a snowmobile vacation. They came upon a sculpture of the Statue of Liberty made out of snow. They were so impressed that they got information about the sculptors and came to see me when they got back to Rockford.

"That sculpture was of such interest to local people up in northern Wisconsin, I thought it would be an excellent thing to bring back to Rockford," Denny said years later.

We agreed that Sinnissippi Park by the greenhouses would be a good site for a frozen piece of art, and between Denny, Ald. Frank Beach, Brian and the Park District, we got the sculptors from Eagle River to come down and carve us a Statue of Liberty, a Liberty Bell and an American eagle. The pieces attracted a lot of attention, even rating a story and photo in the Milwaukee Journal newspaper, besides local press coverage, of course.

The Park District hosts the Illinois Snow Sculpting Contest at Sinnissippi Park each year, thanks to citizens Denny Johnson and Brian Hampton, who brought a sculptor to town in January 1986 to carve this Statue of Liberty. Residents were enchanted with the snow carving and now turn out by the thousands to view entries in the state contest each year.

here on their way to Milwaukee for international competition.

In 2011, we had nine teams in the competition, one just exhibiting and 14 local high school teams. The high school contest is very popular as teams of four students, under the guidance of a teacher who can coach but cannot carve, produce some of the favorite sculptures of the event. The competition comes at an ideal time when we're still in the dead of winter but the holidays are over, the football season (usually) is over and people are looking for weekend things to do.

The princess kisses the frog in this whimsical snow carving.

Snow carvings are large but detailed and, sometimes, delicate. They also are best viewed immediately, because the warming temperatures, wind and snow take a toll.

Lady Liberty eventually melted but the idea of snow sculpting in Rockford did not. Denny had gone to Milwaukee to investigate a snow sculpting competition there and signed us up to host the Illinois Snow Sculpting contest, which we held in January 1986 at Sinnissippi. The participants included teams from France, Italy and Canada.

Rockford, in northern Illinois, was an ideal site for the competition and we've held the contest every year — except for 2003 and 2009 when the weather just would not cooperate. Besides local and Illinois snow artists, we attract sculptors from around the world who "warm up"

You Never Know What You Can Do

Early on I laid out the goals of the Park District as:

1: Offer recreational opportunities citizens want but cannot provide for themselves.

2: Help not-for-profit organizations that have missions similar to ours.

3: Be a voice for those whose recreational needs are not being met.

4: Advocate for unmet park and recreational needs.

Denny Johnson reminded me recently of how important that philosophy has been to Kids Around the World, an organization headquartered in Rockford that has built more than 140 playgrounds in the poorest neighborhoods imaginable in 27 countries. All this while not overlooking their home town, where Kids has put up 25 playgrounds.

Mention of Kids Around the World belongs in this book because of the Park District's role in getting Kids off the ground. As Denny put it, "It goes back to the standard set by Webbs Norman and his staff, the attitude of 'let's do it together.' When we talked to the Park District about putting playgrounds around the world, Webbs said, 'Let's go ahead and build one in Rockford. You can use our staff to help and we'll show you how, we'll train your people.'

"The Park District had influence and expertise. What entrepreneurs and idea people need is the support of people who have financial wherewithal or expertise to make it happen," added Denny. "That's where Webbs and the Park District came in.

"If you went to the Park District with a new idea, they wouldn't say 'you can't do that' or 'that doesn't make sense' or 'that will never happen.' They would say, 'that's a great idea, let's figure out how to make it happen.'"

I'm proud of how we helped Kids get its start, and hope we made a similar difference to other organizations, large and small, through the years.

Marinelli Field for Baseball, and Beer

From its beginning, Rockford has been a baseball town. The game got a boost in the 1860s when soldiers training for the Civil War learned to play at military camps. After the war, they brought the game home.

Here, the Forest Citys were formed and became a team of national renown. Stars included Albert Spalding, a Byron native and Hall of Famer who went on to make a fortune in the sporting goods business, Adrian "Cap" Anson, who went on to a Hall of Fame career with the Philadelphia Athletics and Chicago White Stockings, and Ross Barnes, who later was the National League's first batting champ.

The Forest Citys team was among the earliest in the nation to pay their players, in effect, becoming a professional team. Games were played at the Agricultural Society Fair Grounds, now Fair Grounds Park. The team joined the National Association of Professional Base Ball Players, which later became the National League we know today, in its initial year of

> *"If you went to the Park District with a new idea, they wouldn't say 'you can't do that' or 'that doesn't make sense' or 'that will never happen.' They would say, 'that's a great idea, let's figure out how to make it happen.'"*
> – DENNY JOHNSON

The Dream Reaches Out • 1972 – 2006

Nearly 160,000 fans attended pro baseball games at Marinelli Field when the Rockford Expos played there in 1988.

operation, 1871. Other cities with teams included Boston, Philadelphia, Brooklyn, New York, Chicago, Cleveland, Baltimore and St. Louis.

Rockford had a lousy record and other troubles in 1871, its first year in the National organization, and dropped out to join the Northwestern League, the first minor league in the country. From that time up until the 1920s, the city usually had a minor league team.

In the 1940s, the famous Rockford Peaches[4] played here at Beyer Stadium and from 1947 to 1949, the Rockford Rox provided minor league baseball.

Baseball prospered, however, and the best of it locally was played at the diamond at Blackhawk Park. The Rockford Blackhawks played there and won state titles in 1969 and '70. The diamond was named for their manager, Louis F. Marinelli, who died of cancer in 1971.

The State Legion tournament was held there in 1974, and Rockford East Regional IHSA Baseball Tournament in 1985.

Pro baseball returned only after a typical Rockford argument over selling beer at the ball park. The ball park, Marinelli, belonged to the Rockford Park District, and our stance against the sale of consumption of alcohol was as old as the district. Many folks did not want to make an exception, even for baseball.

Here's what happened. State Rep. John Hallock lobbied long to bring a minor league team to Rockford. In the late 1980s, he stirred some interest and came to the Park Board with a proposal. Boiled down, what it amounted to was we had a good chance to get a team if we invested about $1 million in Marinelli Field and changed our rules to allow the sale of beer and wine at minor league baseball games.

We decided to borrow for the stadium

233

State Rep. Zeke Giorgi (left) and state Rep. John Hallock show off their Rockford Expos jackets. They earned them, helping us get an $800,000 state grant that was partially used to remodel Marinelli Field.

improvements. Bids came in way over budget but we finally got them down to what we could afford. Hallock and our good friend, state Sen. Zeke Giorgi, helped us get a state grant for the work. We remodeled the stadium, just about doubled the number of seats to 3,200 and were ready to go by the spring of 1988.

Before we go on about the stadium, I must tell you the story of how we got that state money. Zeke and John were great to us — well, all our senators and representatives have been.

Now, this was 20-some years ago and communications technology was not what it is now. One Friday night at about a quarter to nine I got a call from Hallock. He said "Zeke and I are having lunch with the governor tomorrow at noon. Get your plans to me (for the baseball field and other projects). We'll get you some money."

I called staff planner Dave Wiemer and said, you've got to get those plans to Springfield by noon tomorrow. Dave put them on a Greyhound bus, they arrived on time, and Zeke and John got $800,000 for us.

No FAXes, no texts, no cell phones, no IPods, but we still got the job done.

A thornier issue was whether we could sell beer at the park. Owners of the team said they wouldn't come here without beer sales. They needed the revenue.

We did a survey of 150 cities which had minor league baseball clubs. All 150 sold beer at the games. We proposed selling beer, while also setting aside a large block of seats as a family section where no alcohol or smoking would be allowed.

Ed Carlson, who headed the Park Board at the time, was against beer sales. Mayor John McNamara and County Board Chairman John Terranova had the opposite view.

"Baseball bogged in beer," said the Register Star's headline over one story.

"I think that is the only way we're going to get a professional team, and I think it is a reasonable request," said McNamara of the beer sales proposal. "I respect Mr. Carlson's opinion, but I think that it would be OK for professional games at one location in a park."

Ald. Tom Przytulski, the 7th Ward Democrat, put it another way: "For a thing to get bogged down on one issue like beer is beyond me. It's a good thing these people weren't around when Jesus Christ had the Last Supper or they would have been thirsty when they got done eating."

Asked Ald. Christie Cacciapaglia, Democrat – 11th, "Have you ever been to a ball game where they didn't sell beer, hot dogs, popcorn and peanuts?"

"Maybe we'd be unique in the minor leagues by having no alcohol in our park, kind of like the Chicago Cubs are in the major leagues by having no lights in Wrigley Field," countered Carlson.

> *"Have you ever been to a ball game where they didn't sell beer, hot dogs, popcorn and peanuts?"*
> – ALD. CHRISTIE CACCIAPAGLIA

At a public hearing June 14, 1987, cries of "Amen" and "Glory" were heard after comments against beer sales. The hearing was supposed to be about whether Rockford should have a team but it focused on beer sales. A teacher warned that selling beer at ball games would lead to children associating alcohol with enjoying sports.

Others insisted no one had the right to legislate the morality of drinking beer at a ball game. A 24-year-old told city fathers if they wanted young professionals to stay in town, they needed to give them attractions like baseball, with beer.

The board voted 4 – 1 to allow the sale of beer and wine for games and got busy on improvements. By spring of 1988, Marinelli Field was ready for the Rockford Expos, the Montreal farm club team which played five years there.

The first year, attendance was nearly 159,000, the seasonal high for the 15 years minor league baseball was played at Marinelli Field. After the Expos' five-year run came the Royals for two years, the Cubbies for four, and the Reds for one. There was no professional baseball here in 2000 and 2001 but in 2002 the Riverhawks, an independent team, opened a three-year stint at Marinelli and then moved to their brand new facility, the privately-owned Road Ranger Stadium near the interstate in Loves Park.

Seasonal attendance at Marinelli was never again as high as it was in 1988, when the team had a sterling 84-win/56-loss record, but it never went below 50,000.

Among the pros who got their careers started in Rockford are slugger Adam Dunn, signed with the Chicago White Sox for 2011, and Mike Quade, who succeeded Lou Pinnella as Chicago Cubs manager late in the 2010 season. Dunn played here in 1999 and Quade managed here in 1989 – 90.

Other pros who played here include Miguel Batista, Archi Cianfrocco, Johnny Damon, Delino DeShields, Scott Downs, Kyle Farnsworth, Sal Fasano, Jon Garland, Mark Grudzielanek, Tim Laker, Brandon Larson, Kyle Lohse, Brian Looney, Rodney Myers, Matt Stairs, Mike Sweeney and Dewayne Wise. If you're a White Sox fan, you know about Wise. He made a spectacular catch that stopped a home run and preserved a perfect game for Sox pitcher Mark Buehrle on July 23, 2009.

Another Rockford baseball rookie, Quincy Carter, turned to football and quarterbacked for the Dallas Cowboys from 2001 – 2003.

Of course, baseball and softball remain a big part of the Park District with diamonds at more than 70 of our properties.

Crossing the River Safely

For years I was concerned about the safety of children and teens crossing the river. Some were going to or coming from Riverview Ice House and, rather than walk to where they could get onto the sidewalk of the Jefferson Street Bridge, they would go down to the river and make their way across by climbing on the bridge supports under the traffic or walking on the ice.

I asked a local engineer to give us a plan for a pedestrian walkway under the bridge and he responded in, shall we say, a less than positive manner. In fact, he came to a board meeting and told commissioners that the idea was the dumbest thing he had ever heard, that such a bridge was nearly structurally impossible and, if it could be done, would cost millions. Guess how that made me feel?

So, I went to see landscape architect John R. Cook, who had helped us on other projects. John's philosophy was that if you wanted to do something badly enough, you could find a way.

And John did, in short order. He figured out that we could fix the walkway on to the piers that were securely anchored in the river and were holding up the bridge. The other engineers said the only way to do it was to hang it from the vehicle bridge. With John's idea, the vehicle bridge wasn't affected at all.

We applied for a grant from the state's Build Illinois program and pointed out the walkway would connect with the Sinnissippi bike path and contribute to the downtown pathways the city was working toward. Build Illinois gave us $700,000 and we got to work.

The walkway was a great success. As with anything new, we had to go through a

This pedestrian bridge under the Jefferson Street bridge ended the dangerous practice of people, especially children, crossing the river on the ice and/or hanging onto the supports of the bridge.

Magic Waters opened in 1984 as a privately-owned facility, but the Park District was involved in its planning.

learning process, in our case getting bicyclists to walk their bikes across and skateboarders to carry their boards across. But the walkway became part of the pedestrian route in the city and remains a safe way to cross the river today for joggers and pedestrians.

We dedicated the walkway in June 1988 with the Phantom Regiment Cadets leading a parade across the bridge before the ceremony. The Register Star editorially called the walkway the city's newest downtown marvel and gave credit to "Rockford's innovative, if not audacious, Park District." The real credit goes to John R. Cook.

In our dedication pamphlet, we said, "This walkway is an outstanding example of the achievements we can accomplish when all of us commit to a common goal and cooperate to improve our quality of life. We extend our respect and admiration to those who have helped…"

Magic Waters a Great Asset to Region

I first heard of wave pools in the 1960s when I worked in Oak Park and met a man named J. Austin Smith, who held a franchise for wave pools in the United States. J. Austin needed to drum up business; at that time, there were no wave pools in the U.S. although they were quite popular in Europe. He wanted me to lead the charge by installing a wave pool in the Oak Park District but I didn't push it. I had never seen one and while I thought they were a good idea, I got cold feet.

After a few years in Rockford, I went back to the idea as part of a regional aquatic center I believed we should develop. I was looking for a revenue-generator and I knew none of the swim pools was big enough or exciting enough to become that. I told the board that regional recreation centers — in this case,

More than 200,000 people, mostly from the Rockford area, western suburbs and southern Wisconsin, enjoy Magic Waters each summer.

an aquatic center — were necessary in the 1980s if we were to grow.

After three years of study, we proposed building a water park in 1980. It would be on 20 acres off of Interstate 90, just east of the former theaters at CherryVale Mall. We figured we could get grants and perhaps a land donation, and pay for the rest through user fees rather than tax money. We knew water parks were money-makers, as opposed to swim pools which cost money.

Water parks were a new feature on the American scene. By 1980, there were only 24 wave action pools in the nation, some still under construction. Europe had had them for decades. Wisconsin Dells was just beginning to build water parks and we knew they would attract people from northern Illinois. As of yet, there was not a wave pool in the state of Illinois. The closest one was in Pontiac, Mich.

We knew there was a local demand for additional water recreation features. We figured a park could accommodate up to 4,000 people at a time, compared with less than half that number at our three pools combined. The Rockford area had a population above 250,000, we pointed out, while the number went to 700,000 if we counted everyone in a 50-mile radius. With a wave pool, water slides, water playground, sun deck, sand beach and a lake for paddle boats, we expected to draw users from that radius and beyond.

We had the usual objections, including, "It's a good idea but the private sector should do it." As it turned out, we had to drop the plan when the Illinois Department of Conservation granted the Park District funding for only one land purchase, and the board decided on Sportscore One. At the time, we estimated a water park would cost $5 million.

The project was taken over by private investors, who adopted our plans with our blessing. The park opened late in June 1984 but things did not go well. The weather was cooler than usual for several summers. Many people said admission was too high; they stayed home. In 1986, the park filed for bankruptcy.

The former AMcore Bank took it back and, in a surprise move, offered it to us. By January 1988, we were deep into discussions with AMcore. The agreement we reached was that the bank would build a third feature attraction and the Park District would pay $2.85 million for Magic Waters, which was valued at around $6 million. If we could make it work, we had a bargain. If not, we could give it back, no questions asked.

After turning down building the park eight years earlier, it seemed the board couldn't wait to try it. I expected some discussion. But when the bank put the Magic Waters proposal on the table, commissioners went right to a vote and accepted the deal.

We opened on May 27, 1988, with admission fees of $6, down from $10, and a

What's better than a slow tube ride down the Lazy River on a hot sunny day?

This little girl is making summer memories at Magic Waters.

new tube slide to go with the 3- and 5-story water slides and the heated wave pool. A month later, we inaugurated bus service to Magic Waters with cooperation from the Rockford Mass Transit service.

The weather gods were with us. The fourth hottest summer on record gave us 43 days with temps above 90 degrees, nine of them with temps of 100 or more. It was so hot that 20 prisoners got early release from the Winnebago County Jail in June when an air conditioner broke down.

At the end, attendance was up 70,000 over the year before, to 210,000. We took in $1.5 million and spent $710,000 in expenses. We could tell residents none of their fun cost a dime in tax revenues.

Today Magic Waters remains one of the money-makers of the Park District. We've added features every two or three years to keep people coming back. We had 206,120 users in 2009 and have become known throughout the Northwest Suburbs as the place to go for summer water fun.

One more thing. You may be interested in how we got the name, "Magic Waters." It came to me one day in the late 1970s as

I rode a bus past Disney World toward Ocala, Fla. A few Rockford folks and I were checking out water parks on a trip hosted by local mall developer Charlie Barnes. Charlie had the group in stitches when he suggested that if we built a water park, its name could be "Wet Dreams."

That got me thinking about what the name really ought to be. As I gazed at Cinderella's castle and the beautiful lakes nearby, I thought about what the words "Magic Kingdom" imply for children of all ages. Suddenly I knew what the name of our water park should be — Magic Waters. And that has been its name since Day 1.

Magic Waters has been a great success for the community. Its location off the Interstate is fortunate; folks driving by see it and form an impression of what kind of city this is. We are one of very few communities in the nation with a water park this size within a 10- or 15-minute drive of our homes.

Serving 'God and Community' Through Golf

One day in 1986 I was sitting in the board room with papers spread out around me doing some work when a man came in and asked for a few minutes of my time. I said of course. He introduced himself as Norris Aldeen and sat down.

We soon realized we had almost met back in 1955 when his company, Amerock, gave $300 for special activities on the last day of a summer rec program I supervised at Sunset Park. Norris told me about his life, how his mother taught him to play golf at Sinnissippi Park and how golf had been part of his life. He had won the Lincoln Junior High Golf Championship in 1931. In college, he started a golf team. He played during his business travels, in places like Afghanistan, Morocco, Saudi Arabia, Sweden and Hong Kong. He had a putting green at his home. He believed strongly in

Norris and Margaret Aldeen, donors of Aldeen Golf Course

The "A" for Aldeen, visible from the clubhouse, identifies Rockford's premier public golf course.

the positive value golf could have on the lives of people, particularly young people.

When he said he and his wife, Margaret, wanted to give the Park District $1 million for a fifth golf course, I had to pinch myself. We knew we needed another course. I had our planner looking for sites and ways to finance one. But we never would have thought of the place Norris was offering, his family's 143-acre farm south of Spring Creek and west of Reid Farm Road.

Before we went public, we had the National Golf Foundation take a look at Norris' idea. Their response was that the Rockford region could handle three more courses, that the northeast location was ideal and the potential was there for an outstanding course.

On Oct. 4, 1988, Norris made his presentation to the Park Board and, when he got through talking, there wasn't a dry eye in the house. He and Margaret wanted to show appreciation to Rockford, where they had lived and raised three children, he said.

Specifically, he told commissioners, "Margaret and I would like to show our gratitude and love for our hometown by contributing a lead gift of $2 million to the Rockford Park District so you can acquire this farm, additional land and have sufficient funds remaining to enable you to authorize the financing and construction of a public, 18-hole golf course of which we all can be proud. The project, he said, would benefit a large cross-section of people and enhance the quality of life here. In so doing, he added, "we believe we will be serving both God and the people of our community."

Norris specified that no taxes be used and that the golf course support itself. He also wanted it to be the premier public golf course in this area, a country club-like course for everyone. We worked hard to make Aldeen just that.

At the time, the Park District had four

golf courses, the 9-hole Sinnissippi course and 18-hole facilities at Ingersoll, Sandy Hollow and Elliot. They were well-designed and well-maintained, and they were busy. A quarter-million rounds of golf were played on them annually, and long waits to get on a course were frequent.

Golfers were ecstatic even though it was clear higher fees would be needed at the new course. We found that out by talking to more than 400 local golfers who came to meetings. Total construction costs were estimated at close to $4 million. In spring 1989, we hired Dick Nugent Associates of Long Grove as architects of the course, with instructions it was to be a championship course that could attract regional and national championships. We raised season passes $20, to $150, and daily fees by $1, to $8 for 18 holes on a weekend, to cover cost of the new course. Construction began in July 1989 after we sold $3.3 million in bonds, to be repaid from golf course revenues over 19 years.

The course would have four sets of tees, water on 12 of the 18 holes, 68 sand traps, a lighted, state-of-the-art practice facility, and a sprinkler system that reaches the roughs as well as the fairways.

Opening Day was July 26, 1991, a day selected because it was Margaret Aldeen's birthday. Ceremonies were held on the back nine with Norris Aldeen among 500 guests. Norris sank a 30-foot putt for a birdie on No. 18, a 480-yard par-5 hole.

Norris was a truly humble man. The

A birdseye view of Aldeen, our newest public golf course, which opened in 1991.

This is the clubhouse at Aldeen Golf Course in northeast Rockford.

occasion inspired this from him: "…I don't like to be overly proud, but I think this time it is justifiably so. This is a beautiful golf course. People seem to enjoy it and are inspired by it and that is what I had hoped. I think it will be quite an addition to the life of the Rockford community."

Whenever I think of Norris and his contribution, I think back to Fred Carpenter, the early commissioner who insisted that golf be "democratized" and made available to everyone. Carpenter's belief led to the Park District's building of courses. What Norris Aldeen believed was that average golfers should be able to play on championship-caliber courses. He raised Rockford's golf culture to a higher level.

Here a Goose, There a Goose, Everywhere …

While it surely existed previously, the first time we realized we had a Canada goose challenge was almost as soon as the Aldeen Golf Club was finished. Too many Canada geese and their "calling cards" appeared on the beautiful new course. Golfers were not happy, and neither was the maintenance staff. The course superintendent remembered reading in Golf Course News about a Connecticut superintendent who had purchased a trained Border collie to

Golfers enjoy one of the city's beautiful courses. This one is Aldeen.

Flash, a border collie who belongs to the Park District, keeps geese from getting comfortable at Elliot Golf Course.

control the goose population. Norris Aldeen got on board quickly and "Blaze," the first dog in the Midwest trained to herd geese, soon arrived.

It appeared the problem in the district had been resolved but of course, it was not. Geese appeared in other locations. As recreational path improvements continued along the river, the geese discovered it. Sweeping to remove goose poop became a daily job, often more than once a day. Commissioners received many complaints. A photo appeared in the Register Star painfully revealing the problem when runners and walkers were unable to avoid stepping in it. Bikers and those in wheelchairs had different challenges.

Who knew where it would lead in 1999 when, over a cup of coffee, I casually asked a business associate if she had any ideas on what to do about the Canada goose challenge. Grouping her with a small group of Park District staff, I stepped away after the first meeting. Soon representatives from GeesePeace and the Humane Society of the United States were invited to talk about the use of humane methods of control.

At public meetings held to discuss the topic, our patrons liked the plan which would, over the years, include addling (oiling goose eggs to help reduce the hatching of eggs), using Border Collies purchased with help from the Humane Society to herd geese both on land and in the river, hand-held lasers, a grass treatment that deters geese, and signage to let people know feeding geese is not helpful, either to the geese or to clean parks. A volunteer added an early educational program for children.

Our Canada Goose Management Program became one of the more successful programs in the United States. By the end of the nesting season of 2010, we had oiled over 18,000 eggs. Experts tell us those eggs would have led to a population of 55,000 resident geese had we not acted. We prevented expansion of the local goose population and contributed to cleaner parks.

There still are some messy areas from geese but not nearly as many as we could have had. And, if people could be convinced to stop feeding the geese, our problem would be smaller still.

Like many other great ideas at the Park District, this nationally-recognized accomplishment all started over a cup of coffee with folks willing to work together to find solutions.

Moving Back Downtown

The Park District had moved into its Sinnissippi Park headquarters in 1971, the year before I came to town. The contemporary style building atop a gentle hill was ideal with its central location and views of our first park (Sinnissippi), North Second Street and the Rock River.

I liked that building but I also became a great admirer of a building downtown, the great edifice at 401 S. Main that housed the U.S. Post Office and Federal Building.

It had been built by the federal government in 1932 – 33 and was as sturdy as any building in town. It also was beautiful, inside and out. Designed by Rockford architects Edward Peterson and Gilbert Johnson, the 93,000-square-foot building was an example of the Neo-Classical Revival design. With its metalwork and marble walls and counters, the interior showed off the kind of craftsmanship tradesmen were capable of in the Depression years. And it was all accomplished for $735,000.

When the main Post Office moved to Harrison Street in 1972, and the Federal Building moved into its own building six years later, the "Old Post Office" building stood largely empty. WQRF Channel 39 television moved in for a time, the Discovery Center Children's Museum opened there, Rockford Amateur Astronomers opened a planetarium and the Post Office maintained a branch office.

Banners now identify the old Post Office on South Main as the Park District headquarters. When I retired in 2006, the Park Board did me a great honor by naming this magnificent building after me.

But the building was not used to its potential. Here was this magnificent edifice, as large, strong and beautiful as anything in northern Illinois. I was convinced it should be housing a vital part of the community.

I advocated buying it and turning it into a Community Resource Center for non-profit organizations. All of them were constantly soliciting citizen involvement but few of them even had a place large enough to hold a public hearing or a roundtable discussion. The idea did not gather steam.

My first proposal to buy it in 1974 went nowhere and the city and MetroCentre bought the building. It became part of our conversation again 20 years later when the Park District had filled up the North Second building and then some. We had offices in seven locations around town.

In 1994, we bought the Old Post Office and cleaned it out — by this time it was being used for everything from a barber shop to storing Cheap Trick's equipment to a bar. We purchased and refurbished it to fit our needs. For the unbelievably low price of $22 a square foot, we had an efficient and centralized Park District headquarters while downtown had a large and stable new anchor.

The location is ideal. With Davis Park across the way, the future development relating to the Stanley J. Roszkowski Federal Building and future development of the riverfront, the Park District couldn't be headquartered in a better place.

In 2006, after my retirement, the Park District did me the great honor of naming the building the Webbs Norman Center. I only wish I were as strong and enduring as the building that carries my name.

Davis Park a Favor Returned

One day in the late 1980s, Judge John E. Sype came to see me and said he represented Morris and Roberta Davis. In their will, Sype said, they had left a sum of money to be used for "… acquiring improved or unimproved property … to be used by and for the benefit of the public…" The funds amounted to $975,000 at the time.

Judge Sype and fellow trustee of the estate, Norman K. Dasenbrook, were charged with interpreting that request and deciding where the money should be spent. They studied suggestions for a year and concluded the money could best be used to develop a downtown park for festivals, concerts and other community events. With cooperation from the Park District, the city and the MetroCentre, we created Davis Park on the west side of the river, just south of Walnut Street.

The park is a testament to the Davises' love for the city and has become one of the riverbank landmarks that so improve quality of life for our citizens. The Davises would have been pleased, we believe.

My daily habit was to stop at various restaurants early each morning, have coffee, read the newspaper and meet with anyone who had something to say. People kidded me about my "office" but this was often the most valuable part of my day. This picture was taken at the old Hollywood Restaurant. (Register Star photo)

The Dream Reaches Out • 1972 – 2006

Davis Park along the east bank of the Rock River is a great site for festivals, concerts, outdoor movies, ice skating and, probably, activities we haven't thought of yet.

Morris had supported the parks for decades, going back to the recreational referendum in 1956.

It was a typical gift for a businessman who had spent a lifetime in Rockford. As Norman Dasenbrook explained, "Rockford was good to Morris. He was just returning the investment."

Davis came to town in 1917 as a soda fountain salesman. He later started his own business, Davis Store Fixtures. He and Roberta were active in the community, with Davis taking a lead role the Community Chest (now United Way), the Chamber of Commerce, Masonic and other organizations. He died at age 93 in 1985.

The seven-acre site was formerly the property of the Lorden and Caster Motor companies. Buildings were demolished except for the Lorden building, which was restored and painted with colorful gears, screws and washers to remind us of the city's industrial roots.

Crowds packed into Davis Park at On the Waterfront. The Register Star building is across the river.

A Bold Attempt to Make a Difference

In May 1992, local activist Ed Wells came to the board with a daring idea. Daring because he proposed taking on a problem with no guarantee of success. And daring because it's a problem that most of us talk about endlessly, then shake our heads, go on with our lives and do nothing.

Ed was concerned about the lack of adult attention to young black boys at risk. They had few positive role models in their homes and few in their neighborhoods. The approach to life they learned at home did not lead to success in traditional schools. After pleading with the School Board in vain for a separate program for these youth, Ed came to the Park District.

He proposed a summer camp to expose young boys who lived in some of the worst environments in Rockford to values that, sadly, were new to most of their thinking. Values like academic achievement, a work ethic, enjoying recreation and the arts, and giving something back to the community. He proposed to do that through a program he called Masai, named after an African tribe that sent young boys to be mentored by tribal elders on the value of family, honor and service. All those things, Ed knew, could give those boys a sense of self-respect and respect for the people and things around them.

> *"Saving young boys and girls who have to endure destructive homes and neighborhoods will take changing our priorities."*
> – Author Webbs Norman

The Park Board bought in. The program started that summer at Lockwood Park, with Ed and Kathy Norman, my daughter, in charge. Ten middle school boys were selected to spend seven days a week, and three nights a week, with Ed and Kathy. They studied, cleaned horse stables, picked up trash around the city, rode horses, cleared debris from the Page Park dam and creek, built a park gazebo and stage, went on field trips locally and to places like Loyala University in Chicago, baled hay, washed dishes and did their own laundry. They had breakfast at 8 a.m. and were kept busy until after dark. They talked about their lives and what choices they had to make.

Many residents said the Park District should not take on such an intensive social program. Well, the first year cost us $4,000. Ed and Kathy worked for nothing. The community donated everything else, from a truck to TVs to mattresses and food.

My feeling was, if we couldn't give these boys a chance to change their lives for that small investment, then we all needed an attitude adjustment.

The program showed success early on. When they went back to school that fall, some of the Masai kids surprised their teachers and families by making the honor roll. Ed and Kathy kept the summer program going four years, and expanded into setting up mentoring programs at the high schools for freshmen boys. But after four years, we dropped the program.

We had done it as a pilot and no one came forward to share the load. The

> *"For indeed, it does take a whole village to raise healthy and successful children."*
> – Author Webbs Norman

support from the community began to dry up and our budget was very tight.

The long term results are sad. Some of the boys died on the street. At least one is in prison. One boy who was building a constructive life died of illness. Our ratio of "success" by traditional standards was low.

But in terms of reasonable expectations, Masai was a success. We gave these boys experiences they never would have had otherwise. We showed them that we cared, and wanted to help them change the cycle they had been born into.

Unfortunately, we couldn't negate the pull from their families, friends and neighborhoods. For most boys, those influences had made a mark before they reached adolescence. The negative impact continued because that's where they spent their lives. We could not separate them from their environment.

"Saving" young boys and girls who have to endure destructive homes and neighborhoods will take changing our priorities in society. Instead of jails, we need to improve schools, offer drug and alcohol treatment, create jobs and programs to help people build better lives. As a community, I can't see that we are ready to do that just yet. I wish we were. For indeed, it does take a whole village to raise healthy and successful children.

The Rock Valley RC Flyers Club opens its field and its hobby to the public several times a year.

Partnering with Hobbyists

Our mission always was to cooperate with citizens' interests in leisure time activities. That philosophy led us to create a flight field for model airplanes at Veterans Memorial Park in 1972. That's the site that today is Sportscore One.

Through the years, the Rock Valley RC Flyers Club, which used the field, had to move it a number of times. Each time, the Park District helped. The last time, in 1985, we found a field that has served well for 25-plus years.

The Radio Controlled Flight Field at 3215 Harrison Road is another partnership. The city owns the land and the Park District helps the Flyers Club with maintenance. The club controls access to the field for the safety of its members and others.

Most days, you can find someone enjoying his or her hobby at the field. The club has 90 some members. Four times a year, the club invites members of the community to come and learn about model airplane flight at no cost.

Lockwood gets Observatory

In 1981, we set our sights on the stars through the eyes of our partners, the Rockford Amateur Astronomers Inc.

The astronomers, formed in 1958, wanted to further interest in astronomy. The club had opened a planetarium for public use in the Rockford Public Library in 1972. When they were asked to move, they found a second home in the Discovery Center children's museum, then housed in the old Post Office.

A permanent solution came about in 1981 when the club opened its observatory in Lockwood Park. This came about after the Park District and the club collaborated on the best way to serve their members and enable them to share their equipment and expertise with the public. The Park District provided the labor and land in Lockwood Park and the club provided money for a domed building, telescopes and other equipment.

Today the facility houses a custom-built, 10-inch refracting telescope, a Pierkowski 10-inch Coelostat solar telescope and several portable telescopes. Thousands of people have used them to observe Halley's Comet in 1986, the moon, Venus, Jupiter, Saturn, Mars and other planets, stars and distant galaxies.

Helping the Pistol Club

When we acquired the land to build Riverview Ice House, the Pine Tree Pistol Club was forced to look for a new home. Founded in 1954, the club had just invested $20,000 in a shooting facility at 115 N. Water St. and members were upset about moving. We didn't need the space right away. We let the club stay there until 1987 when we tore down the building as part of a beautification project. We had agreed to help find a new place.

The Rockford Amateur Astronomers welcome visitors to the observatory at Lockwood Park twice a month.

The Field of Honor is a moving tribute to servicemen and women and others who answered the nation's call during times of war.

In 1988, the club was in the process of building a shooting range at 7301 Auburn St. on land owned by the city and leased to the Park District. Construction was halted by a court order after neighbors complained. A judge ruled the Park District could not sublease the site to the club. The judge also chided the Park District for getting involved with a gun club. This despite the fact that the Chicago Park District had operated the Lincoln Park gun club for 70 years, as had other cities and park districts throughout the state.

A higher court reversed the court ruling but the neighbors continued their legal battle. The Park District and the club decided it was best to find a new site, which we did in an old chicken processing plant on Kishwaukee Road near the airport. The airport leased the land to us and the shooting facility was set up in 1990. But in 1994, the airport needed that space to expand a runway. We then loaned $100,000 to the club to develop a new range at 5454 11th St. In 2005, the club bought the property from us.

We were criticized for being involved with a gun club, but I don't agree. We helped them because they enjoyed that form of recreation and were a community organization. We had forced them out of their original home downtown and we believed there should be a place for gun owners to get training in safe use of weapons, as well as enjoy the art of recreational shooting.

Field of Honor is One Man's Legacy

One of the best days of my tenure was the day before Veterans Day, Nov. 10, 1995, when we dedicated the Field of Honor memorial in Loves Park. That event filled me with gratitude for the likes of men like Art Anderson and the privilege I had of working with him.

The story starts with Art's distinguished service in World War II. He was at the Battle of the Bulge, at the liberation of four prison camps and a concentration camp, at Hitler's palace and at innumerable battle scenes. Art came home with tuberculosis, the loss of sight in one eye and the nightmares, guilt and insomnia that followed many soldiers. He didn't let those things stop him. He started the A.W. Anderson insurance agency, a 50-year marriage to wife Betty Lou and a great family. He also became a leader in civic affairs.

His greatest contribution may have been the Field of Honor, which was inspired by a trip Art and Betty Lou took in 1974 to visit the birthplace of his parents in Sweden. They stopped in London to go to St. Paul's Cathedral because Art wanted to see a memorial for the U.S. airmen based in Great Britain during World War II. The American Memorial Chapel in St. Paul's contained the names of 28,000 Americans who lost their lives in battle. Art and his wife found the names of two

Arthur W. Anderson

The American Gold Star Mothers Memorial recognizes a group of people often overlooked for the sacrifices they endured during war times.

men they knew from Loves Park.

Art was tremendously impressed with what the British had done to honor the American fighting men. He returned home committed to the idea of a memorial in Loves Park. The local heroes deserved recognition, Art believed, and a memorial would serve as a constant reminder of the price of freedom and peace to new generations.

Art recruited a committee to do some brainstorming about a memorial to honor those who fought for the United States during the 20th Century. He teamed up with landscape architect John R. Cook, who studied every war memorial he heard of, driving with Art to see many of them. Art took to heart a suggestion from Diana Rudeen of the VFW Auxiliary that the memorial also honor the mothers of the men who never came home.

When Art started collecting money, most people were happy to help. He got $25,000 from Loves Park, $25,000 and a site in Sand Park from the Park District (Art remarked that was so easy, he wished he had asked for $50,000), $25,000 from Woodward Governor, and $10,000 from the local VFW. Money came from veterans and veterans groups, individuals who sent checks ranging from $10 to $10,000, people from the area and others from around the state and nation.

Local sculptor Gene Horvath started work on the sculptures but died before they were finished. Sculptor Christopher Bennett finished the job. Cook designed the steps, pillars and landscaping, and Sjostrom and Sons did the construction.

It is a handsome and moving tribute. There are five free-standing limestone

The Navy-Marines-Coast Guard memorial in Beattie Park was erected in 1972.

The Greater Rockford Area Korean War Veterans monument ensures these men and their bravery will not be forgotten.

pillars, 10 tons each, representing World Wars I and II, the Korean War, Vietnam War and Persian Gulf War. In front of the pillars are bronze statues of veterans and military support personnel — infantry soldier, sailor, nurse, paratrooper, Air Force pilot, medic, tank battalion soldier, and support person. The 38 flagpoles forming a crescent contain the names of 38 men from the Harlem School District who died during the wars World War II, Korea and Vietnam.

The memorial honors two segments of the population often overlooked. A small column recognizes the sacrifices of the civilian population, especially the Red Cross, Salvation Army, air raid wardens, people who worked in defense industries and even the kids who collected tinfoil to be recycled into war materials. And in its own space is the American Gold Star Mothers Memorial, a 12-foot Swedish black marble and granite obelisk topped with a gold star. The only such monument in the nation, it recognizes the deep sacrifice of mothers who lost sons and daughters in war.

A memorial to Korean War soldiers

The Huey helicopter, lifeblood of soldiers in Vietnam, sits atop a wall listing the roll call of fallen soldiers at the LZ Peace Memorial at the Midway Village site.

next to the main monument was dedicated in 2008. The Greater Rockford Area Korean War Veterans Association erected the monument to honor the 59 men from Winnebago, Boone and Ogle counties who died in that war. Let me offer a special congratulations to Jack Philbrick and other veterans for their dedicated efforts to recognize Korean War soldiers.

Around the Field of Honor are fields of greenery, representing the peace and freedom our veterans preserved. The final element is music, serene and patriotic, and the faint sound of a heartbeat reminding us that our fallen heroes lived among us, and that our lives as Americans should honor them.

More enhancements are planned, among them an eternal flame.

Art put his heart and soul into completing the memorial. It took 30 years but what he envisioned and worked for will forever stand for patriotism and peace here in the Rock River Valley.

What he would ask of you is to remember what the memorial stands for. From the beginning, Art insisted that it not contain a tank or other symbols of destruction.

"I want the park to honor veterans, but not to glorify war," he said.

In honor of Art, we named the seven-acre park the Arthur W. Anderson Peace Park. Art passed away in 2007 but his spirit lives in the hearts and minds of all who knew him.

Navy, Vietnam Memorials

The Field of Honor and Korean memorials are not the only tributes to veterans on Park District grounds.

Beattie Park downtown contains the Navy-Marines-Coast Guard memorial, completed in 1972 with an anchor, jack staff (flag staff) and anchor chain from the USS Tuscaloosa, a ship that had taken part in the Normandy invasion.

I had the honor of visiting with my mentor, Dr. Al Sapora (right) and local activist Jeanine Wortmann as we marked my 20th year here in 1992.

The Dream Reaches Out • 1972 – 2006

The Carlson Ice Arena opened in 1998. It's a popular spot for ice skating by young and old alike and kids love the large indoor Sapora Playworld.

At Midway Village, a Huey helicopter that once ferried soldiers in and out of war zones in Vietnam sits next to a black granite wall. The wall is engraved with the names of 72 Winnebago County veterans who died in Vietnam or later because of war injuries. It was dedicated in 2005. Local members of Vietnam Veterans Honor Society raised the money.

The Midway Village Museum has exhibits on Camp Grant which, of course, trained tens of thousands of soldiers during World Wars I and II.

Another Arena for Dreams of Excellence

By the 1990s, Riverview Ice House was being used to capacity. It was open 18 hours a day and still there were waiting lists for lessons. Classes and programs were scheduled at inconvenient times because that's when we had open ice. Skating and hockey enthusiasts asked for a second indoor ice skating facility.

Developer Kurt Carlson, whose father and grandfather were Park Board members, provided more than $2 million for the second ice house through a donation of land north of Riverside Boulevard and landscaping around the new facility. Friends of Riverview, the ice house downtown, pledged to raise $1 million for the building.

The Park District agreed to come up with $3.5 million and plans were made for a facility close to the Interstate 90 tollway exit. It included a 200- by 85-foot ice rink with seating for 600 spectators, an indoor mega playground called Sapora Playworld for kids aged 1 – 12, a video recreation room and a restaurant.

Carlson Ice Arena opened February 27, 1998. Weekend guests included my mentor Allen Sapora, for whom we named the playground, and figure skating shows by

Would-be hockey players can start young in the Park District program.

made a name for themselves and our city by winning 15 straight prep hockey championships (through 2011).

They are exactly what Janet Lynn had in mind when she talked of what dreams and character can be groomed on the ice.

The Icemen and their enviable record are the result of the Park District's facilities and programs, longtime coach Tim Mattila and his assistants, hockey clubs and dedicated volunteers. It all starts with our learn-to-skate programs for kids as young as 2 years old. From there, those who want to be hockey players — boys and girls — go on to the Junior Ice Hogs, teams led by Park District staff who have one practice and one game a week.

Serious hockey players follow that by joining the Rockford Hockey Club, one of our partners that rents ice time for youngsters who play here and on the road. At high school age, they're eligible to join

Olympians, World Team members and National Medalists with Rockford roots. Included were Sandy Lenz, Caryn Kadavy Lily Lee, David Santee, Kath Malmberg LeBeau, Damon Allen, Lisa Bell and pairs team Brian Geddeis and Julianne Thompson.

Most of the people using Carlson skate for fun — it had 200,000 user visits in 2009 — but the rink also offers the chance to pursue a dream. As Rockford Olympian Janet Lynn said in a letter of congratulations, "What a legacy this rink can become if new dreams of excellence can be born here, and fine human character can be built here through the vehicle of sport."

Thanks, Janet. I couldn't have said it better myself.

Hockey Hotbed

You've heard of the Rockford Icemen, a hockey team of high school students who have

Even on the coldest winter days, kids can let off steam at Sapora Indoor Playworld at Carlson Ice Arena.

the Icemen, another partner organization that has won such acclaim for the city.

Other partners in the program are the Rockford Icehogs and their parent club, the Chicago Blackhawks, who won the NHL's Stanley Cup in 2010. Many of the Icehog players and coaches have worked with kids in our youth programs and the Blackhawks have supported us, too. That helped us renovate the Junior Icehogs building on Madison Street, an off-ice training facility.

The program is the envy of many cities because it literally goes from toddlers to the pros. Along the way, communication and cooperation ensure a smooth transition for young hockey players.

Canine Corners in Searls Park was the district's first park for dogs.

Family of Note

When developer Kurt Carlson stepped up to help us build a second ice arena, he was honoring family tradition.

E.W. Carlson, Kurt's grandfather, was appointed to the board in 1941 to fill an unexpired term and served until his sudden death by heart attack in 1955. He was a key figure in the expansion of our recreation program.

Sixteen years later, in 1971, the Park Board appointed E.W.'s son, Edwin W. Carlson, to fill an unexpired term on the board. The younger Carlson, who served until 1990, was involved in many youth and recreational programs, especially those involving baseball. He was president of the Rockford Boys Baseball organization and built and maintained a baseball field in Carlson-Nelles Park on South Pierpont until the family donated it to the Park District in 1975. Edwin W. helped us bring professional baseball to town and acquire Magic Waters. His wife, Vi, was instrumental in establishing Midway Village Museum Center. And their son, Kurt, of course, generously helped us build our second ice arena.

Families like the Carlsons play a major role in the long-term growth and success of our Park District. Often the board and staff get credit — and they deserve much — but we should not forget the donors who help us build and keep programs going through their largesse and/or their time.

If you use a Park District facility named after someone, you know a generous individual or family made a donation that make it possible for people like you and your family to enjoy life.

Parks for Dogs

In October 2000, we opened our first dog park in Searls Park. As usual, this was in response to a request from a local group. Friends of the Dog Park agreed to raise $8,400 for fencing if we would designate the space.

Friends of the Dog Park was largely started by four women — Paula Christensen,

Mary Sanders, Jean Koernschild and Ellen Franke. They talked up the idea, got support and put together a feasible proposal.

Dog owners had been asking for a place where they could let their pets run without leashes. Not only would the dogs get exercise, but they would learn to socialize with other canines.

There was no such place locally. One Rockton couple told us they drove to Madison several times a week to let their 1-year-old dog run free at a dog park.

Dog owners have wholeheartedly supported their dog parks. We now have two "Canine Corners." In addition to the one in Searls, which has expanded to eight acres, we offer two, 2-acre sites at Elliot Park. All have brush and paths for enjoyable romps for both dogs and owners.

Participants are required to sign up, purchase a $25 a year tag, and obey all rules. For that, they can visit the dog park any day of the year, from dawn to dusk.

Our dog parks now serve nearly 1,000 canines each year, and another park has been opened in Machesney Park's Schoonmaker Park by Harlem Township.

Best friends taking in a sunny fall day, an open field, and each other at Canine Corners.

The Park District will open another one in the spring of 2012 in the new Roland Olson Park. Not only have the dog parks brought enjoyment to pets and pet owners, but the relaxation and exercise might well be extending the lives of both.

Olson Gift Worth $3 Million

Roland and Gladys Olson were among this area's finest citizens. They founded the Lawson Children's Home for children with severe disabilities. Roland often visited there to play with the kids, who called him "Papa."

A real estate developer, Roland Olson clearly believed in sharing his good fortune with the community. He and Gladys had no children of their own and were especially generous to projects that benefitted children and veterans. He sold land cheap for an expansion of Rock Cut State Park and donated land and cash for parks, veterans' groups, churches, schools and more.

After Roland died in 1998 and Gladys passed away the following year, the Park District and community found out just how generous this couple was. In their will, they left a gift worth $3.1 million — their

Roland and Gladys Olson

83-acre home and farm on Harlem Road east of Interstate 90 and a $1.5 million trust fund — to the care of the Park District. It was the largest gift the district had received to that date.

Tiger Woods Comes to Town

I must return to the subject of golf once more to talk about the visit here by Tiger Woods. It was initiated by my friend Tom Warren, author of "An Old Caddie Looks Back." Tom was a lifelong friend of Rockford native Bill Stark, who just happened to be a friend of Earl and Tida Woods and their son, Tiger. Starks and Warren talked over the years about getting Tiger to visit Rockford and decided that their best chance was to appeal to the Tiger Woods Foundation, which conducted a few clinics each year featuring Tiger and his father. Working with the cities of Rockford and Beloit, they submitted a proposal for the year 2000. That was denied. They tried again, and got a commitment for 2001.

To say both cities were excited is an understatement. Tiger was not only a phenomenal golfer but a cultural icon and, at that time, one of the most well-liked athletes ever. He made golf fans out of people who wouldn't know a golf club from a goal post.

The weekend of June 30-July 1, 2001, was unforgettable. We had taken care of some golf course and street improvements because of the visit. Tiger Woods held a clinic for a dozen young golfers at Ingersoll. He and his dad gave a golf exhibition, with more than 4,000 by-invitation-only people at the well-run event.

Earl Woods gave a presentation at Pilgrim Baptist Church. Golf workshops

The Tiger Woods visit here in 2001 created great excitement among local golfers, especially those interested in getting more young people into the sport.

Tiger and his dad, Earl Woods, take part in a press conference at Ingersoll Golf Course.

were held at Beloit College. More than 100 children got help from local pros at another golf clinic.

It was a special time and a message to everyone in Rockford that the great game of golf was for anyone who had an interest in it. We especially wanted to encourage young black boys and girls to try out the game of golf.

The weekend also raised more than $190,000 for local organizations that work with disadvantaged children.

Three years later, we landed a second Tiger Woods clinic, although the golf star himself didn't make a personal visit this time. But 15 local kids flew to Disneyland for fun and a three-day clinic with Tiger, another 75 got lessons from local pros and we held a festival at Levings Park featuring recreation and health. Rockford was the first city in America to host two Tiger Woods Foundation events.

I have been asked how I feel now about Tiger Woods. He is a fabulous golfer, a man who helped us connect with young and minority golfers in our community, and a man who gave the world much in the fields of entertainment, sports and his foundation's work. I still feel honored that the Park District was able to be such an integral part of the Woods Foundation's programs and hope we continue to spread his message, that golf is a game for everyone who is willing to learn it.

Nicholas Conservatory a Tribute to Parents

I mentioned that Dan and Ruth Nicholas gave us start-up funds for our City of Gardens program. Years later, they started another project that is becoming a great source of enjoyment and pride for locals, a reason for people to visit our city, and a model for national botanical organizations.

Dan and I were standing near the old greenhouses in Sinnissippi Park one day,

We filled temporary bleachers at Ingersoll the day Tiger appeared. We had to limit the crowd to invitation only.

The paved path meanders around water features, palms large and small, and hundreds of other tropical specimens. Look up to see orchids and other plants growing on tree branches.

with Dan reminiscing about how important that park was to his family. He and his two brothers grew up in a modest home just west of the park. His grandfather fished in the Rock River from the High Bridge (the old Auburn Street bridge), the Nicholas boys skated on the river in winters, learned to golf at Sinnissippi and spent who-knows-how-many Sunday afternoons with family at the park.

Dan said he had been thinking about how to honor his parents, William and Ruby Nicholas, for all they had done for his brothers and him. Well, I had been thinking, too.

We were about 10 years away from the 100th anniversary of the Park District in 2009 and needed to mark the occasion with a significant project of some sort.

The plan for a conservatory just fell into place. Since Sinnissippi was our first park, it was appropriate to rejuvenate the park and riverfront with a permanent structure. Dan Nicholas was a great admirer of botanical centers and we visited some to get ideas. Then he talked with his brothers, Bill, who also lives in Rockford, and Ab, in Milwaukee, and the three of them offered a generous gift to the community in the form of $2,150,000. That lead gift got us started on a conservatory to be named in honor of their parents.

With the help of local architect/designers John R. Cook, Sam Darby and Gary Anderson, we came up with a plan that would serve many purposes. The 22,000-square-foot building, as high as 52 feet at the peak, contains a beautiful greenhouse filled with

Pineapple, banana and cocoa trees are among the tropical food-bearing plants in the conservatory.

tropical trees and other plants. It is a knockout site for travelers along the river and North Second Street.

There are facilities for school programs on environmental topics, a kitchen, terrace and rooms for meetings, weddings and receptions. The entire cost was $13 million. About $1 million came from government sources but most came from the Nicholas brothers and corporate and citizen donors who gave from $5 to tens of thousands of dollars or more.

Landscaping will tie the conservatory into its setting. The lagoon just north of the conservatory is being rebuilt and will be named the Eclipse Lagoon. Most of the $1.4 million project was financed through a gift from the Perks family, which owns Eclipse Inc., and Eclipse Foundation. The project will include a lagoon overlook, two fountains, a waterfall and prairie plantings. The work, slated to be completed in 2012, also received support from an anonymous donor, a $200,000 gift of services from William Charles Ltd., and fountains from Aqua-Aerobics Systems.

When the landscaping north and south of the conservatory is complete in 2012, it truly will be a stunning facility.

The whole building is LEED (Leadership in Energy and Environmental Design) certified. With solar and geothermal heating and cooling, it will get most of its power from renewable resources. It is, I believe, the only conservatory in the nation that meets LEED standards.

Everyone should take pride in the Nicholas Conservatory and Gardens as a symbol of a generous community that recognizes the value of beauty and education in a hard-working city. It serves as a great symbol of positive growth as we enter the second century of the Rockford Park District.

Passing the Baton

One of my responsibilities under the board's policy governance requirements was to prepare key staff to succeed me. District policy states: "In order to protect the board from sudden loss of CEO services, the CEO may have no fewer than two other executives familiar with board and CEO issues and processes."

Following that, I worked closely with several staffers I considered good candidates for the top leadership post. If for some reason I couldn't come in one morning, there had to be someone who could take over without interruption of programs, planning or building projects.

One of the people on my list of possible successors was Tim Dimke. Tim had been deputy director of operations and had 33 years of experience in the district. He started as a summer employee at age 17, mowing lawns and performing other maintenance tasks. His work performance had been stellar. He had

The conservatory contains more than 3,600 plants of more than 300 species.

Tim Dimke has led the Park District since 2006. He was selected by the Board of Commissioners and recommended by me.

moved up to the position of deputy director and was one of my closest associates.

In 2006, I decided to retire. I had two reasons. One, I wanted to help raise money for the Nicholas Conservatory, the largest project in terms of money the district ever has undertaken. I also wanted to write a book about the history of the Park District. It is so important, I believe, for our board members, staff leaders and others to know and understand the past in order to make intelligent decisions today.

When the board started talking about who would be my successor, I backed off. That is a board decision, not mine. But Nate Martin, then president of the board, asked if I would prepare a written recommendation for the board's consideration on which of our staff was best prepared for the CEO position.

Some of the reasons I gave for recommending Tim are:

1: He was familiar with our form of governance and knew what the past and current agendas contained. He knew the board's role and how commissioners liked to set their agenda. He understood the relationship between the board and the CEO.

2: His 30-plus years in the district gave him knowledge of past and current partnerships and relationships with other governmental agencies, from federal to local.

3: Tim had complete knowledge of internal functions including budget, special facilities, programming, personnel and marketing. Most important, he knew the culture of the district and its core values, which he helped develop and always supported.

4: Tim's experience made me feel comfortable about transferring leadership to him for the planning and development of the Nicholas Conservatory.

5: It would have taken a CEO new to the district three to five years to learn what Tim already knew.

"Tim Dimke does not do everything like I would have done, nor should he. Given Tim's performance in the past five years, I never have been sorry that I recommended his appointment."
– AUTHOR
WEBBS NORMAN

With the advice and counsel of Dr. Ted Flickinger, CEO of the Illinois Association of Park Districts, Tim was selected to become the sixth executive director of the district. The transition to his leadership took place without a blip on the screen. He does not do everything like I would have done, nor should he. Given Tim's performance in the past five years, I never have been sorry that I recommended his appointment. He has done an outstanding job.

Under Tim, the last three years of the first 100 of the district continued to be very busy. Projects accomplished under his leadership include expanding the Discovery Center and Burpee Museum in Riverfront Museum Park, building Nicholas Conservatory and Gardens, continuing close cooperation with Davis Park programs and On the Waterfront, adding attractions to Magic Waters, expanding the Park District Foundation board and its program funding, operating a summer recreation program in cooperation with the Rockford School District, and strengthening the area's tourism promotions with the joint marketing of local gardens including Nicholas Conservatory, to mention a few.

Tim and his staff are looking at exciting developments for the future. Among them could be a major downtown indoor sports center and expanding Sportscore Two with the addition of artificial turf soccer fields.

In the next chapter of this book, Tim reviews how the vision and policies of past boards guide him in governing today's park district. Standards of service remain as high as they ever have been. Times change and the financial constraints of today's world are truly challenging but, as Tim says, paraphrasing a former mayor, "Leave the lights on, we're staying." He then reviews how the district will work with the community to meet park and recreational needs for years to come.

Tim takes a holistic approach to

Bill Taylor, a longtime maintenance staffer at Sinnissippi Park and Golf Course, had a friend named Roscoe the Crow. Roscoe frequently said hello to Bill by lighting on his arm or shoulder.

governing the Park District. As you read, you will gain insight into how the many individual functions relate to the mission, and operate in balance and harmony in providing services. It is must reading for those interested in responsive, effective and creative governance.

The Rockford Park District is in good hands. I know Tim, the board, and the staff embrace the opportunities and challenges to come in the second 100 years with confidence and excitement.

---

[1] Joel Cowen, a researcher at the University of Illinois Medical College in Rockford, began doing surveys every year to measure how citizens felt about services from the Rockford Park District. That still is being done, with the data used to evaluate the kind of work we've done and whether we have earned the trust and respect of the citizens we serve.

[2] Ray Dahlquist was not only a great dad for a couple of ice skating girls but a long-time member of the Rockford Park Board, serving as commissioner for 23 years until his death in 1970.

[3] A vuvuzela is a plastic horn which produces a loud monotone note. Fans used them at the World Cup Soccer match in 2010, to the consternation of spectators and TV viewers around the world.

[4] The 1992 movie, "A League of their Own," told the story of the Rockford Peaches. Some drama was added, of course, but it's a good movie. Better yet, check out the Peaches' exhibit at Midway Village.

GROWTH OF THE PARK DISTRICT 1972 – 2006

Parks acquired 1972 – 2006

1973: Auburn School Tennis Courts, 5110 Auburn, 2 acres*

1973: Booker Washington Park, 500 Blake St., 6 acres*

1973: Guilford Tennis Center, 5702 Spring Creek Road, 3.8 acres*

1973: Midway Village Museum, 6799 Guilford Road, 134 acres (Includes acquisitions through the years)

1974: Taylor Park, 2411 S. Main, 1.4 acres

1974: Terry Lee Wells Memorial Park, 910 Whitman St. at Haskell School, 2.2 acres

1975: Carlson-Nelles Bicentennial Park, 822 S. Pierpont, 14.7 acres

1975: Harlem South Tennis Court, 7356 Windsor Road, 14.9 acres*

1975: Landstrom Park, 3450 Landstrom Road, 14.9 acres

1975: Riverview Park (Ice house, trolley barn, hockey training facility), 324 N. Madison St., 7.2 acres

1976: Founders Park, 326 S. Main, .33 acre*

1976: Peter Olson Park, 1815 Maple Ave., 2.6 acres*

1979: Illinois St. Park, 4500 Illinois St., 6.6 acres

1979: Rockford Arboretum, 1875 N. Mulford Road, 11.9 acres

1980: Joe Marino Park (formerly Waterside Park), 102 N. Water St., .41 acre

1980: Johnson Tract, 5085 Spring Brook Road, 5.2 acres

1980: Luther Esplanade, West State and river bank, .50 acre*

1981: Sixth St. Playground, 2005 Sixth St., .54 acre

1981: Stiles School Park, 315 La Clede Ave., 3 acres

1983: Mullins-Pebble Creek Park, 5350 Windsor Road, 8.6 acres

1984: Civil War Memorial, Main and Auburn, .13 acre*

1984: Jamestown Park, 1823 Sandy Hollow Road, 3.7 acres

1985: Beverly Park, 3414 Parkside Ave., .75 acre (part of Mel Anderson Path)

1985: Ekberg-Pine Manor Park, 3750 Balsam Lane, 6.9 acres

1985: Mel Anderson Recreation Path, along Kent Creek between Talcott Page Park and Searls Park at Safford Road, 37 acres

1985: Riverfront Museum Park, 711 N. Main St., 6.6 acres

1985: Wester Park, 814 N. Main St., .9 acre

1986: Library Esplanade, west bank of river between Jefferson St. Bridge and Mulberry St., .7 acre*

1986: Park-er-Woods Park, 6700 Claremont St., 23 acres

1987: Bresler Park, 3610 Liberty Drive, 3.7 acres

1987: Gambino Park, 4401 Pepper Drive, 9 acres*

1987: Hunter Park, 6689 Barrick Drive, 9.8 acres

1987: Ingersoll Centennial Park, 315 S. First St., 2.5 acres

1988: Magic Waters, 7820 CherryVale N. Blvd., 46 acres

1988: Mulford Crest Park, 5650 Grove Hill, 11.7 acres

1988: Willow Creek Greenway, 6230 Minns Drive, 22 acres

1989: Aldeen Golf Club, 1902 Reid Farm Road, 168 acres

1989: Davis Memorial Park, 330 S. Wyman St., 5.4 acres

1989: Lockwood Park Hill House, 5347 Safford Road, 3.1 acres*

1989: Swanson Park West, 2780 Swanson Parkway, 6 acres (Part of Southeast Community Park)

1990: Oaks Park, 4301 N. Main St., 2 acres

1990: Rock River Greenway South, 3100 block of River Boulevard, 10.3 acres (Acquired with Water Reclamation District for future path)

1991: Patriot's Gateway Playground, 615 S. 5th St. *

1992: Sportscore Recreation Path, west bank of river between Riverside Blvd. to Harlem Road, 3.6 acres

Continued next page

GROWTH OF THE PARK DISTRICT 1972 – 2006

1993: Beyer Stadium, 333 15th Ave., 4.2 acres

1993: Lewis Lemon School Playground, 1993 Mulberry St., Owned by School District; Park District uses for programming

1993: Waterside Plaza (Millennium Fountain), 202 N. Water St., .65 acre

1994: Cherry Valley Path, between Swanson Park West and underpass at bypass, 8.5 acres

1994: Sportscore Two/Indoor Sports Center (Northeast Community Park), 8800 E. Riverside Blvd., 170 acres

1994: Southeast Community Park, 3151 Perryville Road, 78 acres

1994: Webbs Norman Center, 401 S. Main St., 1.7 acres, Park District Administration

1995: Swanson Park East, 7300 Vandiver Road, 37 acres*

1996: Swan F. Anderson building, 1040 N. Second St., 1.1 acres

1997: Saturn Park, 6540 Garrett Lane, 2.8 acres

1998: Carlson Ice Arena, 4150 N. Perryville Road, 9.6 acres

1999: Southwest Community Park, 2004 Ogilby Road, 50 acres

2000: Kaye Anderson Park, 6761 LeaOak Drive, 2.3 acres

2000: Olson Park, 7901 Harlem Road, 88 acres

2001 Northwestern Park, 701 4th Ave., .44 acre

2003: Eddie Greene Place, 114 S. First St., .08 acre

2005: Harlem Community Skatepark, 9400 Forest Hills Road, 33 acres

* Owned by school districts or others, maintained by Park District

PROFILE OF THE PARK DISTRICT 1972 – 2006

Year:	1910	1928	1945	1971	2006
Statistic: **Population**	48,405	91,750	113,410	160,460	205,867
Number of Parks/ Properties	15	45	65	109	173
Park District Acreage	159.47	731.35	2,361.26	3,570.27	4,573.62
Total Budget	$140,343.49[1]	$177,063.00	$150,412.00	$2,965,929.00	$38,615,514.00
Property Tax Revenue	$35,999.00	$160,142.00	$122,837.00	$2,197,237.00	$19,242,500.00
Per Capita Expenditure from Taxes	$0.74	$1.74	$1.08	$13.69	$93.47
Median Family Income	Not available	Not available	Not available	$13,249.00	$47,735.00
Estimated Total User Visits	Not available	Not available	Not available	1,500,000	9,638,217

[1] *1910 budget covered 18 months instead of 12 months.*

THE COMMISSIONERS OF THE ERA 1972 – 2006

Joseph Bean   *Gilmore J. Landstrom*   *John B. Whitehead*   *Gerald Wernick*   *Edwin W. Carlson Jr.*

JOSEPH BEAN
On board 1960 – 1973; president 1971 – 1973

Named acting director of the district in December 1971 following departure of executive director Robert Milne. Led district until Webbs Norman took over as director in March 1972. Beloit College graduate and long-time active alumni. Owned and operated Bean Shoe Service in Rockford and Beloit. After retirement, operated shoe stores at Gunite Foundry and Chrysler Corporation on a part-time basis.

GILMORE J. LANDSTROM
On board 1962 – 1973

"Gilly" served as district treasurer. Managed Rockford Union Foundry, which became part of Sundstrand Machine Tool Company. Was a director of Sundstrand Machine Tool. Financial vice president and secretary of Sundstrand to his retirement in 1963. Landstrom Road Tract named Gilmore Landstrom Park in 1975 in his honor.

JOHN B. WHITEHEAD
On board 1970 – 1983; president 1973 – 1977

President of J.B. and Loren L. Whitehead Inc. Realtors. Served on civic organizations, including City-County Planning Commission, Rockford College board and Rockford Goodwill Industries. Credited for leadership in creating Sportscore One and many other major Park District improvements.

GERALD WERNICK
On board 1971 – 1979

Ran unsuccessfully for Park Board in 1963 but won election in 1971 on campaign promise "to change many of the policies of the present board." Professional photographer. Promoted open discussion of Park District business; board adopted his suggestion to hold evening meetings. Resigned when he moved out of town for business reasons in 1979.

EDWIN W. CARLSON JR.
On board 1971 – 1990, president 1987 – 1988

Son of earlier board member Edwin Carlson Sr. Ran family business, Carlson Roofing Co. Built Little League baseball fields at 900 S. Pierpont Ave. Donated fields to district in 1975. Major player in bringing professional baseball to town with renovation of Marinelli Field, and to district's acquisition of Magic Waters. Wife Vi instrumental in establishing Midway Village Museum.

Continued next page

THE COMMISSIONERS OF THE ERA 1972 – 2006

Alden E. Orput *Jo Baker* *Rolf Thienemann* *Michael J. Delany*

ALDEN E. ORPUT
On board 1973 – 1978

Gained recognition for his co-chairmanship of the Ice Rink Citizens Advisory Committee, the district's first entry into a joint commissioner-citizen-staff feasibility study. President of Orput-Orput & Associates, a prominent local architectural firm. Expansion of the business out-of-town led to Alden's early resignation from board.

JO BAKER
On board 1973 – 1981, president 1977 – 1981

Elected shortly after moving to Rockford, first woman on board. After board service, worked as planner and then as deputy director in Park District. As board member, played a major role in establishing the riverbank recreational/bike path and many other facilities.

ROLF THIENEMANN
On board 1978 – 1997, president 1981 – 1986, 1989 – 1992

Served 19 years, including eight as president. After being commissioner, continued public service as member of Park District Foundation board and Burpee Natural History Museum board. Was president of Muller-Pinehurst Dairy.

MICHAEL J. DELANY
On board 1979 – 1989

Longtime activist in Rockford business, industrial and community affairs. Associated for 22 years with Atwood Industries and Clock Tower properties. Retired as Rockford Clinic's CEO in 1990.

THE DREAM REACHES OUT • 1972 – 2006

William K. Sjostrom   *Michael A. White*   *Fleur C. Wright*   *Bruce T. Atwood*   *Gloria E. Cardenas Cudia*

WILLIAM K. SJOSTROM
On board 1981 – 1993, president 1986 – 1987, 1992 – 1993

Upon retirement from board, Sjostrom cited pride in having helped in cleanup of Levings Lake and adding Standfield Beach, development of Sportscore One, and building Aldeen Golf Course. As board treasurer, improved financial policies and practices. Major supporter in acquisition of Magic Waters. Was vice-president of Smith-Shafer Oil Co.

MICHAEL A. WHITE
On board 1983 – 1989, president, 1988 – 1989

Brought a degree in parks and recreation administration to his board position. Owner of Mike White & Associates for Equitable Life Insurance Co. Enthusiastic supporter of the Magic Waters project.

FLEUR C. WRIGHT
On board 1989 – 2001, president 1993 – 1995

Led effort to revitalize the Rockford Park District Foundation, its board membership and scope of its activities. Influential in establishing First Night celebration. Member of Mayor's Advisory Committee on Gun Control, New American Theatre director of development.

BRUCE T. ATWOOD
On board 1989 – 2001, president 1995 – 1997

Followed tradition of service to Park District started by his grandfather, Seth B. Atwood. Bruce represented board as liaison to the Rockford Park District Foundation. Worked to ensure a broad base of future support for the district and brought new governance system to the district leading to greater effectiveness.

GLORIA E. CARDENAS CUDIA
On board 1990 – 1991

First ethnic minority to serve as commissioner. Followed board service Park District employment, serving as outreach ombudsman. Co-founder and president of Fiesta Hispana, and president and board member of La Voz Latina. Was regional vice-president with A.L.Williams Co.

Continued next page

THE COMMISSIONERS OF THE ERA 1972 – 2006

Kristine O'Rourke Cohn   *Roberta E. Ingrassia*   *Nathaniel Martin*   *Harris H. Agnew*   *Laura Pigatti Williamson*

KRISTINE O'ROURKE COHN
On board 1991 – 1994

Was directing fund development for Rockford Museum Park when elected. Noted for advocacy of long-term planning and inter-agency collaboration. Resigned from board to become Winnebago County chairman. Appointed by President George Bush as regional director of education. Was president of Rockford Recycling.

ROBERTA E. INGRASSIA
On board 1993 – 1999, president, 1997 – 1999

Park Board contributions centered on inter-agency cooperation, strategic planning and effective governance. Served on Rockford Public Library Board earlier. Was headmaster of Keith Country Day School's grade 6 to 12, served on the New American Theatre board.

NATHANIEL MARTIN
On board, 1995 – 1997, 1999 –, president 2004 – 2007

First African-American board member. Career with Rockford School District covered 28 years as teacher, ombudsman, middle school principal and director of secondary education. In 2008, appointed to Illinois park association board.

HARRIS H. AGNEW
On board 1997 – 2009, president, 1999 – 2001

Instrumental in creating Juvenile Court Public Service Work Program, which is recognized nationally for bringing about significant drop in repeat of juvenile offenders. Longtime member of Kiwanis Clubs, which helped start program. Retired from Park Board to serve on Foundation board. Was chief judge of 17th circuit for 11 years.

THE COMMISSIONERS OF THE ERA 1972 – 2006

Daniel J. Nicholas

Charlotte Hackin

Douglas J. Brooks

LAURA PIGATTI WILLIAMSON
On board 1997 – 2009, president 2004 – 2007

Board service emphasized strategic planning, expanded programming for youth, and expanded role of the Park District Foundation. Continued service on committee for 100th Anniversary Celebration and as deputy director, capital planning and asset management for Park District. Served on board of Hunger Connection Food Bank and president of Rockford Gateway Association. Was vice-president with AMCORE Bank.

DANIEL J. NICHOLAS
On board 2001 – 2003

Credited with establishing City of Gardens program. Joined brothers Ab and Bill in donating more than $2 million for Nicholas Conservatory and Gardens, the Park District's Centennial project. Past president of Foundation, was CEO of First Federal Savings Bank, now Associated Bank. Received Rockford Register Star's Excalibur Award for community service in 1991.

CHARLOTTE HACKIN
On board 2001 – 2007

Brought to board her credentials as professional artist and teacher. Former art director at Lincoln Park Zoo in Chicago. Initiated annual Cultural Ethnic Festival. Has made numerous donations of her paintings to support fund raisers in the district and community. Published a book, "Stay Young to 100."

DOUGLAS J. BROOKS
On board 2003 – , president 2007 – 2010

Architect and vice president of Larson & Darby Group. Brought to board broad background of district facilities. Helped his firm do study that determined district's long term maintenance needs.

CHAPTER 5
The Last Chapter
2006 – PRESENT

By Tim Dimke, Executive Director
2006 – Present

Defying the odds

President Thomas Jefferson once wrote, "I like the dreams of the future better than the history of the past." I share his optimism about the future, while being very mindful of the important historical legacy of the Rockford Park District. A debt of gratitude is owed to those who were pioneers in building this park and recreation system, and we are today's caretakers of what they have built. Undoubtedly, the dreams of the future for this organization will continue to improve the quality of life in Rockford area.

In the business world, there is a saying that "Success is hard to manage." Very few private enterprises stay in the top Fortune 500 companies for more than a decade in this competitive global marketplace and ever changing economic environment. The Rockford Park District seemingly has defied the odds of managing success. Our 101+ year legacy of success would qualify us as a Fortune 500 organization.

To continue to succeed every day, innovation and continuous improvement must be expected. Daily we have dialogue on how to keep this nationally recognized and award-winning park and recreation system "the best in North America, as judged by the citizens we serve." Secondly, we think about how to create a future that's sustainable, positive, and progressive for our community. Lastly, we stay mindful about how to stay viable, vibrant, and relevant to the citizens for whom we work each and every day.

Ultimately, our future success depends on the Board of Commissioners who are elected at large and serve six-year terms without compensation. Commissioners provide the vision and direction that drives the entire organization. These five individuals are responsible for determining the

OPPOSITE: *A warm day brings water and sun lovers by the thousands to Magic Waters.*

RIGHT: *Tim Dimke, Executive Director*

services the District provides. It is their collective vision that will continue to bring organizational success for the next 100 years.

Throughout the past 101+ years, the Commissioners serving on the Board have been relentlessly committed to the Rockford Park District's financial stewardship and community investment. They perform a vital role, taking care of what the citizens have invested in as public assets, both in terms of green space as well as bricks and mortar.

It has not been uncommon for Commissioners to serve two or more terms. The Park District has been fortunate to have years of servant leadership from some exceptional individuals. That stability has created an infrastructure that can continuously adapt to improve the quality of living in our great city. As current Executive Director, I pledge to keep the leadership of the Rockford Park District transparent to our citizens. We seriously believe, as does our Board of Commissioners, that the importance of servant leadership and responsiveness to our citizens has contributed greatly to our sustained results.

Our Board of Commissioners have set forth a legacy practice that we must be a citizen-driven organization. Therefore, we continually look for new and effective ways to link with our community. Regularly scheduled meetings occur with other governmental entities (such as city, county, Forest Preserve District, school districts, sanitary district) to keep lines of communication open, and to be certain that all cooperative agreements ultimately benefit the citizens we serve.

The next level of citizen involvement occurs with our established advisory groups. The District collaborates with many groups, such as golfers, hockey families, tennis players, soccer clubs, and any "friends" group that form out of shared passion and commitment. The interactions between these groups with the Board and staff are critical for continuous improvement. Working closely with these users helps us to identify needed services and solve potential problems.

That's really the business the Rockford Park District is in — collaboratively filling needs and creatively solving community problems.

Our business gets accomplished by expecting employee team members to be adaptable in meeting needs and solving problems. Further, this parameter of business encourages everyone in the organization to be absolutely responsive. The expectation is that each and every contact made with a citizen will be a positive experience that builds the credibility of the Rockford Park District. If this happens consistently, the citizens will believe that we are truly servant leaders that listen to their suggestions and recommendations. It is essential to our continued legacy that current and future employee team members understand and uphold our value system that we serve the community first and always.

Annually, we have hundreds of students who will experience their first job

> *As current Executive Director, I pledge to keep the leadership of the Rockford Park District transparent to our citizens.*
> — TIM DIMKE

> *Another reason for our success is found in the diverse mix of individuals who work for the organization — they simply are a reflection of the community we serve.*

Full Staff Picture (2009)

as a Park District team member, and we have employees who have worked for the organization their entire career, several over 40 years. Many of our current employees (including yours truly) began working for the Rockford Park District on a seasonal basis while in high school. Whether one is a seasonal employee or a permanent employee, at the onset of employment the Park District's intangible value system of service must be inherently instilled. When employees are empowered to be flexible in meeting needs and solving problems, they make responsive and more thoughtful decisions.

Another reason for our success is found in the diverse mix of individuals who work for the organization — they simply are a reflection of the community we serve. The talents and expertise they bring to a position must be aligned to the creativity and problem solving approach we expect. We have some incredibly talented individuals on our team, as well as committed volunteers, who all deeply understand the importance of quality service delivery.

In employee orientations, our employees are asked to "treat people not only the way they themselves would like to be treated," but to also take the Golden Rule a step further — called the Platinum Rule — "treat a guest the way the guest would like to be treated." This saying clearly exemplifies how deeply we are committed to satisfied customers.

Team members are always requested to conduct themselves with a demeanor of trust and respect. No matter the guest's request, our goal is to give the benefit of service to the citizen. This is another simple value in our belief system, which demonstrates how we have managed to build trust and respect with others over these past 101+ years.

Managers are encouraged to "think like a CEO," and our leadership teams openly share issues, concerns, "goofs" (we consider these "golden opportunities"), and ideas to improve all areas of operations. In essence, running a golf course (or an ice rink, swimming pool, recreation program, or an internal support department) gives managers many opportunities to operate independently, while still being dependent on the same value system that drives the entire organization. The interdependence we strive for as we work together is yet another strategy for building trust and respect. The management team of the Park District has developed a leadership system to guide our decision-making.

The Leadership System for Maximum Success requires the development, implementation, monitoring, and constant improvement of Park District systems.

There are three phases in our leadership system.

First, a ***Visioning and Planning System*** is in place. Just like any successful sports team, in order to play the game well, the team needs a playbook and game plan. Our organization has a vision of what citizens and customers want us to become, and a plan and program to make that vision a reality.

Secondly, there is a ***Policy Management and Operations System*** that provides the rule book to guide operational decisions. Knowing the rules and staying within the parameters while adhering to laws and ethical practices, provides the framework for high quality, accurate, and timely decision making.

Thirdly, the ***Leadership by Values System*** is a clearly defined system that recognizes the human contribution to organizational success. Achieving the highest level of public confidence and support absolutely requires a concerted focus by all team members to produce high organizational results. Our dedicated team members are the single greatest resource for driving achievement and success.

The three keys to our organizational success are: defining what success looks like through the Visioning and Planning System, establishing operational rules and parameters for team members through the Policy Management and Operations System, and building a caring and supportive team environment for the people that are essential to implement our leadership systems.

Visioning and Planning System

We frequently illustrate organizational concepts by using pyramids at the Rockford Park District. On subsequent pages, our pyramids are presented. The peak is the most important, but the bottom layer is equally important as it is the foundation upon which each section is built. Over the years, the pyramids have gotten taller, and visually resemble the John Hancock building rather than the traditional Egyptian triangular version.

Incorporated into our pyramid visioning and planning system are basic questions of purpose. Examples of our inquiries are: What is the purpose for having park districts? Why do park districts exist? The Illinois State Legislature permitted the forming of park districts in 1895 for the purpose of

The Last Chapter • 2006 – Present

establishing and maintaining a public park and recreation system for the health, well-being, and entertainment of citizens.

The Rockford Park District was formed through public referendum on March 27, 1909, to form a local unit of government in response to the legislature's desire to form park districts in Illinois' communities.

All high performing organizations need to define its vision — what do we aspire to become, and how will we know when we get there? Over the past few decades, the Rockford Park District's vision has been to be "the best urban parks and recreation system in North America as judged by the citizens we serve."

The Rockford Park District has received many prestigious awards as well as state and national recognition over these past 101+ years. However, unless our citizens believe we are "the best" in their eyes, we have not achieved our vision.

The mission statement of the Rockford Park District is "helping people enjoy life." This is accomplished by providing a quality park and recreation system.

Helping people enjoy life means that the District provides access to nature, offers beautiful places to visit, gives people a means to stay healthy, provides respite from the stresses of life, and teaches people lifetime skills so they can make the most of their leisure time.

Many citizens are defined by their choice of leisure interests. How people spend their "free time" can be their defining passion! They may be a weekend warrior on the company's softball team, a golfer who continually strives to lower his/her handicap, a volunteer hockey coach, or a bird watcher in one of our many parks.

It is the daily objective of the team members of the Rockford Park District (and we are most fortunate to work in an industry that is vibrant and fun), to help people enjoy life through offering opportunities to recharge, reflect, and re-energize.

The Board of Commissioners has defined and described what success looks like for the services offered by the Rockford Park District.

 ROCKFORD PARK DISTRICT

VISION To become the best urban park and recreation system in North America, as judged by the citizens we serve.

Global Priority Result Park space and recreation are essential to the quality of life in the Rockford Park District,

Priority Result I
Well maintained park space and recreational facilities meet the recreational needs of this and succeeding generations of District residents.

A Park space acquisition and development priorities:
  i Open space and recreational use along the Rock River;
  ii Neighborhood parks within reasonable walking distance from citizens' homes, with access unhindered by major barriers;
  iii Recreational paths, trails and linear parks are expanded and/or connected.

B Growth in the acreage of parkland or development of facilities for active recreation:
  i Must have identified sources for incremental maintenance and operational costs;
  ii Must incorporate sustainable design in development, construction and operation;
  iii High priority will be given to indoor facilities for year round use.

C Park space meets residents' needs for active and passive recreation
  i A minimum of 10 acres of parkland for organized recreation activities per 1,000 population;
  ii A minimum of 10 acres of natural parkland for passive activities per 1,000 population;
  iii Increased acreage of natural areas for preservation and wildlife habitat.

Priority Result II
Residents are involved in diverse and well supported recreational activities for their health, well-being, and entertainment.

A Residents engage in activities including sports, other types of active and passive recreation, nature study/environmental education and cultural activities.

B Residents develop lifelong recreational skills supported by existing major recreation assets

C Residents engage in well-supported recreational activities in the Rock River Corridor:
  i Fee-based
  ii Free/passive

D Priority is for RPD services/amenities to serve all District residents :
  i Highest priority: Youth ages 3-12;
  ii Second priority: Teens ages 13-18;
  iii Third priority: Adults ages 55+;
  iv During summer and non-school times;
  v Coaching and instruction at introductory/basic levels for lifetime recreational enjoyment;
  vi A clean and safe environment exists at parks, events, buildings, and facilities;
  vii Activities will be accessible at times and locations that meet the needs of diverse demographic populations in a geographically balanced manner.

Approved and adopted by Board of Commissioners 9/28/10

We call these Priority Results. There are four priority results and an overall global outcome that "Park space and recreation are essential for the quality of life in the Rockford Park District, resulting in a high return on investment of available resources."

Parks and recreation services are essential to life, not just something that is "nice" to have if the community can afford it. When the Rockford Park District was formed in 1909, the Rockford Club and the five founding Commissioners were of one voice that parks and recreation were as essential as roads, clean water, and public safety. That visionary planning is still what guides our work today — 101+ years later!

MISSION To **'help people enjoy life'** by providing a quality park and recreation system.

resulting in a high return on investment of available resources.

In the current competitive environment of retaining and attracting new businesses, and for new residents who choose to locate in the greater Rockford community, quality of life is a deciding factor. When people are considering a job change, a residential move, or locating a company here, they consider the amenities offered for arts and culture, recreation, health care, education, and personal growth. The Rockford Park District plays a key role in economic development, tourism, and community viability.

The four Priority Results define what success looks like as we work towards achieving the global outcome desired by the Board.

Priority Result I: Well maintained park space and recreational facilities meet recreational needs of this and succeeding generations of Park District residents.

My interpretation of this policy is that the RPD takes a long term view ("this and succeeding generations of District residents"), including assessment of both population growth trends and geographic distribution, to ensure that both the array of amenities and their proximity help make park space and recreation 'essential for the quality of life' throughout the District, both now and in the future.

Park space is defined as land, amenities, and facilities. Acquisition and development of park space (active and passive use) will be driven by:

Priority Result III
Residents value recreation as essential for a healthy life.

A Residents recognize the importance of and leadership role that parks and recreation play in:
  i A balanced, healthy lifestyle;
  ii Positive use of leisure time;
  iii Beautification, reforestation, conservation, environmentally responsible practices, and engagement with nature.
B There is growth in residents' involvement in and support of their park and recreation system through:
  i Volunteers and friends groups;
  ii Financial support;
  iii Formal partnerships with community organizations.

Priority Result IV
Residents have exceptional parks and recreation facilities, services, and programs at a reasonable cost.

A Priority Results achievement reflects a high return on available tax resources.
  i District residents enjoy parks and a broad array of "core" recreational activities at no additional charge;
  ii Residents receive exclusive discounts for user fees on all programs and services;
  iii Non-resident user fees are comparable with those charged for like programs and services in the marketplace.
B There is growth in visitors and tourists using Park District assets in a way that complements use and offsets costs for residents.

1: The standards the Board has provided.

2: The recreational needs and requests of Park District residents.

All current land and recreation facilities shall be accessible and maintained at the highest level for their intended use and the safety of our users.

Priority Result II: Residents involved in diverse and well-supported recreational activities for their health, well-being, and entertainment.

This Priority Result gives direction to our team to develop a public park and recreation program that offers Park District residents a broad and varied range of park and recreational activities.

"Well supported" is interpreted as meaning that the District has systems and processes in place that provide the level of support required to deliver high quality park and recreation services to our citizens.

The Park District will focus its direct programming in service areas where there are major assets (parks and recreation facilities) to support, and where we have the financial resources and expertise to provide the program.

In service areas where the Park District cannot directly offer the program, support is provided to a partner to offer the program. Priority is given to partnerships that support the District's Priority Results and enhances the expected return on investment to our citizens.

Priority Result III: Residents value recreation as essential for life.

"Value" in this statement indicates that District residents believe that recreation is vital to their health and well being. Residents are aware of recreational opportunities at the District, and understand the value and benefits of park and recreation services in their lives.

It is my interpretation that "residents" to be targeted are those of all ages with priority for resource allocation given to the age groups designated in Priority Result II.

I interpret a key demonstration of "value" to be that residents participate in leisure pursuits including:

- Recreational activities or sports to promote wellness and fitness
- Passive appreciation of beautiful parks, gardens, and natural areas
- Visits to the District's museums and cultural programs

Priority Result IV: Residents have exceptional parks and recreational facilities, services, and programs at a reasonable cost.

Achievement of this end would indicate that residents value the RPD as a good return on their investment through taxes and fees paid. We deliver services to residents in a geographically balanced manner, without favoritism.

"Exceptional" means that each and every District park, facility, service, and program offered will be of the highest quality possible.

"At a reasonable cost" directs that services will be priced at a level to be affordable for residents, with levy and fee structures at or below the average of comparable park districts and fees charged in the marketplace.

> *We deliver services to residents in a geographically balanced manner, without favoritism.*

The Executive Director provides these interpretations for each of the Priority Results so there is a clear linkage between the Board's Priority Results and allocation of resources; these define what services, for which people, at what cost.

Each year, team members have dialogue on what success looks like. We then develop specific, measurable statements called 'Success Indicators.' These indicators tell us what success looks like and are used to develop annual operational plans. Results, achievements, and progress are reported to the Board through regularly scheduled monitoring reports and shared with citizens through an Annual Report of the Commissioners and Citizen Financial Report.

Policy Management and Operations System

This pyramid defines the rule book that guides operational decisions. When the guidelines are clear, decisions are easier and faster to make.

The top level is the Park District Code, enacted in 1947 to codify the state laws which directly govern the powers, duties, and purposes of park districts in Illinois with fewer than 500,000 inhabitants. We are legally bound to observe all state and federal statutes, including additional laws which impact park district operations, such as the Open Meetings Act, Minimum Wage Laws, Americans with Disabilities Act, Smoke-free Illinois, Child Labor Laws, etc.

Residents value recreation as essential for life.

Next, the Rockford Park District Code outlines laws and ordinances governing the operation of the Rockford Park District, including the use and policing of parks and other facilities, personal conduct of patrons and employees, etc.

In the middle of this pyramid, there are Management Limitations Policies that are defined by the Board of Commissioners in partnership with citizens. These policies control Park District operations on a day-to-day basis. These policies direct staff action (do this), establish boundaries staff must act within (shall not do this), and define unacceptable staff behavior and practices.

There are sixteen areas that are currently defined, and these are addressed in annual (or more frequent) monitoring reports indicating compliance or non-compliance.

The sixteen areas involving Management Limitations Policies are:
- General Management Constraint
- Treatment of Customers
- Treatment of Staff
- Financial Planning/Budgeting
- Financial Condition and Activities
- Financial Advisory Committee Recommendations
- Asset Protection
- Capital Improvement Program
- Emergency Executive Succession
- Compensation and Benefits
- Communication/Support to the Board
- Services Logistics
- Partnerships and Grants
- Religious Practices and Activities
- Fund Development
- Museums

Again, there are interpretations provided for each area to illustrate alignment between Management Limitations policies and staff operational policies. These interpretations provide direction to staff on acceptable operational actions, and confirm the means used.

As team members, we are given flexibility and latitude on achieving the ends by a variety of means. The ability to achieve ends flexibly gives staff a clear understanding on what the Board expects and where we need to spend our time, energies, and resources.

Staff Operational Policies are District-wide policies that direct and regulate staff activities and practices to ensure Park District operations comply with the Management Limitations policies.

BUILDING A LASTING DREAM

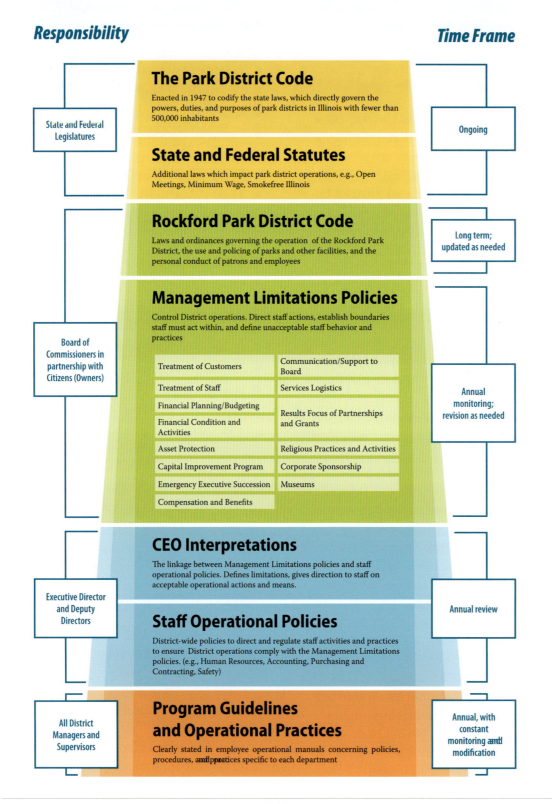

These include human resource policies, financial/accounting policies and procedures, purchasing and contracting policies, and safety policies/procedures.

Finally, the base foundation of this pyramid is Program Guidelines and Operational Practices. These are clearly stated operational manuals concerning policies, procedures, and practices specific to each department and operational area. For example, Magic Waters has an operational manual specific to its operation; park maintenance, golf courses, pools, and ice facilities all have such manuals. These operational manuals are reviewed and updated annually, and all Park District managers and supervisors are responsible for constant monitoring and making modifications throughout the year.

Leadership by Values

Finally, we come to the intangible, philosophical value system on which the Rockford Park District is firmly built. This might be called our "corporate culture." Better described, this is the "heart and soul" of our organization.

Several years ago, I visited and studied at the Mott Foundation in Michigan. I was traveling with several employees of the City of Rockford and Rockford School District. We were learning about strategies to make Rockford a world-class educational system. Gwen Robinson, who was the lead administrator for the City of Rockford's Human Services Department, was traveling with us. She was most familiar with the leadership system of the Rockford Park District. In response to some of the questions posed by the Mott Foundation staff, Gwen made an important observation as I engaged in some of the activities. She commented, "Are you a clone of Webbs Norman? You answered exactly like he would. How do you do that? How do you all stay on the same page?" Gwen did not realize it at that moment, but she had just affirmed our value system at work.

With assurance, we are clearly not Webbs' clones, but our values are definitely shared. Our shared Leadership by Values System is a prominent component within our corporate culture. We may have very different approaches and varied opinions, yet staff operates from this clearly defined system of servant leadership.

Park District employees actually defined the top of the pyramid many years ago. In 1972, Webbs had just been hired as Executive Director when a maintenance strike threatened to divide organizational departments. There were harsh divisions forming between the office staff and those working in the field. It seemed as though the recreation staff and parks staff were never going to find common ground. It seemed apparent that whatever corporate culture existed, it was full of animosity and certainly not one of shared vision.

Once the pending strike was no longer a threat, Webbs brought everyone together to discuss their shared future. He felt it was imperative for staff to work together cooperatively, and regain the trust and respect of the citizens we serve.

Webbs wisely invited staff to ponder what success would look like. He asked them, "What do you want people in this community to think of when they refer to the Rockford Park District?" Almost unanimously staff responded, "We want people to have confidence in us, to support us, to trust us." That need for citizen confidence is what prompted the agreement for internal collaboration.

Ever since, our most important shared core value has been to establish and maintain a high level of citizen confidence and support. Recently we added a qualifying statement with that confidence level. We want citizens to have confidence that they get a good return on their investment with the Rockford Park

BUILDING A LASTING DREAM

ROCKFORD PARK DISTRICT
Leadership by Values System

The Mission of the Rockford Park District is to *"help people enjoy life."* Leadership by Values is a clearly defined system which acknowledges the human contribution to organizational success

- Establish and maintain a high level of citizen confidence and support, as evidenced by a high return on their investment.

- Constantly discuss and refine team members' core values to inspire them to achieve our shared purpose, vision, and mission.

- Continuously communicate and inform all team members of the parameters established by the Policy Management & Operations System.

- Involve all team members in developing and monitoring an operational plan and program to achieve the Board's Priority Results as identified in the Visioning & Planning System.

- Continuously define expectations, roles, and responsibilities for team members to ensure maximum performance and accountability.

- Establish and maintain exceptional relationships with all internal team members and external stakeholders.

- Create a work atmosphere that is safe, healthy, and secure, and is conscious of work/life balance as well as the Park District's goals.

- Align for achievement by recruiting, hiring, developing, supporting, evaluating, rewarding, and promoting competent and service-oriented team members who reflect the composition of the community we serve.

- Pay competitive wages and benefits for like work in the marketplace.

Leadership by Values can only be achieved if all team members are guided by these core values – value centered and mission directed, integrity, truthfulness, trustworthiness, respect, compassion, fairness, internal and external awareness, spontaneity, holism, independence/interdependence, diversity, unity, accountability, and humor

District. This investment includes both fees for service and with the property taxes they pay.

The other seven fundamental building blocks that define our Leadership by Values System are presented on the following illustration. These blocks may only be attained if all team members are guided daily by these core values.

Rockford Park District staff shares a deep commitment to living and breathing these values as we serve our citizens.

Partnerships

The Rockford Park District could not possibly have impacted so many areas of our community without its innovative partnerships. In virtually every area of our organization, partners were and continue to be a vital part of our sustained success. The Park District often receives credit for various projects, but success was actually realized due to opportunities brought to our organization by citizens, donors, local companies, and agencies. Our history is filled with examples of partnerships that were formed from ideas that originated within the community.

In 1979, the Forest City Queen excursion riverboat was given to the Park District by First National Bank. Thirty years later, the boat has ferried over 300,000 people up and down the Rock River.

In 1982, the BMX track at Searls Park was started through the work of the Rockford Jaycees. Today, it is considered to be one of the finest BMX tracks in the nation, and volunteers extraordinaire Jake and Candy Karau operate the track. The track is used by 53,000 riders and spectators annually.

In 1983, Sportscore One opened with eight soccer fields at the persistent request of a small group of British engineers who were employed at Sundstrand. They requested a couple of grassy fields so they could play soccer with their blokes. Today, soccer is played by thousands of area youth and adults on 78 fields throughout the community. Our soccer fields have achieved legendary status, which contributed to a title for Rockford — the amateur sports tournament capital of the Midwest. For 23 consecutive weekends, soccer tournaments fill both Sportscore complexes and overflow hotel rooms within a 30-mile radius.

An important donor and partnership came from the private sector in the late 1990s. Dr. Donald Wedgbury (affectionately known as "Doc") built the Indoor Sports Center in the middle of a cornfield east of I-90, complete with an outdoor stadium, essentially to accommodate club soccer in his back yard. The Indoor Sports Center (ISC) quickly became a popular soccer venue to practice indoors year 'round. The operation was an immediate hit, and while financially successful, Doc quickly discovered he no longer had the time or energy to devote to both the operation of ISC and his sports medicine practice.

Doc Wedgbury approached the Rockford Park District with the desire to keep the operation going without his direct involvement, and was willing to make a substantial donation of land and the opportunity to purchase the facilities he developed for half the cost of the investment he had made in creating ISC.

The Park District had already purchased an adjacent 160-acre site in 1994, and was in the process of creating additional soccer fields surrounding the ISC complex by 2001. The purchase of ISC coupled with the donation made practical business sense, and it's been highly successful and provided a great economic benefit to the community. Hotels, restaurants, and gas stations have greatly benefited from the addition and programming of Sportscore Two. The two Sportscore complexes have made Rockford the "amateur sports capital of the world," or at least that's our vision for creating our future sports amenities.

As the concept of creating a second Sportscore complex was moving forward, a small group of highly committed individuals formed the Sportscore Two Coalition to raise funds to develop the new complex.

> *Almost 40 percent of Park District land and assets have been donated throughout the past 101+ years, and philanthropy continues to play a critical role as the District links the passion of the donor to community needs.*

Attorney and philanthropist Jim Keeling, along with land developer and soccer enthusiast Sunil Puri, together with Wendy Perks-Fisher, the energetic President and CEO of the Rockford Area Convention & Visitors Bureau, raised unprecedented private and public support in the form of donations, gifts, grants, and sponsorship with local corporations and foundations, plus individual private contributions. Sportscore Two was dubbed "The Next Big Thing" for the Rockford Park District, opening for play in August, 2002.

Following this successful fundraising campaign for Sportscore Two, Jim Keeling then devoted himself to developing the next generation of Rockford golfers by founding and leading the Junior Golf Foundation of Greater Rockford that is directly responsible for the creation of the first beginner's course at Ingersoll called The Learning Links, and the First Tee® program at Patriot's Gateway. Jim is a passionate advocate for youth golf and has greatly influenced the expansion of instructional programs at the Rockford Park District.

Another golf enthusiast and great gentleman is a man by the name of Norris Aldeen, who in 1988 stopped by the Director's office, inquiring if he might have a moment of our time to consider a gift of prime farm land, and a donation of $1 million to build it. His inquiry led to the creation of a championship level fifth public golf course that was on par with country club experiences for the working men, women, and children of the Rockford community. Norris grew up playing golf with his mother at Sinnissippi and Ingersoll golf courses, and he never forgot the impact this game had on his family's life.

Donors like Norris and Margaret Aldeen are highly important partners to the District's success. Almost 40 percent of Park District land and assets have been donated throughout the past 101+ years, and philanthropy continues to play a critical role as the District links the passion of the donor to community needs.

Another community advocate is developer, entrepreneur, and businessman Kurt Carlson, who donated prime development land and provided landscaping amounting to $2 million dollars as a donation to create the Carlson Ice Arena. Kurt's father, Edwin Carlson, Jr., had served the Rockford Park District as a Park Commissioner for 19 years and was Board President in 1987 – 88. He and his wife, Vi, are donors of a park named in honor of their parents, Carlson-Nelles Park in Southwest Rockford. Often throughout our history, public service and philanthropy towards the Rockford Park District is a family affair.

Yet another former Commissioner and community beautification advocate, Dan Nicholas, along with his wife, Ruth, created the City of Gardens Program in 1999 with seed money as a gift to the Rockford Park District Foundation in order to plant colorful flowers downtown. The program started with eighteen hanging baskets and has grown to over 250 hanging baskets and street planters.

In 2006, while preparing for the upcoming 100th anniversary year of the Rockford Park District, the Board of Commissioners designated the first park, Sinnissippi and its riverfront area to be the site for a Centennial signature project for the community. Within two weeks, a donor family stepped forward and proposed a substantial gift and asked that the Conservatory and Gardens be named to honor their parents, William and Ruby Nicholas. The Nicholas family of Bill, Dan, and Albert envisioned the Nicholas Conservatory & Gardens as a gathering place for our community and a catalyst for future riverfront development. Construction is now underway with a grand opening targeted for fall, 2011.

Partnerships and Cooperative Planning

The Rockford Park District is somewhat unique among Illinois park districts in the approach undertaken with other recreation providers. Providers such as the Boys & Girls Clubs, YMCA, YWCA, and neighborhood community centers have complemented our success. Our philosophy has been to do what the Park District does best (delivering direct services and providing facilities), helping others be successful at doing what they do best (not directly compete with but support and promote all recreation opportunities to citizens), and advocate for comprehensive recreational services in the community. By doing so, the District has expanded knowledge about the benefits and importance for living a balanced, healthy, and whole life.

The reality is that the Rockford Park District cannot possibly provide all the services and facilities citizens want and need for leisure and recreation. The fact is that the community could not afford to pay for the Park District to be the sole provider of leisure and recreational services.

If, for example, Rockford Little League disbanded, and their core of dedicated volunteers retired, there would be a great need for the Rockford Park District to provide a youth baseball program. Baseball programs are actually provided effectively and efficiently by several groups, including Harlem Community Center, Rockford Pony League Softball/Baseball at Roy Gayle Complex, Ken-Rock Community Center, the Boys & Girls Clubs, and Rockford Little League. Combined, these organizations provide over 4,000 youth the opportunity to play ball for a reasonable fee. The Park District actually owns 35 of the 40 high quality youth baseball diamonds that are operated by these groups.

If Northwest, St. Elizabeth's, Booker Washington, Ken-Rock, or Harlem community centers closed their doors, the Park District would need to step in and serve the needs in those neighborhoods.

Rockford Pony Baseball/Softball has been a highly successful grassroots, volunteer organization since 1962. This summer sports tradition has served over 1,200 boys and girls who play ball at the Roy Gayle Complex on the west end of

> *The reality is that the Rockford Park District cannot possibly provide all the services and facilities citizens want and need for leisure and recreation.*

Rockford. Mike Broski, a tireless supporter and fundraising expert, championed the effort to successfully raise over $400,000 to purchase the land when it changed ownership in order to keep the complex for the youth of our community. We owe Mike and many others an enormous debt of gratitude for their personal commitment and multiple contributions to providing recreation opportunities for families to enjoy together.

It makes dollars and "sense" to support these complementary recreation providers and do whatever is necessary to maintain their successes with citizens. Partnerships are maintained with about 300 organizations and entities each year, and each one is an important and highly valued partner in delivering recreation services to citizens.

Additionally, there are other supporting groups such as Friends of the Dog Parks, Friends of Lockwood Park, clubs for figure skating, hockey, and soccer, that all involve parent volunteers. Imagine the higher cost of programs if the Park District paid wages to everyone who volunteers as a coach, advisor, or museum docent.

The Rockford Park District family of museums is another key partnership for providing recreation for the mind. The six museums are consistently in the District's top visitor attractions, with 1.3 million user visits occurring annually. With a taxpayer investment of $2.1 million, and operating and capital budgets of $10 million, there is a 5-to-1 return on investment. The museums and their entities not only provide a tremendous quality of life for residents of our community, they have tremendous citizen involvement through volunteers and philanthropy. Three of the District museums (Burpee, Discovery Center, and Midway Village) just completed major expansion projects that are propelling them to being even greater community assets and vibrant visitor destinations. Most of the funding was through private donations with some state grants assisting their fundraising efforts.

Much has been accomplished through partnerships with other government, non-profit organizations, and private sector groups to maximize the value of tax resources expended. Tax resources have been leveraged through fee revenue, grants, corporate sponsorships, and private donations to provide a wide range of services throughout the community.

> *Much has been accomplished through partnerships with other government, non-profit organizations, and private sector groups to maximize the value of tax resources expended.*

Facing Future Challenges

Financially, the Rockford Park District is at a pivotal point. Its existing resources have been extensively leveraged and the possibilities for expansion are extremely limited in the current economic environment.

The last tax increase, by referendum, for recreation funding was in 1979 at 5 cents per $100 assessed valuation. That was over thirty years ago. In 1990, voters approved a 10 cent increase for maintenance needs. But when statewide tax cap legislation took effect in 1996, the District could not collect all rates the voters had previously approved. The overall tax rate of the Park District decreased by over 10 cents per $100 assessed valuation since 1996, representing over $3 million that was left on the table, uncollectible, in 2008 alone.

The inability to collect these funds has

been a major factor in the growing backlog of deferred maintenance and replacement needs for District facilities and museums. The estimated costs for maintenance upgrades are more than $12 million for facilities and $2 million for museums.

Further, the funding gap developing between the District's current and future needs and its current resources is widening. It would take a significant infusion of revenue to continue to meet the same service standards that have been historically available to Park District residents.

To address these immediate issues and project a long-term revenue forecast, a Financial Advisory Committee was formed in 2007. Seven citizens with extensive financial expertise met and analyzed current and anticipated needs for the next decade, defined the gap between needs and resources, and developed nine recommendations for the Park District to consider, which they presented to the Commissioners early in 2009. The Board accepted their recommendations, and over $2.2 million in cost savings and $2.2 million in revenue enhancements have been realized in the past two years implementing their recommendations. Sustainability is the key to creating a solid future. We have a history of 101+ years of presenting a balanced budget, maintaining healthy fund balances, and living within the resources the citizens give us to work with.

> *There are about 40 new neighborhood parks needed for new and growing developments to meet the Board objective of a neighborhood park within reasonable walking distance of resident's homes without major barriers or hindrances.*

Land acquisition for the development of neighborhood parks, recreation paths and trails, and public Rock River access is the highest priority for any new land acquisition. The fact is, with an annual budget of $200,000, there are not adequate resources to purchase or develop land. Grants to leverage local dollars are harder to obtain from state and federal sources. Our current policy for new land acquisition requires land banking until money is available to develop or maintain it, even if it is donated. There are about 40 new neighborhood parks needed for new and growing developments to meet the Board objective of a neighborhood park within reasonable walking distance of resident's homes without major barriers or hindrances.

Additional recreational programming is needed to engage today's youth, particularly those youth considered at-risk for success. The Park District provides programs and leverages partnerships with other organizations to better serve this target audience who represent the future face of our community.

Unless the development of new facilities is completely funded by non-tax financial resources (such as grants or donations with maintenance endowments), the District has no available funds for capital additions. Any park or facility development must be leveraged with grants, donations, or private contributions. During the past five years throughout the Rockford Park District, there have been about $30 million dollars in construction projects in development with all but $2 million paid for with 'other people's money.' That's what I mean by leveraging resources and getting a good return on taxpayer investment! This other money includes donations, grants, sponsorships, and other non-local tax sources.

BUILDING A LASTING DREAM

Strategies that have been implemented for financial support were the formation of the Financial Advisory Committee, creating an Audit Committee to provide oversight, and developing more "friends groups" at major facilities. The "friends groups" provide volunteer labor, thereby reducing expenses and administrative overhead.

Leave the Lights on, We're Staying

Often times in our history when circumstances looked their bleakest, the Rockford Park District reinvented itself. In the beginning, five Commissioners pledged their personal assets as collateral to purchase the first park, Sinnissippi. Even though this purchase was criticized for being "too far out in the country that no one would ever use it," developing Sinnissippi Park turned out to be a very wise investment and is a highly valued community treasure.

In the 1950s, local leaders thought it was time the Park District move from a land-only stewardship role to one that provided meaningful recreation programs and services to the community, and a Recreation Tax was approved by voters. Other than the initial founding in 1909, this was the second most significant event that made the Rockford Park District the excellent park and recreation system it is today. From this tax source came many of the recreation amenities within our community. The Park District is renowned for its golf courses, sports fields, free summer concerts, playground programs, indoor skating, waterpark, ,and equestrian center. Not many communities similar to the size of Rockford can boast of having comparable recreational facilities.

The old City Yards on the Rock River was developed into Riverview Ice House where people could skate indoors year around, and it became home to the boat and trolley which offer excursion rides. At the time this project was conceived, it was ridiculed and called "Norman's Folly." The two ice facilities attract and serve over 300,000 people a year.

A once-closed water theme park became a thriving visitor destination which has increased summer tourism, and it has become a favorite summer recreation site for our residents. Magic Waters is the second largest publicly owned water park in the nation and in a normal summer packs in over 250,000 people.

Some swamp land along the Rock River was creatively developed into a sports complex which now serves a million people a year who enjoy playing softball and soccer.

We have a 101+ year history of taking bold, calculated risks with highly successful outcomes.

There are infinite possibilities around us as we forge our future. What does the future of leisure and recreation hold? Some of our current dreams include:

- Completing all phases of the Nicholas Conservatory & Gardens in the riverfront area of Sinnissippi Park, an exciting and vibrant visitor destination
- Skate parks in every quadrant for extreme action sports
- More passive opportunities for people to get closer to nature, enjoy bird watching, and engage in natural studies
- Connecting recreation pathways and trail systems for improved access and providing a means for alternative transportation (ride your bike to work)
- Indoor sports facilities for year-round soccer, basketball, volleyball, soccer,

Opposite: Executive Director Tim Dimke with an architectural model of the new Nicholas Conservatory.

softball, and golf, as well as wheelchair athletics
- Indoor riding arena for year-round equine activities
- Expanded gardens and reforestation throughout the "Forest City"

On behalf of all the men and women of the Rockford Park District, we consider it a privilege and honor to work on behalf of our citizens, and we pledge:
- To be stewards of the natural resources entrusted to us
- To maintain public assets
- To gladly take responsibility for children placed in our care for programs
- To treat financial resources entrusted to us with careful consideration

Thank you for your confidence and support for the past 101+ years. As we have entered our second century of service, we look forward to continuing the shared vision of excellence in parks and recreation in partnership with our citizens.

TIMOTHY E. DIMKE

Tim Dimke is the Executive Director of the Rockford Park District. Tim is a Rockford native who has been an employee of the Rockford Park District for 38 years (as of 2011), where he started as a seasonal maintenance employee. More recently, he has held a variety of leadership positions, including Deputy Director, Chief Operating Officer, and since 2006, Executive Director.

Tim maintains active membership in and is associated with the National Recreation and Parks Association, Illinois Association of Park Districts, Illinois Park and Recreation Association, Natural Land Institute, Pheasants Forever, National Wild Turkey Federation, Jo Daviess Soil & Water Conservation District, Eastern Illinois Athletic Alumni Association, and serves on the Rockford College MBA Advisory Board and Rockford Area Convention & Visitors Bureau Board. Tim was appointed by the Governor of Illinois to serve on the non-partisan Mississippi River Coordinating Council.

He graduated from Auburn High School, received a Bachelor of Science degree in Parks and Recreation Management from Eastern Illinois University, and earned a Master's Degree in Business Administration from Rockford College. Tim has been married for over 30 years to his high school and college sweetheart, Debra. Their son, Derek, attends the University of Illinois and is a member of the football team.

Positions Held with Rockford Park District:
- Seasonal/Crew Foreman, 1973 – 1978
- Manager/Support Services, 1978 – 1980
- Assistant Manager/Riverview Ice House, 1980
- Manager/Riverview Ice House, 1981 – 1985
- Superintendent/Special Facilities, 1985 – 1989
- Deputy Director/Recreation Services, 1989 – 1998
- Interim Executive Director, 1998 – 1999
- Chief Operating Officer, 2000 – 2006
- Executive Director, 2006 to present

PROFILE OF THE PARK DISTRICT 2006 – 2009

Year:	1910	1928	1945	1971	2006	2009
Statistic:						
Population	48,405	91,750	113,410	160,460	205,867	211,538
Number of Parks/Properties	15	45	65	109	173	175
Park District Acreage	159.47	731.35	2,361.26	3,570.27	4,573.62	4,840.04
Total Budget	$140,343.49[1]	$177,063.00	$150,412.00	$2,965,929.00	$38,615,514.00	$35,502,434.00
Property Tax Revenue	$35,999.00	$160,142.00	$122,837.00	$2,197,237.00	$19,242,500.00	$21,683,971.00
Per Capita Expenditure from Taxes	$0.74	$1.74	$1.08	$13.69	$93.47	$102.51
Median Family Income	Not available	Not available	Not available	$13,249.00	$47,735.00	$46,083.00
Estimated Total User Visits	Not available	Not available	Not available	1,500,000	9,638,217	9,213,104[2]

[1] 1910 budget covered 18 months instead of 12 months.

[2] Applies to 2009 only: Programs cancelled at Sportscore One due to flooding.

THE COMMISSIONERS OF THE ERA 2006 – PRESENT

Nathaniel Martin   *Harris H. Agnew*   *Laura Pigatti Williamson*   *Charlotte Hackin*   *Douglas J. Brooks*

NATHANIEL MARTIN

On board, 1995 – 1997, 1999 –, president 2004 – 2007

First African-American board member. Career with Rockford School District covered 28 years as teacher, ombudsman, middle school principal and director of secondary education. In 2008, appointed to Illinois park association board.

HARRIS H. AGNEW

On board 1997 to 2009, president, 1999 – 2001

Created Juvenile Court Public Service Work Program, recognized nationally for bringing about significant drop in repeat of juvenile offenders. Longtime member of Kiwanis Clubs, which helped start program. Instrumental in broadening use of Pard District Sun Singer logo. Retired from Park Board to serve on Foundation board. Was chief judge of 17th circuit for 11 years.

LAURA PIGATTI WILLIAMSON

On board 1997 – 2009, president 2004 – 2007

Board service emphasized strategic planning, expanded programming for youth, and expanded role of the Park District Foundation. Continued service on committee for 100th Anniversary Celebration and as deputy director, capital planning and asset management for Park District. Served on board of Hunger Connection Food Bank and president of Rockford Gateway Association. Was vice-president with AMCORE Bank.

CHARLOTTE HACKIN

On board 2001 – 2007

Brought to board her credentials as professional artist and teacher. Former art director at Lincoln Park Zoo in Chicago. Initiated annual Cultural Ethnic Festival. Has made numerous donations of her paintings to support fund raisers in the district and community. Authored book, "Stay Young to 100."

DOUGLAS J. BROOKS

On board 2003 – , president 2007 – 2010

Architect and vice president of Larson & Darby Group. Brought to board deep background of district facilities. Helped his firm do study that determined district's long term maintenance needs.

THE COMMISSIONERS OF THE ERA 2006 – PRESENT

Jack L. Armstrong   *Tyler Smith*   *Chuck Brown*   *Ian Linnabary*

JACK L. ARMSTRONG
On board 2007 – , president 2010 –

Retired in 1998 after teaching 34 years in Rockford School District. Brought a broad-based environmental interest to the board. Has served as chairman of the Upper Rock River Ecosystem Partnership, treasurer of Severson Dells Foundation Board and Sinnissippi Audubon Society. Also served on Burpee Museum of Natural History Board as president. Honored with Seth B. Atwood Conservation Award in 1990.

TYLER SMITH
On board 2009 –

Owner and operator of Tyler's Landscaping, a full-service landscaping business, for over 22 years. Pledged "to assure our citizens an excellent parks and recreation organization for their taxpayer dollars and for future generations." Active in Ski Broncs water ski organization.

CHUCK BROWN
On board 2009 – 2011

Was director of communications and new media for Rockford College. Commented in the election campaign "as a user of park district facilities, I feel obligated to give back to the community by putting my public service and administrative skills to work for the people." Died in May 2011.

IAN LINNABARY
On board 2011 –

Partner in law firm Reno & Zahm. Extensive board and community volunteer experience. Ran unsuccessfully for board in 2009, appointed in 2011. Avid runner and bicyclist.

PROLOGUE TO THE APPENDICES

A salute to the thousands of people who made the Rockford Park District what it is today.

This history begins in the early 1900s with the dream of Levin Faust that every neighborhood should have a playground for its children and that every parent should be able to take children on a picnic on Sunday afternoons following a long and hard week or work.

Faust made his dream come true. And, thanks to the leadership of 49 Park Board commissioners and their dedicated staffs, along with responsive, active and caring citizens, his dream continues to expand. One hundred and two years later, in 2011, the Park Board's vision remains to develop the Rockford Park District into the best urban park and recreation system in North America, as judged by the citizens it serves.

I'm sure Levin is proud of everyone who has made this continued success possible. Let us all help the vision grow.

I pray that the Park District will, over the next 100 years, enjoy the support it did in the first 100. Without generous Rockford people, a large part of our district would not exist.

Remember that Levings Lake, Anna Page, Searls, Martin, Atwood, Aldeen, Olson and many other parks were donations. Taxpayers didn't buy them.

Now add to that list the Nicholas Conservatory and Gardens, Carlson Ice Arena, Playworks playgrounds, Forest City Queen, Floral Clock, rose garden, Aldeen and Ingersoll golf courses, sculptures along the river, and the many playgrounds built after children, parents and others in the community went out and raised dollars through bake sales and knocking on doors. Don't forget the thousands of snacks and reduced-price field trips the district provided to children in playground programs because some company gave us a check. And never overlook the volunteers who help run special events, raise money for us and keep our parks in good shape.

Without that generous support, we would not be half what we are.

I salute the thousands of people — some wealthy and some not so wealthy – who made our Park District what it is. Perhaps someday you'll join us, whether on the board, as a volunteer or someone who walks into our office and announces, "I have an idea."

Following is a map showing district boundaries and parks, some charts showing our growth, and short biographies on the directors.

We've also included the names of people who have meant a lot to me and the Park District. We've published some of the letters people sent congratulating us on our 100th birthday and telling us what parks mean to them.

Other lists include individuals and organizations that have been honored by the Park District and state associations, staff development instructors who helped our employees do their jobs well, and awards the Park District subsequently won because of the exemplary way those staff members did their work.

OPPOSITE: A young Levings Laker shows off his prize during the Fish Fest at Levings Lake in 2010.

APPENDIX A
MAPS OF THE ROCKFORD PARK DISTRICT

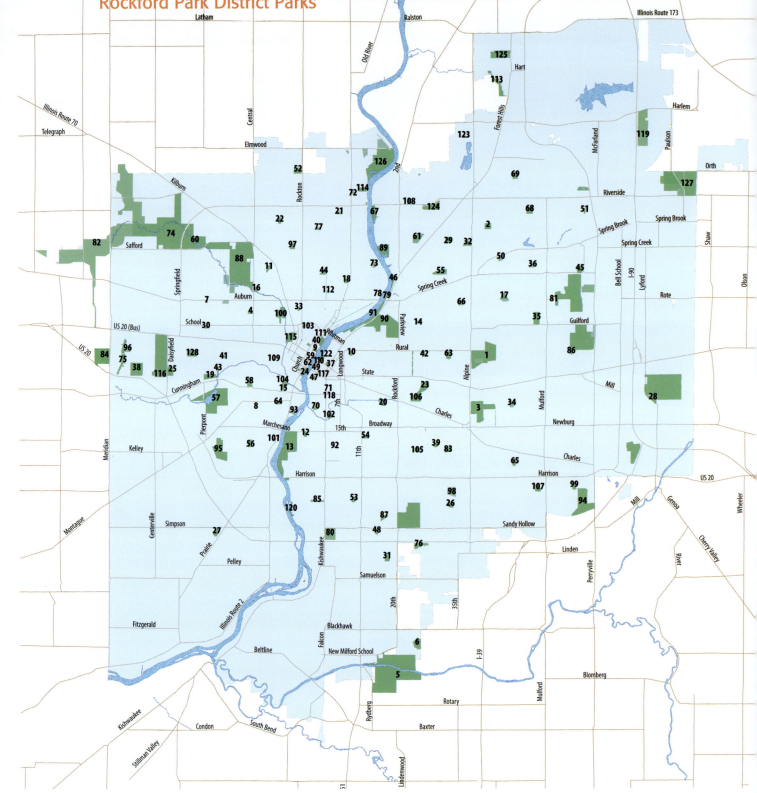

Rockford Park District Parks

Appendix A: Rockford Park District Parks Map

Rockford Park District Parks Key

Aldeen Park 1
Alpine Meadows
    Playground 2
Alpine Park. 3
Andrews Memorial Park 4
Atwood Park. 5
Atwood Park Estates
    Playground 6
Auburn HS Tennis Courts 7
Barbour School Playground . . 8
Beattie Park 9
Beattie Playground 10
Belden St. Playground. 11
Beyer Stadium 12
Black Hawk Park 13
Blackhawk Island Park 121
Bloom School Playground . . 14
Booker Washington Park . . . 15
Bresler Park 16
Brookview School
    Playground 17
Brown Park. 18
Carlson–Nelles Park 19
Churchill Park 20
Collins Playground 21
Conklin School Playground . 22
Dahlquist Park 23
Davis Park. 24
Dennis School Playground . . 25
Eddie Green Place 117
Ekberg-Pine Manor Park. . . . 26
Evergreen School
    Playground 27
Fair Grounds Park 115
Flodin Boys & Girls Club
    at Earl F. Elliot Park 28
Forest Hills View
    Playground 29
Franz Park 30
Froberg School Playground . 31
Gambino Park 32
Garfield Ave. Playground . . . 33
Gregory School Playground . 34
Guilford Center School
    Playground 35
Guilford Tennis Center 36
Haight Park. 37
Hall Memorial Park 38
Harlem Community Center
    Park & SkateWorks 125

Harmon Playfield. 39
Haskell Park 40
Highland Playground 42
Huffman Playground 44
Hunter Park 45
Illinois Street Park 46
Ingersoll Centennial Park . . . 47
Ingersoll Memorial Park . . . 116
Jamestown Park. 48
Joe Marino Park. 49
Johnson School
    Playground 63
Johnson Tract/Garden Plots 50
Kaye Anderson Park 51
Ken-Rock Park 53
Kennedy-Haight School
    Playground 52
Keye-Mallquist Park 54
Landstrom Park 55
Lathrop School Playground . 56
Levings Park/
    Standfield Beach. 57
Liberty Park 58
Library Esplanade 59
Lockwood Park 60
Loves Park Playground 61
Luther Esplanade 62
Mandeville Park 64
Mariposa Dr. Playground . . . 65
Marsh School Playground . . 66
Martin Park 67
Moose Park 114
Mulford Crest Park 68
Mullins–Pebble Creek Park . 69
Nelson Park 70
Northwestern Park 71
Olson Park 119
Oxford Park 73
Page (Anna) Park. 74
Park-er–Woods Park 75
Patriot's Gateway Park 118
Peter Olson Park 123
Puri Park 76
Ray Wantz Memorial Park . 108
Ridge Ave. Playground 77
River Park 78
Riverby Park 79
Riverdahl School
    Playground 80

Riverview Park 122
Rock River Greenway
    South 120
Rock Valley Flight Field 82
Rockford Arboretum 81
Rolling Green School
    Playground 83
Roy Gayle Park 84
Sabrooke Playground 85
Sand Park 124
Saturn Park 86
Sawyer Rd. Playground 87
Searls Park/
    Canine Corners Dog Park . 88
Shorewood Park 89
Sinnissippi Park 90
Sinnissippi Riverfront Park . 91
Sixth Street Playground 92
South Henrietta Ave. Park . . 41
South Horace Park 43
South Park 93
Southeast Community Park . 94
Southwest Community Park . 95
Sportscore One 126
Sportscore Two 127
Stiles School Park 96
Summerdale Playground . . . 97
Swan Hillman School
    Playground 98
Swanson Park West 99
Talcott-Page
    Memorial Park 100
Taylor Park 101
Tenth Ave. Playground 102
Terry Lee Wells
    Memorial Park 103
The Oaks Park 72
Tinker Swiss Cottage
    Museum 104
Twenty-Fifth St.
    Playground 105
Twin Sister Hills Park 106
Vandercook School
    Playground 107
Washington Park 128
Water Works Park 109
Waterside Plaza 110
Wester Park 111
Williams Sports Field 112
Willow Creek Greenway . . . 113

BUILDING A LASTING DREAM

Rockford Park District Facilities and Museum Partners

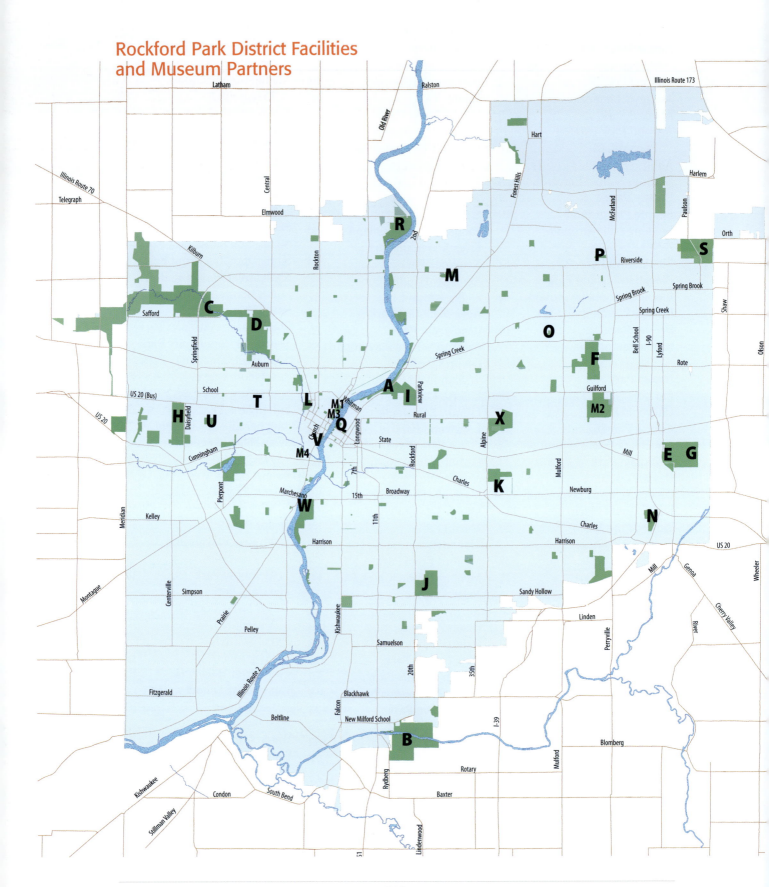

APPENDIX A: ROCKFORD PARK DISTRICT FACILITIES AND MUSEUMS MAP

Rockford Park District Facilities Key

Aldeen Golf Club & Practice Centre .... F
Alpine Pool .... K
Atwood Center .... B
Canine Corners Dog Park – Elliot .... E
Canine Corners Dog Park – Searls .... D
Carlson Ice Arena & Sapora Playworld .... P
Elliot Golf Course .... G
Guilford Tennis Center ...... O
Harkins Aquatic Center L
Ingersoll Memorial Park & Golf Course .... H
Lewis Lemon Community Center .... T
Linda K. White Center X
Lockwood Park Trailside Centre & Children's Farm . C
Magic Waters Waterpark .... N
Marinelli Stadium .... W
Nicholas Conservatory & Gardens .... A
Riverview Ice House .... Q
Sand Park Pool .... M
Sandy Hollow Golf Course ... J
Sinnissippi Golf Course I
Sportscore One .... R
Sportscore Two/ Indoor Sports Center ..... S
Washington Park Community Center ...... U
Webbs Norman Center V

Rockford Park District Museum Partners Key

Burpee Museum of Natural History M1
Midway Village Museum ... M2
Riverfront Museum Park* .. M3
Tinker Swiss Cottage Museum M4

* *Riverfront Museum houses Rockford Art Museum, Rockford Dance Company, Rockford Symphony Orchestra, Discovery Center Museum, and Northern Public Radio*

APPENDIX B
ROCKFORD PARK DISTRICT GROWTH FOR 100 YEARS

How the Rockford Park District has grown through the last century.

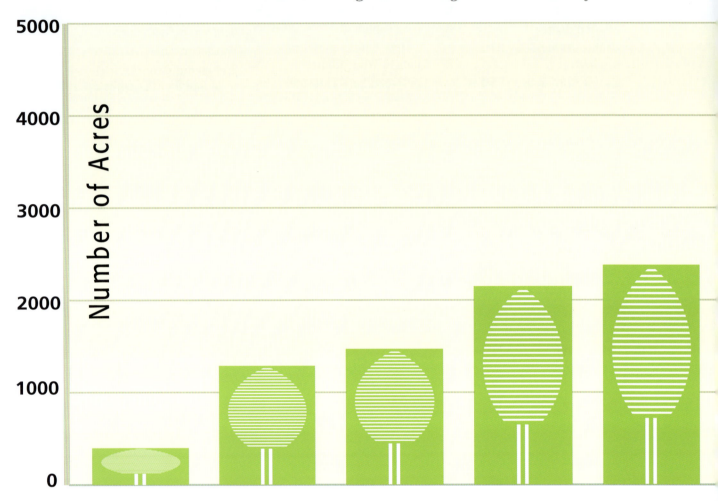

1910s
Blackhawk Park
Brown Park
Fair Grounds Park
Franz Park
Haight Park
Haskell Park
Ingersoll Golf Course
Keye-Mallquist Park
Kimball Triangle
Mandeville Park
Sinnissippi Park
Sinnissippi Golf Course
South Park

1920s
Andrews Park
Beattie Park
Churchill Park
Elliot Golf Course
Franklin Parkway
Garfield Park
Harmon Park
Ingersoll Memorial Park
Levings Lake Park
    & Standfield Beach
Page Park
Sandy Hollow Golf Course
Tenth Avenue Park
Tinker Museum Center

1930s
Alpine Park
Burpee Museum Center
Collins Park
Dahlquist Park
Hall Memorial
Huffman Park
Nelson Park
Talcott-Page Park

1940s
Atwood Park
Martin Park
Sand Park
Searls Park
Wantz Park

1950s
Bloom School Park
Marsh School Park
Ridge Park
Rolling Green School Park
Don Schmid Youth Fields /
    Riverdahl Park
Shorewood Park
South Henrietta Park
Summerdale Park
Twin Sisters Park
Washington Park
    Community Center

Graph is accurate but does not contain complete listing of all Rockford Park District properties.

APPENDIX B: ROCKFORD PARK DISTRICT GROWTH FOR 100 YEARS

1960s
Aldeen Park
Atwood Park Estates
Beattie Playground
Brookview School Park
Flodin Boys & Girls Club
Gregory School Park
Guilford Center Park
Harkins Pool
Sawyer Park

1970s
Auburn School Tennis Courts
Carlson Nelles Park
Founders Park
Guilford Tennis Center
Swan Hillman Park
Illinois Street Park
Luther Esplanade
Midway Village
    Museum Center
Riverview Park
Rockford Arboretum
Terry Lee Wells Park /
    Haskell School Playground

1980s
Aldeen Golf Course
Mel Anderson Rec Path
Rock Valley Flight Field
Hunter Park
Ingersoll Centennial Park
Kennedy Haight Park
Library Esplanade
Magic Waters
Oxford Park
Riverfront Museum Center
Sportscore /
    Veteran's Memorial
Waterside Plaza
Wester Park
Waterside Park

1990s
Beyer Stadium /
    Beyer School Park
Carlson Arctic Ice Arena
Cowell Lots
Davis Park
Northeast Community Park
Post Office Place
    (Downtown Office)
Rock River Rec Path South
Southeast Community Park
Swanson Park West
Sportscore Rec Path

2000s
Kaye Anderson Park
Northwestern Park
Olson Farm Park
Southwest
    Community Park
Sportscore II
Nicholas Conservatory
    and Gardens
Puri Park
Sportscore One expansion
Magic Waters rides
Development Olson
    Swedish Heritage Park
Alpine Hills

APPENDIX C
PARK DISTRICT DIRECTORS

Through its first 100 years, the Park District had six executive directors, as well as an interim director who served for five months. Following is a look at the six leaders who guided the district from 1909 through 2009 and beyond. Two served for 34 years each and one for 18 years. The current director, Tim Dimke, is in his sixth year as of this writing.

PAUL B. RIIS

17 years • March 1910 – June 1927

The district was just under a year old when Paul Riis was hired as its first "superintendent" on March 1, 1910. Born in 1876 in Basel, Switzerland, Riis came to the United States at age 18 and did landscaping in New York and Connecticut. He became a naturalized American citizen in 1904. He worked in the National Park System when it was new, helping to develop Yellowstone and other national parks. An expert forester, Riis was especially gifted in the planting of evergreen groupings. Many of the fir trees on Ingersoll Golf Course are his work. Under his leadership, the new Park District grew to 45 parks on 719 acres. He resigned in June 1927 to become superintendent of the Allegheny County parks system near Pittsburgh, Pa. Riis returned to Rockford in 1932 and worked in landscaping locally and nature studies with Wisconsin environmentalist Aldo Leopold until Riis' death at age 67 in 1944.

CLARENCE T. PEDLOW

7 years • June 1927 – June 1934

Clarence Pedlow was promoted from engineer and expert horticulturist to superintendent when Riis left. C.T., as Pedlow was known, was first hired in 1919. A native of Indianapolis, Pedlow studied landscaping and horticulture at the Missouri Botanical Gardens in St. Louis. He is credited with the original planning for Sinnissippi Gardens. Early in 1934, he suffered a number of medical problems. Disregarding the advice of friends who urged him to take more time to recover, he returned to work where he struggled with the aftermath of a spring drought that brought great damage to shrubs and trees. Pedlow also was directing the district's participation in the Civil Works Administration, which provided temporary jobs to unemployed people. Pedlow died unexpectedly at age 39 in July 1934. Friends believed the strain of work had been too much for him.

EARL F. ELLIOT

34 years • August 1934 – November 1968

Earl Elliot spent more than 40 years with the Park District, starting in 1927 as a landscape engineer after graduating from Iowa State University. Acreage in the district during his years as director more than tripled to 2,615, with the addition of 23 neighborhood parks, as well as major properties such as Aldeen, Alpine, Atwood, Searls, Shorewood, Martin and Sand parks. Just as important, Elliot was instrumental in starting the park-school partnerships, new in the nation at the time, in which playgrounds are built next to elementary schools to serve both the schools and the neighborhoods. Elliot was a member of the Boys Club committee which campaigned for a recreation tax in the district and oversaw the development of a full-blown recreation program in 1956. In 1965, Elliot received the Park Executive Institute's highest honor, the Honorary Fellowship. The capstone to his career was the board's decision to name the district's fourth golf facility after him. The Earl F. Elliot Park and Golf Course opened in May 1968. Elliot retired later that year, and served the district as historian until his death at age 80 in August 1984.

ROBERT H. MILNE

3 years • October 1968 – December 1971

Robert Milne became assistant director of the district in 1960 after working as general manager of the Champaign Park District and director of parks and recreation in Clayton, Mo. A graduate of the University of Illinois, he became director in 1968 and is credited with increasing public awareness of the needs of the Park District and the opportunities for donations. The result was the establishment in 1979 of the

APPENDIX C: PARK DISTRICT DIRECTORS

Paul B. Riis

Clarence T. Pedlow

Earl F. Elliot

Robert H. Milne

Webbs Norman

Tim Dimke

Rockland Foundation, today the Park District Foundation. Milne also was instrumental in establishing the Children's Farm at Lockwood Park. He convinced the board to accept federal funds for the first time to acquire the River Bluff property/Veterans Memorial Park which now includes Sportscore One, boating and park facilities. Milne resigned Dec. 1, 1971, after a year of criticism on purchasing and bidding practices. He went to Phoenix to lead the Maricopa County Park and Recreation Department.

WEBBS NORMAN
34 years • March 1972 – May 2006

Born in Chattanooga, Tenn., Webbs Norman was raised in Morrison, Ill. He earned a bachelor's degree in secondary education in 1957 and a master's in park and recreation administration in 1960 from the University of Illinois. Norman's first professional job, while he was a student, was as a playground leader at Sunset Park in Rockford during the 1955 pilot summer recreation program. He was selected to return in 1956, after a recreation tax had been approved by voters, to direct the first summer of the full-scale rec program in the city. Between his bachelor's and master's degrees, Norman did a one-year internship with the Milwaukee school system. After earning his master's, he went on to serve as director of parks and recreation in Charleston, Westchester and Oak Park. In 1969, he started a park and recreation consulting company, Midwest Planners & Associates. In 1972, he returned to the public sector as executive director of the Rockford Park District.

During his tenure, park acreage grew to 4,574 and the number of parks went from 101 to 173. Numerous programs and facilities were started or taken to new levels, including therapeutic rec, indoor ice skating, museum development, sports fields big enough for major tournaments, pedestrian/bike paths, and more. Several significant awards were won by the Park District during this era: in 1989, the National Gold Medal for Parks and Recreation; in 1995, the National Gold Medal for Therapeutic Recreation; and in 2004, the only city in Illinois named Sportstown USA by Sports Illustrated magazine and the National Recreation and Parks Association. Norman retired in 2006 to become Park District historian, work on this book, and devote time to fundraising for the Nicholas Conservatory and Gardens.

TIM DIMKE
5 years • July 2006 –

Tim Dimke had been with the Park District for 33 years when he was unanimously named executive director in 2006. Dimke worked part-time for the district starting in 1973 while he was in college and joined the district full time in 1979. He has a bachelor's degree in parks and recreation administration from Eastern Illinois University and a master's in business administration from Rockford College. He oversaw expansion of the Discovery Center and Burpee Museum in Riverfront Museum Park, building Nicholas Conservatory and Gardens, adding attractions to Magic Waters, operating a summer recreation program in cooperation with the Rockford School District, and strengthening the area's tourism promotions with the joint marketing of local gardens. Dimke is leading exploration of some exciting sports developments as he leads the district in its second 100 years.

APPENDIX D
PEOPLE WHO MADE A DIFFERENCE

While researching and writing "Building a Lasting Dream," I found that the main thread running through the 100-year history of the district was long-term, meaningful relationships, a value system initiated by Levin Faust in 1909 that continues to this very day. What bothered me the most was knowing so many wonderful people and friends who have contributed to "Building a Lasting Dream" but not having space to recognize their contributions. Therefore, I have developed a partial list of many people who have supported the district, as well as me, through their volunteering, sharing ideas, mentoring, giving donations and, especially, their personal friendships. They have not only greatly enhanced the quality of services offered in the district but they have brought joy and meaning to my personal life. I will always be indebted to the following people. If I forgot anyone, please accept my apologies.

Adams, Mayor Dale
Addis, Chuck & Family
Agent, 0707
Agnew, Harris & Pegee
Agustsson, Jon
Akerlund, John & Betty
Albert, Gerald
Albert, Janyce
Aldeen, Norris & Margaret
Aldeen, Reuben
Alexander, Lisa
Allen, Rev. Mary
Allen, Maggie DiMarco
Allen, Rev. Jesse
Altamore, Alberto
Anderson, Arthur W. "Art"
Anderson, David
Anderson, Gary
Anderson, Geneva
Anderson, John & Linda
Anderson, John B.
Anderson, Laurie
Anderson, Mel
Anderson, Russell D.
Arnold, Dan
Arnold, Dave
Atwood, Seth B.
Atwood, Seth G.
Atwood, Bruce
Bach, Dr. Leroy
Bacher, Cindy
Bachman, Kate
Bachrodt, Lou
Bachrodt, Pat
Bacon, Maichle
Baer, Dick
Baerenwald, Phil
Bailor, Ron & Barb
Baker, JoAnn
Baker, Richard & Sally
Bakke, Wayne & Kim
Baldwin, Cheryl K.
Bannon, Joe
Baptista una Freund, Barb & Family
Barbagallo, Jim
Barber, Diane
Barclay, Jack
Barnard, Judy
Barrie, Vance
Baskin, Dr. Bill & Lea
Bauer, Frank
Beach, Frank
Beach, Jodi & McDowell, Jim
Beaman, Carol and Barry
Beard, Bonnie
Becherer, Jack
Beck, Chris
Beck, John
Behr, Richard
Bell, Howard
Bell, Victory & Carol
Bell, Willie
Bennett, Rev. Perry
Benson, Vicki
Bereiter, Glenn
Berg, Gary
Bergman, Tom
Berman, Dick & Barb
Berry, Mildred
Bernardi, Dick
Biondo, Ted
Bittner, Rev. Denver & Pam
Black, Estelle
Blackwell, Oscar & Annie
Blazer, Cedric & Tara
Blumenthal, Shep
Board, Rev. Kenneth
Bonne, Mark
Bosma, Julie
Bostrom, Dean & Sandra
Bowen, Bill
Bowman, Mickey
Box, Charles
Bracken, Juli
Brademas, James & Than
Brightbill, Charles K.
Brightbill, Fred
Brinker, Richard
Brooks, Chad
Brooks, Douglas
Broski, Michael
Brown, Alan
Brown, Chuck & Becky

Appendix D: People Who Made A Difference

Brown, Lavonne
Brown, Marva/
   Harkins, James
Broyles,
   Jerry & Beverly
Bruce, Thea
Bruehler, Jim
Bruski, Robert
Brynteson,
   Dick & Phyllis
Buck, Roger & Adale
Burden, Bob & Jane
Burfoot, Scott
Burkhardt, Mark
Burnam,
   Jerry & Phyllis
Burzynski,
   Senator Bradley
Butcher, Charles
Butler, Ron
Byrnes, David
Cadigan, Rufus & Elise
Callighan, Paul
Campbell, Stanley
Campos, Andy
Campos, Linda
Cancelose, DeeDee
Cardenas, Armando
Cardenas, Serena
Carlin, Taylor
Carlson, Allen &
   Elizabeth
Carlson, Doug
Carlson, Ed & Vi
Carlson, Jeff
Carlson, Kurt
Carney, Shawn
Carr, Jeff
Carrigan, Patrick
Carroll, Jodi
Carruthers,
   Mary-Stuart
Casazza, Sam
Castrogiovanni,
   Joe & Sue
Castrogiovanni, John
Chadwick, John
Chapdelaine,
   Roland (Chip)
Chapman, Jay
Chapman, Steve
Charney, Bill
Christiansen, Scott
Cichock, Sue
Claeyssens, Dave
Clark, Jim & Libby
Cohn, Kris & Stuart
Cole, Carl
Coleman, Clyde
Collins, Rosemary
Comerio, John
Conard, Bill
Conner, Rev. Bob
Contarino, Joe
Cook, Beryl
Cook, John R. & Marcia
Cooper, Dr. Chuck
Cooper, Jim
Cork, Bob
Cotsones, Rena
Cousins, Flora "Sis"
Cowen, Joel
Crampton, Lew
Cressman, John
Crompton, John
Cudia,
   Gloria and Frank
Cunningham, Linda
Cunningham, Pat
Curran, Patrick
D'Agnola, Louis
D'Castris, Valerie
Dahlgren, Mark
Damon, Dennis
Danielson, John
Darby, Sam
Darda, Jerry
Dargene, Carl
Davis, Ed
Davis, George
Davis, Jan
Davis,
   Nehemiah & Eldora
Dawson, Roy
DeCoster, Ken
Deery, Hugh & Jody
Delanty, Denise
Delany, Michael
Dennis, Linda
Denny, Lorene
DesRosiers, Mimi
Devereueawax,
   Penny & John
DeWitt, Jerry & Pat
Dierks, Ronald
Dimke, Florence
Dimke, Tim & Deb
Dinges, Aaron,
   Jill & Abe
Dixon, Gayle
Dometz, Faren
Dotson, Rev. Earl
Dotson-Williams,
   Henrietta & Mike
Druski, Tim
Duckett, GeorgeAnne
Dudgeon, Dr. Tom
Dufault, Tom
Dunlap, David
Dunn, Mike
Dutton, Ed
Dylak, Karen
Eaton, Phil
Edge, Ken
Eggers, Gordon
Ekberg, Glen
Ellerman, Debbie
Elliot, Charles
Elliot, Don
Elliot, Earl F.
Elliot, Julie
Elliott, Don
Elliott, John
Elliott, Kathy
Elliott, Sue
Ellis, Ed
Ellis, Jeff
Ellis, Mike
Elmer, Paul & Sue
Emanuelson, David
Emerson, Judy
Emmons, Tim
Encheff, Chad
Endencia,
   Jerry & Terasita
Enichen, Ed
Epperson, Chief Chet
Epps, Ronald
Erwin, Dan
Etheridge, Sally
Etnyre, Sylvia
Eubanks, Eugene
Evans, Jay
Faber, Chuck
Fadden, Janyce
Fahey, Ed
Fairchild, Ruthie
Fairgrieves, Richard
Faren, Johnie
Favor, Chuck
Fayram, Dick
Fedeli, Shirley
Felhaber, Jim & Sandy
Fell, George & Barbara
Ferguson, Jackie
Fiduccia,
   Chuck & Carolyn
Fiduccia, Sue
Fiordelisi, Gerald
Fisher, Wendy Perks
   and Roger
Fitzgerald, Diane
Flach, Judy
Flanagan, Nancy
Flickinger, Ted
Flodin, Jim & Kay
Flores, Jean
Foley, Phillip

Ford, Roger & Carol
Forsman, Einar
Fowler, Brad
Fox, Bob
Fox, Patrick
Frankenthal, Charlie
Franzen, Ken
French, Andy
Fridh, John M.
Fry, Charlie
Funderburg, Rob
Funderburg,
   Robert and Mary
Furman, Laura
Furst,
   Thomas & Darlene
Gaffney, Sylvia
Gallagher, Mike
Gambini, Rich
Gambino, Paul
Gasparini, Don
Gasparini, Marc
Gayle, Bunkie
Gaylord, Edison
Geddes, Duncan
Geddes, Gordon
Geiger, DoAnne
Genoways, Becky
Gibbons, Pat
Giese, Todd & Carla
Giesler, Ken
Giest, Bill
Gilbert, Rev. Elderldge
   H.E. & Family
Gile, John
Giolitto, Barb
Giorgi, Amedeo
Giorgi, E. J. "Zeke"
Glavin, Kerry
Glenny, Monica
Glink, Marvin
Gloyd, Larry
Goddard, John
Goddard, Sally
Gomez, Patricia

Gommel, Jacqueline
Gonzalez,
   Kristin Lyons
Goodloe, Sam
Goral, Mickey
Gorski, William
Graceffa, Steve
Graceffa, Tom
Graham, Bill &
   Barb & Kids
Grans, Sue
Gray, Lucille
Gray, Michael & Barb
Greene, Bob
Gregory, Ginny
Groh, John
Guedet, Steve
Guerrero, Isaac
Gulley, Gwen
Gummow, Lori
Gustafson, Rod
Gustafson, Ruth
Guth, John
Hackin, Charlotte
Hackin, Steve
Hagney, David
Hagshenas, Bruce
Hahn, Jennie
Hall, Jim & Debra
Hall, Robin
Hall, Terrie
Hallock, John Jr.
Hallstrom, Dawn
Hamer, George
Hamilton, Lowell
Hamilton, Ricky
Hanna, Don
Harding, Karen
Hardman, Rich
Hardy, Roy
Harner, Dr. Robert
Harnois, Tref
Harrington, Elaine
Harris, Marcella

Hart, Don
Hawks, Lloyd & Mary
Hawks, Pearl
Hawthorne, Rev. Ralph
Hayes, Pat
Hayes, Patrick
Heck, Steve
Heinke, Mariel
Held, Ken
Hendershott, Arles
Herbert, Jan
Hernandez, Linda
Hickey, Vivian
Hicks, Clarence
Hill, Helen
Hilton, Steven
   (The Undertaker)
Himes, Ron
Hlade, John
Hoard, Flossie
Hodges, Lisa
Hoffman, Kevin
Holmbeck,
   Jack & Colleen
Holmberg,
   Gene & Joyce
Holmgren, Janet
Holmgren,
   Marshall & Marian
Holstrom, John
Holt, Jeff
Holt, Don
Holub, John
Holycross, Ron
Horton, Dennis
Howard, Bill
Howard, John
Howard, Karen
Howard, Wray
Howard, Sue
Hoyt, Bill
Hruby, Paul
"Hub"
Hubler, Nancy & Steve
Hubley, Ross

Hughes, Bill
Hughes, Sidella
Hurley, John
Ingersoll Family
Ingram, Tom & Adell
Ingrassia, David
Ingrassia,
   Paul & Roberta
Ingrassia, Ted & Terri
Irons, Keith
Jackson, Bruce
Jacobi, Fritz
Jacobs, Karl & Carol
Jacobson, Bruce
Jacobson, Daniel
Jacobson, John
Jacobson, Leonard J.
Jafari, Jeff
James, Rev. Leonard
Jefferson, Harlan
Jefferson, Rep. Chuck
Jensen, Brad
Jensen, Renee
Johannes, Bill
Johannsen, Jamie B.
Johnsen, Curt
Johnson, Art
Johnson, Brent
Johnson, Chris & Judy
Johnson, Curt F.
Johnson, David
Johnson,
   Dennis & Evie
Johnson, Loren
Johnson, Nancy L.
Johnson,
   Richard & Julie
Johnson, Russ
Johnson,
   Scott & Melissa
Johnson, Sonja
Johnson, Walter
Jones, Bill
Jones, Jan
Jones, Lamont

Appendix D: People Who Made A Difference

Jones, Jim & Ruth
Jordan, Elbert
Jordan, Lewis
Joseph, Charles
Juni, Kathleen
Jury, Gary
Jury, Lefty
Kalchbrenner, Nancy
Kalousek, Tom
Kapotas,
   George & Jean
Karau, Jake & Candy
Kase, David
Kaufman, Suzanne
Kauzlarich, Nancy K.
Keedi, Nabil & Rita
Keegan, Betty Ann
Keeling, Jim & Pam
Kelley, Ed & Lynn
Kelly, Sara
Kendall, Becky Cook
Kennedy, Dick & Pat
Kennedy, Margaret M.
Kerns, Ken
Kilzback,
   Dr. Cary & Dina
Kingsley, Beverly
Kirkpatrick, Bob
Kleber,
   John & Margaret
Kleinman, Steve
Knapp, Dave
Kohlbacher, Don
Kopf, Rebecca
Kostantacos, Peter
Kretzer, Jack
Kunnert, Dick
Kurt, Chuck
LaMonica, Michael J.
Lane, Connie
LaPasso,
   Len & Virginia
Larsen, Steve & Marty
Larson, Marianne

Larson, Randy
Latino, Jim
Laughlin, Thomas
Lawson, Kim
Layng, Laurie
Lemons, Tom
Lenis, Marco
Lewis, Dr. John
Lewis, Elizanne
Lidbetter, Ward
Lind, Roger
Lind, Gloria
Lind, Paula
Lindberg,
   Mayor Darryl & Judy
Lindenmier, Jan
Lindman, Lisa
Lindstrom, Joyce
Lindstrom, Bob
Lindstrom, Randy
Lippert, Tom
Lipsky, Martin
Litterst, Dick
Little, Ruth
Locke, Sandra
Lockwood, James
Lockwood, John & Jan
Loescher, Dan
Logan, Doug
Logan, Lorayne
Logemann, Martha
Logli, Paul
Lorden, Tom
Lunde, Barbara
Lundin, Jon & Gloria
Lundstrom, Nancy
Lundstrom, Randy
Lupton, Frank
Mackiewicz, Chet
Mallquist, Alan
Mallquist,
   Kent & Marty
Malmberg, Ron
Mannery, Jacci

Manzullo, Don
Marino, Joe
Mark, Douglas
Markhardt, Heather
Marquardt, Mary
Marshall, Irene
Martathe, Jack
Martin, John &
   Charlyne Blatcher
Martin, Lynn
Martin, Malcom
Martin, Nathaniel
   "Nate" & Marge
Mastrioianni, Mike
Mateus, Louie
Mathur, Jay
Matilla, Tim
Matranga, Tony
Matzl, Norm
McAfee, Jane
McAley, David
McCarthy,
   Bob & Dorles
McCullough, Ed
McDonald, Cary
McDonald,
   Rod & Jessica
McDuff, Doug
McGaw, Bob & Peggy
McKinney, William
McKiski, Herb
McLaughlin, Neil
McNamara,
   John & Barb
McNeely, Linda
McParlan, Tim
McPheron, Larry
McPherson, Sue
McQueeny, Dave
McWilliams, Lloyd
Mecklenburg, John
Meeks, Richard
Meeks, Thomas
Meinert, Pat
Meuleman, Bob

Meyer, Tom
Meyers,
   Sheriff Richard A.
Millard, Bob
Miller, Al
Miller, Bill
Miller, Howard
Miller, Ruth
Minns, Bob
Mitchell, Harmon
Mohaupt, Mary
Montelongo, Ray
Moore, Stephen
Morf, Judy
Morrissey,
   Mayor Lawrence J.
Mosser, Doris & Don
Moye, Chureia
Mroz, Sue
Mulcahey, Richard
Nason, Mayor Scott
Nelson, Barbara
Nelson, John
Neville, Barb
Nicholas, Albert (Ab)
Nicholas, Bill
Nicholas, Dan & Ruth
Nicholas, Scott & Sue
Nichols, Sharifa
Nielsen, Jeff
Nielsen, Rev. Loren
Niemiec, Linda
Nikolai, Geri
Nivinski, Brett
Noe, Denise
Nolan, Bob & Doris
Nord, David
Noreen, Ron
North, Pat
O'Brien, Bob
O'Brien, Daniel
   Joseph Patrick
O'Donnell, Bill
O'Keefe, Anne

O'Sullivan, Ellen
Oates, Cyrus
Olson, Gerry
Olson, Jon & Dianne
Olson, Nobel
Orput, Alden & JoAnne
Osborn, Lee
Packard, Jack
Pang, Alan
Papich, Bob & Family
Paris, Jerry
Parker, Rex & Carol
Parlapiano, Mike
Patterson, Glenn
Patterson, Linda
Pauly, Mike
Pauly, Ron and Jane
Pearson, Janet
Penniman, Judge A. R.
Perks, Doug
Perrecone, Peter
Perrin, Donald
Perrone, Miriam
Perteete, Charles
Peterson, Delbert
Peterson, Jim
Peterson, John
Peterson, Pastor Jerry
Peterson, Ray
Petty, Gregory
Phalen, Molly
Phelps, John
Philbrick, Jack
Phillips, Kanella
Picchi, Joseph
Picolin, John
Pirages, Jim
Pohlman, Steve
Polcek, Norma
Polsean, Jeffery
Powell, Ann
Powell, Mary
Powers, Jim
Pratt, Don & Marlene

Preece, David & Laurie
Pro, Maxine
Provenzano, Matthew
Provenzano, Peter
Provenzano,
   Vince & Phyllis
Puri, Sunil
Quinn, Gene
Quittschreiber, Ken
Rafferty, Butch
Ramsey, Carla
Rankins, Julius
Rasch, Jim & Kathy
Redd, Maurice
Rehfeldt, Paul & Lisa
Reid, Jim
Reidenbach, Pam Clark
Reichensberger,
   Steve & Fran
Reuber, Tonya
Rhea, Bob
Richards, John
Richards, Stan
Riggs, Judge Bradley
Rix, Doug
Robertson, D. William
Robertson,
   Chief Bill & Sue
Robinson, Doc
Robinson, Mike
Roby, Judy
Roddewig,
   Dan & Jeanne
Roganowicz, Leo
Rogers, Bill
Rogers, Judy
Rohrer, Mark
Roos, Brad
Rosene, Jim
Rosenfeldt, Joel
Roser, Steve & Mary
Rostamo, Rose
Roszkowski,
   Judge Stanley
Rotello, Mike

Rubendall, Ben
Rundall, Dick & Ann
Rundquist, Richard
Russell, Phyllis
Rutherford, Dave
Ryan, Jim
Rydell, David
Saavedra, Daniel
Saavedra, Heidi
Sage, Joan
Salamone, Thomas
Salisbury, Bob
Salmons, Phil
Salser, Chrissy
Saltzgiver, Clyde & Rae
Salvatore, Gino
Sandine, Jay & Liz
Sanford, Dena
Sapora, Allen V.
Sapora, John
Sargent, Robert
Saudargas, Alice
Saunders, Sara
Scandroli, Joseph
Scheffel, Shannon
Scheurich,
   G. Michael & Mary
Schier, Frank
Schleicher, Mayor Ben
Schou, John
Schwerin, Rev. Gary
Scott, Mayor Doug
Scott, Sandy
Shaheen, Tom & Joann
Shannon, Bill
Sheley, Frank & Judy
Shepard, Press
Shields, Bill & Judy
Shipley, Ralph
Sibley, Richard
Sidney, David
Simmon, Hans
Singer, Bob
Sinkiawic, Mayor Joe

Sjostrom,
   William & Jenny
Smith, Mary Ann
   and Gordon
Smith, Cynthia
Smith, Jeff
Snively, Julie
Sorensen, Sorrie
Spear, Fred
Spitzer, Wayne
Squire, Calvin
St. Angel, Frank
St. Angel, Jasper
Staaf, Ken
Stark, Bill
Stark, Steve
Starks, Marshall
Starks, Becky
Stavros, Peter
Steffan, Wally
Steinberg, Jessica
Stieglitz, Dr. Thomas
Steingraeber,
   Scott & Katrina
Stocker, David
Stonecipher, Harry
Stoner, Chip
Strandin, John
Stubblefield, Guy
Sullivan, Elsie
Sullivan, J. R.
Swanson, Don
Sweeny,
   Chuck & Cherene
Sydney, David
Sylvester, Nancy
Symes, Steve
Sype, John & Ruth
Syverson,
   Senator Dave
Talbert, Stacie
Tarro, Dorothy
Taylor, Edna May
Tegland,
   Michele & Emily

Appendix D: People Who Made A Difference

Terraski, Don
Teske, Melissa
Thacker, Jim
Thiede, Bill
Thienemann, Rolf
Thomas, Pastor Mike and Tammy
Thompson, Curly
Thompson, Cyndi
Thompson-Kelly, Ann
Thomas, Brian
Thoms, Chuck
Tilson, Bob
Timm, Bill
Tobias, John
Tower, Sandy
Towns, Carl
Tracey, Linda
Tracy, Jim
Tucker, Constance
Turner, Phil

Turpoff, Glen
Updike, Brett & Shirley
Uphouse, Alice
Uram, Sandy
Vails, Terry
Van Drie, Karen
Van Pernis, David
Vance, Mike
Vanderwerff, Joe
Vandewalle, Ray
Vaughn, Linda
Verni, Vic & Kathy
Verni-Lau, Gary & Barb
Venable, Jerry & Donna
Vernon, Tonya
Vitale, Jimmy
Vogl, Bob & Sonia
Voll, Dan
Voneida, Diane
Waddell, Jim

Wait, Ron
Waldorf, Nancy
Walgren, Howard & Elizabeth
Walter, Frank
Ware, Ed & Virginia
Warren, Tom & Mim
Wasco, Carl
Watson, Gary
Wehrstein, Frank
Weis, Karen
Weisensel, Yolanda
Weissbard, Rev. David
Wells, Ed
Wells, Walter and Willie May
Werner, Al
Wernick, Gerald
Wescott, Fred
Wheeler, Kim
Whitby, Norma

White, Michael & Linda
White, Terry
Whitehead, John B.
Wiemer, David & Wanda
Wilkins, Pat
Willhemi, Bill & Judy
Williams, Coleen
Williams, Dr. Allen
Williamson, Walt
Wilson, Henry
Winters, Rep. Dave
Wise, Linda
Wolf, Sarah
Wood, Jennifer
Wood, R. Ray
Woodard, Fines
Woodworth, Gene & Lois
Wortmann, Dr. Don & Jeanine
Wyatt, Laura
Young, Larry
Zais, Alan
Zapke, Cliff
Zenoff, Hon. Kathryn E.
Zies, Margie & Bill
Zimmerman, Brad & Julie
Zook, Gail

Swans and other fowl always attract crowds at the lagoon.

APPENDIX E
DISTINGUISHED SERVICE AWARD RECIPIENTS

Presented by the Rockford Park District

Recipient Name	Date Award Received
A & D Electric	April 11, 1995
Agnew, Harris	March 20, 1997
Alberts, Ronald	December 18, 1987
Aldeen, Norris	October 12, 1991
	June 5, 1995 (by Webbs)
Allen, Maggie	September, 2007
Almquist, Sheryl	February 11, 1992
Ambroz, Karl	June 29, 1989
Anderson, Arthur	November 13, 1990
Anderson, Russ	February, 2005
Arco, Joe	January 9, 1996
Baer, Richard	May 13, 1997
Baker, Joanne	January 30, 1992
Balsam, Marilyn	July 12, 1983
Barber, Diane	June, 2006
Barnard, Judy	August, 2004
Bee, Steve	Dec. 13, 2011
Behr, Richard	February 9, 1993
Bell, Howard	May 10, 1983
	December 18, 1987
Bell, Victory	April 28, 1994
Berry, Mildred	March 29, 1989
Blazer, Cedric	June 12, 1984
Blazer, Tara	January 9, 1990
Blunt, Dennis	May 9, 1995
Board of Commissioners	April 13, 1982
Bowen, Bill	1994
Box, Charles (Mayor)	September, 2008
Boy Scout Troop 400	August 11, 1987
Brademas, James	June 14, 1996
Brandt, Claire	August 14, 1990
Brewington, Alfred	November 22, 1991
Brooks, Chad	December 14, 1990
Boys & Girls Club	October, 2008
Brown, Alan	April, 2003

Recipient Name	Date Award Received
Brovary, Citizens of	February 28, 1996
Bruans, Casey	May 14, 1985
Burzynski, Brad	Feb. 22, 2011
Canfield, Robert	February 13, 1996
Carlson, Cheryl	March 30, 1990
Carlson, Edwin	March 30, 1990
Carpenters Local Union 792	January 9, 1990
Cave, Tom	September 11, 1979
Claeyssens, David	May 14, 1985
Clark, Dick	July 13, 1982
Coca Cola	April 11, 1995
Cohn, Kris	December 15, 1994
Collman, Clyde	July 19, 1984
Compensation Advisory Committee	November 27, 1985
Connell, Steve	September, 2005
Cook, John R.	June 24, 1988
Cosentino, Jerry	August 23, 1988
	May 9, 1990
Cowen, Joel	Oct. 11, 2011
Crampton, Lew	August, 2007
Cratty, Jack	November 13, 1990
Cudia, Gloria Cardenas	April 9, 1991
Dawson, Roy	April 28, 1994
	February 22, 1996
Delany, Michael	April 24, 1989
Delaporte, Edward	June 19, 1980
Denny, Lorene	July 21, 1994
	June 14, 1996
Dinges, Mary	August 19, 1981
	July 19, 1994
Divine, Charles	November 13, 1990
Edgren, Gary	February 9, 1993
Edwards, W.	February 6, 1990
Electrical Workers Local Union 364	January 9, 1990

Appendix E: Distinguished Service Award Recipients

Recipient Name	Date Award Received
Ellerman, Debbie	September 28, 1987
Elliot, Donald	November 7, 1985
	March 9, 1993
Elliot, John	September 8, 1987
	September 27, 1988
Emmett, Judy	January 11, 1985
Enichen, Ed	June 14, 1994
Entrikin, Ronald	July 20, 1980
Espenscheid, Harry	May 26, 1979
Etier, Karen	September 11, 1990
Faber, Chuck	August 15, 1978
Fancher, Bill	June 23, 1995
Faulkner, Bill	July 31, 1986
Ferrell, Larry	May 14, 1985
	March 28, 1996
Festival of Lights Committee	January 9, 1990
Field, Ann	September 13, 1994
Figure Skating Club	February 9, 1993
Finley, Jerry	February 9, 1993
First National & Trust Co.	October 10, 1978
Fisher, Wendy Perks	December 11, 1979
	2006
Flach, Judy	September, 2008
Flickenger, Ted	March 19, 1997
	March, 2009
Foote, Barbara	April 8, 1990
Fore, Jason	November 28, 1994
Frary, Lee	May 12, 1992
Freeman, Evelyn	July 12, 1983
Gambini, Rich	June 10, 1997
Giorgi, Zeke	September 25, 1987
Goodson, Bill	September 26, 1996
Greene, Robert	May 21, 1986
Grubb, Gerald	June 29, 1989
Hackin, Charlotte	June, 2007
Hall, James	November 8, 1983
	November 3, 1984
Hallberg, Ron	September, 2008
Hallock, John	September 25, 1987
Hand, Larry	June 29, 1989
Hanna, Donald	1991-1992
Harnish, George	April 12, 1994
Harris, Creston	November 13, 1990
Hart, Maxine	June 12, 1984
Heinke, Mariel	September, 2005
Hendricks, Phillip	December 19, 1986
Herbert, Jan	September 27, 1988
	August 14, 1990
Hicks, Clarence	September 10, 1991
	August, 2008
Hoffman, Wayne	February 28, 1986
Holmbeck, Colleen	May 14, 1991
Holmberg, Joyce	September 25, 1987
Holt, Don	July 15, 1993
Holub, John	October 11, 1989
Horvath, Gene	February 9, 1993
Hurley, John	September, 2006
Ingram, Adell	July 21, 1994
Ingrassia, David	November 13, 1990
Jackson, Arlene	August 18, 1992
Jacobs, Karl	January 20, 1989
	July 25, 1997
Johnson, Arthur	October 9, 1984
Johnson, Dennis	February 10, 1987
Johnson, Don	December 16, 1988
Johnson, Herbert	January 9, 1979
Johnson, Marvin	June 5, 1995
Johnson, Vivian	December 11, 1984
Johnson, Walt	October, 2003
Jones, Jim	December 9, 1980
Jordan, Elbert	September 27, 1990
	July, 2006
Kalousek, Thomas	December 6, 1986
Kapala, Fred	June 29, 1989
Kelly, Edward	June 4, 1982
Kelly, Lynn	June 4, 1982
Kizilbash, Cary	November, 2004
Koberg, Sylvia	July 10, 1979
Kowal, Connie	September 13, 1993
Kutska, Betsy	November, 2005
Larsen, Steven	April 29, 1997
Larson, Randy	September, 2006
Latino, James	November 13, 1990

Recipient Name	Date Award Received
Lind, Paula	January 25, 1995
Lindbeck, Gary	December 11, 1984
Lindeman, Roger	September, 2008
Little, Romayne	May 21, 1984
Logan, Doug	December 1986
Lotzer, Ray	September 28, 1987
Lupton, Frank	May 11, 1993
Mahlberg, Milton	October 12, 1982
Mahnke, Robert	October 9, 1984
Mallquist, Kent	Oct. 25, 2011
Malmberg, Richard	February 9, 1993
Marinelli, Jeanne	August 13, 1982
Marino, Joe	January 13, 1981
Mark, Jan	September 11, 1990
Martin, Nathaniel	May 15, 1997
May, Ellis	December 28, 1990
McCarty, Dan	May 10, 1983
McCullough, Ed	October 14, 1980
McGaw, Robert	April 14, 1981
McGill, Rob	June 5, 1995
McNamera, John	March 31, 1989
Medrano, Jesus	April 21, 1996
Meulman, Bob	February 22, 1995
Millard, Robert	December 14, 1990
Moors, John	June 24, 1988
Musholt, Maurice	May 28, 1993
Nelson, Mary	September, 2008
Nihan, Ray	July 11, 1985
Nikolai, Geri	May, 2008
Norman, Kathy	August 27, 1992
Norman, Patty	February 11, 1993
North Towne Bank	October 10, 1978
Olson, Gerald	November 13, 1990
Owens, Rhondell	December 14, 1981
Palmquist, Marvin	October 20, 1994
Paul's Crane Service	January 11, 1994
Perrone, Miriam	July 31, 1982
Peterson, Craig	July 14, 1981
Peterson, Delbert	July 9, 1985
Phillips, John	December 19, 1988

Recipient Name	Date Award Received
Pizzuto, Mike	January 25, 1996
Pratt, Don	March 25, 1988
Puls, Sue	July 24, 1985
Puri, Sunil	October 11, 1994
Quinn, Eugene	September 24, 1996
Reed, Anthony	August 27, 1992
Reichensperger, Steve	January, 2008
Rhymer, Jesse	July 24, 1985
Riggs, Judge Bradner	June 29, 1989
Robinson, Mike	June, 2003
Robertson, Bill (Chief)	June, 2008
Rockford Area Convention & Visitors Bureau	April 28, 1994
Rockford BMX Club	December 13, 1988
Rockford Garden Club	August 14, 1979
Rockford Noon Lions Club	July 6, 1995
Rockford Police Department	February 28, 1990
Rockford Ski Broncs	July 13, 1986
Sanderson, Genie	February 14, 1989 April 9, 1984
Sapora, Al	March 27, 1992
Scandroli Construction Company	January 9, 1990
Scheurich, Mike	June 14, 1994
Schmid, Donald	November 3, 1984
Shields, Judy	September, 2002
Shinn, William	December 27, 1986
Sink, Richard	June 29, 1989
Sinkiawic, Joseph	April 27, 1997
Sjostrom, William	1992? (no date noted)
Sjostrom, Genny	June 8, 1982
Smith, David	June 29, 1989
Snively, Julie	January 9, 1990
Sorensen, Helvig	October 8, 1982
Speer, Fred	December, 2002
Standfield, Joe	September 6, 1990
Stegall, Larry	August 13, 1982
Stevens, George	April 14, 1992
Stone, Bob	October 15, 1992
Stringer, Phyllis	October 9, 1984
Sullivan, Jim	June 9, 1994

Appendix E: Distinguished Service Award Recipients

Recipient Name	Date Award Received
Telling, Carol	December 12, 1995
Thienemann, Rolf	December 11, 1984
	May 21, 1984
	May 15, 1992
	June 9, 1992
Thompson, Carol	July 24, 1985
Tower, Sandra	April 18, 1994
Vee, Steve	December 13, 2011
Vietnow	June 29, 1989
Vourliotis, Spero	November 13, 1990
Waldorf, Nancy	November 16, 1986
Wales, Robert	December 11, 1979
Washington Park Improvement Assoc.	September 8, 1987
Wells, Ed	August 27, 1992
Wernick, Gerald	March 12, 1979
White, Michael	April 24, 1989
White, Linda	June 19, 1997
Whitehead, John	June 18, 1983
Wiemer, David	June 29, 1990
Wigner, Jim	October 20, 1994
Williams, Michael	December 2, 1989
Wolf, Georgia	August 13, 1982
Wolven, Ken	July 10, 1979
Wortmann, Jeanine	November 13, 1990

APPENDIX F
ALLEN SAPORA PLAQUE

This plaque honoring Al Sapora hangs near the Sapora Playworld in Carlson Ice Center. It recognizes his deep contributions to the Park District in these words: "As a result of Dr. Sapora's vision, creativity and leadership, for more than 40 years, Park District citizens have been afforded an ever increasing number of recreational opportunities to enjoy life year-round in a Park District that has become a national leader. This creative playground is a tribute to 'Doc Sapora' who inspired all leisure professionals during more than five decades of leadership at the University of Illinois, and is dedicated to the enjoyment of all kids who will learn and grow through play for decades to come."

APPENDIX G

ILLINOIS PARK AND RECREATION ASSOCIATION/ILLINOIS ASSOCIATION OF PARK DISTRICT COMMUNITY SERVICE AWARDS TO INDIVIDUALS

Awards presented by the Rockford Park District.

Recipient Name	Year Received
Aamodt, Jim	2010
Adcock, Douglas	2003
Allen, Mary	1996
Anderson, Art	1996
Anderson, Christina	2010
Anderson, David	2006
Anderson, John	1996, 2004
Anderson, Russ	2002
Atwood, Bruce	2002
Au, Joe & Anna	2003
Aumann, Ray	1996
Bachelder, Laura	2004
Bacon, Dr. Maichle	2002
Barnes II, Earl	2009
Barrett, Bill	2005
Beach, Frank	2004
Beaman, Carol	1996
Beck, John	1998
Becker, Sheila	2009
Beckstrand, Armour	1999
Behr, Dick	2009
Benedict, Roger	2003
Bender, Gus	2001
Bergman, Tom	2003, 2008
Bitner, Rev. Denver	2002
Bitner, Bill	2001
Black, Gail	2000
Blair, Rickey	2010
Blunt, Dennis	1996
Bonne, Mark	2002
Bowen, Bill	2006
Boyd-Gustafson, Ruth	1998

Recipient Name	Year Received
Box, Charles E.	1996, 2001
Brace, Howard	2001
Brame, Naomi	2001
Brierton, Ron	1996
Broski, Mike	2003
Brown, Marva	2005
Brown, Russ	1995
Bulfer, Carol	2001
Burdick, Kevin	2008
Burzynski, Brad	2001
Cabrera, Robin	2006
Cardenas, Armando	2002, 2003
Carlson, Kurt	1996, 2004, 2009
Carlson, Dr. Mark	2004
Casazza, Sam	2000
Cassady, Edwin & Cleta	2004
Castrogiovanni, Joe	1996
Cesario, Mike	1998
Chance, Joshua	2001
Christenson, Paula	2001
Christiansen, Scott	1997, 2007
Cichella, Carol	1997
Claeyssen, Jim	2007
Coe, Jeanne	2003
Cohn, Kris	2000
Cole, Carl	2007
Cole, Marylon	2010
Collura, Dale	1996
Contreras, Sharon	1999
Cook, John R.	2006
Cook, Rebecca	2000
Cooper, Birdia	1996

Appendix G: IPRA/IAPD Community Service Awards to Individuals

Recipient Name	Year Received
Cowen, Joel	2008
Craig, Lewis	2010
Crampton, Lew	2003
Crowley, Bill	2002, 2009, 2010
Cusimano, John	2009
Custer, Kim	2005
Dahlgren, Mark	2004
Dahlquist, Bruce	2002
Dargene, Carl	2002
Davie, Lori	2010
Decourey, Verne	1999
Delacey, Bob (Robert)	2009
Delaporte, Ed	1995
Demarco, Bev	2000
Derry & Friends, Jim	2000
Denzer, Chris	2004
Diamond, Chuck	1999
Dierks, Ron	1996
Duenser, Mike	1998
Dundore, Tina	2001
Dunlap, Lisa	2008
Dunn, Mike	2010
Easton, Kathy	2001
Edgcomb, Kim	1997
Edwards, Venzella E.	2002
Eggers, Gordon	2002
Ekern, Todd & Vicki	2005
Elke, Robert	1999
Elsbree, Phil	2008
Emerson, Sylvia	2000
Engen, Rich & Lana	2010
Epperson, Chet	2007
Ernst, Steve	1999
Escamilla, Leticia	2002
Espenscheid, Harry	2005
Ewaldz, Jean & Mary	2006
Fadden, Janyce	2007
Fahrenwald, Jeff	2007
Fairchild, Ruth	2007
Fedeli, Shirley	2004, 2008
Fehlhaber, Jim	2002
Findley, George	2003
Findley, Linda	1999
Flemming, Jeff	2005
Flodin, Jim	2003
Flowers, David & Lottie	1998, 2000
Foley, Tamara	1995
Forsman, Einar	2009
Fox, Pat	1996, 2000
Fowler, Brad	2001
France, Todd	2003
Franke, Ellen	1997
Franklin, George	1995, 2006
Fraser, Brett	2010
Fraser, Linda	2010
Frichtl, Dennis	2009
Fritz, Mimi	1995
Fruechtenicht, Brian	2008
Funderburg Jr., Rob	2007
Furst, Tom & Darlene	2009
Gaffney, Tim	2009
Gannon, Andy	1995
Gardner, Fred	2010
Geddeis, Laurie	2000
Geiger, Do Ann	2003
Gendron, Pat	2001
Gibbons, Patrick	2004
Gibbs, Laura	2008
Giles, Dr. Jeffrey	1998
Gill, Matthew	2010
Gillenwater, Grant	2002
Glenny, Tom	2006
Glover, Theo	2005
Goodwin, Tim	2009
Graham, David	2000
Gray, Mel	2005
Green, Tom	2005
Groh, John	2003
Gufstason, Lori	2008
Gull-Clemons, Dr. Ann	2004, 2008

Recipient Name	Year Received
Ha, Master Tae Eun	2005
Hagshenas, Bruce	2006
Hallberg, Ron	2001
Hamm, Kim	2004
Harbaugh, Scott	2003
Hartsfield, Kip	2008
Hayes, Donna	2010
Hazzard, Mark	2001
Held, Ken	2003
Hendee, Scott	2003, 2009
Helland, Dr. David	1995, 2001
Hebron, Michael	1996
Hill, Helen	2009
Hilton, Steve	1998, 2001
Hodges, Greg	2001
Holmes, Mike	2000
Holub, John	2007
Horvath, Phyllis	2004
Hosseini, Javad	2004
Howard, Wray	2000
Hundt, Gerald	1996
Hundt, Mary	1995
Hutchinson, Cora	2003
Hughes, Ray	1995
Ingrassia, Ted	2002
Ingham, Mark	2008
Ingram, Adell	1995
Jack, Deborah	2001
Jacobi, Fritz	2006
Jacobs, Karl	2002
Jacobson, Dan	2005, 2006
Janssen, Pat	1996
James Sr., Rev. Leonard	2000
Jefferson, Chuck	2001, 2007
Johnson, Dennis	1995, 2004
Johnson, George	2003
Jones, Duwayne	2010
Jones, Lamont	2005
Jones, Linda	1995
Jones, Monique	2010

Recipient Name	Year Received
Jordan, Lewis	2002, 2003
Jury, Lefty	2003
Kaltenbach, Kevin	2003
Karau, Jake & Candy	1997, 1999
Key, Dottie	1996
Keeling, Jim	2000
Keller, Kerry	2001
Kendall, David	2010
Kidd, John	2010
Kinkaid, Bruce	2010
Kirksey, Maggie	1999
Konitski, Cheryl	2003
Koerber, Steve	1996
Koelling, Scott	2010
Koernschild, Jean	2001
Kopf, Rebecca	2003
Kretzer, Jack	1995
Krieger, Mel	2000
Kroll, Mary	2008
Krueger, Stacy	2008
Krupke, Beth	2002
Krug, Barbara	1995
Labrant, Lou	1998
Larson, Dale	2004
Larson, Michele	2010
Larson, Tim	2009
Lenox, Margaret	1997
Lindberg, Darryl	2001, 2007
Lindley, John	2001, 2005
Lindeman, Roger	1996, 2008
Linsky, Grant	1999
Lockinger, Chuck	1995, 2006
Loescher, Dan	2010
Logsdon, Scott	2001
Long Jr., Bob	2010
Long, Nancy	2005
Lowe, Robert D. "Bob"	2008
Lubbert, Gary	2007
Lundin, Gloria	2007
Lundin, Jon	2001, 2002

Appendix G: IPRA/IAPD Community Service Awards to Individuals

Recipient Name	Year Received
Macdonald, Jessica	2009
Mallquist, Kent	2002, 2008, 2010
Mannery, Jacqueline	1995
Manzullo, Don	2005
Martin, Nate	1997
Martin, John	2006
Martin, Paul	1997
Marino, Joe	2007
Marzorati, Gary	2002, 2004
Mattila, Tim	1995, 2001
Maule, Gene	2002
Maxwell, Jimmie	1997
May, Don	2001
McCarty, Dan	1997
McBride, Pat	2000
McGuire, Brian	2005
McKiski, Tom	2003
McIntosh, Steve	1995, 2001
McLaughlin, Rick	1996
McLamarrah, Marilyn	1997
McParlan, Tim	2001
McPheron, Larry	2001, 2003
McWilliams, Lloyd	2003
Medrano, Jesus	2000
Meeks, Tommy	2003
Meyer, Anne	2005
Miner, Bill	2005
Mitchell, Diane	1996
Mitchell, George	1996
Mitchell, Martha	1997
Miller, Calvin	2010
Miller, John	2003
Moczynski, Lynn	2010
Mohar, Bob & Denise	1997
Mohaupt, Rick & Mary	2000
Moore, Bob & Bev	1997
Morrissey, Eileen	2003
Morrissey, Larry	2003, 2007
Mott, Merrit	2001
Munson, Linda	2001
Murray, Mark	2005
Nelson, Mary	2008
Netto, Alice	1996
Nice, Laurie	1999
Nicholas, Dan	1996, 2003, 2004
Nicholas, Scott	1999
Nikolai, Geri	2007
Nielsen, Dr. Norman	2003
Nielsen, Chief Jeff	2006
Noble, Jan	1995
Noel, David	1995
Nord, David	1995
Ohalla, Anna	2003
Olson, Gerry	2008
O'Neil, Rick	2009
O'Neill, Riley	1996
Parker, Rex & Carol	1999, 2009
Panzer, Marty	2003
Patterson, Linda	2001
Paulson, Brenda	1996
Paulson, Jerry	2004
Pensabene, Jill	2006
Perrin, Don	2002
Perteete, Phil	2007
Petty, Ryan	2001
Peterson, Becky	1999
Peterson, Diane	2004
Peterson, Mark	2007, 2009
Philbrick, Jack	2007
Polzin, William	2005
Ponds, James	2010
Powell, Mary	2006
Powers, Matt	1999
Pratt, Don	1996, 2003
Pro, Maxine	1995
Provenzano, Peter	2010
Powers, Jim	2004
Pugh, Steven	2005
Puri, Bharat	2009
Puri, Sunil	2001, 2008

Recipient Name	Year Received
Quinn, Eugene	1996, 2000
Rasmann, Lori	1997
Reif, Tom	1995
Reinke, Jeff	2006
Rhea, Bob	2006
Rogers, Barb	1997
Rogers, Kim	1995
Rosene, Jim	2000
Rudey, Rick	2001
Rudie, Ryan	2000
Ryan, Jim	2006
Salvatori, Gino	2000
Sanders, Mary	2000
Saporiti, Christine	2003
Sarver, Charlie	2006
Schafman, Nancy	1999
Scherrinsky, Doug	2010
Schoembs, Ross	2002
Schoonhoven, Tom	2009
Schier, Frank	2004, 2008
Schlehuber, Gary	2001
Schubert, Verna	2000
Schrama, Bret	2008
Scott, Brazz	2010
Scott, Mayor Doug	2001
Squire, Calvin	2005
Sharp, Ed	1996
Shannon, Bill	2004
Showers, Mila	1995
Sinkiawic, Joe	2004
Sjogren, Michael	2001
Skerkoske, Mary Lib	1995
Skorzak, Kirk	2001
Smith, Adam	2007
Smith, Jeffery	2001
Sockwell, Curtis	2009
Sockwell, William	2009
Spellman, Ivonne	1996
Stanfield, Ossie	1995
Stark, Bill	2007
Sully, Steve	1996
Sutton, Terry	1995
Swan, Kevin	2001
Swanson, Armer	1996
Swanson, J.J.	2003
Sweeny, Chuck	2007
Syverson, Dave	1999, 2001
Szegda, Don	1996
Tanner, Dave	2010
Tanner, Carol	2010
Taylor, Edna May	1996
Taylor, Greg	2005
Tegland, Michele	2003
Thiede, James	1995
Thiede, William	2001
Thienemann, Rolf	2006
Thompson, Austin	1999
Thornton, Kristen	1997
Tietsort, Ron	1996
Timko, Dan	1995
Timmer, Diane L.	2002
Timm, Mike	2001
Tokoto, Jean-Pierre	1995
Toleski, Scott	2003
Tulley, Mike	2002
Turner, Phil	2009
Upton, Whit	2009, 2010
Van Pernis, David	2001
Vicau, Shelly	2007
Villagomez, Mary	2006
Vitale, Jean	2007
Vitale, Jim	2001, 2009
Vogl, Andy	2009
Vee, Steve	2001
Wagner, Cheryl	1996
Wait, Ron	2001
Walden, Phil	2004
Walker, Curtis	2001
Walker, Jeff	2008
Watkins, Louie	1995

Appendix G: IPRA/IAPD Community Service Awards to Individuals

Recipient Name	Year Received
Ward, Marjorie	2000
Warren, Tom	2007
Weber, Kathy	2009
Wedgbury, "Doc"	1999
Weller, Stuart	2003
Wenzel, William	1995
Wentland, Stan	2002
Wessels, Terry	2003
White, Sheri	2009
White, Terry	2008
White, Tracy	2009
Whitlock, Sharon	1997, 2004
Williams, Aneda & Henry	1998
Williams, Susan	1996
Williamson, Laura	1996
Winters, Dave	2001
Wisley, Mike	1998
Wolf, Sarah	2000
Wysong, Jeri	2005
Zais, Alan	2007
Zamora, Jose	2001

These kids were enjoying an Easter egg hunt at Lockwood Park sponsored by the Park District and The Undertaker (aka Steve Hilton). In 2005, Hilton organized a hunt for 292,686 filled plastic eggs in Searls Park. The event held the record — for a couple of years — in the Guinness Book.

APPENDIX H
ILLINOIS PARK AND RECREATION ASSOCIATION/ILLINOIS ASSOCIATION OF PARK DISTRICT COMMUNITY SERVICE AWARDS TO ORGANIZATIONS

Organization Name	Year Award Received
Alpine Veterinary Hospital	2001
American Red Cross Homeless Shelter	2001
Arachnid	2000
The Arc	1995, 2003
Arby's	2004, 2005
Attain Program	1995
Aldeen Foundation	2002
Badger Popcorn And Concession	2010
Barbara Olson Center Of Hope	2000
Beyer School PTO	2005
Blackhawk Chapter Of Trout Unlimited	2006
Blue Cross Blue Shield Of Illinois	2010
Boylan High School "Green Club"	2001
BVRH Board Of Directors	2002
BVRH Volunteers & Instructors	2000
Camaraderie Arts	2002
Canine Corners Advisory Committee	2008
Center For Sight And Hearing Impaired	1995
City of Loves Park	2002, 2008
CherryVale Mall	2007
City of Gardens Advisory Committee	2004
City of Rockford Human Services Dept.	2008
Coca-Cola	2007
Comcast	2008
Community Foundation of Northern Illinois	2005
Council of Neighborhood Organizations	2000
Creative Pig Minds	2000
Crimestoppers	2008
Culvers	2007
Discovery Center Museum	1998
Earthbeat	2004
Easter Seals	
Children's Development Center	2003
Espejo Newspaper	2006
Fairgrounds Advisory Committee	2002
Fatwallet, Inc.	2008
Festival of Lights Committee	1995
First Northern Credit Union	2006
Fourth of July Committee	1995
Fox-39 Kids Club	1998
Friends of Riverview	1996
Friends of Lockwood	2005
Funderburg Farms	1997
G & O Landscaping	1997
Gander Mountain	2009
Geese Peace	1997
Gilles Orthopedics/Sports Institute	2000
Graham Spencer, Inc.	2000
Greater Rockford Blues Fest Committee	2000
Grindstar	2009
Harlem Community Center	1996, 2005
Heart Solutions Inc.	2007
Home Depot	2000
Hunger Connection	2003
Illinois Youth Soccer Association	1997
Insight Communications	1999, 2000
Ipsen	2008
Kaboom	2010
Keith Creek Neighborhood Association	2010
Kids Around The World	2001
Klhem Arboretum And Botanic Garden	2005
Korean War Veterans	2007
Laidlaw Education Services	2003
The Larson Group	2004

Appendix H: IPRA/IAPD Community Service Awards to Organizations

Organization Name	Year Award Received
Luz Latina Newspaper	2003
Lonnie's Carpet Max	2008
Lowes Home Center	1997
LPGA-USGA Girls Golf	2007
Lutheran Social Services	2007
Mcclure Engineering	1998
Mcdonalds Corp	2006
Metlife Foundation	2010
Midway Village & Museum Center	2003
Millennium Fountain Committee	2003
NAACP (National Association for the Advancement of Colored People)	1998
National Association of Women In Construction	1997
National Association of Negro Women, Rockford	1998
Nicholas Conservatory & Gardens Steering Committee	2008
Nicolosi & Associates	2000
Northern Illinois Food Bank	2008
Northwestern Illinois Area Special Olympics	1995
Orchid Neighboorhood Association	2008
OSF Saint Anthony Center for Sports Medicine & Health Fitness	1998
Patriots Gateway	2005
Pepsi-Cola Bottling Company	1997
Petco	2006
Project First Rate	2002
RAMP	2003
Rehab Associates Of Northern Illinois	2002
River District Association	2004
Riverside Community Bank	2003
Rock River Bank	2004
Rock River Fly Casters	2006
Rock Valley College	2008
Rockford Amateur Astronomers, Inc.	2001
Rockford Area Convention & Visitors Bureau	1995, 2005
Rockford Area Gardeners of America	2001
Rockford Area Mexican Business Association	2006
Rockford Blacktop Construction Company	1998
The Rockford Boys & Girls Club	1996
Rockford Chariots	2003
Rockford College MBA & Business Administration Dept.	2000
Rockford Community Foundation	1997
Rockford Dance Company	2010
Rockfordfishing.Com	2009
Rockford Health Council	2008
Rockford Health System	2005
Rockford Hockey Club	1995
Rockford Ice Hogs	2004
Rockford Ice Hogs Charitable Foundation	2006
Rockford Jaycees	1996
Rockford Lutheran Ministries	1998
Rockford Masters Commission	2007
Rockford Memorial Development Foundation	2003
Rockford Park District Foundation	2004
Rockford Pickleball	2009
Rockford Pony Baseball	1997
Rockford Pro/Am	2002, 2004
Rockford Public Library	2006
Rockford Public Schools – Facility Department	1999
Rockford Register Star	2005
Rockford Sanitary District	2001
Rockford Speedway	1997
Rockford Sports Coalition	1997
Rockford Sportsman's Golf Association	1995
Rockford Women's Golf Association	1995
Rockton Bus Company	1999
Rosecrance Adolescent Program	2010
Preferred Fencing	2008
Salvation Army Millennium Center	2001
Saturn Of Rockford	1996, 2002, 2008
Schlichting and Sons Excavating	1997

Organization Name	Year Award Received
Sentry Integrated Home Care	2002
Seventh Street Area Development Council	2000
Ski Broncs	2002
South Park Development Group	1997
The Station	2009
Robert R. Stenstrom, Inc.	1997
Swedish American Health System	1997
Tiger Woods Foundation	2001
U.S. Cellular	2006
United States Golf Association	2000
United Way Of Rock River Valley	2002
Van Matre Rehab Center	1995
Village Of Cherry Valley	1999
Whiz Kids Enrichment Center	2004
WIFR -TV	1999
Winnebago County Sheriff's Department	1999
Winnebago County Health Department	2010
Winnebago County Landfill Company	2008
Woodward Governor	2008
WREX - TV	1999, 2005
WROK Radio	2009
WTVO/WQRF - TV	2009
YMCA	1998
YWCA	1995

APPENDIX I
STAFF DEVELOPMENT INSTRUCTORS

Much of the success of the Park District is a result of its commitment to providing consistent and effective staff development programs — programs that allowed all team members an opportunity to develop the skills needed to be successful in their daily responsibilities. Special recognition goes to the following instructors who provided learning opportunities to all those who wanted to grow and serve. This is a partial list.

Jodi Carroll	Jon Lundin	Nancy Sylvester
Bill Charney	Mike Mastroianni	Terry White
Dr. Robert Henry	Steve Mongelluzzo	Jeanine Wortmann
Keith Irons	Gerry Olson	
Prof. Cary Kizilbash	Jim Pirages	

APPENDIX J
ROCKFORD AREA GOLF HALL OF FAME

The Rockford Area Golf Hall of Fame is organized as a means of recognizing, preserving and promoting the heritage of golf in the Rockford area. Many individuals have made extraordinary contributions and have had incredible accomplishments in the lifetime sport of golf. The Rockford Area Golf Hall of Fame honors the contributions and accomplishments of these individuals who are worthy of recognition as examples for others to emulate.

Each year, those selected to enter the Hall of Fame are invited to play in a Hall of Fame Golf Play Day, along with sponsors and other dignitaries. The honorees are inducted at a dinner banquet following the golf outing.

Class of 2011
Jamie Hogan
Gunnar Nelson
Rockford Sportsmen's Golf Association
Conny Sjostrom Sr. and Irene Sjostrom Youth Golf Foundation

Class of 2010
Carl Dargene
Webbs Norman
Mary Holton Reid
Mark Taylor

Class of 2009
Christian Beto
Ken Kellaney
Scott W. Nicholas
Lois Jean Dahlquist Woodworth

Class of 2008
Shirley M. Dommers
Robert "Butch" Pegoraro
Robert A. "Bob" Reitsch
Rockford Pro-Am

Class of 2007
David J. Claeyssens
Brad Fowler
Mike Johnson
Junior Golf Association of Greater Rockford – James W. Keeling

Class of 2006
Steven Hare
The Hogan Family
Dean Lind
Rockford Women's Golf Association
Mary Wilder Welsh
Salley Wessels

Class of 2005
Margaret and Norris Aldeen
Georgalee George
John Holmstrom Jr.
Nancy Joan Kauzlarich
Roger Lindeman
Lloyd McWilliams
Kay Rossmiller
Ken Scott
Mary Lib Skerkoske
Don Terasaki
Tom Warren
Alex Welsh

APPENDIX K

MAJOR AWARDS TO THE ROCKFORD PARK DISTRICT OR SHARED BY THE PARK DISTRICT

Past 25 Years

1986 – 1989: Illinois Association of Park Districts (IAPD) Gold Medal Finalist

1989: National Recreation and Park Association (NRPA) Gold Medal Winner

1993 – 94: IAPD Gold Medal Finalist (therapeutic recreation)

1994: Midwest Regional Championship (Soccer)

1995: National Safety Council; Iowa/Illinois Safety Council

1995: NRPA Gold Medal Winner for Therapeutic Recreation

1999: Western Illinois University

2000: NAACP (Continuing Support)

2003: Government Finance Officers Association (GFOA) Excellence in Financial Reporting

2005: America in Bloom Winner

2006: All America Rose Selection for Outstanding Rose Garden Maintenance

2007: Inducted into Rockford Area Convention and Visitors Bureau Hall of Fame

2007: America in Bloom and Governor's Hometown Award

2008: World Waterpark Association Awards in 3 categories to Magic Waters

2008: Golf Digest Magazine Awards 4 ½ stars to Aldeen Golf Club

2008: Ellis & Associates Platinum Award to Aquatics and Gold Award to Magic Waters

2008: GFOA Excellence in Financial Reporting (2005 – 2006)

2009: World Waterpark Associations Award, highest award for employee recruitment, retention and training

2009: Illinois Parks and Recreation Association, Illinois Association of Park Districts (IPRA/IAPD), state award for photography

2009: IPRA/IAPD First Place Agency Showcase, 2007 Annual Report

2009: IAPD Best of the Best, Top Journalist of the Year, WREX-TV

2009: IAPD Best of the Best, Outstanding Citizen Volunteer of the Year, George Franklin

2009: Excellence Level from Park District Risk Management Agency

2010: Mike Cassidy Commissioner Service Award to Nate Martin from IAPD/IPRA

2010: New Professional of the Year Award to Breane Cory by Illinois Therapeutic Recreation Section

2010: Broadcast Award from IPRA for 30-second TV spot about low-fee programs

2010: Catherine H. Sweeney Award, American Horticultural Society, to Nicholas family for philanthropic support

2010: GFOA awards for excellence in financial reporting (2008) and 2008 annual report for citizens

2010: United States Specialty Sports Association award for Outstanding Performance in League Organization to Marianne Larson and Sportscore One

2010: Best of the Best Awards, IAPD, Charlie Sarver, Citizen Volunteer of the Year; Tim Larson, Skyward Promotions, Friends of Illinois Parks

2011: New Professional of the Year Award from Illinois Therapeutic Association, Abby Billips

2011: Citizen/Volunteer of the Year Award from IPRA/IAPD to Marva Brown

2011: Excellence in Financial Reporting and Popular Annual Financial Reporting for 2009 from GFOA

2011: One of four finalists in nation for Gold Medal Award from National Recreation and Parks Association

2011: IAPD/IPRA Best of the Best awards, Good Sportsmanship to Ken Held, Roy Gayle baseball complex; Green Practices, Nicholas Conservatory

Opposite: This dressed-for-spring little girl is flying a kite at the district's Kites in Flight day at Southwest Community Park in May 2011. It is hoped the kite day can be held every year.

APPENDIX L
LETTERS FROM PATRONS

Most of these letters were written in 2009 when the Park District observed its 100th birthday.

'Make this place better'

My life is better, thrice over, because of the Rockford Park District.

In 1947 I purchased my first district-sponsored Junior Golf Permit. The stiff brown wallet-sized pass with rounded corners and black print gave me easy access to countless hours on Rockford's courses. It cost one dollar for the year! This gesture of support for the youth of Rockford encouraged me to seriously dive into the fascinating game of golf. I did. The benefits have lasted a lifetime.

In 1960 as a college student home for the summer, I worked at Sinnissippi Gardens. The highlight of the season was a massive hail storm that shattered 1,500 greenhouse windows. We spent weeks cleaning up the shards while tending to our bloody fingers. As vivid in my memory, I observed a high morale team of employees join in to, in the words of our supervisor, "Make this place better than ever."

In the late 1990s, I had the privilege of working with the district to bring the Tiger Woods Foundation to town. Inspired by this experience and in collaboration with the Park District Foundation, I wrote a book about Rockford called "An Old Caddie Looks Back: Reflections from a Town that Loves Golf … and Tiger." In developing it, I learned something about how Illinois statutes allow for fiscal independence and creativity in local park districts. I can testify that Rockford's district has fully realized these possibilities. A half-century after my junior golfing years, my admiration was re-confirmed and expanded.

— Tom Warren

'Experiences shaped me'

I grew up in the Haight Village neighborhood. There were plenty of guys to hang out with (it was the Baby Boom era). Every family seemed to have at least six kids. My buddies and I loved to play softball and baseball at Tenth Avenue Playground. One little quirk with that field was that a rapid creek ran along the first base line. Our team did not possess the most accurate throwing arms, nor was our first baseman a Gold Glove candidate. I wore the "tools of ignorance" as the catcher, probably because I was the smallest and didn't know any better.

Well, when the ball got by the first baseman, which was pretty often, I would have to race over and jump in the creek to save the ball from being lost downstream. When I did not succeed, my older and bigger teammates would really get on my case. In the afternoon, we would swim at Tenth Avenue Pool.

When my family moved to the northwest end of town, it was Brown's Park where I helped the "Parkie" as a Junior Leader. I even met my first girlfriend there. I realize how these experiences helped shape me as a person.

As an adult, I had the privilege of serving two internships at the RPD, which included recounting the history of how Dr. Allen Sapora and a group of students from the University of Illinois (including future Park District Executive Director Webbs Norman) convinced a skeptical Park Board into getting behind passing a recreation tax, which led to the multi-faceted district we enjoy today. I also served on the Marinelli Stadium Design Committee, which answered a boyhood dream for me. The Park District has, and will continue to be, an important part of my life. Come summer, I will dust off my golf clubs and bicycle to enjoy two of my favorite pastimes.

Thanks for the memories and Happy 100th Anniversary!

— Paul Elmer

Letters from Patrons

'My park, my neighborhood'

It was my park — in my neighborhood — Brown Park in north-west-central Rockford. It was a source of playground sports and games, making lanyards, splashing in the spray pool and, during one winter, teaching myself to ice skate on the park's outdoor ice rink. Why was the ice rink so important? It led in later years to an avocation of being a certified youth hockey referee. From the all-ages kids of the Rockford Hockey Club to Division 3 NCAA hockey games, it was Brown Park that made it all possible.

— **Bob Kirkpatrick**

'Place for dreams to come true'

Ours is a beautiful, loving and sharing community. No where is this more greatly epitomized, in our eyes, as in the Rockford Park District and Park District Foundation.

For 100 years, the Park District has offered us a place to come together as family and friends in nature, recreation and joy. It has given us a sense of hope and harmony as we walk through its woods and gardens, swim in its pools, run and bike along its paths, skate upon its ice and golf upon its courses. The Park District offers a place of imagination and a place for dreams to come true. It gives us an opportunity to store memories that help us work through the difficult times. Whether you're reflecting upon a brook of the gently flowing Kent Creek as it meanders through Page Park or gaining a better sense of service as you reach another goal at the Guilford Tennis Center, you find a greater appreciation for life.

My own life and that of my family has been enhanced and improved through our relationship with the Park District. It has given us weddings and a place to pay tribute, a garden to stroll and a place to work and grow. It has offered us a stage to perform upon and seat in which to sit back and enjoy the show, a world in which to create and recreate within. Midst sunshine or clouds, in summer heat or wintry days, the Rockford Park District has given us a place to be. And for that, we are eternally grateful.

— **Brett H. Nivinski**

'Best of the Best'

The nationally-renowned Rockford Park District has served the residents with distinction for more than 100 years. The district has met the diverse needs for wellness through recreational programs as well as the protecting of natural resources and wildlife habitats, historical and cultural facilities.

The Park Board and professional staff have a "Citizen First" attitude. They lead the nation for park recreation and conservation agencies in many areas but none more important than citizen involvement. There are a minimum of 50 advisory committees and organizations under the umbrella of the Park District.

The Rockford Park District has all the makings of greatness through superb leadership. Webbs Norman molded the district to be a model to emulate by other agencies. Under his tutelage as the executive director, the district repeatedly won the coveted National Gold Medal Grand Award for parks, recreation and conservation management. In addition, Webbs, the Park Board and highly professional staff have been recognized by the Illinois Association of Park Districts, the National Recreation and Park Association, and many other organizations for the unparalleled services they have rendered to the citizens of Rockford. Tim Dimke succeeded Webbs Norman and has kept the traditions alive. The Park District has continued to be successful because of Tim's excellent management skills and the public support.

What do residents say about the Rockford Park District? Ask them. We did. The answers have been a resounding "GREAT… OUTSTANDING…WE LOVE OUR PARK DISTRICT."

We salute the Rockford Park District Board of Commissioners, staff and citizens for making their agency the BEST OF THE BEST. Congratulations and Happy 100th anniversary.

— **Ted Flickinger, Ph.D.**
Past president of the National Recreation and Park Association and CEO/president of the Illinois Association of Park Districts

Continued next page

'Operating without ego'

The men and women of the Rockford Park District hold a very special place in my heart. The RPD generously opened their doors to me, welcoming me, first as a member of a partner organization, and now allowing me the honor of doing a case study of the RPD and its leadership over the last three decades for my Ph.D. dissertation. In researching leadership in action, I have worked the closest with Webbs Norman, a true mentor and friend, whose gift is to inspire and encourage everyone he meets to believe in his/her own value. And, ultimately, that is the core of the RPD's operation — management by values.

I have observed the RPD in action, operating without ego, reflecting care, generosity, respect, integrity and appreciation for our community's diversity on all levels — embracing our ethnicity, talents, interests and challenges. Balancing everyone's needs, that has to be one of the greatest challenges for a public service agency. We inhabit this world together and so often struggle to share the world while honoring our different points of view and unique interpretations, our individual capacities and talents. These differences may contribute to conflict, suffering and dissension in the world. Or they may contribute to the creation of organizations, partnerships and collaborations that allow and, even more, encourage all of our differences to manifest creative, healthy and productive solutions, helping expand everyone's opportunities for self-expression.

I am inspired by the RPD's visionary, even transcendent leadership — by how they have developed a vision that embodies and reflects these core values of service. The RPD has led the way in our community and set an example for park districts around the country. But for me, the RPD has taught me that leadership and service are inseparable. Thank you and Happy 100, Rockford Park District.

– Maggie Allen

'The very best neighbor'

As a resident of the Rockford Park District, I have always enjoyed the district and the benefits of living in the district. We live on the bike path and get to see the use of that path everyday — 24 hours a day/7 days a week/365 days a year!

My youngest daughter, Holly, has cerebral palsy. When she was very small, we, with the therapist's assistance, were trying to teach her how to throw an object — a difficult skill. We used to ride on the bike to the pond at Sinnissippi and she would feed the fish while practicing "throw" and "let go."

Living on the river next to the park, we frequently observed children and young adults playing in the park, near the river, and not always playing safely. When I observed unsafe behavior, I would call the Park District office and they would quickly send out the park police who always handled the situation beautifully.

There was no question in our mind that the Rockford Park District was the very best neighbor one could ask for.

I always thought I understood the value of the Rockford Park District. But when I served as interim president and CEO of the Chamber of Commerce, I realized I had not understood the full value of the Park District. In that position, I got the opportunity to understand the contribution that Park District makes to the business community.

The Park District is a major factor when businesses are looking to relocate in the Rockford area. When people see our parks, our park programs and our Park District golf courses, they are extremely impressed and see the true benefit of living in the Rockford area. The vast majority of the businesses already located in the area realize the benefit that the Park District brings to their business and their employees. The business community continually benefits from the Park District.

Probably the greatest single asset of the Rockford Park District has been Webbs Norman who served as its executive director for 34 years. Not only was he a great leader during his time as executive director but his leadership style was so effective that his philosophies and influence on the district will be felt for many years to come.

– Nancy Sylvester

Letters from Patrons

'Unseen things make it work'

In 1981, I was hired for full-time employment at the Rockford Park District. At that time, I had no idea of the scope of the "adventure" awaiting me. For the next eight years, I learned so much — not only about myself (which was considerable) — but even more about the district's contributions, not only to the city of Rockford and surrounding areas but also to the lives of people coming from much further distances. The district's vision of "Helping People Enjoy Life!" and its ability to establish and maintain a high level of citizen confidence and support became a distinct reality for me.

The foresight of the district's director in those years, Webbs Norman, and the board members who both envisioned and met needs, resulted in the district procuring land and building much-needed sports and recreational facilities we are now so familiar with.

Today, almost 30 years later, those community needs are being met in a myriad of ways:
- Many beautiful, safe and well-maintained parks.
- Concerts in the parks and at the Sinnissippi Band Shell.
- Numerous summer programs in the parks.
- Swimming pools and the water theme park, Magic Waters.
- Extraordinary golf courses.
- Recreational paths.
- Sportscore complexes.
- Riverview Ice House and Carlson Ice Arena.
- Sinnissippi Gardens and the Nicholas Conservatory.
- Guilford Tennis Center.
- Atwood Environmental Center.
- Lockwood Park Equestrian Center and Children's Farm.
- Forest City Queen riverboat and the Trolley Car.
- Sapora Playground.
- Museums — Burpee Natural History, Rockford Art, Discovery Center, Midway Village and Tinker Swiss Cottage.

The list is extensive and, of course, highly visible to all. But it is the unseen things which make it all work:

The dedication of the district's past and present directors and board members and the staff who have embraced the vision and mission and give their all to see it carried out.

The behind-the-scenes support given by the district — of not only their facilities — but of materials and time to enhance so many other community events.

The bottom-line mentoring of staff on both personal and professional levels to ensure that every employee was and is fully-equipped to carry out both the vision and the mission.

We are fortunate people indeed to have "right here in river city" one of the top, if not the very best, park district in the country.

My life and the lives of all who have been touched by this park district have been enriched through the carrying out of the unity of purpose in its vision to help people enjoy life. We have been greatly blessed by the Rockford Park District's presence in all of our lives.

– **Janet M. Pearson**

'Positively impacted'

I was positively impacted by the Rockford Park District at several stages of my life. I want to take a moment to note a few memorable instances of such impact.

When I was in grade school at Julia Lathrop Elementary, I participated in one of the summer programs. I learned how to play knock hockey and did several art crafts and enjoyed an ice cream social at the end of the program.

As a young adult, I used the Levings Park roads as a track for walking and enjoying nature. As a minister of the House of Refuge Church, I used that same park for several church picnics. On several of those occasions, we held public water baptisms for people who had received Jesus Christ through our ministry.

Our church has also received help from the Rockford Park District in the form of a park property which was adjacent to our church property being donated to the ministry. We turned that under-used asset into one which is used as a parking lot daily for our ministry.

I think that the Rockford Park District is one of the best in the nation. Congratulations on your 100th anniversary.

– **Rev. Mark T. Williams**
General Overseer Banner of Truth International

Continued next page

'Unique Standout'

Some of my fondest memories are the days I spent with the residents of Rockford and the staff of the Rockford Park District while doing a study of National Gold Medal Award winners of which Rockford was one of the standout recipients. As I recall that visit in my mind, the terms that continue to shape my recollections are "uniqueness" and "standout."

The Rockford Park District is a "standout" in the best sense of the term. Whenever I am asked to isolate those attributes or actions that empower a public park agency to become a standout, I always recite the "unique" aspects of the Rockford Park District.

— Congratulations to an organization that has its priorities in the right place by making the community and its residents the center of its purpose and actions; it is not about the district and its successes, but about what is best for the community.

— Continued success to a district that has retained the ability to think BIG while simultaneously ensuring participation and engagement one person at a time; how else to explain a vision for an arboretum while offering free and low-fee opportunities for families and children.

— Admiration for one of the more unique ways in which the Rockford Park District is a standout through the power of partnerships; the Rockford Park District sets the standard for not only the number of partnerships, but the genuine collaboration among the district and its multitude of community partners.

— Genuine gratitude extended to an organization that not only remembers the roots of public parks and recreation's role in a community but practices it day-in and day-out.

Congratulations to the Rockford Park District on its 100th anniversary! Long may it continue to retain its uniqueness and standout status as the basis for continuing to serve its community and residents so well and as a role model for other public agencies.

– **Ellen O'Sullivan, Ph.D.**
Chair, Center for Public Recreation and Parks
Professor Emeritus,
Southern Connecticut State University

'Using the parks for devotionals'

The Rockford Park District has played a very important role in the history of the Baha'i Community in Rockford. I have lived in Rockford for about 35 years and ever since I moved here, the community has used public parks every year for some part of their programming. Long before we acquired a center in 2001, the Baha'is would hold some of their meetings in a mix of homes and public places. In the summers, we often planned meetings in parks. In the '90s, when we started giving the Race Unity Awards, we always chose a public park for our potluck picnics at which we handed out the awards. The shelters at Levings Lake or Page Park were filled with people of all races enjoying food and hospitality together.

One of the interesting ways we observed one of our holy days for several years was to visit 15 or 20 parks in small groups and say prayers for the Rockford Community. We would leave a rose with a short quote from the Baha'i Sacred Writings somewhere in the park. We also frequently went to a park for the culminating session of our Sunday school.

For the past several years, the Rockford Township Baha'i Community has planned a series of summer devotional programs focusing on various topics such as "The Oneness of Humanity," "A Life of Service," and "Spiritual Aspects of Agriculture." They are always held in parks in the area, along with a potluck picnic. Because of the Faith's strong support for nature, it is fitting to use the parks for these devotionals because they give the participants an opportunity to interact with nature as they meditate and pray.

One recent summer a group of Baha'is held a junior youth group and children's classes weekly at Black Hawk Park for over 30 children who were recent immigrants from countries like Myanmar, Burundi and Iraq. The children were learning to get along with people of all cultures different from their own and learning English, arts and games. These are just some of the many ways we have used the parks over the years. The parks are one of Rockford's greatest assets!

– **Judy H. Moe**

Letters from Patrons

'Sinnissippi Park influence'

As I was driving down North Second Street recently, I noticed the recent statue, Sinnissippi Guardian, in Sinnissippi Park looking out toward the Rock River. I began reminiscing how much Sinnissippi Park has influenced my growing up years in Rockford and continued through my adult life as well.

In 1936, my family moved to Rockford, and the very first night we spent here, Dad took my two sisters and myself on a tour of the city, beginning with Sinnissippi Park to make us familiar with our new hometown. He knew we would really enjoy the rolling drive and curves as we drove through Sinnissippi Park. I had no idea at that time what a major part Sinnissippi Park would play in the future.

For graduation from Rockford High School in 1940, my uncle gave me a set of golf clubs and I spent many years from then on enjoying the recreational opportunities there as I learned to play at Sinnissippi as well as other Park District courses, besides enjoying the playground programs available, and the Concerts in the Park.

As though to complete the cycle in my adult life, I had the opportunity to work for the Rockford Park District as an employee in the pleasant office building in Sinnissippi Park overlooking North Second Street, for many years. It was an enlightening experience working in that beautiful and relaxing park setting where I learned how many residents enjoyed the facilities and recreational opportunities at Sinnissippi Park and other district facilities the far-sighted commissioners provided in the community. The recent addition of the conservatory just continues a century of progress for the Rockford area.

– **Lucille M. Gray**

'Special for everyone'

Sinnissippi Park is in my earliest memories. I have a black and white photo of myself taken in 1947, surrounded by cousins and some of my six siblings, dressed in our "play clothes," at Sinnissippi.

I grew up near Sandy Hollow Road, a distance from Sinnissippi, but the park was our choice for annual family reunions.

We all got together. Some of them took the bus. They would bring dishes of food and hot dogs for the kids and we picnicked all day long. There would be at least 30 of us. My mom was the youngest in a family of seven girls.

On the hill of Sinnissippi Park, the adults let the kids run, swing and go across North Second Street to feed the ducks. That meant the adults could eat, relax, catch up on the news, relive the old days and share their lives, all day long. It was special for everyone.

We went to Sinnissippi for my dad's company picnics, too. He worked at Rockford Drop Forge. I remember the summer I was 5, my dad won a tricycle for me at his company picnic.

We went to Sinnissippi in winter, too, to ice skate on the lagoon. Once I fell through thin ice, all the way up to my knees, and was stuck until my dad and brother came to the rescue.

My husband, Jim, recalls visiting Sinnissippi as a school boy from Stillman Valley. We still enjoy many of the parks and forest preserves in the area and we're at Sinnissippi, every Tuesday and Thursday night in the summer, for the free concerts. We often get people to come with us and they become regulars, too.

– **Helene Parker**

Helene Parker is the smallest child, in front, in this group. The picture was taken in 1947 during a Rollins family reunion at Sinnissippi Park.

BIBLIOGRAPHY

Cunningham, Pat. Rockford: *Big Town, Little City*, Rockford Newspapers Inc., 2001

Elmer, Paul. *The History of the 1956 Recreation Tax and Subsequent Development of Recreation in the Rockford Park District,* 1987

50th Anniversary Toolkit. The President's Council on Physical Fitness and Sports, Department of Health and Human Services.

Gangewere, R.Jay. "Allegheny County Parks." *Carnegie Magazine* July/August 1986

Hamilton, Lowell. *The History of the Rockford Park District.*

Johnson, Eric A. *Rockford 1900 – World War I, Postcard History Series.* Arcadia Publishing, Charleston, S.C., 2003.

Johnson, Eric A. *Rockford 1920 and Beyond, Postcard History Series.* Arcadia Publishing, Charleston, S.C., 2004.

International Snowmobile Manufacturers Association. *Snowmobiling Fact Book,* www.snowmobile.org/facts

Leaf, Brian, "Atwood; manufacturing, banking, real estate, hospitality, Rockford. (Focus: Influential Families) *Crain's Chicago Business, Crain Communications, Inc.* 2005. HighBeam Research. June 5, 2010. <http://www.highbeam.com

Lundin, Jon W., *Rockford, An Illustrated History*, Windsor Publications Inc., 1989.

Nelson, C. Hal, editor, *Sinnissippi Saga*, Winnebago County Illinois Sesquicentennial Committee. Wayside Press, Mendota, Il., 1968.

National Public Parks Tennis Association. *Tennis, Historically Speaking.* www.nppta.com/History.htm

Nelson, C. Hal, editor. *We the People of Winnebago County*, Winnebago County Bicentennial Commission. Wayside Press, Mendota, Il. 1975.

Newspaper writers. "75 pages of significant Rockford and world history." *Rockford Morning Star.* 20 March 1963.

Rockford Historical Society. *National Avenue history.*

Snowmobiling Fact Book. International Snowmobile Manufacturers Association, Web site snowmbile.org/facts

Super, John C. and Irons-Georges, Tracy. *The Seventies in America.* Salem Press. 2006.

Swanson, Don. *Life in Rockford's 'Swede Town'*

The Associated Press. *1950s,* http://olderthanme.blogspot.com/2008/01/how-experts-think-well-live-in-2000-ad.html

Warren, Tom. *An Old Caddie Looks Back: Reflections From a Town That Loves Golf ... and Tiger.* Amphitryon Press, Rockford. 2007.

West, Myron. *The Rockford Plan*, Rockford City Plan Commission, 1918.

Wiltse, Jeff. *Contested Waters: A Social History of Swimming Pools in America.* University of North Carolina Press. 2007.

INDEX

A

Ackerman, Deb 183
African Methodist Episcopal Church 42
Agnew, Harris 196, 218, 270, 294
Agnew, Terese 216
Aldeen Golf Club 240-243, 265, 298, 300
Aldeen, Norris 25, 92, 99, 240-244, 286
Aldeen, Reuben A. 129, 138, 142
Alpine Meadows Playground 140, 299
Alpine Park 82, 83, 117, 126, 299, 302, 303
Alpine Pool 124-128, 186, 300, 301, 303
America in Bloom 206
American Federation of Labor 112
American Gold Star Mothers Memorial . 252, 253
American Park Builders 42
Americans with Disabilities Act 179, 281
Amerock 99, 134, 142, 240
Anderson Art 251-254
Anderson, U.S. Rep. John B. 101, 132, 166, 167, 194
Anderson, John and Linda 215, 216
Andrews Memorial Park 60
Andrews, Harry B. 63, 66, 84
Angel of Hope 217
Anna Page Park 63, 82-84, 155, 299, 302
Art Association 75-77, 221
Anderson, Arthur W. Peace Park 251-254
Armstrong, Jack 295
Atwood Environmental Center 66, 107-109, 300, 331
Atwood Park 65, 81, 106, 107, 109, 140, 298-300, 302, 303
Atwood Park Estates Playground . 140, 298-300
Atwood Soccer Center 228
Atwood, Bruce 122, 269
Atwood, Seth B. 59, 63, 65, 66, 72, 81, 82, 84, 99-102, 107, 108, 118, 120, 122, 136, 141, 269
Atwood, Seth G. 122
Auburn High School 292
Auburn School Tennis Courts ... 169, 265, 303
Augustine, Dallas 209

B

Babe 54-56
Baby Boomers 122
Badminton 69
Bailey, Bill 154, 157
Baker, Jo 1, 166, 188-192, 196, 222, 268
Barber Colman 174
Barbour School Playground 140, 299
Barnes Mansion 77
Barnes, Ross 232
Baseball 26-30, 36, 38-40, 42, 53, 59, 69, 92, 93, 105, 120, 121, 126, 143, 172, 187, 195, 201, 225, 232-235, 257, 267, 287
Basketball 38-40, 53, 100, 104, 119, 120, 136, 170, 179, 186, 227, 229, 291
Basketry 38
Bastille Day 46
Batista, Miguel 235
Bauer Memorial Path 191
Baur, Mike 217
Beach, Frank 230
Bean, Joe 139, 142, 148, 149, 152, 154, 267
Beattie Is 214, 219, 220
Beattie Park 44, 60, 204, 205, 214, 217, 219, 220, 253, 254, 299, 302
Beattie Playground 44, 60, 94, 299, 303
Beattie, Anna 44, 218
Beattie, James 167
Behr, Richard A. 216
Bell Bowl 45
Bendelow, Thomas 23-25, 46
Bengston, Folke 90
Benjamin, Brad 25
Bennett, Christopher 253
Bennett, William 35
Bernardi, Dick 169

335

Beverly Park 265
Beyer Stadium 120, 233, 266, 299, 303
Bicentennial Bicycle and
    Pedestrian Path 187-192
Black Hawk Park 22, 29-31,
    35, 40, 41, 46, 53, 54, 56, 60, 80, 121, 161,
    163, 212, 298, 299, 332
Blackhawk Bike Club 190
Blackhawk Valley Riding Club 181
Blackwell, Oscar 170
Bloom, Henry C. 32, 78
BMX 206-208, 285
Boehland, Gustav J. 204
Boitano, Brian 168
Booker Washington Community Center . . . 170
Booker Washington Park 265, 299
Boustead, Thomas P. 100
Boys Club Association 4, 10, 92-98, 101
Brademas, Jim 59, 93, 95,
    96, 102-111, 152, 169
Bresler Park 265, 299
Brightbill, Charles 93
Brooks, Douglas 271, 294
Brookview School Playground . . . 140, 299, 303
Broomball 168
Brown Park 8, 42, 60, 299, 302
Brown, Chuck 295
Brown, Edward. W. 8, 9, 62
Brown, Joe 199
Buehrle, Mark 235
Burnam, Jerry 185
Burpee Museum of Natural History 74-77,
    220, 221, 229, 294, 301
Burpee Trust and Art Association 77
Burpee, Harry 76
Butler, George 99

C

Callihan, Harold 93
Camp Grant 15, 40,
    44-46, 79-81, 107, 255
Camp Sunshine 176-178, 226
Canine Corners 257, 258, 298-301

Carlson Ice Arena 101, 205,
    255-257, 266, 286, 297, 300, 331
Carlson, Edwin W. Sr. 85, 141, 143, 257
Carlson, Edwin W. Jr. . . . 143, 234, 235, 257, 267
Carlson, Hal 40
Carlson, Kurt 255, 257, 286
Carlson, Vi 1, 257
Carlson-Nelles Bicentennial Park 257, 265
Carpenter, Fred E. 14, 15, 17, 19, 23, 61
Carter, Quincy 235
Centennial Methodist Church 42
CEO Interpretations 277, 282
Chamber of Commerce 33, 54,
    71, 100, 146, 148, 166, 247, 330
Charles Street Community Path 191
Charles Woodward Martin
    Memorial Park 80, 117, 118
Charles Street Community Path 191
Chautauqua 173
Cherry Valley Path 266
CherryVale Mall 145, 238
Churchill Park 60, 92, 117, 299, 302
Cianfrocco, Archi 235
Citizen Information Form 159
City of Gardens 33, 34,
    204, 206, 260, 271, 286, 322
City of the Lighted Schoolhouse 147
City-County
    Planning Commission 135, 143, 267
Civic League 91
Civilian Conservation Corps 79
Cleveland, Frank L. 62
Cohn, Kristine 270
Colehour, Francis H. 142
Collins Playground 83, 299
Colman, Howard 50
Community Welfare Council 98
Conklin School Playground 140, 299
Cook, John R. 167, 190, 236, 237, 252, 261
Coots, Lt. Gene 197
Cryer, Robert 1, 121
Cubbies 235
Cudia, Gloria 212, 214, 269

Index

D

Dahlquist Park 83, 299, 302
Dahlquist, Ray 142, 160-163, 264
Dahlquist Sisters 160-163
Damon, Johnny 235
Darrow, Clarence 41, 48, 63, 84, 141
Dasenbrook, Norman K. 246
Davis Memorial Park 246, 247, 265
Davis, Morris and Roberta 246, 247
Deery, Hugh 125, 137, 191, 307
Delany, Michael J. 268
Dennis School Playground 60, 299
Denny, Loreen 119
Depression 8, 34, 65, 67-69, 72, 79, 81, 87, 88, 245
DeShields, Delino 235
Dick Nugent Associates 242
Discovery Center 211, 213, 221-223, 229, 245, 250, 264, 288, 301, 305, 331
Don Schmid Athletic Fields 140
Downhill Skiing 104
Downs, Scott 235
Dunbar, Michael 217
Dunn, Adam 235
Dunn, Dr. E. C. 76
Dutch Elm Disease 21, 115

E

Easter Egg Hunt 184, 321
Eastman, A. Reyner 113
Eddie Greene Place 266
Effigy Mound 218-220
Ekberg-Pine Manor Park 265, 299
Elliot Golf Course 124, 125, 129, 130, 164, 244, 300-302
Elliot Park 140, 164, 167, 258, 298, 299, 302, 304
Elliot, Earl F. 72, 82, 87, 89, 92, 93, 97, 103, 110-112, 116, 129, 131, 137, 139, 304, 305

Ellis, Don 93, 103, 105
Elmer, Paul 1, 99, 110, 334
Environmental education 66, 81, 103, 107, 109, 112, 278
Equestrian Center 181, 291, 331
Erickson, E. N. 74
Espenscheid, Harry 183
Esplanade, Beattie Park 204
Essington, A. V. 69
Evergreen School Playground 299

F

Fair Grounds Park 11, 25-27, 30, 36, 37, 51, 52, 57, 60, 96, 125, 232, 301, 302
Fairbanks, Ortho 217
Farnsworth, Kyle 235
Fasano, Sal 235
Faust, Levin 7-20, 32, 34-36, 43, 44, 46, 48, 51, 52, 59, 61, 69, 84, 124, 193, 297, 306
Federation of Teachers 100
Feliciano, Jose 113
Field and Track 38, 179
Field of Honor 251-254
Financial Stewardship 274
Fitness 4, 136, 188, 189, 194, 280, 323, 334
Fitzgerald, Diane 211
Flachs, Norman 119
Flack, Roberta 113
Fletcher Barnes Home 73
Floberg, Adelbert R. 50, 63, 84
Floral Clock 202, 203, 297
Folk Dancing 38, 39, 104
Football 29, 38, 39, 95, 119, 225, 227, 229, 231, 235, 292
Forbes, Judge Seely P. 100
Forest City 27, 40, 42, 112, 115, 129, 164, 204, 205, 209, 285, 292, 297
Forest City Lodge 42
Forest City Queen 112, 164, 204, 205, 209, 285, 331
Forest Hills Country Club 137
Forest Hills View Playground 140, 299

Fortune 500 Companies 273
Foster, David 217
Founders Park 265, 303
Franz Park 60, 299, 302
Friberg, Leonard A. 100
Fridly, George R. 90, 91
Friends of Lockwood 182-184, 288
Froberg School Playground 140, 299
Froehlich, Raymond J. 100
Funderberg, Robert 214
Furst, Tom and Darlene 217

G

G.A.R. 36
Gagliano, Charles 154, 155, 157
Gambino Park 265, 299
Garber, Josh 217
Garfield Ave. Playground 60, 299
Garland, Jon 235
Gaylord, Robert 99
Getaway 212-214
Gibson, Bert 129
Gill, Jim 178
Gillett, A. J. 24
Giorgi, Sen. Zeke 125, 234
Global Priority Result 277
Graham, Bill 190, 196, 210, 215
Grant, Ulysses S. 27
Greater Rockford Bicycle Committee 190
Greene, Robert E. 144, 192-195
Greenlee Brothers 12
Gregory School Playground 140, 299
Gregory, Howard C. 85
Grudzielanek, Mark 235
Guilford Tennis Center 169, 265,
        299, 301, 303, 329, 331
Guilford Township 53
Guilford Tennis Center 169, 265,
        299, 301, 303, 329, 331
Guinness Book of World Records 184, 321
Gunite Division of Kelsey Hayes Co. 210
Gymnastics 38, 39, 179

H

Hackin, Charlotte 271, 294
Haight Park 60, 299, 302, 303
Hall Memorial Park 83, 299, 302
Hallock, Rep. John 233, 234
Hallstrom, Herman 32
Hamilton, Lowell 1, 136, 308, 334
Hamilton-Sundstrand 209
Hampton, Brian 230
Harkins Pool 125, 303
Harlem Park Amusement Park 53, 54
Harmon Playfield 60, 299
Harris Bank 229
Harry and Della Burpee
    Art Gallery Association 76
Hart, Don 157
Haskell Park 60, 299, 302, 303
Henie, Sonja 161, 163
Hennigan, Patricia 167
Henry, John 214
Hess, Jim and Sharon 209
Hicks, Clarence 185
Highland Playground 80, 83, 299
Holmberg, Gene 196
Holub, John 165
Hoover, Cove 136, 137, 156
Hope VI 120
Horner, Frank S. 43, 62
Horvath, Gene 215, 216, 217, 253
Howard, Wray 193
Huffman Playground 79, 83, 299
Hunter Park 265, 299, 303

I

Ice Skating 5, 27,
        104, 106, 161-169, 255-257, 264, 305
Illinois Emergency Relief Commission 67
Illinois Street Park 299, 303
Illinois Youth Commission 119
Indian Terrace Neighborhood Association . 219
Indoor Sports Center 227-229, 264, 266, 285

Ingersoll Centennial Park 265, 299, 303
Ingersoll Golf Course 47, 260, 302, 304
Ingersoll, Lt. Clayton C. 46
Ingersoll, Winthrop 44, 46, 47
Ingram, Mrs. Tom 119
Ingrassia, Ald. David 194
Ingrassia, Roberta 270
Institute of Rehabilitation 177
International Teamsters 154

J

J. L. Clark 85, 95
Jacobs, Dr. Karl 150
Jamestown Park 265, 299
Jane the Dinosaur.................. 221, 223
Jarnstedt, B. G. 171
Jaycees 190, 207, 285
Jefferson, Thomas 273
Joe Marino Park 265, 299
Jogging 136, 188, 189
Johnson Tract 265, 299
Johnson, Denny 230, 232
Johnson, Gilbert 245
Johnson, Oscar J. 32
Johnson, J. Seward Jr. 216
Julin, Jim 217
Junior League 118, 213, 223
Junior Chariots 179

K

Karau, Jake and Candy 206, 207, 285
Karney, Rex 108
Karpowicz, Terry 217
Kaye Anderson Park............ 266, 299, 303
Kelly, Ed 149
Kennedy, John 188
Ken-Rock Park 83, 299
Ken-Rock Center 100
Kent Creek 26, 27, 51,
    68, 70, 71, 78, 82, 120, 123, 191, 224, 265
Keye-Mallquist Park 60, 302

Kids Around The World 232
Kiefhaber, Christoph 217
Kjellgren, Martin 17
Klehm Arboretum..................... 229
Knight, Gladys (and the Pips)............ 113
Kullberg, Fred J. 100
Kuller, Bengt and Mary 217

L

Lake Louise 128
Laker, Tim 235
Landstrom Park 143, 265, 267, 299
Landstrom, Gilmore 129, 143, 267
Larson, Brandon 235
Lathrop School Playground.......... 140, 299
Lathrop Tract 117
Lathrop Woods 29
Leadership by Values 276, 283-285
Leathers, Robert 211-214, 223
Leave the Lights On 264, 291
Lee, Joseph 8, 101
Lenz, Sandy 168, 255
Leopold, Aldo 50, 304
Levasseur, Napoleon 32, 62
Levings Lake Park 57, 65,
    68, 151, 153, 199, 205, 302
Levings, Thomas G. 43, 68
Lewis Lemon School Playground 266
Lewis, Fay 48, 63, 66, 69, 84, 141
Liberman, Alexander 214, 215
Liberty Park................... 140, 212, 299
Lindgren, Charles O. 121
Linnabary, Ian 295
Lockwood Park 112, 132,
    133, 140, 179-184, 229, 248, 250, 265, 288,
    298-301, 305, 331
Lockwood, James E..................... 182
Logan, Arthur 91
Logo 195, 196, 294
Lohse, Kyle 235
Looney, Brian 235
Loves Park Lions Club 136

Loves Park Playground 117, 140, 299
Lundberg, Lewis B. 114
Lundstrom, Milton 114
Lupton, Frank 103, 107, 110, 309, 314
Lynn, Janet 161, 168, 256
Lyons, Leo 39, 53

M

Mace, Cpl. David 200
Machesney, Fred 71, 72
Magic Waters 112, 143,
    201, 229, 237-240, 257, 264, 265, 267, 269,
    273, 283, 291, 298, 300, 301, 303, 305, 331
Mahlburg, Milt 74, 77
Manarchy, Frank 137
Mandeville Park 22, 30,
    31, 60, 75, 220, 299, 302
Mangionne, Chuck 113
Mangold, Robert 217
Manny Mansion 76, 77
Mantello, Joe 178
Marijuana 122-124
Marinelli Stadium 201, 232-235
Marinelli, Louis F. 233
Mariposa Drive Playground 140
Marsh School Park 302
Martin Park 116-118, 190, 200, 299, 302
Martin, Nathaniel 270, 294
Maud Johnson School Playground 140
Mazzie, Marin 178
McCanna, Ed 191
McCarthy, Sen. Joseph 108
McCauley, Robert N. 216
McFarland, J. Horace 56
McGaw, Mayor Bob 149, 166, 193
McNamara, Mayor John 234
Meehan, Michael 135
Mel Anderson Recreation Path 201, 265
Mendelssohn Club 45, 113
Mezey, Bob 209
Midway Village Museum 1, 143, 170,
    172-174, 255, 257, 265, 267, 300, 301, 303
Mike Quade 235

Millard, Bob 173
Millennium Fountain 266
Mills Brothers 113
Milne, Robert 131, 137, 138, 142, 267, 304
Mission 8, 23,
    25, 93, 95, 110, 131, 151, 153, 158, 212, 249,
    264, 277-279, 284, 331
Moore, Melba 113
Morning Star....................... 10, 13,
    16, 18, 41, 62, 69, 91, 92, 106, 117, 121, 124,
    129, 154-156, 185, 190, 191, 334
Mounds 218-220
Muldoon, Bishop Peter James 35
Mulford Crest Park 265, 299
Mullins, Harley W. 143
Mullins-Pebble Creek Park 143, 265, 299
Murphy, Jim 167
Music in the Park 41, 67, 70, 112
Myers, Rodney 235

N

National Committee,
    Arts for the Handicapped 178, 226
National Golf Foundation 241
National Guard 34, 79
National Recreation and
    Park Association 49, 326, 329
Native Americans 220
Nature Study Club 31, 75
Nauert, Robert 191
Nazi 201
Nelson Park 60, 83, 299, 302
Nelson, John 20, 83, 171
Nelson, O.G. 85, 141, 142
Nicholas Conservatory 1, 89,
    159, 205, 206, 216, 217, 260, 262-264, 271,
    287, 291, 297, 301, 303, 305, 331
Nicholas, Dan and Ruth 34, 206, 260-262
Nicholas, Dan 271
Nierman, Leonardo 217
Norman, Webbs 5, 59,
    139, 142, 147, 232, 246, 263, 266, 267, 283,
    300, 301, 305, 325, 328-331

Index

Northeast Community Park 266, 303
Northlands Association for
    Special Recreation 178
Northwest Tollway 145
Northwestern League 233
Northwestern Park 266, 299, 303

O

Oaks Park 140, 265, 299
Olson Park 258, 265, 266, 303
Olson, Dr. Alfred 32, 62
Olson, Roland and Gladys 258-259
Olson, Jon 150, 164, 165
Orput, Alden E. 268
Outdoor Winter Sports Association 39
Oxford Park 60, 299, 303

P

Packard, Lawrence 129
Page, Anna R. 80, 82
Park-er-Woods Park 265, 299
PDRMA 210, 211
Pederson, Helen 103
Pedlow, Clarence T. 50-52, 67, 72, 304, 305
Pedlow, George 79, 204
Perrecone, Pete 149
Perrone, Miriam (Miggie) 175-179
Perryville Path 191
Peter Olson Park 265
Peterson, Edward 245
Peterson, P.A. 9
Physical fitness 188, 194, 334
Plant Raid 92
Policy Management 276, 281, 282, 284
Progressive Labor Party 201
Project Playworks 211-214
Provenzano, Vince 152
Puri Park 299, 303
Puskac, Bill 209

Q

Quarry Hill Park 133, 181
Quoits 38

R

Rawls, Lou 113
Reckow, Louis M. 9
Recreation Tax 38, 90,
    99-102, 110, 139, 146, 150, 182, 291, 304,
    305, 328, 334
Register-Republic 72, 74, 101, 108, 121, 127
Reitsch, Arthur 50
Rew, Robert 10, 13, 14
Ridge Avenue Playground 117
Riis, Paul B. 20, 22,
    24, 26, 28, 33, 35, 42, 49-51, 304, 305
Riler, Carol 168
Ripolles, Juan 217
River Bluff Nursing Home 131, 132
Riverby Park 140, 299
Riverdahl School Playground 140, 299
Riverfront Museum Park 192, 211,
    223, 264, 265, 298, 301, 303, 305
Riverhawks 229, 235
Riverview Park 265, 301, 303
Riverview Ice House 163-169, 204,
    236, 250, 255, 291, 292, 300, 301, 331
Road Ranger Stadium 235
Robinson, William G. 74
Rock River Greenway South 265
Rock River Recreation Path 187-193
Rock Valley Kiwanis Club 7
Rockford Arboretum 85, 139, 265, 299, 303
Rockford Area Convention
    and Visitors Bureau 220, 226, 229, 292
Rockford Art Museum 75, 76, 217, 224, 229, 301
Rockford Arts Council 219, 223
Rockford Boys Club 4, 10, 92-98, 101
Rockford BMX Club 207
Rockford Central Labor Union 42
Rockford Club 8-12, 14, 33, 61, 279

Rockford College 59, 103, 143, 145, 216, 217, 267, 292, 295, 305
Rockford Community Fund 67, 89
Rockford Concert Band 129
Rockford Country Club 23, 74
Rockford Dance Company.......... 221, 301
Rockford Expos 233-235
Rockford Family Campers Association 108
Rockford Federation of Labor............ 100
Rockford Figure Skating Club 142, 160, 163
Rockford Ice Skating Club 163
Rockford Industrial Athletic Association 39, 80
Rockford Jaycees 207, 285
Rockford Lawn Bowling Club 92
Rockford Lions Club................... 113
Rockford Mass Transit 239
Rockford Museum Association 170
Rockford Natural History Association 75
Rockford Newspapers 136, 137, 334
Rockford Park District Foundation ... 205, 206, 269, 287
Rockford Plan 43, 61, 187, 334
Rockford Rotary Club 208
Rockford School District 66, 143, 149, 264, 270, 283, 294, 305
Rockford Square Dance Association 88
Rockford Symphony................ 221, 301
Rockford World Cup 208
Rockland Foundation 205, 305
Rolling Green Garden Club 95
Rolling Green School Playground . 117, 140, 299
Rood Woods 9, 12, 18-20, 62
Roos, Emanuel 41
Roosevelt, President Theodore 10
Roper, George.................. 14, 15, 17, 19, 32, 40, 42, 43, 50, 61, 187
Roque 38
Rose Garden 151, 202-204, 216, 297
Rotary Club 15, 137, 208
Roy Gayle Park 299
Rugby 227, 229
Rusk, Dr. Howard 177
Ryan, Walter 137

S

Sabrooke Playground 80, 140, 299
Sackett, Edith 38, 59
Salisbury, Robert 144, 148, 149
Sand Park 65, 71, 80, 83, 123, 125-127, 136, 174, 175, 186, 197, 252, 300-302
Sand Park Pool 123, 125, 175, 197, 300, 301
Sandy Hollow Golf Course 58, 60, 73, 74, 298, 300-302
Sapora Playworld 101, 255, 300, 301
Sapora, Allen V. 93-101, 254, 255
Saturn Park 266, 299
Sawyer Road Playground................ 140
Scandroli Construction 314
Schleicher, Robert F. 66, 85, 141
Schulte, Fred 40
Scott, Sandy...................... 211, 310
Sculptures 214-217
Searls Park 65, 80, 81, 184, 206, 257, 265, 285, 298, 299, 302
Searls, Emily J. 82
Seaver, Frank........................ 74
Servant Leadership 274, 283
Severin, Carl 171
Shaheen, Thomas 148
Shields, Judy 206
Shorewood Park 118, 140, 299, 302
Shuffleboard 69, 120
Simmonds, O.C. 21
Sinnissippi Golf Course 22-25
Sinnissippi Park 7, 16-19, 22, 23, 34, 41, 49, 51, 60, 62, 65, 73, 76, 92, 113, 114, 128, 135, 136, 142, 158, 162, 169, 188, 190-192, 201, 202, 208, 214-216, 221, 230, 240, 245, 260, 264, 287, 291, 299, 302, 333
Sinnissippi Lagoon 87, 162
Sixth Street Playground 299
Sjostrom, Eugene 137
Sjostrom, William K. 269
Skateboarders 150, 237

Index

Ski Broncs 118, 295
Smith, J. Austin 237
Smith, Jean Kennedy 178
Smith, Tyler 295
Snow Sculptures 230, 231
Snowmobile 132, 180, 181, 230, 334
Soccer 4, 29,
    38, 39, 179, 225-229, 264, 274, 285, 286,
    288, 291
Sorensen, Sofus. 217
South East Park 28, 36
South Henrietta Avenue Park 80
South Horace Park 60, 299
South Park 28-30, 37,
    42, 60, 80, 198, 299, 302, 324
South Park Lutheran Church. 42
Southeast Community Park . 265, 266, 299, 303
Southwest Community Park 266, 299, 303
Sportscore One 132, 140,
    143, 191, 192, 225-230, 238, 249, 267, 269,
    285, 293, 298, 300, 301, 303, 305
Sportscore Two 227-229, 264,
    266, 286, 298, 300, 301
Sportscore Recreation Path 265
St. Angel, Frank 166, 173
Stairs, Matt 235
Stefanelli, Don 209
Strader, Rick 190
Strike 4, 137, 139, 154-157, 160, 163, 283
Submerged Lands Act 8
Summerdale Playground 117, 140, 299
Sun Singer 195, 196, 294
Sundstrand Tool 95
Sunken Gardens 18, 22, 54, 92, 142
Sunset Park 28, 32, 38, 60, 95, 240, 305
Suspension Bridge 107, 132, 224
Swan F. Anderson Building 266
Swan Hillman School Playground 140, 299
Swanson Park East 266
Swanson Park West. 265, 266, 299, 303
Swanson, Harry O. 66, 85
Swanson, Wayne 90
Swedish Salvation Army Band 41
Sweeney, Mike. 235
Symbol 214-216

T

Taft, William Howard 27
Talcott-Page Memorial Park 83, 299
Taylor Park 265, 299
Team Members 158, 255,
    274, 276, 278, 280, 281, 284, 285
Tebala Shrine Temple 94
Tennis 10, 22, 26,
    28, 38, 39, 54, 69, 102, 104, 120, 136, 151,
    152, 168-170, 186, 187, 265, 274, 298-301,
    303, 329, 331, 334
Tenth Ave. Playground 60, 299
Terranova, John 234
Terry Lee Wells Park 144, 193-195, 303
Thienemann, Rolf 268
Thomas, Atty. Chuck 181
Thompson, L. W. 37, 38
Tiger Woods Foundation 259, 260, 328
Tinker, Robert H. 10, 14,
    15, 19, 22, 37, 38, 61
Tinker Swiss Cottage. 1, 10,
    14, 60, 77, 78, 170, 204, 229, 299, 301, 331
Title IX 189
Toboggan Run 82, 106
Track and Field 38, 179
Trailside Centre 179, 181, 300, 301
Tri-County Planning Commission. 150, 164
Trolley 164, 169, 208-210, 265, 291, 331
Twin Sisters Park 104, 106, 200, 302

V

Van Pernis, David 219, 311
Vandercook School Playground 140, 299
Velie, Dr. Robert 77
Veterans Memorial Park 132, 140,
    225, 249, 301, 305
VFW Auxiliary 252
Victory Gardens 79
Vietnam Veterans Honor Society 255

Vietnam War 129, 253
VietNow 218
Vigiaturo, Silvio 217
Volleyball 38, 40, 69, 104, 227-229, 291

W

W. A. Whitney 95
Wagon Wheel 161
Wagstaff, Charles D. 74
Walgren, Howard 163
Waller, Edward 18
Wantz Park 302
Warren, Tom 1, 23, 67, 259, 328, 334
Washington Academy 31
Washington Park Community Center . 118-120, 140, 301, 302
Waterside Plaza 266, 299, 303
Watson, Jill 168
Webbs Norman Center 5, 246, 266, 301
Welfare Council 98, 100
Wendell, C. A. 12
Wernick, Gerald 129, 136, 137, 143, 149, 166, 267, 311, 315
West, Myron Howard 42
Wester Park 265, 299, 303
Westerg, Ernest 90
White Stockings of the Northwest League . . 27
White, Bruce 217
White, Michael 269
Whitehead, John B. 124, 137, 143, 166, 267
Whitney, W. A. 95
Wiemer, Dave 188, 196, 234
Williams Sports Field 83, 299
Williams, Henry W. 14, 16, 61, 62
Williams-Manny Insurance 16, 99, 143
Williamson, Laura 271, 294
Willow Creek Path 191
Wills, Richard 99
Windsor Lake 128
Winnebago County Forest Preserve 25
Winnebago County Housing Authority 120
Wise, Dewayne 235
Wise, Linda. 184
Woodward Governor 95, 99, 117, 253
World War II 65, 68, 70, 79, 80, 87, 88, 150, 251-253
WPA (Works Progress Administration 70
Wright, Fleur 205, 269
Wright, Frank Lloyd 111-114
WROK Radio 40

Y

Yacht Club 80
YMCA 66, 97, 113, 190-192, 204, 215, 287
Young At Heart 118
Youth Recreation Council 212, 213

Z

Zack, Arthur 113
Zoo 54-56, 133, 271, 294
Zoological Society 54

OPPOSITE: Children wade in Kent Creek at Page Park. Such adventures in Rockford's peerless parks become cherished memories of youth and guide people to become keepers of the Dream in adulthood. For 100 years, each new generation has embraced the challenge to preserve and expand the Park District's resources. I have every confidence the Dream will endure.

NOTES

Notes

ABOUT THE AUTHORS

Webbs Norman first appeared on the Rockford Park District scene in 1955 and 1956, working in summer playground programs. He returned to the U of I, where he earned a bachelor of science degree in education in 1957 and a master's degree in parks and recreation administration in 1960, and then worked in park districts in Chicago's west suburbs and around Illinois.

In 1972, Webbs returned to Rockford to begin a 34-year career as executive director of the Park District. His first challenge was facing a strike by maintenance workers. After that and a thorough reorganization of the district's internal workings, the agency embarked on three decades of growth that made the district one of the best in the nation.

Webbs wasn't a 9 – 5 office administrator. People joked about his "offices" in local coffee shops, where he met daily with citizens and community leaders. A sign on his office door at the Park District read, "Interrupt us, please." Webbs believed communication was the start of anything meaningful. To him, a custodian's view on policy was just as important as that of a deputy director. A day was wasted if he didn't hear from at least one Park District patron. If that person had a complaint, great. To Webbs, a complaint was an opportunity.

Webbs' open mind to any and all ideas led to Park District innovations, programs, generous gifts and partnerships that saved taxpayers millions of dollars.

Webbs received many park association and community honors before his retirement in 2006. And that "retirement" is a bit of a joke. He remains active in community affairs and, yes, you can still find him every morning at a coffee shop somewhere around town.

Geri Nikolai, a graduate of the University of Wisconsin – Eau Claire, was a newspaper reporter and editor for 39 years, working at the Wausau, Wis., *Daily Herald* and the *Rockford Register Star*.

She is retired but continues to write gardening/nature columns and feature stories for several publications and pursue her interest in history, both local and beyond. She is a mother, grandmother, gardener, fan of all teams Wisconsin and, though a newcomer to Rockford 25 years ago, a booster of what the city provides thanks to the Rockford Park District and many other organizations.

If you have comments or questions, please contact **Webbs Norman** at the
Rockford Park District
401 S. Main Street
Rockford, Illinois 61101
or email me at:
webbsnorman@rockfordparkdistrict.org

Visit our Website at **www.rockfordparkdistrict.org**

Use QR Code above to view website